ESCAPING SCIENTOLOGY:
AN INSIDER'S TRUE STORY

# ESCAPING
## SCIENTOLOGY

### AN INSIDER'S TRUE STORY

#### MY JOURNEY WITH THE CULT OF CELEBRITY SPIRITUALITY, GREED & POWER

## KAREN SCHLESS PRESSLEY

BAYSHORE PUBLICATIONS, 2017
NOKOMIS, FL

Published by Bayshore Publications, Nokomis, FL.
www.bayshorepublications.com

*Library of Congress Cataloging-in-Publication Data*
Pressley, Karen Schless
Escaping scientology: an insider's true story / Karen Schless Pressley.
Includes index.
Library of Congress Control Number: 2017913442

ISBN-13: 978-0-9990881-0-4

ISBN-10: 0-9900881-0-6

Bibliographical references, glossary, and additional book content published at www.escapingscientology.com

*Book cover design by Jefferson Hawkins, Skyhawk Studios*

First Edition: September 2017
Printed in the United States of America.

*I dedicate this book
to my mother, Alice Markovic,
the most tenacious woman I will ever know.
August 24, 1922 - May 4, 2015*

The Scientology organization failed numerous attempts to get me to disconnect from my mother. After Mom helped me make my final escape in 1998, she and my family and I enjoyed the last 17 years of her life together.

*This book is also dedicated to the ex-members of Scientology,
especially the survivors of the Sea Organization and the Int base:
May you enjoy your freedom, find your voice,
and share your story to help others.*

# CONTENTS

## PART II
### OVER THE RAINBOW

## PART III
### ESCAPING SCIENTOLOGY

Glossary, references, and additional content and photos are
available on www.escapingscientology.com

# ACKNOWLEDGEMENTS

RECOVERY FROM SCIENTOLOGY—especially as a radicalized member of its extremist group, the Sea Organization—is no walk in the park. Starting life over as a middle-age adult after sixteen years in this group would have been even more challenging without special people who surrounded me with love, compassion and encouragement. Because of them, I found my life compass.

Coming home to family was like docking in a safe harbor after a war. You were my solid foundation for rebuilding my life. *Mom, your tenacious spirit lives in me, so there was no way I was going to remain trapped. Then you hounded me to get this book out. I only wish it was out in print before you passed away.*

I am especially grateful to my trusted friend Chaz, my accomplice who went above and beyond to provide for me, to ensure I was safe, and to make it possible for me to rejoin my family. *Chaz, you are a man of character who has continued to influence me by your selfless, giving nature.*

Two professors at Kennesaw State University, Dr. Miriam Boeri and Dr. Anne Richards, who became dear friends, mentored me through my undergraduate degree and master's degree. They were my models for becoming a professional woman who could achieve anything I wanted. *Thank you for helping me view my past not as wasted years, but as an opportunity to learn from my experiences as a springboard to my future.* Our writing group at KSU, with dear friends Anne, Sandy, Laurence, and Jessica, kept my manuscript warm like a newborn baby in an incubator. Your feedback, edits, and friendship have been invaluable.

To the many people who left Scientology who had the courage to expose its abuses by giving media interviews, blogging, posting YouTube videos, filing legal affidavits, writing books, hosting websites and private Facebook groups: Thank you for the forums you have provided that helped me to connect with reality, find truth, and reconnect with friends. This list would take up several inches if I named everyone, but I give special thanks to Janis Gillham Grady, Mike Rinder, Roger Weller, Jeff Hawkins, Spanky Taylor, Doug Parent, Karen de la Carriere, Jeffrey Augustine, Gary Morehead, and Tony Ortega's tonyortega.org.

Extra special thanks to Leah Remini and A&E for creating *Leah Remini: Scientology and the Aftermath*. Leah, thank you for being a courageous voice for so many who have been harmed and bullied by Scientology. Your tenacity inspired me to become an activist again. My mother would have loved you. Thank you for the opportunity to contribute on your show, coincidentally filming on the day of my 19th anniversary date of escaping Scientology.

Thank you to Mike Rinder and Steve Hassan for writing a foreword to my book. As the former spokesman for Scientology and head of its Office of Special Affairs, Mike had been instrumental in my husband Peter Schless's disconnection from me; he publicly criticized me after doing TV interviews, and blocked my books from coming out in 2000 and 2006. Mike's own break from Scientology in 2007 required a similar "Sophie's Choice" as mine to leave loved ones behind when choosing life outside of Scientology. For Mike to now help me is, as Mike wrote to me, "both ironic and karmic...and satisfying and cathartic." *Mike, I thank, respect and appreciate you for redirecting your efforts into exposing Scientology's abuses that are touching thousands through your blog, Something Can Be Done About It, and the lives of millions, through Leah Remini: Scientology and the Aftermath.*

Steve Hassan's book, *Combating Cult Mind Control*, was the first "cult recovery" book I read along with Jon Atack's *A Piece of Blue Sky*. Although Steve wrote about leaving the Moonies, I found my own life experiences on his pages as he described his mindset in the cult, the group's use of thought control, and his break out, recovery and conclusions that he now uses to help others regain their freedom of mind. *Steve, thank you for encouraging me to stand up and be counted as an ex-member with valuable experiences to share that could help others. I appreciate your compassion toward people breaking free from the undue influence of cults without judging them as having character flaws that caused them to join the cult originally.*

The special man I met at a most unlikely time in my life extended friendship to me that became a special relationship I could trust and embrace. We opened our worlds to each other and found we could share our pasts and enjoy life as a loving partnership. Greg is the most thoughtful man I've ever known, and I dearly love. And he rearranged his life so I could complete this book without other obligations. *Greg, I wouldn't have become the woman I am now without your resilience through challenging times, your unending support, and your unconditional love.*

# FOREWORD ONE

WHEN IT COMES TO A SUBJECT as complicated and difficult to navigate as scientology, it helps to have a guide. Ideally, she would be well versed in the subject, and her knowledge would not be based solely on academic study, but on personal experience.

She would also be able to translate that experience and knowledge—and the often impenetrable forest of words and acronyms that litters scientology—into understandable and interesting English.

It would be even better if your guide had a compelling personal story to hold your interest and be a foundation for the insight imparted.

And this brings me to Karen Pressley (whom I knew as Karen Schless before she left the Sea Org).

Karen takes her readers on a journey from the world of professional musicians and Hollywood, through introduction to the teachings of L. Ron Hubbard, the first steps of his "Bridge to Spiritual Freedom," to becoming immersed in the scientology "celebrity" orbit, to arriving at the top and gaining entrance to the innermost sanctum of the organization. There, she worked directly with scientology's worldwide leader at his secret international headquarters.

She ultimately escaped from the mental and physical prison – but like so many others, she had to make a Sophie's Choice, abandoning her husband in order to break away from the organization's control.

And then the fallout: daring to speak about her experiences and becoming a target for the notoriously vindictive organization in its efforts to silence her.

Sadly, I was part of those efforts before I too reached the breaking point and escaped. It is somewhat ironic, but certainly karmic, to now be writing a Foreword to Karen's book. This is the same book I had worked so hard to prevent being published since the early 2000s. And to know that in some way, I have been able to encourage and assist Karen to tell her story to the world now is both satisfying and cathartic.

It is a great read by a talented woman. The old adage that truth is stranger than fiction might have been coined for this book. Some of it is too incredible to be true. But it is. Every word of it.

MIKE RINDER
May 2017

Mike Rinder, former Executive Director of the Church of Scientology's Office of Special Affairs (OSA) and international spokesperson, has become the foremost critic of the Church of Scientology International since he left Scientology in 2007. A second generation Australian Scientologist, Mike worked with L. Ron Hubbard in the Sea Organization aboard the Flagship Apollo since 1973. He remained in the Sea Org until 2007, when he concluded that there was no way he could change the culture of violence and abuse that had become endemic under its head, David Miscavige. Since Mike left Scientology, he has worked to bring about change that ends abuses within the church. Mike has appeared in the Emmy-award winning HBO documentary *Going Clear: Scientology and the Prison of Belief* by Alex Gibney (2015) and works as a consultant to *Leah Remini: Scientology and the Aftermath* (A&E Channel, 2016-2017).

# FOREWORD TWO

IT'S AN HONOR FOR ME TO WRITE THIS foreword to Karen Pressley's memoir. As a licensed mental health counselor, I strongly encourage people to read this book carefully and thoughtfully, to realize the degree that Scientology has long been exploiting well-known social influence methods and techniques. They knowingly look for high profile, attractive, creative spokespeople to help present the brand in the most positive light, who could be used in Scientology recruitment videos and utilized in their indoctrination scenarios. I *so* want people to understand undue influence and mind control, and how Scientology's influence infiltrated Hollywood, and thus Hollywood fans, while Hollywood is now reclaiming its power.

Karen and I originally connected by email after she escaped from Scientology in 1998, after she read my book, *Combating Cult Mind Control*. She said that reading my experiences leaving the Unification Church (where I had become a leader who recruited for the Moonies in the 1970s) helped her come to terms with her own circumstances as a former celebrity recruiter for Scientology. We finally met in Montreal in July 2012, when we were each to lead sessions at the International Cultic Studies Association conference for people recovering from past membership in cultic groups—the same week that Katie Holmes left Tom Cruise and took baby Suri with her.

When the news about the Cruise-Holmes separation hit the news, a CNN crew came to Montreal to interview each of us about how Katie's bold move would affect her and Suri's safety, considering Scientology's known policies of vindictive attacks against ex-members and disconnection that breaks up families. I admired Karen's courage and willingness to stand up and be counted, to do media interviews and share her experiences of how deeply involved she was in Scientology—experiences that are not easy to discuss in public settings.

Karen taught a writing workshop at the conference, using her workbook "Coming to Terms With Your Story: Writing to Heal." She showed them how to use writing as an effective method for personal healing and to tell their stories. As a recovery counselor, I believe "narrative therapy" is incredibly valuable. This helps people to recover as they step out from the present, look back to see the younger self, and remember facts and circumstances surrounding different events so they can put the pieces together again. Narrative therapy is integral to reclaiming one's sense of self that may have gotten displaced while being involved with a controlling, high-demand group. There's also a synergistic quality to healing when former group members share stories with each other, because they tell you their memories that might trigger your own memories.

I appreciate Leah Remini giving me the opportunity to participate in one of her *Reddit: Ask Me Anything* specials with journalist Lawrence Wright and attorney Ray Jeffrey. This was a surreal opportunity for me to reflect on my 40-plus years of close association with Scientologists and members of other cultic groups. This brought me a powerful emotional marker of how far we've come— that there can be a high-profile celebrity such as Leah saying the likes of "With the help of the former Number 3 man (Mike Rinder), we want to expose this group and pull back the curtains. We want everyone to know the truth, how they are harming people, how they are breaking up families, how they are ripping off the public, how much deceptive recruitment is involved…" There is a synergistic effect as people get out, tell pieces of their stories and put it all together, and heal. That's one of the biggest roles Leah Remini has right now with *Aftermath*. She's interviewing people sharing key points that many members have experienced, and it's helping them heal.

As I said during the segment I was in on her show but it was edited out due to time constraints: We also need to help people recover by explaining undue influence and mind control, explaining that things like Scientology's TRs (training routines) are hypnosis, explaining phobia programming and how to undo phobias. It's important for people who have left a group to learn about these things to help them heal.

Undue influence is any act of persuasion that overcomes the free will and judgment of another person. People can be unduly influenced by deception, flattery, trickery, coercion, hypnosis and other techniques. Similarly, mind control refers to a specific set of methods and techniques, such as hypnosis or thought stopping that influences how a person thinks, feels and acts. Mind control becomes destructive when the locus of control is external, and it is used to undermine a person's ability to think and act independently. A person's freedom of choice becomes compromised by influential authorities or techniques such as persuasion, coercion, conformity, compliance, control or fear arousal, that modify your perceptions, motives, and cognitive or behavioral outcomes.

The four components of control—Behavior, Information, Thoughts, Emotions (BITE)—are my model to help people understand mind control as a complex phenomenon aimed at creating a new cult identity. Destructive mind control can be determined when the overall effect of these components promotes dependency and obedience to some leader or cause. Such influences used to keep people mindless and dependent is unhealthy, and can result in social isolation, acceptance of dominant ideologies from authoritarian leaders, and extreme threats or promised rewards that are deceptively orchestrated. Use the BITE model to help people exit as well as recover from abusive and high-control cults.

A destructive cult is a pyramid-shaped authoritarian regime with a head or group of people that have dictatorial control over members. It uses deception to recruit new members, and does not tell them what the group actually believes or what will be expected of them if they become a member. It uses undue influence to keep people dependent, obedient, and loyal. People who leave cults also have to break through the phobias that have been implanted by the group. Scientology instills a phobia in its members to not see mental health professionals, and to not call the police when they witness a crime within the Scientology organization. Hubbard developed phobias for his Scientology members because he wanted a monopoly on influence techniques. He didn't want people to know that if you've been traumatized, reliving it over and over and over again in a session until the needle floats is *not* the best way to heal trauma; in fact, Scientology's auditing process makes you numb and disassociated—the opposite of what real trauma healing is about.

Research has been demonstrated repeatedly—from the Asch conformity study (of individuals yielding to a majority group and the effect of those influences on people's beliefs and opinions), the Milgram obedience study (measuring the willingness of participants to obey an authority figure who instructed them to perform acts conflicting with their conscience) to the Zimbardo prison study (investigated the psychological effects of power discrepant roles in a BITE model human test tube)—that shows how we are social organisms, how we have mirror neurons, how we are constantly taking in information, and how we are being impacted by our environments. This research speaks to the central significance of the need to use our critical thinking, our ability to engage in reflective, rational and independent thinking, and be able to detect inconsistencies and mistakes in reasoning, while questioning any person or group that says: *I have the only way; I have the Truth; don't talk to those ex-members, don't talk to those critics, don't read their books, don't look at their websites because they are bad people.*

For people involved with Scientology or any cultic group, I'll address why people remain in them, as Karen's story highlights: Many stay for fear of losing their family, friends and career connections if they leave. Most groups inflict destructive practices against apostates such as shunning and disconnection that destroys families and friendships. However, the toll is also very high for staying in while not being able to be your true self, and not being happy with yourself.

Our investigative journalists have the responsibility to present the public with truth based on checked facts that will help people make informed decisions about groups that practice mind control techniques. Anderson Cooper's 2012 interview of the Scientology wives on CNN left people hearing that the women were married to top leaders and swear that nobody was abused by David Miscavige—contrary to the testimonies made by their former husbands. Yet, the consumer needs fact-checked findings to decide who was right. Presenting both sides without fact-checking both sides has turned into normalizing harmful practices—the burden of proof for a cult's lofty promises falls on the consumer who must subject him/herself to the group's policies and practices to find out whether the group's claims are true, at their own expense. And this expense can be tolled in loss of mental well being, loss of years of their life, loss of money, even the loss of a family member.

To reverse this problem, the burden of proof should be placed on the organization making a claim, not on the consumer to disprove it. If a group such as Scientology that calls itself a religion is making extraordinary claims such as "We can heal psychosomatic illnesses, eliminate mental dysfunctions, and enable you to achieve extraordinary superpowers," the burden of proof should be on Scientology to demonstrate those claims to be provable in double-blind studies. An organization that affects the lives of humankind shouldn't be able to say that they have different criteria for living or for discipline or for creating miracles without at the same time being obligated to prove their claim and comply with the laws of the land—whether it's a used car and how much mileage is on it, or a group that says we are a church and we can do faith healing so you don't need doctors or vaccinations. This is not meant to tamper with freedom of religion, or the individual's right to believe and practice as they choose, but it is meant to protect citizens against organizations with unscrupulous practices that bring harm, such as physically or mentally abusing staff, destroying families, and robbing people of life savings, under the banner of religious freedom. We see this protection in many other countries that have banned Scientology, but we are waiting for the American government to take action.

Karen's book holds another powerful message: There is life after cult. This story is not about rehashing and reliving the trauma of the past. It's a story coming from a survivor/thriver, from a place of "I am a good person, I have important things to do with my life. I can reclaim the altruism and idealism that I had when I was in the cult thinking that I was helping the world. Now I can actually help the world in a constructive effective way." Karen's story and others like it by ex-members is going to help people better understand how young people become radicalized by extremists, whether it's a neo-Nazi group, white identity cults, ISIS, political cults, or multi-level marketing cults. We need to raise people's consciousness about the human mind, and how we are hard-wired to respond to people who we think are legitimate authority figures; how we are hard-wired to respond to our peer groups with whom we identify.

Karen, I care about you, and respect and admire you. I salute you and all the other heroes who stand up and put the pieces together to heal themselves and help others heal through sharing their stories.

STEVEN HASSAN, M.Ed., LMHC, NCC
Boston, MA - May 2017

Steven Hassan has been on the forefront of cult awareness activism since 1976, and is one of the foremost authorities on undue influence in high-control groups. He is the Founding Director of Freedom of Mind Resource Center, a coaching, consulting, and training organization dedicated to supporting individuals to freely consider how they want to live their lives. He understands the subject from the perspective as a former cult member and as a clinical professional who has worked full time in this field since 1975. He authored *Combating Cult Mind Control: The #1 Best Selling Guide to Protection, Rescue, and Recovery from Destructive Cults* (1988, 1990, 2015); *Releasing the Bonds: Empowering People to Think for Themselves* (2000); and *Freedom of Mind: Helping Loved Ones Leave Controlling People, Cults and Beliefs* (2012, 2013). His web site is www.freedomofmind.com.

# INTRODUCTION

## Gulf Coast USA, Summer 2017

ERNEST HEMINGWAY AND RED SMITH are both quoted to have said, "There is nothing to writing. All you do is sit down at a type-writer, open a vein, and bleed." I can relate. Writing a story about a personal journey through Scientology would have been a lot more pleasurable if I had been writing a comedy story or a lifelong love letter. But weeks bled into a few annual calendar turnovers as I portrayed Scientology's legacy to me.

A person who gets involved in Scientology can fall down a rabbit hole in many ways without seeing it coming, like we did. Re-flecting on my twenty-something state of mind when my then hus-band, Peter Schless, and I detoured from building our lives to-gether in the Hollywood entertainment industry to journey into Scientology, is a perplexing experience for who I am now. We saw ourselves as interested participants, not victims, but no one knows they are being deceived while they are being deceived.

Fewer seats were taken by A-list celebrities in Scientology's course rooms and counseling seats than by artists like Peter and me. We were not household names, but we had achieved some success. Our greatest accomplishments by that time were our hit song, "On the Wings of Love" composed by Peter Schless, with lyrics and recording by Jeffery Osborne; and "Peace in Our Life," the theme song to "Rambo: First Blood Part II," composed by Pe-ter with lyrics and recording by Frank Stallone. As a fashion de-signer, I enjoyed working with celebrity clients, including Lisa Blount, co-star of "An Officer and a Gentleman," a Carol Burnett

Show comedienne, a Beverly Hills fashion boutique, a private collection, and a growing client portfolio.

Ours is a one-of-a-kind story of two artists enticed by Celebrity Centre's siren song who walked out of Hollywood careers to join Scientology's extremist group, the Sea Organization and work in the inner sanctum of Scientology's leader, David Miscavige. We didn't plan to land near the top of the empire. Becoming a Scientologist was like getting absorbed into the script of a complicated reality show based on a story line authored by L. Ron Hubbard, the main character and protagonist. His self-appointed successor, David Miscavige, who entered the scene disguised as another protagonist, revised Hubbard's story line with his own ideas of how Scientology is supposed to go. Hubbard's plot for his characters (the customers and staff who enroll) is straightforward and linear: customers pay their money, read and absorb the materials without question, follow the rules written in stone, achieve the stated outcomes of each level of the bridge to spiritual freedom, and ultimately dedicate their lives to the Sea Org for a billion years to preserve Scientology in the endless universe.

But Hubbard's and Miscavige's story line is filled with flaws. Scientology imposes its will on its characters (the individual customers and staff) through undue influence, while convincing participants they are achieving spiritual freedom. But they grossly underestimate the power of free will in those of us who want to author our own story line and determine our own outcome. These people—the departed celebrities and other followers, the media professionals, public officials and police, lawyers and psychiatrists, religious leaders, ex-members turned critics, and even the "never-ins"—become the antagonists who stand in opposition to the protagonist's goals. We are not the bad guys as Hubbard & Miscavige would have everyone believe. But by authoring our own outcomes, we bring on the wrath of the group that tries to shut us up and defame us.

It began for us as it does for many new people in Scientology, with an innocent reach for some Scientology appetizers—short, inexpensive self-help courses. These led us to indulge in their impressive buffet of spiritual-enhancement services at Scientology's temple of the gods, the Hollywood Celebrity Centre. In this fortress for artists, we learned about achieving greatness and commanding influence so we could change world conditions. Brick by brick, we built the walls of our own mental prison while becoming Scientologists.

Scientology artists and celebrities are protected, understood, gratified, and revered simply for showing up. It was easy to become drunk with self-importance from CC's signature cocktail: A mix of Hubbard's ego-boosting words that elevate the artist who is seen as a special breed of human, the most valuable in earth's social strata, the dreamer of dreams who alone can elevate the tone of a society above all others. Add the luxury Celebrity Centre oasis, its privileged services to its array of celebrity followers, garnished with the attitudes, values, beliefs and lofty promises embedded in its spiritual pursuit system, and we have intoxication from daily engagement in celebrity spirituality.

A few celebrity faithfuls from our era—Tom Cruise, John Travolta, Anne Archer, Kirsti Alley, jazz musician Chick Corea, Nancy Cartwright (the voice of Bart Simpson), writer/director Paul Haggis—have been joined by several of the young rising stars from the '80s who moved to A-list success including singer Lisa Marie Presley, Leah Remini ("King of Queens," "The Talk,"), Elizabeth Moss ("Handmaid's Tale," "Mad Men"), Juliette Lewis ("Cape Fear", "The Firm"), Jenna Elfman ("Dharma and Greg"), Giovanni Ribisi ("Avatar," "Friends").

A short list of later additions includes: actress Laura Prepon ("Orange is the New Black"), comedian Jeffrey Tambor, actor Jason Lee ("My Name is Earl"), musician/songwriters Isaac Hayes, Edgar Winter, Billy Sheehan, Beck, David Campbell, David Pomeranz, Mark Isham; Erika Christiansen ("Traffic", "Parenthood,") Michael Fairman ("Hill Street Blues," "The X Files,") award-winning British author Neil Gaimon, photographer/film producer Michael Dovan, actor Jason Beghe ("Chicago P.D."), actor Geoffrey Lewis ("Return of the Man from U.N.C.L.E."), news anchor Greta van Susteren and her Washington lawyer husband John Coale; film/TV actresses Nazanin Boniadi, Katie Holmes, Nicole Kidman. The latter three left the group after a relationship with Tom Cruise. The revolving doors continue to spin out the back with the departures of Tambor, Lee and Gaimon, as well as Haggis, Beghe, and Presley who have become open critics. Leah Remini has become the foremost celebrity ex-Scientology critic in their history. Actors Christopher Reeve, Patrick Swayze, Sonny Bono, Lisa Blount and Karen Black, and musicians Isaac Hayes, Al Jarreau, Nicky Hopkins (Rolling Stones, Beatles "Revolution" album) passed at a young age, not experiencing the life-prolonging benefits that Scientology promised. Celebrities also dabble in Scientology and leave after a few courses, such as Leonard Cohen, William S. Burroughs, Demi Moore, Brad Pitt, Jerry Seinfield, and Catherine Bell.

Peter and I were striving to be at the top of our game, recruiting artists and celebrities for Scientology, before I beheld the honor of succeeding Yvonne Gillham Jentzsch, the founder of the Celebrity Centre Los Angeles, as the Commanding Officer of the CC Network. Peter walked out of his music career into obscurity as a musician for Scientology, and I joined him at Golden Era Productions. That marks our transition from being world changers through the arts to entering a war zone triggered by the *Time* Magazine story, "The Thriving Cult of Greed and Power."

The crux of that *Time* story really did identify what I discovered at International Management. After Hubbard's death, David Miscavige's headship of Scientology coincided with the entrance of Tom Cruise into Scientology and the church going under Cruise Control. At the Int base, we inevitably intersected with the Miscavige family, including David and his wife Shelley, brother Ronnie Jr., and father, Ron Sr., along with the elite staff working at the headquarters. I expected to find ultimate Operating Thetans (advanced Scientologists), the most superior and able beings who demonstrated the highest intellectual acumen and emotional tone levels while working to achieve the aims of Scientology: a world without war, insanity and criminality. We did find a beautifully groomed estate with some luxurious interiors—albeit behind chain-link fences topped with barbed and razor-topped wire—but the luxuries belied the Int base's dystopian world.

The management of Scientology operations parallels the Netflix series, "House of Cards" that portrays ruthless manipulation and cold-blooded leveraging of power. As Scientology's head who monopolizes control of Scientology and the empire's wealth, David Miscavige mirrors Kevin Spacey's character, Frances Underwood, a power-hungry politician who will stop at nothing to gain power and control over Washington. Underwood espouses that you either dominate or you submit; you either create and exploit fear, or you succumb to it. Heather Dunbar (Attorney General), who abhors President Underwood's cunning ways, faces off with Underwood asking, "Is this how you live with yourself, by rationalizing the obscene into the palatable?"

"Rationalizing the obscene into the palatable" portrays the mindset of the Int base culture: rationalizing physical and psychological abuse, overboarding, sleep deprivation, abortions, prison camp assignments, divorces to prove loyalty, cover-ups as acceptable acts that have become normalized. This wear-and-tear on staff's mental and physical condition seems like an effort to destroy people's subjectivity so that Scientology can perpetuate with Miscavige at the center of its universe. I've had a front-row seat watching misogyny play out as he dismantled women from power positions and turned other leaders and staff into ash while transforming Hubbard's Scientology into Miscavige's brand. Staff are immunized from certain hurtful actions against church enemies, by not being told what is really going on in the outside world regarding deaths, suicides, lawsuits, and shrinking membership numbers in Scientology, and instead being told Scientology is the fastest growing religion on earth.

While Tom Cruise and John Travolta are known as Scientology celebrities, far less is known about how celebrities are seduced by Scientology's siren song with promises of achieving immortality. And that key people strategize celebrity recruitment, and utilize them as mouthpieces with social capital to bring in more recruits and income. Even less is understood about the role of artists in Scientology, their responsibilities for making this a better world through Scientology, and how they are to recognize and deal with Scientology's long list of enemies from police, doctors and media to psychiatrists, journalists, critics and ex-members, and defend Scientology against attacks.

Behind all of this is the masterminding of the Scientology empire emanating from the secretive International Management headquarters in the southern California desert for more than 30 years. Two decades of experience at the Celebrity Centre level in Hollywood and at the highest levels of Scientology management exposed me to the inner workings of both, where the strategies are crafted and the plans are implemented in a do-or-die environment. My story answers the question, how does Scientology transform artists into zealots, and staff into extremists? And how does Scientology hide its crimes behind the banner of religious freedom?

It took three escapes to finally get out, when the doors to my world of Scientology friends and loved ones slammed shut from the disconnection policy. I've heard it said that if you're afraid to speak out against tyranny, then you are a slave of it. As a survivor, I've found that writing about my experiences has helped me to recover from the uneasy balance of my Scientology life, having walked that tight rope for 16 years, and outside since 1998. As a critic, I've had experiences that you wouldn't want your children to experience. The organization stopped my first two book publications in 2000 and 2006, using threats and lies to intimidate my publishers. Instead of rebounding with a counter-attack, I completed my undergraduate degree, got a Master's degree, spoke at more than 100 events, from churches and youth groups to university classrooms, and did media interviews on NBC *Dateline*, CBS, CNN and others. Scientology sought vengeance by fair gaming me further, but they only diminished their own reputation as a result.

Since the mid to late-2000s, when stories from people who had escaped more recently than me became a focus in the media, I receded as an activist. In late 2016, the A&E Channel aired Season One of *Leah Remini: Scientology and the Aftermath,* with Mike Rinder, former head of Scientology's Office of Special Affairs and international spokesperson, as a consultant. Leah's show has caused an upheaval in Scientology's previously untouchable empire. Scientology has bullied ex-members into silence for years, but the recent testimonies about human rights violations opened the floodgates for people to learn the truth and for many of us to tell our stories with less fear. *Aftermath* served as a call to action that inspired me back into activism. I echo Leah's belief that every story matters, whenever it happened. I share her conviction that I can't let the Scientology bullies harm people and do nothing about it. *That* is why I got this book out.

Scientology's membership numbers are shrinking, but they continue to affect people who have nothing to do with it, such as teens who join and then disconnect from their parents who don't support Scientology. A growing network of people "never in" join with ex-Scientology critics online as part of a growing voice that speaks up for those remaining trapped inside, and that informs "never-ins" from getting involved or getting harmed by the group.

This story is written chronologically to the best of my memory. It covers three decades, starting prior to Scientology membership,

16 years in Scientology and 12 years in the Sea Organization, and about 15 years of aftermath. People and events that appear in my story directly impacted Peter's or my life in some way. All statements are drawn from my direct knowledge, observation, and experiences to the best of my recollection. Conversations with staff or friends from twenty or so years ago, whose name or date of conversation is unknown, is unable to be documented.

Please note that I've added commentary that reflects my current thinking about those past events, so you will read about something from twenty years ago while also reading my current thoughts about it. Steven Hassan said "Unless you work on your own personal recovery and integrate your Cult Self with your Authentic Self, the Cult Self can continue to exert unconscious negative influence." Adding current commentary to past events has helped me to diffuse the effects of those events.

I have no intent to harm any people named in this story. I changed only two names for their protection. I make criticisms, but I seek no vengeance. I left 19 years ago and have created a great life since then with no desire or need for revenge. Scientology affects everyone differently, so I'd be glad to hear from you if you want to write me. Scientology may try to "dead agent" me (defame me in the public eye) once this book comes out. You'll find my reports about their actions on my book website, among other places.

Since I have attributed various books, websites and other sources directly in the text throughout the story, I have not provided separate reference pages. I define almost everything in the text, so I do not include a glossary in the book. Please visit the book website for a glossary, or write me with questions.

Scientology is a genre of fantasy that transports participants across religion, magic and the occult, science fiction, self-help practices, and psychology, adding up to the world created by L. Ron Hubbard. To get an answer to "What is Scientology?" read memoirs like this one; read stories by others who have lived through it, and read well-researched journalistic and academic coverage, to get a complete answer.

Every true story is another thread woven into the tapestry of testimonies hanging in the gallery of the public eye. Cruise or Travolta could single-handedly end Scientology's abuses by facing off with the organization's leadership and delivering some ultimatums: end the abuses or I'm out of here. For arcane reasons, they continue using it for personal benefit despite its abuses. But if my story can help just one person break free of Scientology or help one family reconnect after being separated by Scientology's disconnection practices, then the efforts to publish this book were worth it.

My goal was to stop writing when I finished a complete account of my journey. When the book came to 800 pages and 240,000 words, and I still wasn't done, I abridged some of the chapters in the interest of readers who prefer a shorter book size. If you are interested in reading more details wherever I abridged a chapter, please visit the book website. Also let me know if you have any questions.

I hope this book raises questions such as: What other church do you know of that runs separate buildings for its celebrity followers, like a Catholic Celebrity Centre, or a celebrity Jewish temple? Do you know of any other church that calls its followers a recruiter to whom they pay commissions on the money spent by the recruiter's selectees to that church? Do you know of any other church that sells self-help services at fixed prices? Is there another church that enforces their followers to get abortions to prove their loyalty? What about routinely covering up child abuse behind the banner of religious freedom? We know that other cultic groups practice "shunning," which Scientology practices extensively. At what point will our justice system, which is here to protect us, step in and halt the crimes this group commits under the guise of religious protection?

# PART I

## CELEBRITY SPIRITUALITY

# 1

## HAPPY VALLEY

"No one shall be subjected to torture or cruel, inhuman or de-
grading treatment or punishment."

> \- United Nations
> Declaration of Human Rights (1948), Article 5

**Southern California desert, 1990**

*Come back!*

Gravel crunches under the car's tires as I listen to it back away
from the Great House. Its headlights glare at me against the inky
sky over Happy Valley, blotting out my vision of the driver's face.

A uniformed security guard from the Church of Scientology's
International Management base has just deposited me at a ram-
shackle building that houses its prison camp, eleven miles from the
base. As he heads back toward the main highway, the red taillights
of his car diminish. I hear the car wrenching at every pothole,
shocks creaking, violating the desert silence. And I don't want
those hideous sounds to stop.

Through this rusty window screen from inside a front room, I
can barely make out the vehicle anymore. Terror stabs my gut. I
can't chase after him; it's pitch black out. *Get me the hell out of here!*

*This is all wrong. Come back damn you!* Why bother to scream through the window? No one will hear me. *Bastard.*

The compliant guard will dutifully follow that road for eleven miles until he arrives at the base and reports that he has delivered me to the RPF, the Rehabilitation Project Force, a public relations name for Scientology's prison camp. I am now a non-person without rights, and he has complied with his order. He is trained to be indifferent to my feelings. He and Jeff Walker, Scientology's highest technical official, the Senior Case Supervisor International, who signed off on my paperwork to route me to the RPF, probably believe that I got what I deserved.

At 38, I am now a detainee in the Scientology's gulag in a southern California desert. The Great House, circa 1940s, stands alone on the former Soboba Indian Reservation, and serves as the rooming house for RPFers. The guard must have brought me to this God-forsaken place in the dark so I couldn't see breaks in the fences along the perimeter of the property as possible escape points. I would have a heck of a time finding my way out of here if I tried to break out. Former detainees cautioned me about the rattlesnakes and scorpions out here, so a midnight trek was unlikely. I heard that former Int base execs Jesse Prince, Spike Bush, Vicki Aznaran, probably others had escaped from HV, but I wondered how.

My husband, Peter Schless, and I have been forced to stay in separate quarters for nearly one month. Only troublemakers end up at the Old Gilman House (OGH) on the west edge of the Int base, or the RPF. People like me who fall from grace with Scientology's leadership are sequestered, off-loaded, or "RPF'd" when officials deem us to be treasonous or dysfunctional. I am considered treasonous. I "blew" the base headquarters—I took an unauthorized departure, left without permission—as if I were an enlisted military member who had gone AWOL.

Before I took off, I had begged Peter to leave with me. My husband lacked the ability to see through the bubble in which he dwelled at his Golden Era music studio. I thought of it as his gilded cage. Or maybe he just didn't have the guts to take the risk even when a door opened. At the headquarters of the Church of Scientology International—the Int Base, known to the public as Golden Era Productions—it's safer to wear blinders and maintain status quo and get stroked for it, than to question leadership and stand up for what you believe.

As a member of the Sea Organization, the elite corps of Scientology management who makes a billion-year commitment to safeguard Scientology, I had to physically escape to get out. I couldn't just leave if I wanted out, couldn't just say, *I've changed my mind and want my old life back, so goodbye, thanks for everything, I'm done.* No. I relinquished my rights to control my mobility when I signed that eternal contract in 1986. Policy says that I have to get permission to leave, go through an in-depth interrogation process, sign volumes of papers to "route out" on Scientology's terms, and get the whole mess approved, if I wanted out.

Before I blew, I had wanted out so desperately that I refused to waste anymore of my life trying to do anything on the Sea Org's terms. I had been in the Sea Org at Celebrity Centre since 1987, but Peter and I had only been at the Int base one year. I had seen enough to realize that the planet could not be cleared through the actions of Int Management, where modus operandi included physically abusing staff and psychologically bringing staff to their demise through sleep deprivation and slave-like working conditions; requiring women to get abortions, and requiring spouses to divorce to prove their loyalty to Miscavige. Leaders at the Int base had no moral compass and I could not consider this the most ethical beings on the planet or a religious organization. It didn't take rocket science to figure out that we had made a bad and even stupid choice coming here.

Once I realized that I couldn't convince Peter to leave with me, after countless secret conversations about leaving the Sea Org, I had to make moves independent of him. My best option was to escape in the middle of the night when there was less of a chance that anyone would see me. Feeling like a slave on the run or a convict breaking out of a prison, I had to steal back the rights to my life instead of freely claiming them. But being on the run is better than being dead.

Before dawn, without waking Peter, I tossed a few clothes and toiletries into some white plastic garbage bags with yellow drawstrings. Russ and Linda Greilich were sleeping in the other bedroom while I crept quietly out the front door with my dog, Toby. If anyone else saw me walking outside around 4am toting garbage bags, they'd think I was taking out the trash or the dog, so they wouldn't stop or question me. And Gold crew came home at all hours of the night, so there would be nothing unusual about me being up and around outside.

As I neared my car parked by the garbage dumpster, Bruce Hines, who had audited Tom Cruise from the Senior C/S Int's office, was just coming in. I didn't want to draw attention to myself by waving, but I did make eye contact with him. He nodded and said, "Taking out the trash?" After I smiled and nodded, he passed me by, probably writing off my actions as what I hoped them to look like. I watched Bruce enter the building before I put my bags in the trunk and Toby in the back seat.

I took a deep breath, hoping no one else would see me as I drove through the parking lot toward the gate. Since Peter had been on the "OK to drive list" we had a remote control for the gate in the car. The trick was, guards were on watch 24/7 at the Devonshire Apartment gates. But I was in luck! Security guards must have fallen asleep, or maybe they were changing shifts and not paying attention to the gates. My throbbing heart leapt up my throat as the gate rolled open.

No one stopped me. The miracle of driving through those gates unnoticed and with ease belied my sense of feeling like a convict breaking free.

We were outside the gate now, with no plan. Which way to go? I turned left into Hemet, and chose back roads through Moreno Valley toward Orange County. Anaheim? There would be a lot of people in Anaheim. There would be no Disneyland stops, no time, nor could I pay for admission. I just wanted to be surrounded by a lot of people, in case Security came after me and I needed help.

Anaheim felt meaningless. Crowds of people, mostly families and couples having fun together, made me feel so alone. I needed to be somewhere that mattered. San Diego? Peter and I had great memories there. We once stole away to Le Meridien Hotel on Coronado Island for Christmas, our only day off all year. I had no funds for Le Meridien. My white plastic trash bag held only a pair of jeans, a t-shirt and some undies, so I needed some clothes. My Nordstrom's credit card would come in handy right now, a carry-over from my pre-Sea Org life, something I couldn't use much since I rarely had time off. Did I have the nerve to walk into Nordstrom in this state, an AWOL runaway? Heck with it. I was sick of being without, living as if I didn't deserve to fulfill my needs. I left the downtown San Diego Nordstrom store after a reprehensible shopping spree, carrying a few bags of clothes and shoes that would be part of the new me—Karen Schless, the ex-Sea Org member.

Where could I stay? I had enough cash to pay for about two nights in a reasonably priced hotel. I couldn't use a credit card, because Security would access my charges through Peter and see where I was traveling. I drove along the Pacific Coast Highway and discovered a rustic resort outside of La Jolla, overlooking the Pacific Ocean. I checked into Torrey Pines, not knowing that this was a famous golfer's hotel. The oceanfront setting might offer some stress relief through the views and sound of the waves. Not bad for $89 per night.

I called Mom to tell her I had just left Gold, without Peter. She offered to fly from Atlanta to help me. My thoughts turned to the many times that Scientology ethics staff had tried to get me to disconnect from Mom. Thankfully I had been defiant enough to refuse. Had I complied, I would have no one to turn to right now.

While awaiting Mom, I explored a small stretch of the Pacific Coast Highway, all four windows open, my hair whipping at my face. I filled the rest of the day with moments of little pleasures, basking in the magnificence of time to myself—a rare commodity since I joined the Sea Org in 1987—soaking up ocean views, tasting the sweetness of freedom. I stopped to watch a group of people hang-gliding in La Jolla, leaping off the cliffs to soar over the ocean, trusting their lives to the wind. I wanted to know what it felt like to enjoy such reckless abandon again, without fear. I wanted to know what it felt like to freely be myself without asking permission or feeling guilty.

I found an inexpensive place to eat, since I was low on cash. When I returned to my hotel, I scanned the parking lot for familiar cars and uniformed Sea Org staff before I parked. Security teams would be fired out to hunt me down, once they detected my location though their travel reservations computer system. Teams would scour airports, train and bus stations quickly enough to prevent me from successfully leaving the LA area.

Mom arrived the next day. After we got through our tears, and then rehashed everything that happened, she tried to help me reason through my circumstances. She understood why I wanted to leave the Sea Org, but what was I going to do about Peter? We stayed at Torrey Pines another night before she and I set out on the 2,500-mile drive to her home in Atlanta.

Somewhere outside of Gallup, New Mexico, at a roadside motel, I broke down because I wanted to talk to Peter. I could barely stand to be away from him another minute. Being apart from him was like separating two layers of skin.

"It's not Peter I am trying to leave, Mom, it is the Sea Org. You know that."

"I'm sure Peter's worried about you," Mom said, "but are you sure it's wise to call?"

Calling Peter meant that I had to call the Int base through Gold reception, since direct lines and cell phones were prohibited. All incoming and outgoing calls were monitored by security; we *never* had private phone conversations. Peter would have been working with Security trying to track me down.

"Golden Era Productions, how can I help you?"

"This is Karen Schless. I want to talk to Peter."

"Just a moment." No questions were asked. I knew that the Gold receptionist had been given my name as a security risk--a blown staff member now on the Perimeter Council list--so when she put me on hold, she was sending my call to the security booth, where Peter would mostly like be camped out.

"KK? Where are you?" Peter's voice strained. I knew a guard was listening on the line.

"I'm with Mom, we're at a motel. I thought you might be worried about me. Are you in the security booth?"

"Yes, dammit, I've been trying to track you down. KK, are you crazy? What are you doing?"

"You knew I wanted to leave the Sea Org! You wouldn't listen to me. I'm going back to Atlanta with Mom. We're in Gallup, New Mexico right now."

"No, you stay there. I'll fly out there, and we'll talk. We'll work this out."

The next morning, Peter arrived at our desert motel, but didn't arrive alone. Two khaki uniformed security guards and Ken Hoden, the Gold public relations port captain, flanked Peter as they walked toward me. Peter and Hoden wore their winter blue pseudo-military Sea Org uniforms. Their shiny black shoes, navy blue pants, long-sleeved blue naval shirts, black ties, black and gold striped shoulder epaulettes, and white naval caps with black brims contrasted freakishly with the travelers wearing vacation clothes in 90 degree weather. Worse, the two men wore knee-length navy blue trench coats like X-men or comic book characters from *Batman's* Gotham City. Mom was frightened by what she called their Gestapo appearance. I felt like I was watching a scary scene from a bad movie that I didn't want to have a role in.

My husband's clothing didn't say, this-is-you-and-me-talking, sweetheart. His extremist image spoke loud and clear: he had come first as a Sea Org member, on duty to recover an escapee, and second as a husband who cared about his wife and marriage.

Instead of feeling happy to see him, I felt betrayed. I had imagined us hugging and I wanted to look into his eyes and see a flicker of compassion. There would be none of that. Nor would there be private time to talk, because Hoden wouldn't leave us alone. I flared up over Scientology's extremist demands and intervention into our life. Hoden didn't give a damn about our marriage. This visit was only about putting things right in the interest of the Sea Org. My complaints about Scientology's control were never seen as reasonable requests for a right to privacy. I felt furious at Hoden's insistence on being a part of our conversation and wanted to tell him to fuck off.

I won the small battle of having a private conversation with my husband, but it happened on his terms. Hoden let Peter and I sit in a booth in the motel coffee shop, while Hoden kept a watchful eye on us from a nearby booth.

"KK, you are living in the past. The Sea Org is our life now, and you signed a billion year contract. Doesn't that mean anything to you?"

As I watched Peter's facial expressions and listened to his tone of voice, I saw a man sold out to the Sea Org. In a strange way, I admired his level of commitment, twisted as it was, but I didn't share that with him. Peter and I had talked numerous times about the extreme conditions at the Int base when I had pleaded with him to leave with me and start our lives over. For him, leaving was not an option.

"What about our marriage vows? We said 'yes, until death do us part' before joining the Sea Org! Doesn't that mean anything to you?"

"Yes, but the point is, we made a decision to come into the Sea Org together! So are you going to throw this away and leave? I love you, KK."

He had me at KK. He still used this intimate nickname that reminded me of when we met in 1977 and had been crazy in love since. I didn't want to leave my husband; I only wanted to leave the Sea Org. And I wanted us to leave together and knew we could make it on the outside. I felt emotionally toxic, mentally broken. But like clay on his potter's wheel, he shaped my emotions. He persuaded me to return to the Int base and get myself sorted out.

Clinging to my hope that Peter would come to his senses and eventually leave with me to recover our lives, I ignored the signs that Peter's loyalty had shifted from our marriage to the Sea Org.

Who had betrayed whom? I stifled my rage. Any efforts at personal autonomy seemed futile. I didn't know anything about psychological manipulation then, but felt like I was being twisted like a pretzel to conform to what he and the Sea Org wanted. I didn't believe that Scientology used brainwashing, or that thought control existed. But I had no reasonable explanations—other than loving my husband—for why I succumbed to this coercion, or why I abandoned my efforts to regain my freedom.

I found Mom and lovingly but guiltily informed her of my decision to go back to the base with Peter. She was torn by seeing how much I cared about our marriage, and advising me to carry out my plans to leave the Sea Org. But before she could effectively argue to bring me to my senses, Hoden booked her a plane ticket. One of the security guards drove her to the nearest airport. The trench-coated men departed for their return to the Int base.

Scientology authority stole my hope for spending time talking with Peter while driving back to the base together. How could I have been so weak as to let them put my mother on a plane and fly her back to Atlanta? Worse, how could I have allowed Hoden to accompany me in my car back to the Int base, while Peter left with the security guards?

Hoden tried to commandeer the route I took back to the base. Instead, I drove back via the Grand Canyon, defying his efforts to prevent me from getting one last view of one of my favorite places on Earth. All Hoden cared about was returning me as fast as possible. Despite Hoden's protests, I drove to one of the shops near the rim and bought a copper Indian bracelet that I clasped on my wrist.

I thought I might not be able to travel again for years, and my bracelet would keep me connected to my memory of this place and time.

Once back at the base, instead of rejoining Peter to sort things out as Hoden promised, I was made to park my car near Peter's music studio, where it would be convenient for him to use. Peter and I were not allowed to see each other, and I was sequestered on the northwest side of the property in the Old Gilman House under 24/7 security watch.

I only stayed a little bit sane while under watch at OGH by re-living memories. Until just one year ago, I had been recruiting celebrities for Scientology and running the Celebrity Centre Network from our Hollywood headquarters. Before that, my design portfolio was growing with celebrity clients but I parked my design career to set up our music publishing company so we could retain more shares and rights from his recorded compositions. Just a few years ago, we were celebrating our biggest career achievement with "On the Wings of Love" becoming a hit song, and then getting "Peace in our Life" accepted as the theme song to "Rambo: First Blood Part II." Though these were Peter's works as a musician and composer, I call them our achievements because from my supporting roles as his music publisher, studio manager and wife, we achieved it all together. We had tasted success together. And then made a bad choice that let it all slip through our fingers.

I've asked myself over and over, what happened to Peter and me as artists who wanted to help build a new civilization by popularizing Scientology through the arts? Why did my husband, an award-winning composer, trade a successful career for professional obscurity? Why did we find the exclusivity of the remote desert base so alluring, as to give up everything we had for L. Ron Hubbard, Scientology, and the Sea Org?

And why are outsiders so unaware of this gulag on this hidden reservation along the San Jacinto Mountains between Gilman Hot Springs and Palm Springs? Maybe because this stretch of land holds not much more than dusty paths, tumbleweeds, and a few old buildings crying out for repair. But in the daylight, anyone could see the hundred or so black-clothed RPF detainees running from one place to the next, carrying out their orders in the desert heat. And if anyone meandered deeper into the property, they would see what Scientology was really trying to hide. The old Castille Canyon Ranch houses a more pathetic sight to behold: the children of the Int base Sea Organization staff who live and work there. Hold the hand of one of these shunted children to get a sense of a Sea Org child's daily life, void of a parent's nurturing, attention and love. They attend Scientology "school," whose product is to instill blind allegiance to Scientology, as if shaped by the Hitler youth training. I avoided having to watch the kids line up at muster like little soldiers. These kids are second generation Scientologists, unaware that there is any other way of life. They spend their formative years in a militaristic boarding-school setting, toiling like adults, robbed of a playful, joyous childhood and proper education.

Hubbard says that people with young bodies already know everything but have just forgotten; they've lived many past lives and just need to remember how to do things again. They grow up believing they are big spiritual beings in little bodies, powerful enough as thetans who were able to pick their mother who is a Scientologist, and come back into Scientology this lifetime. At best, the kids see their parents once a week on Sunday mornings, sometimes only once every few weeks. My friends Pat and Sarah placed their daughter Gayla and their son Gavin at the ranch, and tried to see them every other Sunday morning when possible. Gavin didn't adjust well to this parentless Ranch life, and was sent to the kid's version of the RPF in a remote camp in Los Angeles. Jenna Miscavige, daughter of Bitty and Ronnie Miscavige and niece of Scientology's leader, David Miscavige, was raised there, too, without parental nurturing or supervision. What a perfect place to shunt distracting children and imprisoned staff where few would think to look or ask what's going on here.

*Breathe*, I told myself. I have no idea what time it is. I am thirsty and the temperature is dropping. During the day, I was used to the hot Santa Ana winds blowing sheets of sand across the Moreno Valley. This cool night breeze now coming through the ragged window screen gives me chill bumps.

A white rattletrap school bus pulls up, and dozens of people spill out. RPFers run past me in the Great House wearing dirty black t-shirts, black shorts, black socks, black sneakers. Soon, I'll wear all black. It's Sea Org policy that everyone must look alike to express the unity, the oneness of our organization. The black clothes of an RPFer scream degradation, debasement, dehumanization. The daily uniform for Sea Org members in good standing looks like a U.S. Navy uniform, with light blue military shirt with shoulder epaulets and navy blue pants for men and women, decked with insignia and regalia that symbolizes officer status, ethics presence and Sea Org honor. Anyone like me, who lands here with no black clothes, has to dig through a barrel of used clothing discarded by former RPFers, to get dressed, until we somehow manage to acquire our own black gear.

*Breathe.* I fumble for the compact in my bag, needing a mirror to find the specks of sand lodged under my contact lenses. A crushed-looking woman with vacant blue eyes, straggly long brown hair, and smudges in the creases of a downturned mouth, stares back. Ugh. Whatever happened to me, the artist, Karen Schless? To living my dreams as an artist, a fashion designer, a wife, a music publisher?

We should have never left our home near the top of Coldwater Canyon above Studio City, overlooking the San Fernando Valley below. How and when did I lose myself?

The only way I am going to survive here is to live within my memories of the very real world called my past. It's the only way I can cling to life and prove to myself that I still have my wits about me. If I didn't stay connected to my past, I would have lost myself, like Peter did.

# 2

# RISKY BEGINNINGS

## Houston, 1976

TEXAS WAS THE LAST PLACE I had ever imagined living, after growing up in urban Chicago with a huge family that shaped my world. Except for a short stay in Gainesville, Florida, my life compass never pointed south or west, or to this city where oil is treated like gold.

My friend Mick, a fresh Marine Corps vet, lured me with an opportunity to help him start a new venture. After he had seen my Plant Lady business in downtown Bowling Green, Ohio, he talked me into coming to Houston to help him create a similar enterprise. It wasn't hard to entice me with Houston's warm climate after eleven feet of snow topped by an ice storm had just blanketed northern Ohio.

I sold off my business, held a moving sale to empty my apartment, and traded in my old van for a new Toyota SR5 hatchback. Unburdened with only luggage, some personal artwork, and a AAA travel map, my terrier Jessie and I headed to Houston. Jessie ended up saving my life at a motel in Little Rock, Arkansas that first night. She woke me up barking wildly as she stood on the end of my bed, her eyes riveted toward the window. Through the curtain, I could see a man's figure outside my door. Jessie and I heard him twisting and jiggling my doorknob. Her shrill bark and my screaming at the window drove him away before a guard arrived responding to my call to the front desk.

Our two-day journey ended with a safe arrival at Mick's place, but brought surprising news. His small business loan didn't get approved for the funds he needed to supplement his personal investment money. With only enough to cover a few weeks of salary and set-up costs, he lost me as a partner within the first month.

Going back to Ohio was not an option. I landed a day job doing temp secretarial work and a night gig serving drinks at a fancy Chinese restaurant. The local flavors of Luther's barbeque and steamed crawfish, along with the beaches at Galveston and Corpus Christi, plus interesting people within the city's diverse culture helped me to get to know Houston, Texas like a new best friend.

I landed a weekend job as a cocktail waitress at Spiro's, a new Houston nightclub that dressed its servers in off-the-shoulder mini-togas. A disco DJ filled the dance floor nightly, which kept the customers drinking, but the owner really packed the house once he switched to a live band. On opening night, a nine-foot ebony grand piano graced the front stage, awaiting the ten-piece Johnny Williams band. I was so busy serving cocktails I didn't notice the musicians moving into position behind their instruments until the lights went down. From my spot near the bar, above the heads of the crowd surrounding the stage, I could see the three-piece horn section, the drummer, and the lead singer on risers.

Once the crowd took their seats, I noticed the piano player sitting on his bench, though only from the back. He unleashed those keys with such passion that I couldn't keep my eyes off of him. His solo drew wild applause, including mine. I forgot about my drink orders until the bartender shouted "KK!" At the first break, I sent the piano player a message on a napkin via another server, complimenting his performance.

The pianist made his way to me through the crowds, holding a glass of Southern Comfort on the rocks. He was about 5'8', about two inches taller than me. His dark-brown, curly rock-star hair fell to the shoulders of his tan, three-piece suit, captivating me by the unlikely yet stunning combination of the two. I caught just a glimpse of his lake-blue eyes in the club's dim light. His northern accent sounded similar to mine, his from New York and mine originally from Chicago, which brought comfort in contrast to the twang of my new hometown.

With little time to talk during the break, Peter Schless said he'd find me again after the next set. I accepted his invitation to a midnight breakfast after work. We missed the closing of my favorite late-night diner, so we resorted to a drive-through. He cleared the couch in the back of his blue Dodge van and set up the table. As if we had known each other for ages, we talked non-stop, comparing stories while dining on burgers and fries from paper bags.

Peter had jammed or played with some of the greatest southern rock and blues musicians including the Allman Brothers, B.B King, a 13-piece jazz-funk band called Music Machine that performed along the eastern seaboard, and the Florida band, Power. He had just been on the road with Rainey, a funky R&B band from New Orleans that he loved. Rainey, the lead singer, had a voice easily mistaken for Aretha Franklin's or Chaka Khan's, with the added spice of her Memphis-N'Orleans dialect. Rainey wanted her band members to leave Houston and move together to Hollywood with the hopes of getting a record deal. Peter didn't want to leave Rainey, but declined the opportunity, saying he would only go to LA with a definite gig already secured.

Peter was just as curious about me, so I shared some bits and pieces. I grew up in a "Leave It To Beaver" family of the '50s. Dad brought home the bacon, while Mom took care of the kids and our home in a Chicago suburb. Dad told WW II army stories while my parents played cards with my brothers and me on Friday nights. Dad built us a summer cottage on Goose Lake and took us on fishing vacations. Mom was an avid reader, and a talented craftswoman and seamstress, which influenced my early love for reading and exploring art and clothing design. I wanted to major in Art and get a college degree, but that hadn't happened yet.

"That's cool, KK. Sounds like your family was close."

"Yeah, but things changed…" My parents plucked me from my Chicago high school to move to Toledo, Ohio, so Dad could start a new business. The move ended our frequent family get-togethers with cousins, aunts, uncles and grandparents, and broke up our close relationship with Tom and my new sister-in-law Paula, and my first nieces, Kimmy and Krista, and my nephew Adam. This break from our Chicago family began the regretful trend that family closeness could be put aside for job opportunities.

"Something like that happened to me after my dad died, when I was seven," Peter told me. "I was born in Plattsburgh, grew up in the Adirondacks in upstate New York. When my Mom moved our family to Florida, my little brother Ely and I were just kids, but my brother Beau and sister Lacy were almost in high school. We had these big age gaps."

"What happened to your dad?"

Bob Schless had been a pilot, a lover of jazz, a dreamer, and an inventor of toys, ingenious gadgets, and modern furniture, among other things. His artistry brought the Schless family comfortable wealth and interesting friends like Buckminister Fuller who designed the first geodesic dome, and musician friends Lambert, Hendricks and Ross. But his father didn't seem to know how to create family harmony. He was often gone or living in his own imaginative world. Bob Schless used to fly a single-engine plane between their home in Elizabethtown and New York City, where he would escape family life over weekends. He loved hanging out with beatnik musicians at jazz clubs. On one trip co-piloting a flight home in a late night fog, he was killed in a crash landing.

"Ever since my dad died in that crash, I have wanted to learn how to fly a plane."

"But why?"

"I have always wanted to know what it felt like to live like my father." Peter gazed at me, as if seeking comfort for not being able to know the phantom parent who had vanished from his boyhood. "But living at our camp at Lincoln Pond in the Adirondacks was good. My grandfather Obbie taught me how to do all kinds of stuff that I couldn't learn from my dad."

"When did you start playing piano?"

"I was about three. I'd sit on the bench and just started finding notes. I grew up taking lessons, but played better by ear. I really got into music after we moved to Florida and met so many musicians. Did you go to college?"

"Some." My parents called me a dreamer of dreams with my head in the clouds. My vivid imagination kept me entertained as a kid envisioning things like graphics and fashion in colorations that I would draw. My love for reading and writing stories led me to become the Art and Feature editor of my high school newspaper. No one in our family had gone to college. Their strongest objection to college for me was that being an Art major wouldn't lead to a good paying job. I won the battle of getting one year at Ohio State University. After that year, the conflict of going away for more years of college became a breaking point for us. I moved to Bowling Green and got a job at the university so I could take classes. "What about you?"

"I went to music school at North Texas State for their incredible jazz program. I didn't finish because I wanted to marry my girlfriend Diane. We went on the road together, but that brought our marriage to an end, actually just recently. So you want to finish college?"

"Some day. I want to teach, but my family genes say I'll be an entrepreneur whenever I can." I had been a business owner since my early twenties, and told him about my freelance graphic arts business and my retail shop, The Plant Lady. A local paper featured a story on me as the youngest business owner in downtown Bowling Green. Then there was Mick's business debacle in Houston.

"And here you are at Spiro's, wearing this white toga minidress serving cocktails."

"And here you are in Houston playing piano with the Johnny Williams Band."

I liked that we were both from the north, and only in Texas for some phase of our journey. Peter and I had each landed in Houston, converging paths only because of risky opportunities with others that hadn't worked out to our best interests. Maybe leaving Ohio and moving to Houston had been a right move. Maybe it was perfect timing. We spent hours getting to know each other. It had to be after 4:00am when I stepped out of Peter's van.

Peter drew me into his musical world, and I willingly transformed from a casual concertgoer to an audiophile with Peter as my musical director. I switched from listening to folk rock like Joanie Mitchell and Simon & Garfunkel, and got into jazz and R&B. I came to love Aretha Franklin, Chaka Khan, Weather Report, Stevie Wonder, Quincy Jones, Joe Sample, Chick Corea, Spyro Gyra, Herbie Hancock, Pat Metheny, John Coltrane, and on.

Music was in Peter's DNA and he lived for funk. This Johnny Williams band was not a good fit for Peter. Their scripted performances with limited piano solo opportunities cramped his style. One night at Spiro's on break, Johnny commented to a few other servers and me that the way Peter Schless drew attention to himself at the piano was distracting, so he was thinking of letting him go.

I tipped off Peter to Johnny's plan so he could find another gig before he was out of work. Peter was an awesome keyboard player, so it was easy for him to get gigs, but they didn't always satisfy the level of musicianship he desired. Peter sought greatness, so he wanted to play only with musicians as good as him and preferably better, so he could continuously improve.

Peter's desire to get off the road and develop his studio work coincided with my desire to have our own home. We bought a condo near the Houston Galleria, with just enough room to hold his rented, upright piano in the living room, with a second bedroom for my sewing studio. Peter and I were my best advertisements. He wore my jackets and shirts to studio and club gigs, and I wore my designs. Entertainers became my first customers for stage clothes, added to the private clientele I had developed. If only I had some financial backing and could have pursued clothing design full time, I could have immersed myself in it like Peter did in music.

## Glimpses of Scientology - Houston, 1978

From the front window of our sunroom, Peter and I noticed a skinny man in a black rubber body suit running past our house in the sweltering Houston heat nearly every late afternoon. Peter or I would say, "There goes that lunatic in the black suit again."

One day, we hailed the guy and asked him why he was running in the heat wearing what looked like a surfer's wet suit. We learned that W.C. Langdon played drums in a local band, so Peter made a new connection. But the rest of W.C.'s story intrigued us, so we invited him into our kitchen to talk.

"The rubber suit causes me to sweat excessively. I'm exercising as part of a purification process at the Church of Scientology," W.C. explained.

"What's Scientology?" Peter and I echoed. I had never heard of Scientology—good, bad, or otherwise. Peter had some recognition of it. He said that in the early 1970s, he had gone back stage after a Chick Corea "Return to Forever" concert. When Peter introduced himself, Chick extended his hand and asked if Peter had heard of L. Ron Hubbard. Peter said this event had always lingered with him.

"And what do you mean by purification process?" Our kitchen guest gave us some vague details about Scientology, and said he felt more clear minded by not drinking alcohol or doing drugs, which helped him feel more focused as a musician. I pointed out that quitting drinking and drugs was not an original idea from Scientology, and anyone could make this choice for himself.

W.C. said that he got started in Scientology by taking a personality test that showed him what had been ruining his life.

"What do you mean by 'personality test'?" Peter wanted to know. And I asked, "Did you think that was ruining your life before Scientology told you it was?"

W.C.'s explanation of the Oxford Capacity Analysis (OCA) sounded like it delved into deeply personal issues. "The questionnaire shows you the exact things that are wrong with you and Scientology can handle it," W.C. said. "I've been going there ever since."

I later discovered that the OCA had nothing to do with Oxford University. Peter and I couldn't connect "personality test" with "church" and "rubber sweat suits" with "purification." It seemed strange, but we liked W.C. Langdon. These two musicians discovered that they had a lot in common, which led to playing together in some studio gigs.

The Houston music world was small and tight. Musicians who worked in studios got each other gigs on record albums or in clubs. Their girl friends or wives adopted each other like family, went to each other's parties, and took care of each other. I ate crawfish and others suck the heads off them was at Freddy Fender's birthday party; the first time I saw a cowboy get his butt kicked by a bucking bronco was with musician friends at Gilley's nightclub in Galveston while *Urban Cowboy* was in production.

Peter's first shot at becoming a recording engineer was at Huey Meaux' and Mickey Gilley's studio in Galveston. That led to playing keyboards on Crazy Cajun record label albums, starting with Freddy Fender, then other Texas country albums by Roy Head, B.J. Thomas, Savoy Brown, and Dr. John. Peter loved his night gig at Cody's, a Houston jazz club, playing with amazing musicians including vocalist Tamara Matoesian. Tammy's husband, Bill Champlin, was a Grammy-winning songwriter and singer for the band, Chicago. Tammy and Bill did vocals for the *Urban Cowboy* movie soundtrack starring John Travolta and Debra Winger, filmed at Gilley's. Thanks to Tammy and Bill, Peter played piano and keyboards on that *Urban Cowboy* soundtrack.

We had heard that John Travolta had been involved in Scientology, but didn't understand it. We knew of Travolta as Vinnie

Barbarino on *Welcome Back, Kotter,* and as Vince Manero in *Saturday Night Fever,* so we were fans. If Travolta had talked to Peter about Scientology, we might have been interested, because whatever had been inspiring or boosting the success of one of our favorite actors might have appealed to us, too.

\* \* \*

To help our finances during Peter's transition between playing in clubs to full-time studio work, I took a day job at Skidmore, Owings and Merrill as secretary to architect Richard Keating, co-designer of the Sears Tower in Chicago, then the world's tallest building.

In 1979, Peter took me home to Warm Mineral Springs, Florida, to meet his mother. As we drove down along the Gulf, Peter stopped near one of the jetties at Venice Beach so we could stretch our legs and walk Sugar, our cockapoo. At the end of the jetty, with the January wind gusting off the ocean and whipping our hair, Peter took me by complete surprise. He had to nearly shout above the gusting wind and waves slapping at the jetty for me to hear him.

"I stopped at this spot because I wanted to show you the jetties where I used to hang out when I was a kid...and I love you, KK. Will you marry me?"

"What? I love you too—Yes!" We hugged with Sugar between us.

"I don't have a ring for you yet, KK, but I wanted to propose before we got to Mom's."

That night over dinner with Shirley Egglefield Schless Royal, Peter announced our upcoming marriage. Her pleasure in our news struck me as sincere happiness for her son settling down. He and Diane had not survived road life, partly because Diane wanted to have a family, while Peter saw life on the road as his route to success before he had children. Shirley told me she remained in touch with her ex-daughter-in-law who, coincidently, was also a clothes designer like me.

I enjoyed Shirley's brash transparency, glad to be included in their family tradition of storytelling. She spun one yarn after another about the Schless family from Old Germany, relatives who still owned a vineyard in France that bottled a famous label champagne, and another who was a professor at an Ivy League university on the East Coast. Her father had opened the first Ford dealership in upstate New York that put the Egglefield family on the map in regional history and wealth. Every turn in our conversation led to another good story. Peter had not only brought me into a world of music, but into a family legacy with a storybook background. As a young girl, I followed my mother's routine of spending hours a day with my nose in books, a way to travel places and experience things that I otherwise couldn't. I loved to connect with adventurous people who journey off the beaten path and tell their stories. The Schless family began a new chapter in my life.

Back home in our Houston condo, friends packed our tiny living room, the chapel for our marriage ceremony. We asked a Methodist minister whom we didn't know to perform our ceremony with Christian vows, despite the fact that neither of us embraced a religion. Our marriage ceremony centered on love and personal commitment, not on a religious covenant or denominational dogma. We shared our vows, and exchanged rings of knotted silver that we bought at an artisan jeweler's shop. After a fun reception with friends, we enjoyed our wedding night at a fine downtown hotel.

## On the Road, 1979

Peter and I each desired greater opportunity and advancement. His interest in Texas country music waned as opportunities for recording other types of music diminished in Houston recording studios. He seemed restless from living in one city for several years. I didn't have road fever like he did, but I was, for sure, always interested in advancement.

While looking for opportunities outside Houston, Peter took a gig with an R&B band playing in Colorado ski lodges over the Christmas season.I sold my Indoor Gardener business to a friend, packed my sewing equipment into trunks that we loaded with the rest of our condensed life into our blue Dodge van, put everything else in storage, and went on the road.

Drummer and lead singer Michael Jay Dahoney looked like Mick Jagger and had a deep, sultry voice. The incredible lead guitarist, Randy Cobb, was crazy fun to hang with, so life would never be dull. Listening to great musicians play R&B tunes in ski lodge bars every night was like a paid vacation, but we didn't last long. We expected better accommodations, and didn't enjoy listening to romantic sound effects through the paper-thin walls of our hotel room, where band members on both sides of us entertained multiple women through the night.

## Michigan, 1980

Christmas was the perfect time to see family, so we headed to northern Michigan. A piggy bank stashed under the tire well of our van held the last of our savings, which wasn't quite enough to cover the gas for the trip. Dad wired us some money to help us with the rest of the journey.

This story detours into a year of living in Northern Michigan near my family. If you'd like to read about it, please visit the book website.

After a year, we became restless again, looking for bigger and better opportunities. As if in answer to our dreams, we got a phone call from Peter's friend, guitarist Les Dudek. Les tracked Peter down after no contact for 10 years, to lure him to Los Angeles and go on tour with Cher's new band, Black Rose. Geffen Records produced the first album for Casablanca, so the label was ramping up for a promotional tour. Peter had always said he would only go to LA for a definite gig. We discussed Les's invitation for about thirty seconds before we called him back to say yes.

In the early '70s, Les and Peter had played in the southern rock band, Power. The band broke up after their friend Duane Allman died in a motorcycle accident, when the lives of nearly all their mourning musician friends fell to a complete lull. Dickie Betts, a friend of Peter's who played with the Allman Brothers, had told Peter that they were looking for a guitar player, so Peter and Les jammed at the Allman's farm in Macon, Georgia. Les played on the Allman's *Brothers & Sisters* album, and went on to play with Boz Scaggs and the Steve Miller Band before connecting with Cher.Saying goodbye to family was not easy. I wanted to help Mom and Dad's shop succeed. Jim and Denise had their first child, Joshua. Sugar had given birth to eight puppies, with one survivor that we named Toby. Most of Peter's band members decided to stay in Michigan until something better came up.

We packed up our life, invited everyone to visit us in California, and headed to Hollywood.

# 3

## WELCOME TO LALA LAND

**Los Angeles - 1980**

THE HOLLYWOOD SIGN APPEARED through the LA haze as we navigated our way into the San Fernando Valley. Peter's New Orleans friend Rainey and manager-guitar-player husband Robert Haines welcomed us into their little home in Burbank. We slept on their storage room floor for several weeks, happy to have a safe haven while we got our bearings.

Peter spent days and nights in recording studios with Les Dudek and Cher, or listened to the master recordings of the *Black Rose* album to get the feel of the music he would be playing on tour.

I did temp secretarial work to make extra money. My first assignment took me to Aaron Spelling Productions as a script typist for *The Love Boat* show. The next-door office housed the *M\*A\*S\*H* show staff, and the secretary, Marie Kleidon, and I became friends. Marie and I strolled around the studio lot during lunchtime or we'd eat in the canteen where Alan Alda, Henry Morgan, Loretta Swit and other actors grabbed a bite.

Evenings, I'd go to studios with Peter and meet musicians and singers whose names I recognized from credits on record albums. That first night, I met Cher, the lead singer from Toto, and John Lennon's recording engineer. Seeing famous people behind the

33

scenes in their working environment reduced the awe I had always felt about Hollywood stars. I began to see them less as a starstruck fan, and more as regular people who had achieved a high level of success. My ability to achieve my dreams started to feel more within my reach.

Cher's Black Rose tour opened at the Forum in Los Angeles, with (I think) Motley Crue as the opening act. Peter was crazed to play with Cher but especially Les again, reminiscent of their southern rock days. On opening night, Peter wore the black-and-white striped satin baseball jacket I designed for him, which thrilled me to see on stage. One night after a concert, the band joined Cher backstage for Chastity's birthday party. Other nights we'd walk through the Forum's underground caverns and witness the glories of road life, seeing things like tour buses being deloused and fumigated.

Cher's home in Benedict Canyon had become Les Dudek's home, and also their rehearsal spot. When Les invited Peter to come over to practice, I'd sometimes go along. Les toured us through different rooms, lavishly decorated with exotic Egyptian influences that matched Cher's captivating mystique. Her marble-lined meeting room held an exquisitely carved drinking fountain in the stone wall that spouted water from a solid gold cobra head. A Franco Zefferelli-designed glass ceiling opened to the sky by remote control above a massive, square table centered under the glass. The immaculate, industrial-style kitchen held an immense, white marble island for food preps, and I caught a glimpse inside her commercial stainless steel fridge filled with vegetables. I happened to be at her home one day during a delivery of dozens of towering palm trees imported from Egypt to line her canyon driveway, fitting for a residence of royalty.

Coming home to our little place after visiting Cher's mansion dwarfed our level of living. But the fact that we were moving forward in dream careers kept us motivated. Steady income helped us move from Rainey's storage room to a one-bedroom apartment, then to a two-bedroom stucco house with a yard and garage. Our new abode on palm-tree lined Alameda Avenue was near Glenoaks in Burbank, in the Verdugo Mountains' foothills. We rented a white baby grand piano that filled most of our dining room, with a compact desk where Peter could score sheet music.

Peter's younger brother Ely, a motorcycle racer and inventor who had Peter's blue eyes and dark curly hair, moved into our living room. His addition to our home gave Peter and me the comfort of family that we both desired.

The musician's roller-coaster ride of recording and performance was sweet at the top through the duration of a gig; but there could be downslides of no work. Peter stayed with Black Rose through the tour, but found other work once he heard the album lacked the action on the charts the record label had hoped for. He landed keyboard spots on the movie soundtrack *All the Right Moves*, Les Dudek's 1981 solo album *Gypsy Ride*, Tim Bogert's album *Progressions*, and Janis Ian's *Uncle Wonderful*. He also played on Glen Hughes' (singer from Deep Purple) and Pat Thrall's album for Epic Records, produced by Andy Johns, who produced several records of Led Zeppelin and the Rolling Stones.

The Hollywood entertainment industry felt similar to Houston's, a small world where only a select number of session players worked. But here we found a fine calibre of musicianship. Rainey had been gigging with her Houston musicians and some new handpicked studio musicians, and asked Peter to rejoin her group. She secured a house gig at The Flying Jib in Sherman Oaks on Ventura Boulevard, while she composed songs for her upcoming album. Iconic musicians and local recording artists would sit in with their band nearly every night. The Jib rocked, and I enjoyed Rainey performing in costumes I had designed for her.

On one of these nights, Jeffrey Osborne, the lead singer from the R&B band LTD, sat in. Peter had already been an LTD fan, but that night Jeffrey's vocal power and range blew him away. Jeffrey told Peter that he was working on his first solo album with A&M Records. The next day, Peter bought copies of Jeffrey's LTD albums to study Jeffrey's voice. He decided to compose a song specifically for Jeffrey's vocal range that would enable him to hit the highs, lows and mid range notes that would bring out Jeffrey's vocal power. Peter intended to place this song on Jeffrey's first solo album, produced by George Duke.

\* \* \*

Peter met people in the music business who told him how Scientology could help to remove creative blocks in our careers and improve our ability to communicate as artists. One avid recruiter,

Bob Fisher, worked as Peter's roadie transporting musical equipment between studio sessions and live gigs. Bob regularly shared his experiences with Scientology that evidently appealed to Peter.

"KK, we gotta check this out." Peter said Scientology could help artists like us. He gave me a copy of a Way to Happiness booklet, with Bob's name written on the front.

"What does it do, exactly?"

"Bob said their communication course is really helpful to get started with. It's only $50." Since we lived with self-imposed pressures to succeed in a competitive and intimidating business, the course appealed to us.

"What do we have to lose?" I agreed to find out more. Scientology had intersected with our life through Chick Corea, John Travolta, W.C. Langdon, and Debbie Harvey by this point. It held no repute with us, other than weird feelings we got from W.C.'s explanations.

Bob introduced us to Robbie, a Scientology field practitioner in Silver Lake. He taught us some Scientology basics, starting with the communication course, and then a marriage course. These couldn't have come at a better time, since Peter and I both felt plenty of tension about career challenges. Robbie also talked to us about buying some auditing (counseling) called Life Repair, saying this would help us deal with problems and stress. But auditing costs thousands of dollars for blocks of 12 1/2 hours, so that was not an option.

I once arrived at Robbie's home when he was sitting on his front porch wearing jeans unzipped at the waist, revealing his white underwear, and no shirt. What an odd flirtation, since Scientology was a path for spiritual advancement based on strengthened morality. Not exactly professional, I ignored the scene below his neck, my first experience with inappropriate sexual innuendos in Scientology. Our services with Robbie began to drag, although we were interested in moving ahead in Scientology. Bob's friend, Gerry Simons, saw our interest drifting and recommended that we visit the Scientology center nearest our home, the Valley Organization in Sherman Oaks. Gerry took me there for an orientation to Scientology's "grade chart," and I learned the steps we could take to ascend the bridge to total freedom.

The outdated interiors of the Valley Org and the staff's low standard of dress turned me off. This should have tipped me off to the fact that they weren't earning much money here. But the potential for spiritual growth swept me over, and it was more organized than Robbie's practice. Peter wanted to make faster progress than what we had accomplished with Robbie. I put together a loan application for $8,000 to buy a training package so I could become an auditor, or spiritual counselor. Being an auditor seemed to be the best way to learn to control life, and help others move up the bridge to achieve the state of Clear and gain special spiritual abilities. Peter was upset about going into debt for Scientology, but we bought an L. Ron Hubbard library of books and tapes anyway.

I called Robbie to share the great news about my investment in Scientology training.

"YOU WHAT????" Robbie's otherwise calm voice transformed into a loud shriek, and I found myself getting screamed at. "I invested all that time in you and Peter and this is what you do to me?" he shouted. My first learning experience about the money motivation of the Scientology world nearly caused me to disinvolve myself on the spot.

"Why did you buy TRAINING? You were supposed to buy your AUDITING from me!" What he meant was, he lost out on thousands of dollars in auditing fees plus an $800 commission that was now going to Gerry.

Field Staff Members (FSMs, volunteer sales people who recruit people into Scientology) like Gerry were rewarded with a 10 or 15% commission for ushering their "selectees" into the orgs and started on services. Field practitioners like Robbie were supposed to deliver introductory services and refer their customers to the big dogs, Class Five Organizations, that competed with each other to move paying customers along Scientology's spiritual path.

The traumatic screaming incident led me to tell people at Valley Org how this disillusioned me about being a Scientologist. A spiritually advanced field auditor like Robbie should be in greater control of his emotions. The ethics officer made Robbie apologize to me over the phone. This incident scratched the surface of learning about money motivation within Scientology.

Bob Fisher slipped from credibility when we discovered he had been contributing money to a church enemy, David Mayo's splinter group. Mayo had left his role as Scientology's highest technical authority, Senior Case Supervisor International, to practice Scientology outside church control. Although we were new and uninformed about Scientology's problems and dark side, we had heard of this "suppressive person" Mayo. Knowing nothing about Mayo's reasons for leaving, we had already drank enough Kool-Aid to believe that anyone who left the good graces of Scientology to deliver their own version on the outside was a "squirrel," an enemy. With that mindset, we disconnected from Bob.

Peter and Karen enjoyed Texas wildflowers on a day trip outside of Houston, 1977.

Peter and Karen moved into their first home in Burbank on Alameda near Glenoaks by the Verdugo Hills circa 1981. In this home, Peter wrote "On the Wings of Love" and Karen launched her fashion design business.

While Peter performed keyboards in Melissa Manchester's world tour in 1993 in Australia, Karen joined him in Melbourne. She is backstage with one of the back-up singers (left) and the sax player. (Right): Peter and Karen went to the wildlife preserve in Coolangatta where they made friends with a kangaroo.

Peter and Karen moved to their first home on Alta Mesa Drive in Coldwater Canyon around 1982 after Wings hit, also around the time they transferred from the Valley Org to Celebrity Centre.

Peter and Karen never had children, but they dearly loved Sugar, their cockapoo (left) and Toby, their beloved mutt (right), offspring of Sugar. The dogs loved to travel and went everywhere with them.

Karen having fun with her FSM, Gerry Simons, who recruited her into Scientology's Valley Org, circa 1981.

**Why is Peter missing from these photos?** When Karen escaped Scientology, she left with nothing. Peter did ship her some boxes of clothing and personal possession but few photos. Karen had sent some pictures to her mother over the years, which Alice saved. Most photos with Peter in them got discarded after Peter and Karen divorced in 1999. Alice left Karen her entire family photo collection when she passed away in 2015, where Karen found many photos from her past.

# 4

## SQUEEZE THE CANS

**Sherman Oaks, California, 1981**

MY ORIGINAL INTEREST IN SCIENTOLOGY was not as a seeker of religion, but as an artist looking to improve my creative abilities along a path of spiritual development. My passion for creative expression also synchronized with Hubbard's description of the artist's role in society. Creativity identified our essence as a couple, so Peter and I set our sights on transferring to the Celebrity Centre when the time was right. Meanwhile, the Valley Org was closer to home. Becoming super-literate through Scientology's courses carried strong appeal because I aspired to finish college. Hubbard's statement, "The real barbarism of Earth is stupidity," and that knowledge of self brings responsibility and control, helped me believe I could flourish with a Scientology education that enhanced my life.

### Experiencing Scientology

The Scientology world offers a place for everyone through four primary avenues: as a paying customer who is an active Scientologist, a volunteer field worker or Scientologist entrepreneur, a contracted staff member who works for an org or mission, or a member of the Sea Organization. There are vast differences in mindset and lifestyles between each of these groups of Scientologists.

General customers comprise the "public" of Scientology. Celebrities are also public Scientologists, but they attend Celebrity Centres and receive special services compared to general public who attended Scientology missions, or Class IV organizations, such as Valley Org. Celebs live in their own homes, have a personal career, and raise their families. They lead private lives, except for the infiltration of Scientology that permeates their life choices. An "onsource" Scientologist fulfills their obligation to take a course or receive auditing for 12 1/2 hours weekly, and is routinely asked to make donations to the International Association of Scientologists or one of the social betterment programs, to prove their support of Scientology.

Scientologist entrepreneurs and volunteers working in the field are also paying customers, but they apply some specialized skill they learned within Scientology by donating their time to a Scientology cause or earn a living from it. This includes Field Staff Members (FSMs) who recruit people into Scientology and earn a commission on their selectees' purchases; Volunteer Ministers (VMs) who donate their time to apply Scientology in their community, from giving touch assists to people, to helping at a disaster scene; Field Auditors who are members of I-HELP and charge a fee for auditing his/her own customers; WISE consultants who earn fees for using Scientology policies to run a dental, chiropractic, accounting or any other kind of business entity. The sector of The Association for Better Living and Education (ABLE) includes the Scientology workers under Applied Scholastics, Narconon, Criminon, and The Way to Happiness Foundation, which are usually paid jobs. Others work directly with organizations going out on tours to promote Flag services, bring in donations for the IAS, being an OT ambassador to activate the field, and on. Scientologists who receive special awards such as the IAS Freedom Medal tend to come from these field workers. These Scientologists are often exploited in Scientology marketing materials, showing simple acts of kindness like giving a Way to Happiness book to a children's group in a third-world country, that get blown into monumental proportions as if a country is being transformed by TWTH because of these small efforts.

The contracted staff members carry a major responsibility for front-lines delivery of Scientology courses and auditing at the Class IV orgs. They drive people into their building by body routing, selling books at airports and street corners, supervising course rooms, running the auditing and ethics areas that service the paying customers, and supervise the FSMs who recruit people. Contracted staff members are good-hearted people who want to help change the world. In return, they hope to receive Scientology auditing and training for "free." It's easy to forget that they are giving their time for next to no pay and then think that they receive "free" services. These people work for low wages, typically 60 hours or more per week, and sign contracts to serve for 2 1/2 years or 5 years. These are prime candidates for Sea Org recruiters, because the Sea Org provides housing, meals, uniforms, transportation, and Scientology services that contracted staff struggle to pay for.

The most fanatical of Scientologists are the Sea Org (SO) members, Scientology's extremist group called management's "elite corps." SO members pledge their eternity in billion-year contracts. They relinquish private lives to work as dedicated soldiers who get ethics in on the planet so the planet can be cleared through Scientology/ They believe they will come back for many more lifetimes, so they work to make this a better world they can come back to. The money earned by the Scientology empire is accomplished on the backs of Sea Org members. Hubbard personally raked in millions of dollars from his organizations managed by Sea Org members who sacrificed their personal lives, families, and even mental health.

Peter and I had learned some of the Scientology basics through Robbie's field practice, but the heavy indoctrination set in at Valley, where we laid the foundation of our Scientology mindset.

## Basic Indoctrination

As students, we were expected to immerse ourselves in "the tech"—the books, tapes, policy letters, films, and the beliefs and practices that comprise Scientology philosophy—and apply it through our thinking processes and behavior. The thought control system starts with the Scientology appetizers—short, doable courses that teach the basics of Scientology in practical contexts. We were to apply in life what we learned in class, such as how to study a course, maintain a successful marriage, communicate well with others, handle children, handle problematic relationships, analyze and handle problems, organize a business, create art, handle finances, and on. The appetizers led to the main course, when the Scientology magic would happen behind closed door of the private auditing sessions when the auditor would say "squeeze the cans" and the journey into the mind begins.

I had always been an avid reader and loved education, so I had no problem reading Hubbard's mountain of books. I wish I had been as aware then as I am now of how this "education" in Scientology was a manipulative strategy by a writer who, in some chapters, appears to be quite articulate, but is mostly all over the place with his thoughts. Trying to make sense of his key points is like finding my way through a labyrinth while connecting the dots, and having "cognitions" along the way. Had I realized that this whole process would create a similar derangement as what existed in Hubbard's mind, I would have stopped at the beginning.

I liked Hubbard's approach to life that contrasted with my Christian education. There, priests and nuns serve as the bearers of divine wisdom who interpret God's word for people, telling parishioners what Biblical scripture means and how it should be used in life. In contrast, I was intrigued by Hubbard's words, "What is true for you is what you have observed, and when you lose that, you have lost everything..." His approach put me in the driver's seat, helping me to make connections between what I studied and how it relates to being successful. If Christian educators developed a similar system where students learned Biblical concepts in the context of practical living, it might revolutionize the religious upbringing that I left.

My eager attitude for change and desire for new ideas paved the way for a gradual dismantling of my prior attitudes, values and beliefs, replaced by a Scientology world view. For example, Scientology teaches that man is basically good, so humans are not considered sinners by nature. People are capable of doing anything they decide to do, and learn to confront others and overcome all odds to achieve their goal. In contrast, Christianity teaches that people are born with original sin and a sinner's nature, inherited from Adam and Eve. People should turn the other cheek, practice meekness and humility, let God be in control, and be forgiving when others transgress against them. Scientology and Christianity couldn't be more opposite.

Everything learned in a Scientology classroom is printed or recorded under the name L. Ron Hubbard, "Source." I didn't realize it then, but the use of the word "source" was probably the most destructively influential word in the Scientology vocabulary. Herein lies the core of Scientology brainwashing: Hubbard is the origin for Scientology, and thus, the origin of truth. Truth won't be found in anyone other than Hubbard. Question him and you are in trouble; you are either word-cleared until you change your mind, or you are interrogated, or you are a disaffected, potential trouble source connected to a suppressive person. The conclusion is that you are not source, I am not source, no one other than Hubbard is source. The use of this word goes hand in hand with Scientology's doublethink of saying something and meaning another within the same term. Hubbard offers a key datum in Scientology, "What is true for you is what you have observed. And when you have lost that you have lost everything." But in reality, this cannot play out in a Scientologist's life unless what you have observed aligns with the way Hubbard says things are.

Scientologists strive to discover themselves as an immortal being, with a way to unlock the mysteries of the universe within a social system to live a better life. Peter and I moved along on Hubbard's carefully taped path that unfolds a mystery here and there. We read how other religions and mental health practices throughout history have failed humankind. Hubbard's writings resonated with me where they reminded me of some bad experiences within Catholicism. Instead of being focused on hellfire and damnation, Hubbard offers solutions to revert man's downward spiral of moral and mental depravity so that humankind could discover inner truth, regain our true inner powers, and live lifetime after lifetime.

As a baby Scientologist, I couldn't yet learn answers to the mysteries in the advanced levels, since those secrets would be revealed as I moved up the bridge. Beginning Scientologists read one set of Hubbard's materials; a separate set of confidential materials exists for the advanced "OT" (Operating Thetan) Scientologist that a pre-Clear (pc) cannot access. Other materials exist only for Sea Org members, and within Sea Org materials, there are confidential items designated for certain eyes only at various levels of the hierarchy, such as LRH Advices for the International Management base, for Golden Era Productions, for dealing with celebrities, and for internal legal operations. Never one to enjoy being limited by anyone or anything, I wanted to break all barriers and know all there was to know.

The Hubbard Qualified Scientologist (HQS) course put the first notch in my belt as a Scientologist learning the basics and kept me in a constant state of curiosity and intrigue. I learned Scientology's applied religious philosophy, basic study skills, how to use the tone scale, how to give touch assists to help relieve a person's pain, how to see my life compartmented into eight different dynamics. It touched on some of the mysteries in the advanced levels of the bridge to total freedom through the *Technical Dictionary* and the readings.

The most adventurous part of the HQS course was learning how to communicate the Scientology way, using the TRs—training routines that control communication, and then the Upper Indoctrination TRs that develop an advanced level of control through spiritual intention. It was no accident that Hubbard required us to read lines from Lewis Carroll's *Alice's Adventures in Wonderland* and *Through the Looking Glass* while practicing these communication drills. The sane little girl, Alice, was lost, confused and argumentative in the story, while demanding Wonderland make sense. There we were as students of Scientology, confused by these bizarre Scientology teachings, while demanding that they made sense. For the drills, we would practice getting our questions answered, and would ask our partner, "Do birds fly?" Our partner would read a line from *Alice in Wonderland*, "Off with her head!" We'd repeat, "Do birds fly?" Our partner would read, "I'm looking for the way out." We'd repeat "Do birds fly?" Until our partner said "yes, birds fly." This drill builds the ability to stay focused on your question and never vary or give up until you get an answer.

This course taught me how to listen extremely well, and taught me specific skills to control communication. I did build confidence that this part of Scientology was workable and helpful, leading me to trust that other things I would learn in Scientology would have a positive effect in my life. Not until years later did I realize that Hubbard had betrayed my trust because herein lies the basic brainwashing of early Scientology, a form of hypnosis through repetitive actions, such as:

- Give a command to our partner and then physically navigate the person to execute the command. *Walk over to that wall. Thank you. Turn around. Thank you. Walk over to that wall. Thank you...* and on, requiring us to physically push, pull, stop, or turn our partner's body to do what we commanded. The goal is to be able to get someone to do what you want them to do, whether they want to or not. This skill is referred to as "8C", required for an auditor who might have to control a pre-clear in a session, such as preventing the PC from leaving the room before the session was completed.

- Sit in a chair facing another chair holding an ashtray. I had to shout at this ashtray, *Stand up. Thank you. Sit down. Thank you...*and on, until a coach gave passed me on my laser-precise Tone 40 intention. The goal is to be able to get people in your life or in an auditing session to execute your commands, without being able to successfully resist you.

Even at the most basic level, the courses I took and topics or terms I learned, brought about my Scientologist state of mind. I didn't realize at that time that my Scientologist state of mind was shaped largely through the hypnotic repetition of commands and drills, and the replacement of concepts and words with Scientology language and ideas.

Ex-Scientology readers already know the Scientology basics, from mystery sandwiches and cleared cannibals to wogs, learning how to learn Hubbard's way, the sci-fi aspects of Scientology, and on. Visit the book website if you are interested in reading more.

# 5

# GOING CLEAR

**Valley Org - Early 1980s**

I WANTED TO REACH THE STATE OF CLEAR and beyond, which could be achieved through training to be an auditor, or by receiving auditing from another trained auditor. If I became an auditor, I would learn to use the e-meter and gain knowledge about the mind and spirit, acquiring skills that would help me with my own spiritual progress while I audited others. The value of training is emphasized over the value of receiving auditing. An auditor controls life, self and others.

A pre-clear, someone who receives auditing, is being controlled by the auditor and isn't gaining any technical skills in the process. To "go Clear" costs tens of thousands of dollars, starting with Life Repair, and then each of the required auditing levels in sequence. Blocks of auditing hours cost $2,000 per a 12 1/2 hour intensive. I chose to train to become an auditor, which is why I borrowed only $8,000 for the auditor training package. But my FSM Gerry Simons thought I should get a little taste of auditing first so I knew what it was like. I got started with *Dianetics* Book One auditing, which doesn't involve the e-meter, and only costs about $50 to start.

My Book One auditor took me into session in a scadily furnished but well-lit room. We sat in comfortable chairs, facing each other. He began asking questions, getting me to recall an incident, and then an earlier similar incident. It was interesting, but frustrating. I sensed that he hadn't done this often, and lacked confidence. But by the second session, I remembered things that had happened to me when I was three years old. He asked me to recall the moment I was born, coming through the birth canal.

Remembering the "birth incident" is a goal of Dianetics Book One auditing. The intent is to get the person to recount all the pain and sounds and smells of this "engram," or moment of great pain recorded in the mind with all the various senses while being born. Erasing the "birth engram" eliminates those moments of pain and unconsciousness, no longer able to be triggered by something in present time. This is why Scientology parents have "silent" birth deliveries. Silence prevents the baby from recording what is said in the room by the mother or the doctors, thus eliminating the possibility of the words said at birth having any future effect on the baby, such as "I'll never forget the pain he caused me," "Isn't she fat and sassy!" or "I couldn't wait to get him out."

After the first session, my Book One auditor left me in the middle of some mental gyration. I felt terrible for the next several days. My friend Gerry called me one day and asked me how the Book One auditing was going. I told him that I hated Scientology auditing and would never go back.

An hour later, Gerry was at my door, insisting that I go into the Valley Org. He had arranged for the Book One auditor to take me back into session, and complete the process. I don't remember the details of that session, and felt a little better about it afterwards, but still wasn't happy with Book One auditing.

The Executive Director arranged for me to receive metered auditing to repair that bad Book One auditing. That was my first session on an e-meter (electropsychometer). Metered auditing is an expensive counseling process that must be done precisely as dictated by Hubbard's rules. I sat in a private room at a desk with an auditor trained to listen, who writes on worksheets what I say, while also controlling the e-meter. I held an empty metal can in each hand, connected by leads or electrodes to the meter, through which a light electrical charge ran between the meter and me, while the auditor operated the meter. The auditor says, "Squeeze the cans, please." She set up the meter with the proper sensitivity and tone arm position. A dial on the meter shows a needle that reacts to my thoughts. The needle movement shows resistance to mental charge and also the release of it, in response to questions the auditor asked me. The auditor watches and "reads" the needle reactions—every needle's movement means something different and the auditor is supposed to know what to do next depending on that needle's movement.

For example, if the needle "floated" it moved cleanly, rhythmically, sweeping back and forth across the dial. This is called a "floating needle" (F/N) and indicated that I have had a spiritual/mental release. If the F/N was accompanied by me looking happy and winning, this is called "very good indicators" (VGIs). If the needle ticks, stops, or looks wildly erratic, each needle movement means something different. It's up to the auditor to interpret the needle reaction. "F/N VGIs" is the objective of an auditing session at the end.

Auditors must be highly trained; there is much to know about the reactions of the mind, operation of the e-meter, recognizing the meaning of different needle movements, understanding the indicators of the customers, how to carry out the many different processes, and how to control an auditing session. This was also my first glimpse at realizing just how flawed the whole auditing process could be. My skepticism told me, no auditor is perfect. The potential for errors is high, not only from flaws in the mechanical operation of the meter itself, but in the auditor's ability to interpret the needle reaction correctly, listen to the customer, and correctly perceive the indicators of the customer. Could I trust it?

While the metered auditing ended up as an okay experience, I was unhappy about paying hundreds of dollars for it. It wasn't my fault that the Book One auditor had messed up, so why should I have to pay to fix it? This introduced me to the money-motivated procedures of Scientology, where nothing is free. You pay every step of the way, even when the mistake is theirs. It also introduced me to the no-responsibility caveat of the Scientology organization. If something goes wrong in session, the customer has to be responsible for all outcomes. The church is never at fault, even when an auditor makes a technical mistake. Customer satisfaction doesn't count in Scientology, like it does across the world when anyone buys a product or service. Poor quality of auditing does not result in a free repair or repeat of the process to the customer's satisfaction. If a customer requests a refund, then that customer is declared a suppressive person and expelled.

My intrigue about going Clear won over the risks. Who wouldn't want to have a mind freed of engrams, pain and unconsciousness erased from my past that blocked my ability to fully be myself? A Clear was supposed to be healthy, without colds, with better vision, and exemplify high abilities in life. Most of all, this was the launching pad for becoming an Operating Thetan, where I would become fully causative over all areas of life.

I converted some of the money I had on account for my training to auditing. To go Clear, I had to complete all the preparatory steps and levels first, and move up the grade chart by doing my "Grades." The end phenomenon of each grade was appealing: Grade 0 - Ability to communicate freely with anyone on any subject; Grade I - Ability to recognize the source of problems and make them vanish; Grade II - Relief from hostilities and sufferings of life; Grade III - Freedom from the upsets of the past and ability to face the future; Grade IV - Moving out of fixed conditions and gaining abilities to do new things; Grade V Ability to handle power.

As we audited through each level, the auditor gave specific commands. For example, one level was about problems. She'd say, "Recall a time when you had a problem..." and I would recall something from my past that answered the question. I would have to "view" all the sensory aspects of the event—what I heard, felt, thought at the time. She would then ask another question, "Recall an earlier similar time when you had a problem..."

I recalled a memory of a horrific accident and the problem in it:

On my first day at Ohio State University in 1971, my boyfriend Steve and I were going to his fraternity party. His friend was driving with his girlfriend next to him. Steve and I sat in the back. We were in a nearly blinding downpour of rain. Our car merged onto the freeway. In my left peripheral vision, I barely glimpsed the oncoming car that smashed into us broadside. I recalled instant blackness. I recalled being outside of my body, in desperate confusion. So much pain in my body, I couldn't be in it. I recalled an awareness that if I didn't go back into my body, it would die.

I gained consciousness, lying in a hospital bed, with my mother and father sitting next to my bed, crying. I could barely feel my body. I drifted in and out. I couldn't move my left arm, leg or foot. No idea how much time passed until I asked Mom what happened. I had been in a terrible accident.

The crushing impact of the collision on the left side where I had been sitting had thrown the car doors open on the right side. My body flew outside more than twenty feet. The police found me lying in a field of mud. My left arm and side of my face were packed with chards of glass. Miraculously, I had no broken bones. The left side of my body was so compressed that my left thigh was indented about 1/2 an inch. I recalled hearing a policeman tell my parents there was no explanation for why I was not dead. Dad vomited after he saw the pictures of our vehicle in the police report, because our car was compressed like a soda can crushed to half its size. The policeman told my mother it was a miracle that I survived, and there was no explanation for why I was alive.

My auditor asked, "What was the problem?"

I recalled an actual moment, after the impact of the car hitting us, the moment of pain and the actual cognitive moment when I knew that if I didn't go back into my body, it would die, and the cognitive moment of not wanting to do that because my body was so full of pain that I didn't want to be in it. *That was the problem.*

But I had solved the problem myself at that moment when I had made a choice to rejoin my body. And that's why I didn't die.

The session ended after I realized I had solved the problem myself. I remember walking out of the session, amazed after recalling that accident and being aware of myself as separate from my body. I was astounded that I had recalled the actual moment of choosing to live rather than die. I wondered if my body had already died immediately upon impact of that car and had I, as a spiritual being, exteriorized from my body? How was it that I was able to pose myself a choice at that moment after the impact, and make the choice to rejoin my physical self? I thought about Hubbard's statement that people *are not* their body, they *have* a body. And Hubbard taught that something was only true if it was true to you because you had observed it. This was the first significant claim in Scientology that I believed to be true. However, Scientology auditing had not helped me solve the problem—it only helped me remember how I had already solved it.

## Attesting to Clear

My auditor told me that I bypassed a release point several times. Evidently, I reached the "end phenomenon" (EP) of each level easily. I attested to the state of Natural Clear without doing all of the grades. This means that I knew that I created the content of my own reactive mind, knew that I was in control of my own condition, and knew I created my own reality. The process of attesting to the state of clear was not a blowout phenomenon like I saw in the church's marketing photographs of people achieving this coveted state. For me, it was more of a relief from not having to hunt around in my mind any more to address disabilities that didn't exist.

To rehabilitate the certainty of reaching the state of Clear, I did the Sunshine Rundown, a "solo" auditing action before doing the advanced OT levels. My Case Supervisor handed me the instructions. I went to my favorite place, the Griffith Park Observatory, an expansive space where I could extrovert, aware of myself having direct perception of my present time environment. I would be "in communication" with my environment, without my reactive mind in the way. I stood on a high point overlooking Los Feliz and Hollywood merging into Los Angeles, where I had a panoramic view. All this space seemed to be mine. I felt huge, as if I had no limits. I felt calm, with no random thoughts, an awareness of being aware of just being me.

I remember writing a success story, but it didn't blow me away. I think the whole process had been too hyped up beforehand. It irritated me to pay more than $2,000 for this rundown to confirm what I already knew, but I didn't complain.

I wondered if Scientology makes it a habit to suggest to people that they have certain conditions that don't actually exist…and is Scientology all about making itself the solution to these nonexistent conditions? Figuring this out was going to be part of the journey.

By that point, our generation knew great musicians dying from overdoses like Jimi Hendrix, Janis Joplin, Jim Morrison, and on, and we wanted to change our lives. Peter and I had already stopped doing recreational drugs that had been part of our music business life. We learned about the Purification Rundown to cleanse our bodies of drug residuals, and decided to take the plunge. We endured the rigorous program of exercise, sweating in a sauna, and taking intensive amounts of vitamins and oils. I don't recall any licensed doctors overseeing us, yet we were given daily instructions of how much vitamins and oils to take, which required medical knowledge. I remember Peter saying he had some hallucinations turn on. I finished in two weeks because I had a light drug history; Peter finished in about five weeks and raved about its effects.

Peter wanted to go Clear at CC, but the Valley Org didn't want us to transfer. A registrar told me that Peter belonged at CC, but I should stay at the Valley Org. I noted the invalidation and moved on. Scientology organizations, like any business, don't like losing customers who have the potential for spending a lot of money.

# 6

# CHÂTEAU SCIENTOLOGY

## Hollywood, 1982

IN MY PRE-CELEBRITY CENTRE DAYS, friends and I enjoyed a cappuccino at La Poubelle, a sidewalk bistro across the street from Scientology's castle at 5930 Franklin Avenue. We'd gaze at this intriguing French-Normandy building, whose seven stories loomed over us. Its weatherworn peaks and turrets stood tall, as if reaching for a higher deity.

The Manor Hotel, formerly a coveted Hollywood address near Franklin Village, showed years of wear in need of repairs, reminiscent of WW II movies showing war-torn great houses in Europe occupied by soldiers. Its once stately stone walls were now crumbling in an endearing sort of way. Swaying palms and tamarind trees framed the castle like an Elysian paradise. Then and now, it sought to be a place of bliss for beautiful people, a sort of temple of the gods.

Celebrity Centre's setting at the Manor mimics a luxurious Beverly Hills hotel, off-putting to friends who don't feel comfortable in the company of high-profile people. While the Manor Hotel needed massive renovations, it served as the only hotel in Los Angeles exclusively for Scientologists. I didn't know of another religion with a separate building to distinguish its celebrity followers from their general members, like a celebrity Catholic church or a celebrity Jewish temple.

CC tour guides touted the château's history, underplaying the 1950s era when it was the Fifield Manor retirement home. CC seemed to prefer resting on the laurels of the castle's 1930s Hollywood lore. The fact that Humphrey Bogart, Clark Gable, Katherine Hepburn, Edward G. Robinson, and other Hollywood elite had rented apartments or stayed in its hotel rooms fifty years prior had no connection with Scientology, but this seemed to be part of the self-aggrandizing script for presenting Scientology to the special people of Hollywood, part of casting the vision that American idols would once again fill its halls. In the front foyer, framed head shots of celebrity followers such as John Travolta, Karen Black, Amanda Ambrose, Diana Canova, Priscilla Presley, Lee Purcell, Bobby Lyons, Chick Corea and others adorned the walls, like pics hanging in Sunset Boulevard restaurants for tourists. We noted small groups of people talking together in settings marked by vestiges of romance and beauty in its turrets, gardens, niches and hidden hallways. Antique furnishings, art, and once beautiful but now threadbare rugs, filled the main floor rooms.

The pseudo-military uniformed staff added to the battleground sense of the fortress, and walls adorned with elaborately framed pictures of L. Ron Hubbard showed how CC memorialized Hubbard, starting with an office dedicated to the presence of "Source." Bronze busts of LRH and photos from his early days accented the halls, classrooms, and public spaces. Hubbard was Scientology's first celebrity, clearly the object of awe. Ample materials provided info about Hubbard as a humanitarian, writer, philosopher, cinematographer, master mariner, and on. Scientology publications share nothing of his dark side, but tout his celebrity status that started with the sale of his first screenplay, *Secrets of Treasure Island*, to Columbia Pictures in 1937, and carried on as a pulp fiction writer of hundreds of stories. He established Bridge Publications in Los Angeles and New Era Publications in Denmark as his personal publishing houses to ensure his works are freely disseminated worldwide, not subject to an outside publisher's scrutiny, control, or profit sharing. He also self-published his fiction books, including *Battlefield Earth* and his satirical science-fiction dekalogy, *Mission Earth*. Over the years, we were urged and sometimes even strong-armed by staff to buy some of these books. I remember being rounded up with other Scientologists to buy *Battlefield Earth*, *Mission Earth* volumes, or some other new release like a *Ron Mag* so we could drive up the sales statistics. After all, any Scientologist worth their salt wanted Hubbard to be a best-selling author.

My first impression? A total refurbishment was needed to complete the grandeur the group obviously desired. But the alluring yet questionable concoction of religion, luxury hotel, silver-platter treatment for celebrities and the arts served up an intoxicating potion when Peter and I first walked through its doors. It was easy for us, and I believe it was easy for many of my artist friends, to become drunk with the self-importance suggested by Hubbard's writings that emphasize the value of people who have an aesthetic mind. Friends who filled the seats in Celebrity Centres every day were there for reasons similar to mine: we wanted to help clear the planet through Celebrity Centre, our oasis, a fortress where an artist is understood, protected, gratified, elevated, and even revered.

Hubbard's descriptions of artists in *Science of Survival* elevates the artist, regardless of the level of one's celebrity status, above all others. Artistic people are treated as a special breed of thetan, able to function above the level of the common analytical mind. We grew in belief that our considerations are senior to the limits of our mind and body. Hubbard says that artistic types are able to deal with the nebulous field of art and creation because we possess a great deal of theta, our endowment of free-flowing spiritual energy through our aesthetic mind, giving us the potential to be great musicians, designers, and the like. Theta, or élan vital, life force, spiritual energy, empowers us to work toward peaceful revolution as world changers, to be the change we wanted to see. Scientology promises limitless levels of power, knowledge and abilities to control life, thought, matter, energy, space, time, and form—a god-like role in life.

I saw more pictures of A-list members on the walls than in person strolling the grounds or sitting in the class rooms, but still got a strong sense of Hollywood clubbiness there, the small-world feeling like the Houston music scene and the LA music industry. It's that sense of being in a tight, somewhat selective community, a cultural group that makes you feel less-than when you're not part of it, and makes you feel like you matter when you are in it. Up and coming writers and musicians of the time, as well as children of celebrities filled the halls in those days, such as Paul Haggis, Jason Beghe, Leah Remini, Elizabeth Moss, Juliette Lewis, Giovanni Ribisi, Jenna Elfman, Bodhi Elfman, Lisa Marie Presley, David

Pomeranz, John Novello, Jeff Pomerantz, to name just a few. There was always a buzz about who was coming into CC LA, or CC New York where Superman Christopher Reeve slipped in and out before he died. We became friends with New York celebs enrolled at CCNY including cinematographer Lee Hopp and Broadway dancer Christina Kumi Kimball from *Cats*.

Any prospect who walked in the door and met the criteria of being an artist or celebrity was treated as one of Earth's top strata of beings. This helps to explain why, in the fiercely competitive environment of Hollywood, artists and opinion leaders of all levels are comfortable here. CC is perfectly situated in the hub of American Idol culture where people turn to star power for everything from creative inspiration and cultural trends to political responses and spiritual guidance.

At the CC, high-profile celebs also receive special treatment not afforded to general Scientologists, such as special entrances into designated rooms, private lounges, classrooms, and even rooms for auditing separate from general Scientologists. Special schedules were offered to accommodate recording or filming schedules. This contrasts with general public who must commit to specific days of the week to fulfill their weekly hours of Scientology. Others, like Tom Cruise and Nicole Kidman later did, received the Gold platter treatment at the International Management base for one-on-one, private auditing and training.

Peter set up a mini-recording studio in the lower level of the CC as a place for songwriters and musicians to meet and work on demos of songs they wrote together, with the intention to recruit them into Scientology. Years prior to Peter arriving at CC, musicians jammed in the lobby at night, which sometimes attracted outside musicians. Doug Parent headed up a group with Thad Corea, Sonny Khoeblal, Kanga LaVrado, Sean Wiggins, Maxine Nightengale and Margie Nelson. Peter's group usually included Mel Nelson on bass, Gordy Gale on drums, Bill Lorentzen on guitar, Margie Nelson on vocals.

We organized the Manor's Renaissance dining room into a club on weekends featuring different bands and solo artists. Peter kind of monopolized or controlled who could play there when he first came on the scene, which likely offended some of the musicians who had been CC public long before he arrived. He was all about LRH, and expected that the Scientologist musicians who he performed with would be focused about disseminating and clearing the planet, and not be overly focused on themselves. This affected who he would call to play at CC. I guess it was normal for musicians to sometimes be intimated by other good musicians, but I noticed Peter seemed to exert a power play around certain people, such as Jamie Faunt, a well-known bass player, whom Peter didn't even introduce one night after a solo. Eventually, the schedule opened up to many more musicians and singers.

We were always on the hunt for new recruits and openly told our contacts in the entertainment business about Scientology. We brought in Frank Stallone, through whom we tried to reach Sylvester Stallone. Peter and Frank co-wrote the theme song to *Rambo: First Blood Part II*, so we spent times in the studio with Frank when Sylvester would come in to listen to the tracks. Body guards surrounding Stallone made it difficult to reach him personally, so we missed that opportunity. We brought in Garnett Rolie, wife of Santana and Journey keyboardist and singer, Gregg Rolie; Santana drummer Michael Carrabello and percussionist Greg Enrico; Marie Kleidon from MASH, and others who do not want their names mentioned.

I knew that Scientology wasn't for everyone, and never told my contacts that you could be a Scientologist and a Christian, Jew, Buddhist, etc., at the same time, because that didn't make sense to me, even though we were trained to say that. This line was meant to help people get around the issue of having to choose between their lifelong religion and Scientology as a new religion, and instead, to think of Scientology as an add-on to present beliefs. This premise, however, was utterly misleading. At a certain point, a Scientologist has to forsake "other practices" and beliefs, and in no way, shape, or form would a Scientologist ever be allowed to move up the bridge into advanced levels while professing faith in another religion or spiritual practice.

## Plenty of Profit for Celebrity Recruiters

A recruiter (called a Field Staff Member or FSM) who could bring in enough celebrities and artists for services could quit their day job by relying on commission income. This commission system pays 10% to 15% commission on each customer's purchases. Just as Gerry Simons brought us into the Valley Org and earned commissions from services Peter and I paid for, I saw recruiters making oodles of cash by bringing new people into the CC, and watching over them to ensure they continued to buy Scientology courses, auditing, books, and e-meters. For example, paying for the steps to "go Clear" might cost $50,000 or more. That's about a $5,000 commission on that package for the FSM, and more if they bought books and tapes.

Celebrities move on from CC to do advanced levels up through OT VII at Scientology's mecca, the Flag Land Base in Clearwater, Florida or the Advanced Org Los Angeles (Big Blue). To operate at Tone 40, full throttle as a spiritual being, with or without a body to control life, and achieve OT VIII, a Scientologist goes to the Freewinds, Scientology's cruise ship, usually docked in the Caribbean. Making this confidential level available only at sea was a smart way for the church to kill two birds with one stone— the Freewinds was a safe base for the International Association of Scientologists, that collects millions of dollars in donations for the Scientology "war chest" in free international waters outside governmental regulations. And getting Scientologists to spend hundreds of thousands of dollars to pay for OT VIII plus ship accommodations was a clever business decision to finance the Moneywinds' operations. But the recruiters were pocketing the likes of $50,000 in commissions when their selectee paid for all the steps up through the advanced levels that cost more than $500,000. That exceeds an average real estate commission. Can you imagine any church paying commissions on tithes thrown in the Sunday collection basket?

The big payoffs came by recirculating the advanced Scientologists, who were made to redo basic or advanced level services whenever church leader Miscavige told the Scientologists they hadn't really achieved the outcome of the level, and had to redo their services, such as what happened whenever he would release a new "Golden Age." Or, whenever Hubbard's books were repackaged and "all errors removed," everyone would have to buy the latest versions of books and CDs. The price tag on those services and materials could be in the tens to hundreds of thousands of dollars.

## The power of celebrity

The Celebrity Centres drive the strategy behind the power of celebrity in Scientology, and manipulate the outcomes for the profits of Scientology. The highest hopes of Scientology management were to convert celebrities into walking success stories to become mouthpieces for Scientology. The goal? American consumers who listen to celebrities praise Scientology will make the success equation: *If Scientology worked for that celebrity, it could work for me too.* As a brand, Scientology is obviously not alone utilizing celebrity endorsements as marketing collateral. But this notoriety further builds Scientology's social capital.

But before celebs would become mouthpieces, they had to be satisfied with their results in Scientology auditing and training. They had to be able to share wins honestly, or they wouldn't be able to converse with media, recruit other celebrities, or talk to public in general as a confident Scientologist. Celebrity Centres are charged with the intense responsibility of achieving this outcome in each of its paying customers.

Scientology wants to be viewed as the savior to social betterment with its celebrities speaking to community and government officials about how their social reform is religious in nature. Scientology directs the International Association of Scientologists (IAS) members—the entire Scientology world—to get LRH tech into society through their social betterment programs such as Narconon, The Way to Happiness, Applied Scholastics, and Citizens Commission for Human Rights (CCHR). Every Scientology front group wanted to utilize CC's biggest names to forward their particular program. Prior to Tom Cruise, few celebrities did media interviews because of being unable to handle critical journalists, which is why we see a scarce number of famous faces publicly supporting Scientology. John Travolta made presidential connections to get LRH study technology into public schools in the '90s through the Clinton administration. Kirsti Alley shouldered the Narconon drug-rehab promotion for many years, but in the advent of numerous lawsuits against Narconon for wrongful deaths, this may have affected Kirsti's support of the program. Jenna Elfman and Kelly Preston promoted Applied Scholastics, and Jason Beghe and Paul Haggis had been strong supporters of CCHR.

In later years, no mission seemed to be impossible for Tom Cruise. As Scientology's boldest rebel against the non-Scientology status quo, he seemed out to prove that he could win any battle, including Scientology's battle against Enemy #1, psychiatry. I remember watching Tom Cruise belittle Matt Lauer on the *Today Show* (2005) for being glib and having an inferior understanding about the destructive effects of psychiatry and "psych drugs" like Ritalin and Prozac. To say the least, his arrogance and bullet-like comments reflected poorly on his ability to handle the communication of his show host. He seemed intent to steamroller Matt Lauer and interrupt and invalidate him. Cruise's rude arrogance spoke loudly about the personality of an advanced Scientologist. Not to mention his later criticisms of Brooke Shields for taking an antidepressant psych drug. Then there was his episode of jumping on Oprah's couch while expressing his love for Katie Holmes, and his infamous video with his strident laughter about how Scientologists are the only ones who can help someone in trouble. Well, even "the best" aren't perfect. But I can't recall any subsequent public displays with such outbreaks. I can only imagine how David Miscavige or a designated official might have addressed Cruise about refraining from such behavior for a while.

# 7

## "ON THE WINGS OF LOVE"

### Burbank, California - 1982

OUTSIDE OF OUR SCIENTOLOGY WORLD, life centered in our little Alameda Drive hub of creativity. Peter lived and breathed practicing piano, listening to music, and composing. Lately he was spending hours on the piano accompanying Jeffrey Osborne's songs to get a feel for his vocal style. I dwelled in my design studio from morning until night designing, drafting patterns, and sewing. My most favorite moments at home with Peter were days like this, with me designing a new piece while listening to Peter play a free-flow of notes and chord progressions, like spontaneous musical poetry. One afternoon after Peter practiced scales, he broke into improvisation that escalated into some passionate moments on the keys. I heard him play the most beautiful combination of notes that flowed out of some deep melodious well, that made me drop what I was doing.

I called out, "Hey, play that again. Those last few bars, what you just played." He didn't find those notes at first. I went into his room and hummed what I had heard, the notes were so memorable, even though I had only heard them once.

Peter retraced his steps on the keys. "That! Right there—that!" I would say when he recaptured those same notes.

"This?" He worked the keys, played out a few note patterns, repeating and then building on the original notes.

"Beautiful. You ought to do something with that," I told him. Peter retraced his keys and tapped into the well of those notes. It was as if the finished melody had always been there, it just hadn't yet been mined and released. He threw himself into that piece, working on nothing else for days. He'd replay some of Jeffrey's recordings just to listen to his vocal range, and then he would go back to his piece to rework the notes to take them higher and some lower, to give Jeffrey the vocal challenge that would bring out the power of his voice. Peter finished the intro, the melody, and the bridge of the most beautiful piece that became the first song he pitched to Jeffrey Osborne for his first solo album. We put together a package for Jeffrey, with a tape of Peter playing the full melody on piano, along with sheet music that held Peter's full score for the song with other instruments added to the arrangement. Peter delivered it to Jeffrey's house in North Hollywood.

Two weeks later, Jeffrey called to tell us he had written three sets of lyrics to Peter's music. He asked us to come over to listen to the lyrics and music together. The next day we were standing in Jeffrey's music room.

"Peter, your music is so visual—the range, the highs, the lows...this music suits me, I can stretch out vocally—man, it's what I was looking for." Jeffrey gave Peter a huge grin and slapped him on the back with a hug from the side.

I watched Peter's face react to Jeffrey's response with smiling eyes. I knew how much Peter had poured himself into creating something that he had already decided would land on Jeffrey's album. "Well, I love your voice, man, I mean, I know where you can take it. So, thanks." Peter squeezed my hand, and told Jeffrey, "Let's hear what you got."

Jeffrey started tape of the music to sing the first set of lyrics. "I'm calling this version 'At the Rainbow's End.' Listen to these words."

Peter and I nodded to each other as we listened to how the lyrics matched the movement of the music. "That was beautiful, man," Peter nodded at Jeffrey.

Jeffrey sang the second set of lyrics to our music track, but I don't remember the words; they didn't strike either of us. "OK, here's the third set. I think you're gonna like this." Jeffrey started the tape over again.

"Just smile for me and let the day begin...you are the sunshine that lights my heart within...and I'm sure that you're an angel in disguise...come take my hand and together we will rise..." Peter's piano notes crested to the chorus. "On the wings of love, up and above the clouds, the only way to fly, is on the wings of love..."

I nearly floated, listening to Jeffrey belting out these lyrics to Peter's melody, that elevated and crested as if born to move together as one. Tears spilled down my cheeks. I looked at Peter as he put his head down, squeezing his eyes, while a smile stretched across his face.

Jeffrey stopped the tape when he finished singing the "Wings" lyrics to the music. "I think I like this one the best, 'On the Wings of Love,' yeah, I think that's the one. What do you think?"

We laughed with tears on our cheeks. "That's the one, Jeffrey. You slayed it man. I love it."

"I love it too, Peter," Jeffrey said. "I'm going to play this for George Duke. He said we needed a ballad, a love song like this—everything else we're putting on the album is funky or faster tempo. I'll let you know what he says. And Peter, thank you so much."

Jeffrey told us that at one point, Duke had debated whether "Wings" would make it on the album as a ballad. We were sweating it out before Jeffrey gave us the news a few weeks later. "It's gonna make the cut! He loved it." A&M Records released one song from Jeffrey's first solo album, *Jeffrey Osborne,* before releasing "On the Wings of Love" as a single.

"Wings" flew up the *Billboard Top 100* charts. Every week, Peter and I drove to the newsstand at Ventura Boulevard and Sepulveda to buy the latest copy of *Billboard.* We'd nearly rip the paper apart until we came to the Top 100 chart to see where "Wings" had placed. We'd jump up and down screaming out loud every week it moved another position up the charts. Each significant step meant we could request another advance from A&M Records. I got to know Neil Portnow, a Vice President at A&M, through my bi-weekly visits to pick up our checks. Neil was a great guy who made every artist feel like they had hung the moon. He was not an arrogant record company exec like other musician friends complained about. He was good at his job, particularly good dealing with artists.

The taste of success was a sweet injection of pleasure, and we were becoming addicted.

## Coldwater Canyon - 1982

After Wings hit, Peter and I headed for the Santa Monica Mountains above the San Fernando Valley in search of a new home. We found our first place in Coldwater Canyon between the Valley and Beverly Hills. Avenida del Sol branched off Coldwater to Alta Mesa Drive as a steep, tightly wound canyon road, with houses jutting vertically from the mountain cliffs above canyon walls. Our sand-colored stucco ranch house was partially built into a cliff, the kind of house I used to think people were crazy living in. But I learned that houses on stilts were more flexible in earthquakes and less likely to crack and break as the earth shifts.

We lived three doors down from songwriter and keyboard player David "Hawk" Wolinski, who had produced Chaka Khan and Rufus' last hit album, and down the road from jazz singer Al Jarreau. This small-world feeling of the neighborhood was home to a community of musicians and artists who were living out their dreams.

Our home had a finished lower level, built into the canyon wall, with a flow of rooms we converted to our dream spaces. My design studio with parquet floors and massive windows filled the large center room. Peter's music studio fit into a side room lined with brick walls, with a private entrance from the driveway. Ely moved into a suite of rooms at the other end of the house. We had another guest room and bath that rotated visiting friends and relatives. Peter's twin cousins, Lori and Lynn Egglefield, moved in for a while, as did Kris, an Australian friend dating Ken Rarick, keyboard player for Air Supply. With plenty of room for our bustling household, we never lacked family and friends around. "On the Wings of Love" was, at this point, providing both help and pleasure to many of our loved ones.

"Wings" seemed to be playing everywhere in stores, restaurants, elevators, you name it. The success of "Wings" ushered us into an artist-label relationship with A&M Records, along with all the paperwork that goes with registering a song with a record label and on an album. Since Peter's career was hitting big, and I knew that artistic careers were all about timing, I parked my design career to support his.

I quickly learned that a songwriter has several channels for revenue when original music is recorded by an artist—songwriting, publishing, and copyright revenue. I set up a music publishing company as a corporation to protect Peter's rights and income as a composer. That way, we would earn shares of publishing, song writing and copyright, more of the share than what most songwriters typically earn. I wanted to fast-track learn how to become a music publisher. I paid our Beverly Hills music attorney for several hours of his time to show me the ropes of music publishing, and to teach me the basics about copywriting music, filing forms with record companies, the Library of Congress, and anyone else with whom we needed to be affiliated. He recommended two books for me to study and use as legal references for the novice music publisher. He helped me set up Schlessmusik Inc., as the umbrella organization for our recording studio and music publishing company, Lincoln Pond Music.

Lincoln Pond, the Schless family's beloved camp in the Adirondack Mountains, held two cabins built by his grandfather Obbie and one built by Peter's mother, our headquarters for summer vacations every year since we had been together. Going to camp held deep family significance, a ritual that called for an annual family mecca, most fitting for our company's namesake.

We joined Broadcast Music Inc. (BMI) that represents and protects songwriters and music publishers in song performance matters such as royalty collections and song licensing. Now so focused on music publishing, I learned the steps of music administration, how to file Peter's musical compositions with the Library of Congress, file copyrights, everything. Without doing this, we would have lost out on significant shares of income that we have been collecting in royalties since day one of our first recorded song.

One year later, we moved to a five-acre estate at the top of Alta Mesa Drive, near the top of Coldwater Canyon just under Mulholland Drive. We rented this 3,500 square foot tudor home that was like a private resort for about $3,000 per month, not yet able to buy real estate in that area priced out of our reach. A 100' brick terrace with lounge chairs and a jacuzzi for twelve spanned the width of the house facing the San Fernando Valley. We'd relax in the spa at night with a glass of wine, overlooking millions of twinkling lights below.

Our home held two master suites, each with a balcony facing the Valley at opposite ends of the house. Ely lived in one side while Peter and I enjoyed the other. We converted the expansive living room on the main floor into Peter's recording studio. With tile floors, open beam ceilings, and glass doors facing the valley view, the space was perfect for even A-lister recording artists that Peter hoped to host. We set up banks of keyboards and sound equipment, and purchased a new mixing board and all the gear needed to make the studio work.

Jeffrey Osborne's successful record deal with A&M and his first solo album catapulted Jeffrey's career. He moved his family to a beautiful home in the west end of the Valley, where he opened his new recording studio, "Wings West." Jeffrey was invited to perform "On the Wings of Love" at the next Grammy Awards. What a surreal experience to sit in that special room of the Biltmore Hotel in Los Angeles, watching Jeffrey belt out the song that Peter had just composed. This event marked the peak of Peter's career, and also mine through my supporting role.

Meeting famous songwriters and performers whom we had previously admired from a distance turned our first Grammy night into a surreal experience. Surrounded by the icons of the music world, and now a part of that group of songwriters, Peter and I moved through the night in a dreamlike state, even though "Wings" was not a Grammy recipient. "Up Where We Belong" performed by Joe Cocker and Jennifer Warnes won in the "best pop performance" category that year, along with Men at Work's "Land Down Under" for the best song award.

I'll never forget the moment when Peter and I met mega-songwriter David Foster, a 14-time Grammy Award winner with 44 nominations. In his career, he produced some of the most successful artists in the world including Celine Dion, Mariah Carey, Chicago, Whitney Houston, and Michael Jackson. In front of several other nominated songwriters, Foster said to Peter in a serious tone, "There's one big thing wrong with 'On the Wings of Love'."

Peter took Foster literally. Like a humble grasshopper to a sage, he asked, "What's wrong with it?"

Foster laughed and slapped Peter on the shoulder. "I didn't write it, man, that's what!" The other guys laughed, while Peter didn't take his comment as the complementary chiding it was meant to be. Peter reddened, smiled at Foster, and turned to walk away instead of starting a conversation with this icon that he had always wanted to meet. Under his breath, Peter told me that Foster was a jerk who he would never work with if he had the choice. It was as if he felt whittled down a notch in front of peers. My reaction was the opposite. I saw the moment as an opportunity to connect with an icon, since Peter now had an open door to collaborate with just about anyone in the business. A huge missed opportunity. Stepping into the role of a recorded songwriter was unfamiliar, and seemed even somewhat uncomfortable for Peter at first. He was learning the ropes of how to hang with the big guys before he fully realized that he had become one of them.

## New York, 1983

A year after "On the Wings of Love" became the top hit from Jeffrey Osborne's solo album, Peter received the recording industry's cherished Broadcast Music (BMI) composing award, "Most Played Song of 1983." This BMI Songwriter Award acknowledges the authors of the music, not the performers or the record producers.

The Grammy's in Los Angeles had been amazing the year before, but the thrill of this BMI event at the Plaza Hotel in New York surpassed the Grammy's. Icons of the songwriting world filled the seats at the adorned dinner tables of the Plaza ballroom. Some of the Jackson's were seated at the table to the right of ours. If we had ever doubted whether we could be successful in the competitive music world, the acknowledgements that night showed us that Peter had moved to the top of his game as a composer; I took pride in knowing that my supporting role contributed to his success.

The atmosphere was electric. Song intros flooded the room as icon after icon in the world of hit songwriters moved to the stage to receive their awards. These were the peers Peter had always wanted to be part of, who had kept him motivated along the way. When the announcer called Peter's name, I watched my husband make his way through the tables and up the steps to the podium, while "On the Wings of Love" filled the room.

Peter rightfully enjoyed that moment of glory. I believed he carried within him a bottomless well of talent and imagination, and there was nothing this composer couldn't accomplish.

After he rejoined me at our table, Peter was like a full cup overflowing with water. He facial expression said, the rest of this event is too much to absorb. I could see he wanted to revel in the accomplishment privately. He whispered, "Let's get out of here."

"What do you want to do?"

"Lets take a horse-drawn carriage ride through Central Park."

We slipped out of the ballroom doors, and decided that we needed some cigars for this ride. We found the Plaza's cigar shop, where we perused the collection as if we were connoisseurs, and made our selections. We raced passed the doormen and climbed into an empty carriage. Our driver headed us into the park while we languished in our seats and lit our cigars. Not a smoker, I nevertheless savored the rich taste in my mouth. Peter blew smoke rings between moments of reflection and outbursts of laughter. We tipped our ashes over the side, listening to the rhythmic clip-clop of the horses. I don't remember exchanging any words. The pure contentment in Peter's blue eyes that night will forever remain in my memory. I hoped I would see that look in his eyes again and again.

Peter and Karen moved into their second Alta Mesa Drive Home in Coldwater Canyon around 1985 after "On the Wings of Love" became a hit song. Their recording studio was the location for the photo shown on the Celebrity Magazine below

Peter and Karen moved into the Manor Hotel in 1986, showing their increased involvement in Scientology.

Above: Celebrity Centre featured Peter and Karen on its Celebrity magazine cover with a story about their participation in the Religious Freedom Crusade.

Right: "On the Wings of Love" became a hit song in 1982, was featured at the Grammy's, and won Peter BMI's songwriter award "Most Played Song."

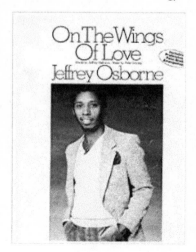

# 8

# LIVING THE DREAM

## Los Angeles - 1982/83

❧ PETER'S SUCCESS WITH SONGWRITING was a dream come true for both of us. But entering my design studio brought me into my private dream domain. It was just a small second bedroom, but its old, polished hardwood floors gleamed, and ample window light fell on my design table. I stuffed the closet with bolts of fabrics, patterns, and sewing supplies. We built a massive cutting table where I could unroll bolts of cloth and craft my patterns. Peter bought me a high-end Viking sewing machine, and a professional Baby-Lock surger that finished the inside edges of seams. Work lights clamped to the edges of my work table burned into the late hours of many nights, often twelve hours a day. I was living my dream, designing one-of-a-kind pieces for my growing clientele, proud to add new photos of my growing gallery of clients to my walls.

My friend from Aaron Spelling Productions, Marie, began referring clients to me. I designed my first creations in LA for Richard Dreyfus's fiancée, actress Kristi Kane, who also became a friend and referred other actors to me. My first appearance in the *Hollywood Reporter* highlighted my young design career in Los Angeles with a blurb and photo (except they goofed and listed Marie's name under my photo) after three celebrity guests wore my designs at a party held in honor of Randi Oakes, a TV star appearing in

*Fantasy Island, The Love Boat,* and *CHiPS.* I built my design clientele through personal referrals, including a Carol Burnett Show comedienne, Miriam Flynn, and Scientologist actresses such as Lee Purcell, and Lisa Blount who co-starred in *An Officer and a Gentleman,* who chose several of my designs to wear in her promotional photos. The manager of the New Christy Minstrels hired me to design several outfit changes for their next tour. One of my favorite clients was our good friend, wildman guitarist Steve Ferris, whom Peter met playing with Kenny Loggins band, who wore my stage clothes playing with Mr. Mister.

Marie and I organized a photo shoot at Marina Del Rey and also in Brandt Park near Glendale to feature a few pieces from a collection I was creating, with Marie and me as the models. We chose my Asian-influenced tunic, an off-the-shoulder black midi dress, and a loosely flowing purple silk top and pants to start with. Garrett, our photographer, captured some good shots, but could have done a better job on the lighting. Nevertheless, those photos started my design portfolio that I showed to potential clients.

Garrett and I had met on Sunset Boulevard, when he suddenly approached me and asked rather haphazardly if he could shoot my photo some day in his studio. When I asked this stranger why I would want to do that, he said, "Because I am building up my portfolio and you would make a perfect model." I thought, well this is a new line for a come-on. He opened his art case filled with prints of various people he had shot and developed. After seeing some of his work that appeared to be quite credible, we were impressed and decided to give him a try. Peter and I visited Garrett's studio, where he composed a "beauty shot" of me wearing a shirt with shimmery silver threads that he provided, and soft lighting that was quite artistic. He actually created a beautiful portrait that I have saved to this day. We continued to ask Garrett to take shots of Peter wearing different stage clothes I had designed for him, and we referred his photography work to others.

Marie quit her job at *M\*A\*S\*H* and Aaron Spelling Productions to become my business manager. I had designed a collection of clothes that would be my first retail exposure under my label, Kaké, (sounds like "KK"). The logo looked like Japanese brushstroked letters, gold on black, reflecting an Asian influence and simplicity that marked my style. We also signed on with Shuki, a Scientologist artist manager, whose clientele were Scientologists.

We held one uneventful show out of Shuki's office, and cut ties after seeing that his monthly fees delivered next to no services.

Marie and I contacted a buyer at Bendel's in New York, where I dreamed of selling my line. We made the mistake of taking the trip with only a tentative appointment that didn't pan out. Back in LA, Marie organized another party featuring my designs, and also tried to drum up some interest through some investor friends of hers, but didn't land the $200K we sought to get started. I wasn't interested with the business end of things and just wanted to focus on designing; Marie was a beautiful, charismatic woman whose heart was in the right place, but her newness to entrepreneurship didn't support the business end we needed.

I had also introduced Marie to Scientology. I talked Scientology all the time, and she seemed okay with it at first, but skeptical. She started a basic Scientology class that she discovered wasn't for her. She disliked it so much that it drove a wedge into our friendship. She said we couldn't work together if Scientology was involved. I told her I was a Scientologist. She quit the class, and I lost her as a business manager and friend.

Aside from designing for entertainers, I created one-of-a-kind pieces and commissioned design work for several retail clothing stores. One of a Kind on Beverly Boulevard featured a few of my pieces, but Meryl's of Studio City, that later moved to Little Santa Monica Boulevard in Beverly Hills, was my biggest account, until Voltaire.

I'll call the other account Voltaire, an exclusive mobile collection that traveled between Las Vegas and LA for showings to private customers, mostly the wives of casino owners. Voltaire's owner, whom I will call Carmela, was the daughter of a former casino manager who, she said, had allegedly been a Mafia man. Her father was deceased, but her mother still resided in Beverly Hills. Carmela brought me to her mother's home, lavishly adorned in a rustic elegant Ralph Lauren style that seemed to spare no cost with decor. Her mother handed me a roll of light grey striped silk, and asked me to make her a full circle skirt. I don't know why I only charged her $75; she probably wouldn't have batted an eye at a $750 bill.

My designs comprised one-third of Voltaire's total collection, featuring mostly silk and linen separates. My silk t-shirts sold for $350, linen and silk pant-skirts for $500, jackets for $400. I'd travel with Carmela and the collection in the silver Voltaire van, customized inside with silver carpet and chrome clothing racks. Carmela set up appointments with these casino wives she had met through her parents. We'd wheel our collection into stunning Vegas mansions, and show the clothes in the privacy and comfort the customer's dressing rooms. The women, who mostly wore sizes 2 through 6, tried on their selections with their own jewelry and shoes to get a complete picture of the outfit. A typical sale for an afternoon's visit awarded us about $5,000, usually in cash.

At first, I enjoyed casino visits with Carmela, whose Las Vegas lover owned the Black Jack machines in a major casino. We'd stop at a craps table where he'd tell me to roll him some nines. Naive me. I rolled nines. Next, he'd tell me to roll him elevens. I'd roll elevens. I didn't question the source of his magic over the dice. He'd cash in chips from the winnings, and I'd walk away with $500 in my hand after a few rolls of the dice, about as much as I earned in a week.

He treated us to dinner one night at Caesar's Palace in a private room with several of his friends. A gloved waiter stood behind each guest attending to our every need as we ate at a lavishly dressed round table. The $700 dinner tab was taken care of without a blink of an eye. But the perks of the job didn't outweigh my discomfort with the arrangements. One night, the three of us rode in his limo when he noticed Carmela's eyes light up at the sight of an attractive blonde girl walking the strip. Sugar Daddy asked Carmela if she wanted the driver to pull over and invite that woman to come home with her. I had always excluded myself from their sexual escapades, as well as that night's adventure. We parted ways a few days later after Carmela called to persuade me to leave my husband and move in with her and Sugar Daddy.

With Voltaire and Carmela in my past, other showings, parties, and photo shoots filled my schedule. I invited Peter to come to some of my events to share this excitement with me, but he usually declined, saying he had to rehearse or perform. He paid little attention to my design career other than modeling or wearing the stage clothes I made for him. I had been his biggest fan and staunchest supporter since 1977, throughout the development of his career in studio engineering, and as a composer and studio musician. Was he going to be my fan?

## World Tour

1983 brought more opportunities for Peter, starting with a gig playing keyboards for Melissa Manchester's world tour, with the first leg in Australia. Spouses were welcome on the road with Melissa's band, so I joined him in Melbourne. For three weeks, we explored Melbourne, Sydney, the Dandenong Mountains, and the Brisbane coast near the Great Barrier Reef. In Coolangatta wildlife preserve, I met my first wallabee that licked me on the cheek. The kangaroos would come out of the forest if we stood quietly, and Peter captured pictures of one that walked right up to me. We had a blast driving on the wrong side of the road through the round-abouts in a rental car that had a steering wheel on the left side of the car.

Manhattan Transfer opened for Melissa's show for the Australian leg of the tour. Janis Siegel and Cheryl Bentene were beyond amazing singers, but they were also warm, friendly and down to earth on the tour. We hung out at the Auckland airport, where they bought up New Zealand sheepskin boots and bags that were out of my price range. Peter received an offer to join their tour playing keyboards, but he was happy with Melissa's gig, so he declined.

When Melissa's tour headed back to the U.S. for the east coast, I joined them in New Jersey. We traveled in their tour bus through the Boston-area concerts, starting with the Cohasset Music Circus. We'd stop at roadside food trucks and eat the most amazing fresh clams with a cold beer, when I'd sometimes tell the musicians about Scientology. I had to stay pretty light about it, after I discovered that most of the band members had heard negative things. Peter and I sometimes even felt ostracized from some of the musicians we met, because of Scientology's reputation. One friend once told us that Jeffrey Osborne didn't want to collaborate with Peter again because Christianity and Scientology did not align.

During Melissa's stint at the MGM Grand, I'd drive to Vegas on weekends. We'd hang out back stage before and after shows with performers who'd come over after their shows in other hotels. Back stage life was how a lot of entertainers made friends, made connections for future gigs, and had some semblance of family life or stability despite their transient careers. That's when I first met Randy Jackson, who then played bass guitar for Journey. This was thirty-plus years before Randy became a judge on *American Idol.* I loved getting into spiritual conversations with Randy, who openly shared his ideas. He believed in Rosicrucionism, so he and I would compare and contrast that with Scientology. He lived in the San Francisco Bay area and had known many people who looked into Scientology. Randy expressed an inclusive, positive attitude toward people, which drew others to him. Everyone around him seemed to love him. But about Scientology, he'd say, "Aw, KK, do you really believe all that by L. Ron Hubbard?" Randy never criticized it, but would pose penetrating questions to me that expressed a concern about my choices.

Melissa's U.S. tour ended in Lake Tahoe at Harrah's. During the day, we'd explore around town, or ride horseback trails up the snow-covered Sierra Madre Mountains, bundled up in the warmest clothes we had with us. From a small mountain plateau near the top, we looked down over Lake Tahoe where people sunned at the beach in swimsuits. Come rehearsal time, we got to know Billy Crystal, Melissa's opening act. Billy was a perpetually funny guy, always on, and I never knew when he was kidding or serious.

## Mom & Dad's Visit to Flag

Apart from the parties and making new friends, living out of a suitcase got to be old, so Peter was glad to finish the tour. We fell back into our routine of being in the course room every night at the Celebrity Centre, and then went to Flag in Clearwater for a special event.

My parents had moved from Michigan to Florida, where the balmy weather offered an easier lifestyle than the snowy northern winters, so Mom and Dad came to Flag to see us. We gave them a tour of the Scientology facilities that also gave them a full explanation of Scientology's grade chart and the steps to total spiritual freedom.

One of the most regrettable moments of my life happened next.

My mother seemed to be interested in the learning process. Though Mom and Dad hadn't had the opportunity to finish high school, Mom was nevertheless bright and a voracious reader. Dad was bright and very capable, too, he just hadn't pursued much interest in education. Dad was the first to comment after the grade chart orientation.

He turned to Mom and said, "Hon, I really don't think this is for me. But I think that if you are interested in it, you could do this." My heart went out to Dad because I sensed that he was putting himself down, as if learning Scientology was over his head.

Dad said, "Karen, I'm sure all this is really helping you. You've always been smart, and I'm proud of what you are doing in your life."

To this day, I would give anything to redo my actions that followed. Peter and I had to leave for the airport to catch our flight back to LA, so we didn't get to talk much with Mom or Dad about getting involved in Scientology. I walked away filled with regret, even feeling shameful. This experience opened my eyes to the chasm that had developed between us as a result of my involvement in Scientology and living in California that excluded my family. I should have spent time alone with them on this trip to Florida, instead of using up our time together on a tour of Flag and the grade chart. I should have made sure Dad knew that I had no expectations about them pursuing Scientology. Most of all, I didn't want Scientology to come between us.

The next evening, I received a phone call from my brother. Dad had a heart attack at home that afternoon. He had been with some friends playing cards, walked into the bathroom, and crumpled on the floor, dead. Smoking and hardening of the arteries caused his final heart attack at age 64. Dumbstruck, I tried to climb out of my ocean of regret about not being in closer touch with Mom and Dad. It was too late. The opportunity to make up for lost time had slipped through my fingers. I felt ashamed, filled with regret. I wasn't sure what effect the Scientology orientation had on Dad, and wondered if it had overwhelmed him.

I mentioned this to some friends at CC. Someone commented, "Well, he dropped his body the day after he learned what Scientology was about. Maybe that's a good sign, that he'll come back to be a Scientologist." Scientologists put little significance on death. It just means that a spiritual being has dropped a body, and would soon take on another body in a new lifetime. There's not a lot of grieving after someone dies, and sometimes people say things like "Fly high!" or "See you next time." As if I wasn't supposed to feel grief for losing my father, and should just be analytical about it and not show human emotion and reaction (HE & R), I don't remember shedding a tear when I first heard the news of his passing.

A few days later, Peter and I flew to Florida for Dad's funeral. I expected Mom to be distraught, but she was more than a wreck.

Dad had been her life companion since 1945, so the loss of her one and only love was monumental. Our family put together a wonderful service for Dad. A Christian minister addressed our gathering before Peter got up and read a funeral ritual from the Scientology handbook. Peter's reading ended with, "Go John, go now to your next place..." or some such that had an afterlife message. I sat next to Mom and couldn't contain my tears because she wasn't containing hers. But Mom told me later that she liked what Peter said. It had a peaceful effect, as if encouraging Dad to move on to heaven, which gave her closure. Scientology doesn't believe in heaven or hell, just a continuation of spiritual life until taking another body. But I didn't explain that to Mom until later.

Mom continued to be severely distraught about losing Dad, and being alone. I felt concerned about leaving her alone, and wanted to help bring her some kind of relief. I contacted a Scientology organization in Tampa and arranged for her to receive an auditing session. Hours later, she came out smiling. She told me that the auditing helped her to face the horrible memories of her father's death when she was young, and some fears that had plagued her dreams about dead people. Mom said that she felt like she arrived at some kind of peace about Dad's death, not that she was over the loss of him, but she felt she wouldn't be afraid of being alone at home where she had found him, crumpled on the floor in their bathroom.

Peter and I returned to LA feeling like we had helped Mom deal with this huge loss, and had done a good job introducing Mom to Scientology auditing. I left with hope about her actually coming over to my side in beliefs.

## Schlessmusik rocks

After "Wings," Peter cranked out other great new songs. I stayed busy on the administrative end with Lincoln Pond Music, and made sure the Schlessmusik studio was booked solid. We placed several of Peter's songs with recording artists, including the theme song for *Rambo: First Blood Part II,* "Peace in Our Life" performed by Frank Stallone; a song on the soundtrack for *All the Right Moves;* "Bad Night," a cut on Frank Stallone's album; and a release of "My Heart" recorded first by Mark Spiro and then by Englebert Humperdinck in Europe, where it went gold on the charts.

We expanded our studio clientele in Schlessmusik by Peter producing and recording song demos performed by some great artists including Al Jarreau, Peter Aykroyd, Frank Stallone, Janet Planet Morrison (Van Morrison's former wife), and others. Lots of other opportunities opened up for Peter as a studio musician playing on other people's albums, including Kenny Loggins. We stayed so busy that we hired Garnett Rolie as a studio assistant for Peter, and a part-time accountant to keep everything straight. I now worked full-time as a studio manager and music publishing administrator, and Peter was happy to have my full-time dedication. For Schlessmusik, I took care of marketing and public relations, promoting our studio services, booking clients for studio time, and networking with other recording artists, songwriters, and musicians.

As exciting as this work was, I missed working in my own passion as a designer. Maybe my time would come. I counted on my auditing and training at Celebrity Centre to help me with that.

Lisa Blount, co-star of "Officer and a Gentleman" wears Karen's designs in her promo photos, early 1980s. Lisa was a Scientologist, and jumped to her death in 2010. (Photographer unknown).

Miriam Flynn, actress in National Lampoon's Vacation, comedienne on the Tim Conway show, and starred in ABC show Maggie, wears Karen's designs in her promotional photos, early 1980s. She was not interested in learning more about Scientology. (Photographer unknown).

Karen modeled one of her designs for a photo shoot at Marina del Rey, 1982. Photograph by Garrett.

Guitarist Steve Ferris and Peter Schless met in a studio when Steve played with Kenny Loggins and Mr. Mister. Steve wore a variety of Karen's designs when he performed, and would shop with her to pick out fabrics. He rejected Karen's recruitment efforts about Scientology. Photo by Garrett.

# 9

## RELIGIOUS FREEDOM CRUSADE

### Portland, Oregon - 1985

❦ CELEBRITY CENTRE PRESIDENT Sue Young McClay called Peter and I one day with an unfamiliar franticness in her voice, asking us to come to CC immediately. She burst into a frenzied explanation of how Scientology was under attack and we needed to help. Between incessant phone calls from Author Services Inc. and the Office of Special Affairs, Sue said the Church of Scientology was under lawsuit filed by a disgruntled Scientologist, Julie Christopherson-Titchborne, in Portland, Oregon. According to Sue, this $10 million lawsuit threatened not only the church's survival, but the freedom of all religions.

The church was being challenged by Christopherson's attorney, Michael Flynn, whose alleged goal was to break the church's bank. Former Sea Org members unhappy with Scientology—major SPs, according to Sue—had been deposed as expert witnesses, including Laurel Sullivan, Bill Franks, and Gerry Armstrong, who would testify in the trial. These were all people we had heard about, who had allegedly committed horrendous crimes against the Church of Scientology. We didn't know what they had done or why they left the Sea Org. We only knew that they were to be treated as SPs with no rights in the eyes of the church. Not until years later would we realize that Scientology had objectified Julie Christopherson as a sup-

suppressive person through church PR efforts and thus dehumanized her, dissuading anyone from having any compassion for her grievances against Scientology. Some of her complaints were similar to earlier legal cases, such as Homer Schomer's, saying that Scientology misrepresented who Hubbard really is that led to her realization that Scientology was a fraudulent organization that had milked thousands of dollars from her while making L. Ron Hubbard and the Scientology organization rich.

Sue wanted us to help her implement CC's role in the strategy to win the battle by issuing a call to arms of all Scientologists to fight for "religious freedom." Her plan was to start with celebrities who could wield the most influence in the media and on the general Scientology public. She asked us to activate musicians and singers to go to Portland and perform in public events held in parks and venues, to draw media that would cover the church's efforts to overthrow the case.

Peter and I accepted the mission, and started with one of the biggest names we knew at the time—Frank Stallone, brother of Sylvester Stallone. We woke up Frank around 11:30 p.m. to ask him to take a stand for religious freedom. At first he was ticked that we asked him to support Scientology, because Frank had already told Peter he wasn't interested in it. But Peter appealed to Frank's sense of religious freedom, with this being a great opportunity to take a stand for something meaningful, that no American should have to battle for, whether they were a Scientologist, Christian, Jew or whatever. Frank called Peter the next morning to let him know that he was in.

We had also rallied twelve other musicians and singers who were jumping on the religious freedom crusade bandwagon. Within 24 hours, we had assembled singer Frank Stallone, Santana percussionists Michael Carabello and Greg Enrico, Stevie Wonder's keyboard player, Tina Turner's bass player, Lenny Macaluso, and more. We also enlisted dozens of other Scientologist friends who were not performers but who would go to Portland as activists.

The next day, our musical entourage boarded a private jet filled with musicians and band equipment, along with some church Public Relations staff, and flew to Portland. The plan was to perform a few concerts in the park that weekend to draw media to our religious freedom crusade. The court case dragged on, but the call to arms worked. Thousands of Scientologists came to Portland from around the world to support religious freedom, filling hotels for blocks in the downtown area. That weekend stretched to thirty days of performing, picketing, assembling, and rallying for religious freedom.

Scientology strategists, particularly Vaughn Young, RTC and OSA staff, with President Heber Jentzsch as a key front man, had turned this issue into a blanket attack on religious freedom. They appealed to other religious leaders including Sun Myung Moon of the Unification Church and Rev. Jesse Jackson to support religious freedom, as if this court case challenged other religions. I heard that Heber Jentzsch did gain Moon's collaboration, but Moon didn't present himself. I had heard about the Unification Church members, "Moonies" who believed that Moon was the present-day messiah of Christianity. I thought, *whew, those people are really off the deep end. Now that is a cult and we are not anything like them.*

While Earle Cooley and opponents battled it out in the courtroom, more musicians arrived to perform in the concerts including Stanley Clarke, Chick Corea, Edgar Winter, and Nicki Hopkins, along with more Scientologists who donated to support the cause or who physically came to participate in crusading. At one concert, Stephen Ambrose from Stevie Wonder's band got Stevie on the phone through a live feed that was broadcast into the park. Stevie sang a few bars of a song in praise of crusading for what we believed in, "I just called to say I love you..." Crusaders applauded and shouted as if Stevie Wonder was endorsing Scientology.

I gained an unusual opportunity to be in the courtroom one day while Michael Flynn battled our lawyer, Earl Cooley. I had tripped on a curb in a park during one of the concerts and sprained my ankle, which caused me to wear a light cast and use a crutch for a few days. Ken Hoden, a church public relations man, rounded up a wheelchair. With me in it, he settled me in the courtroom like a prop near the front side of the room among other viewers. He told me "It would help to have a wheelchair in the courtroom; it would show that even a crippled Scientologist would come and support their church." Though I was glad to be privy to the controversial battle inside the courtroom, I regret to this day my participation in that charade.

Peter and I worked closely with Sea Org members who had come to Portland from the Int base, including the Golden Era musicians. They had come from that mysterious, confidential location with an aura of elitist power. Meeting staff from "over the rainbow" was like connecting with the sovereign gods of the Scientology world. We found ourselves in the sweep of daily decision-making with many of them, and worked hand in hand on everything from logistics to event set-ups. The Int base staff considered the crusade a nightmare, not only because the church's bank was at risk of being broken that could crack the empire. They also had to fund hundreds of thousands of dollars for crusade operations along with manpower, so they sent many RPFers to Portland to do the work, basically as slave labor. Peter and I didn't know any of those people, but we observed how effectively they worked individually and together. They operated as if they could accomplish anything they set their minds to.

I had only one negative experience with a Sea Org member in Portland, Jason Bennick. I had been working closely with Jeanine Boyd, an enthusiastic Int base staff member in charge of celebs at the Crusade (aside from Sue Young from Celebrity Centre). Jeanine asked me if Peter and I would put up a credit card so they could check celebs into the main hotel as they arrived. I said yes, because she assured me that they'd keep putting money on the card as they raised funds, to cover the costs. One day I discovered that our card carried $10,000 of charges, so I asked Jeanine to arrange a payment on it. She said she would take care of it, but this evidently caused a "flap" at the Int management level.

The Corporate Liaison In-Charge from the Religious Technology Center, Jason Bennick, came down from the Int base to speak with me personally. Jason exuded an arrogance that was quite off-putting and perplexing, considering the general sense of high-spirited cooperation that the volunteers on the ground in Portland had been working with. He asked me to explain why I needed a payment onto our credit card. I made it clear that our card had served as a convenience for check-ins to float the funds until the church raised money to make a payment on it. (The bill was paid, but in 1990, I would discover that Jason Bennick had become my rival.)

After nearly a month of courtroom battles and crusading, Scientology won the battle. To me, the victory was multifaceted. I knew little about the full legal significance of this case at the time, much less the true battle being fought behind closed doors of Scientology leaders, attorneys, OSA and Hubbard. But I believe that all the Scientology participants could see just how powerful we could be as a group united in one cause. We were the foot soldiers deployed at a moment's notice to do whatever was necessary to bring down our enemy. This resulted in tremendous unity among Scientologists and the church. We saw an incredible resurgence at CC after the crusade, when more people joined the Sea Org. LRH issued the Executive Directive "Winning" that acknowledged all the OTs who contributed. The document was so special, it was framed and played on an easel in CC's lobby.

Once Peter and I returned home five weeks after we had dropped all of our work to go to Portland, we faced our abandoned studio and a pile of bills. We hadn't earned any income for a month, and the bills that poured in required at least $8,000 monthly income to pay. We looked at the bills blankly, feeling more swept up in Scientology's goal to clear the planet than in our professional work. After the intense feeling of unity and power from crusade efforts, we started thinking that competing in the Hollywood music and fashion industries was unimportant compared to the sense of worth we felt after dedicating ourselves to the higher cause of religious freedom.

A month after the Crusade, Peter and I were featured on the cover of *Celebrity* magazine. Our interview emphasizes how we had discovered our purpose in life at the crusade, which deepened our belief in and dedication to Scientology. By then, I had already begun losing myself as a lover of creative expression and all things artistic. Instead, we both began to express that fixed, dedicated glare for which a dedicated, on-Source Scientologist is known, that same expression we saw in Sea Org members.

Broke, and somewhat confused about careers, we packed up our home and studio in Coldwater Canyon and moved into an apartment at the Manor Hotel that housed the Celebrity Centre. The rent was only $700 per month compared to our $3,000 home. The Manor hoped to fill the apartments with other celebrities, as if trying to re-capture the 1930s heyday of the Chateau Elysee. Actor Jeff Pomerantz soon moved into a sixth floor suite directly under ours.

It needed drastic restoration, but it met our needs, at least temporarily. Our new domain filled the seventh floor penthouse suite, which was not fancy and needed renovations. Our living room gave passage through two sets of French doors to a fenced rooftop terrace, where we enjoyed a dramatic view of the Holly-wood Hills. We put plants and a table and chairs out there for moments of occasional languishing at night when the view was most spectacular. Peter set up a smaller version of his recording studio in CC's lower level, deciding to use his studio as a draw to get more musicians and songwriters into Scientology.

We started throwing parties with Celebrity Centre friends as our guests, and someone would bring in a non-Scientologist who, we hoped, would get interested in Scientology. In one get-together, we hosted Russian rock star Sasha Malinan, introduced to us by David Pomeranz. That night, Edgar and Monique Winter, Jeff Pomerantz and many of our musician friends, David Pomeranz and Sasha filled the floor and seats of our living room where David and Sasha led us in song. Peter, David and Sasha co-wrote and published a song after that. Sasha received some Book One audit-ing, but that's where his Scientology involvement ended. While our Scientologist artist friends wanted to expand Scientology through the arts, not everyone wanted to dedicate themselves to its ultimate purpose of becoming a Sea Org member.

# 10

## CHANGING OF THE GUARDS

**Los Angeles - January, 1986**

AS THE MAN WHO ULTIMATELY INTENDED to lead the Scientology world, David Miscavige emerged publicly by announcing the death of L. Ron Hubbard. Hundreds of Scientologists gathered at the Hollywood Palladium to news that rocked the Scientology world. Peter and I watched the broadcast through a video feed at the Celebrity Centre where a thousand Scientologists packed the exterior grounds.

My conclusion? Deception and cover-ups defined life in the Sea Organization, at the highest realm of leadership—not to be understood by me until starting in 1990.

Since this is an historical event that is well-documented in many other online sources, I posted my account of this event on the book website for readers who'd like to know more.

Left: Peter Schless and Karen rallied all the musicians and performers they knew to come to Portland, OR to support Scientology's Religious Freedom Crusade in 1985, in response to the Julie Christopherson lawsuit against Scientology. Peter and Karen dedicated four weeks full-time to perform and organize daily events in the park.

Edgar Winter, Michael Carabello, Al Jarreau and Frank Stallone rehearse for a night's performance at the Crusade. Peter and Karen brought Michael and Frank into Scientology. Edgar and Al were on the Celebrity Recovery Project.

Stephen Ambrose, Michael Carabello, Frank Stallone and Peter Schless call Steve Wonder from the Portland Park at the Religious Freedom Crusade. Stevie sings "I Just Called To Say I Love You."

Celebrities and supporters of the Religious Freedom Crusade filled the ships as they paraded down the Sacramento River to publicize Scientology's Religious Freedom Crusade.

Jeff Pomerantz, Peter Schless and hundreds of Scientologists marched daily through downtown Portland with picket signs.

# 11

## CELEBRITY SPIRITUALITY

### Hollywood Celebrity Centre

I HAVE OFTEN BEEN ASKED, what attracts opinion leaders and artistic types to Scientology? How does Celebrity Centre transform garden-variety artists into celebrities, and into dedicated Scientologists who become mouthpieces for the church? My answers would have been different when I was a young Scientologist versus at the time I'm writing this. Peter and I had personal experiences at Celebrity Centre with training, auditing, and socializing that, I believe, typify what many before us and after us experienced. So I can best answer those questions through personal stories and interpretations of Scientology terms and concepts.

Let me first put our experiences into context: Celebrity Centres provide the ultimate *inclusive* environment. Our journey had escalated within the bubble of celebrity spirituality at Scientology's temple of the gods. We found CC to be a fortress of safety in the competitive Hollywood environment, where artists are protected, understood, gratified, and revered simply for showing up. Celebrity Centre's purpose includes helping artists achieve to greatness, to command influence and to change world conditions to favor Scientology. Years later, I came to see it as the ultimate *coercive* environment, long after I had already been lured by Scientology's siren song.

In the beginning, it was easy for us, and I believe for many of our friends, to become drunk with self-importance from CC's seductive spirituality cocktail: A mix of ego-boosting words from Hubbard that elevate the artist, who is seen as a special breed of human, the most valuable in earth's social strata, the dreamer of dreams who alone can elevate the tone of a society above all others. Add the luxury Celebrity Centre oasis with an array of celebrity followers, garnished with the attitudes, values, beliefs and lofty promises embedded in its spiritual pursuit system, and we have intoxication from daily engagement in celebrity spirituality. I developed a personal mission statement: To improve the world through peaceful revolution using Scientology in the arts.

When you see how the lives of celebrities unfold, they are just real people with families, lives, and problems, just like anybody else, and they opt to manage every aspect of their life with the teachings and mindset of L. Ron Hubbard. But also realize that they've been being shaped on this potter's wheel by the hands of management through a strategy of indoctrination. I believed myself to be entirely self-willed, making self-determined choices every step of the way. Others who knew us well might have seen how we became more and more dependent on Scientology's beliefs, dogma, rules, regulations, traditions, practices and vows, for answers to life—a slow and steady indoctrination to believing that only Scientology offers answers that resonate with real-life issues. I think most of my CC friends shared my goals, and couldn't see this codependency about themselves, either. It's hard to see a bubble surrounding you when you are within it.

My early days at CC were spent fairly oblivious to the underlying strategies of Hubbard and Scientology leadership. In retrospect, Peter and I were more like clay on a potter's wheel, shaped by the hands of the extremist Sea Org staff that knew exactly what to say and do to move us across the bridge to a point of greater dependence on Scientology for spiritual fulfillment. Scientology influenced us at an aesthetic level that supersedes the real world. The constant immersion in the tech of training and auditing fostered an obsessive urge for knowledge about self. This dependency on Scientology to fulfill my obsession was like being on an intravenous drip of self-absorption, while thinking that we were actually becoming more spiritually aware. I didn't realize that we weren't becoming more spiritually aware; we were just becoming better Scientologists.

## Religion or business?

Being surrounded by Scientology artists and celebrities gave us a big game, a way to be involved in something bigger than ourselves. Nothing was more important than clearing the planet, starting with handling our own cases, and helping others secure their keys to eternity. But those keys came at a high price, adding up to an expensive addiction that emptied our wallets and cost us decades of our lives.

That last statement points to an ongoing issue with which I struggled—was Scientology a religion, a business, or an approach to spirituality? Its interplay of business, spirituality, and applied religious philosophy makes for interesting debate. *Religion* is an institutionalized system of beliefs and practices that involve worship of a deity or the supernatural, based on dogma, traditions, rituals, and even vows, rules or regulations. Religion shows itself through people's behavior, translating life experiences into a deeply felt framework. *Spirituality* is a search for meaning as an eternal spirit or soul, perhaps connected to a power greater than ourselves, through values and a way of being. Spirituality seems to be more of a choice, whereas religion seems to be enforced or controlled because someone is there organizing it and running it as a system. *Business* is the exchange of goods and services for money. Then, we were not free to debate the answer to this question about whether it was a religion or a business; we were, however, supposed to know the 10 points of Keeping Scientology Working.

As a Scientology couple, I often felt like we were a balancing act walking a tightrope. What could I believe of Hubbard's claims? What was real to me? What was real to Peter? What was the Scientology organization, really? One can be spiritual without being in a religion. One can be in a religion without being very spiritual. Businesses can capitalize on religion and spirituality. Religions can capitalize on business, as various groups like Scientology and Christian Science have done, to name just two.

In my early days, I had a hard time referring to Scientology as a religion because it didn't—and never has—involved the worship of a deity, unless we want to count self-worship. We revered Hubbard as Source, but we spent less time focusing on him compared to focusing on our *self*. The Scientology journey is about delving into one's "case"—the whole sum of all mental charge from events in our current life to all our past lives—to an obsessive focus on all aspects of the *self*, so the concept "deification of self" could fit here.

Scientologists revere LRH, whose name, physical image, and legacy as Source were prominent throughout every Scientology building and in all Scientology materials. In his book, *Hymn of Asia*, Hubbard writes of himself as the Metteya, the much-awaited Buddha with red hair. Hubbard knew what he was doing when he wrote this book while eastern mysticism was becoming part of our '60s and '70s counter-culture, influenced by Beat writers Jack Kerouac, Allan Ginsberg, and William S. Burroughs, by the Beatles, by anti-establishment college student culture seeking transcendence, and on. Through *Hymn of Asia*, Hubbard offers transcendence, which lures people into Scientology.

I wasn't looking for a relationship with a deity, although I was curious about his interpretation of God. Early on, I never thought of Hubbard as a deity, a Messiah, or an object of worship. Loyal Scientologists *never* outwardly question the validity of L. Ron Hubbard's identity. We were not free to question or discuss such controversial details. From the beginning, I viewed Hubbard as a prolific writer and man of ideas, with the smarts to package and sell the concept of immortality as a commodity with a system to deliver it. Years later, after reading Napoleon Hill's *Think and Grow Rich* (and knowing that Hubbard named Napoleon Hill as an early influence), I could see that this book had contributed to sparking Hubbard's *one* idea that Hill says anyone needs to grow rich. Hubbard's idea, as we know, was to invent a religion as a means of making millions of dollars. Over the years, more about a whole new identity opened up about Hubbard beyond the materials provided by the church, that I discovered in the first few books I read after Scientology: LRH's son, L. Ron Hubbard Jr (aka Ron DeWolf), said in *L. Ron Hubbard: Messiah or Madman?* that Ron regarded himself as the successor to occultist Aleister Crowley, self-proclaimed "Beast 666," the anti-Christ. Jon Atack's excellent book, *A Piece of Blue Sky,* exposes an identity of Hubbard as a charlatan with evidence that Scientologists will never learn. More on this later.

I eventually agreed with Hubbard's premise that the world had gone mad and was at risk of extinction through nuclear weapons—a Cold War fear to which Hubbard hitched his Dianetics and Scientology wagon and captured many takers since the 1950s. Everything seemed to be about war, and war seemed to be everything in

Scientology. At first, Peter and I didn't succumb to this fear so much as we were just being artists who wanted to build a better world, without threat of nuclear destruction looming upon humankind. Our pre-Scientology lives had been more connected to a culture focused on the natural struggle of earning a livelihood; our Scientology lives became a culture of turmoil and the inter-human struggle of being at war.

Celebrity Centre was a perfect fit into Hubbard's dangerous environment strategy to absorb the masses. CC was responsible for expanding the number of celebrities in Scientology by recruiting the opinion leaders into Scientology. Maria Ferrara, the *Celebrity* mag editor, told me that in the early days, to attract the wannabe actors and recording artists, CC staff used to place ads in publications like *Variety* and the *Hollywood Reporter,* promoting workshops to "make it" in the entertainment industry. Once the wannabe's come in, CC's job is to ensure that artists become celebrities who expand in their area of power. Once in, the recruits would learn of the danger and paranoia that Hubbard claimed filled the world. And if they were being well taken care of, they would feel thankful that Scientology was there to save them from this dangerous environment.

For many Scientologists, including Peter, Hubbard is worthy of being idolized, although I never shared that view. I'm embarrassed by some of the things I remember doing: I stood in course rooms and event halls with dozens to hundreds or thousands of Scientologists, facing a bust or photo of Hubbard, often with Peter next to me, with everyone clapping enthusiastically for at least three minutes straight while someone shouts "hip hip" and everyone else shouts "hooray," inciting everyone to hoot, whistle, and clap harder and longer. Peter was always a loud, long clapper. If I didn't clap while everyone around me clapped, I would have stuck out like a sore thumb and might have been hauled away for my "bad indicators" of not applauding LRH, so I clapped along, oftentimes beyond the point I wanted to stop. This applause overkill was part of the groupthink of a Scientology crowd, as if we were wind-up toys or marionettes on puppet strings. This routine reminded me of scenes in WW II movies where Nazi supporters stood en masse, dutifully clapping for Hitler, with probably many afraid to not clap for fear of being tormented by the SS. When I reflect on times that I participated in group praise of LRH like that, I'm ashamed of my disingenuous acts, when privately thinking *thank you for the help in my life* would have sufficed.

When I started at CC in the '80s, I remember Leah Remini, Elizabeth Moss, Giovanni Ribisi, Juliette Lewis and other young artists just getting started, many who were second generation Scientologists, born into Scientology families. Peter and I were friends with Juliette's father, actor Geoffrey Lewis who performed with musician friends of ours in Celestial Navigation, and Elizabeth's father Ron Moss, who managed Chick Corea's band. Since Remini, Ribisi, Moss and Lewis were just getting started in careers, I recall some CC staff quarreling about counting them and others like them as "celebrities" in their weekly statistics, such as "CBIS, celebrity bodies in the shop." Hubbard himself said that the entourage of a celebrity should also be treated as celebrities. So the rising stars at Celebrity Centre were nurtured through the system and many went on to became A-listers. *That* is the job of the Celebrity Centre.

## What informs celebrity spirituality?

Certain Scientology books influenced the development of the celebrity spirituality mindset, along with specific concepts and ideas from Hubbard. The most influential was *Science of Survival* (SOS), published in 1951. Science of Survival is the survival handbook, the most vital of Hubbard's texts to master. Per Hubbard, surviving in this dangerous environment of earth requires expert understanding of and complete control over human behavior. A particularly alluring statement describes the artist as a "rebel against the status quo" who accomplishes peaceful revolution and creates future realities by imagining and creating changes in the present. This helped me believe that becoming a world changer was within reach with support of the organization. Hubbard envisioned a culture as being only as great as the dreams of artists who elevate it to its highest heights. To accomplish such lofty goals requires a masterful command over human behavior, so the book is packed with tools and concepts for how to achieve this.

Changing beliefs and ideas across humankind requires revolution. Peaceful revolution, or being the change that one wants to see in the world, becomes the heart of any Scientology artist, as it was mine, although we didn't call it that. Revolution becomes a state of mind—Keeping Scientology Working—a deep personal drive to clear the planet, and change the environment before the suppres-sors in the environment become too powerful or too effective over self. War becomes everything, and everything becomes war, with the personal goal of *survival* for self and *defeat* for the opposition. Yet this peaceful revolution is a life of stress, attack and defense, and even paranoia, versus finding ways to be at peace with human-kind overall, much less one's parents or the guy next door who doesn't like Scientology. Hubbard's writings drive home the point that our enemies are everywhere, and since the majority of people were against Scientology, we had to do whatever it takes to pre-serve it. In essence, working to save humankind was actually a mis-erable process, but we had to show that we loved it.

I'd often re-read SOS's Book One Chapter 27, "Method Used by Subject to Handle Others," Book Two Chapter 18 "Level of Mind Alert" and any sections where Hubbard discusses the role of the artist in society, and how artists are treated by others. In these sections you can find some of the best and the worst characteristics about being human, from Hubbard's perspective. I did quite an in-depth exploration of SOS for this manuscript, covering Hubbard's view of human extermination, the emotional tones, particularly the lower tones where he categorizes the homosexual, the critic, and the fascist. If you'd like to know more, please visit the book web-site for interesting details.

**Moral exclusion**

Prior to the Internet, it was hard for general public to learn how Scientology practices moral exclusion. Hubbard's writings have always lead Scientologists to believe that it is a dominant group in society, whose norms were superior to everyone else's. SOS and many policies contain statements and even orders to belit-tle, marginalize, exclude and even dehumanize certain types of non-Scientology or ex-Scientology people. In SOS, the grouping of gays, lesbians and critics with extremists such as fascists and com-munists, all called degraded low-toned people, doesn't stop at just being dehumanizing hate speech. It illuminates Scientology's asser-tion of its own superiority over people they consider to be expend-able, undeserving non-entities. He positions these people outside a moral boundary as if without rights, like history reflects in the Nazi party, for example, that treated Jews without rights, and eliminated them to create a more pure society for Germany.

International Management is the dominant group of the Scientology world that sets the tone and policies for attacking critics. Scientologists are trained to believe that the norms of the Scientology world are superior to all others. This develops the sense of entitlement Scientologists feel to belittle, marginalize, exclude, and even dehumanize targeted groups such as ex-Scientologists, ex-Sea Org members, and media critical of Scientology, that justifies their vigilante justice.

As more and more ex-members testify about Scientology's moral exclusion and hate tactics exerted toward them, only then will the facts be visible in the public arena, and in the justice system. To say that all signs point to Scientology as being subversive to freedom and democracy in America is an understatement. It is confounding that our government grants this organization the rights to carry on as they do, under the cloak of religious protection with tax-exempt status. Other governments, such as France, Germany, Russia, Belgium and on, wisely deny Scientology's "religious" status and call it a for-profit business.

## God, gods & beliefs

Scientology's war is played out on the battlefields of the mind, ironically supported by Hubbard's statements that only Scientology can create a world without insanity, criminality, and war. Wars are with enemies, but wars also lie within each Scientologist who must win the battle over the reactive mind, fighting whole track evil purposes, and overcoming all odds to attain a divine nature. It's all about self-awareness, self-knowledge, self-control. Scientologists are constantly looking at the present self and past-life selves, recalling incidents along millions of years of lives. Isolating and erasing or "as-ising" engrams, false purposes and other troubles in the mind and spirit is supposed to set people free from all disabilities that keep a person from being his/her true self. Like the mythical Greek youth, Narcissus, who loved to gaze into a pool to admire his reflection, the myth says he can't stop looking at himself. For a Scientologist, this obsession of looking at self is no myth. It's a routine.

A new member might not at first perceive the war-like nature of Scientology, much less its system of gods and god makers, until one advances up the bridge. One's craving to be fully OT—an omnipotent, omniscient operating thetan—becomes an obsession for these god-like abilities. We progressively move up the path of spiritual awareness as an OT, acquiring greater self-control with increased self-knowledge. This obsession for OT abilities pinnacles at the most advanced level, OT VIII "Truth Revealed," where one comprehends one's true nature, basically as a supreme being. This level compels the Scientologist to forsake any remaining belief in any messiah or ultimate being such as Jesus Christ, Allah, Buddha, and the like, finally coming to realize who is god through personal cognition. This also negates the possibility of being a Scientologist and a member of another religion at the same time.

Scientology sales people push members to believe that "going free" is so vital to do right now, before Earth is blown up and it's too late, that handling one's case is paramount over anything. This is a mental health approach to self-help, not religious. Scientology is essentially in the business of selling self-help services and materials to self-venerating individuals. I'm not suggesting that all artists and celebrities are narcissists, but with such obsession on self-development at all costs to become the ultimate actor, musician, writer, designer and the like, it's no wonder why creatives are attracted to Scientology, like Peter and I were.

I once heard Nancy Cartwright, a Scientology celebrity (the voice of Bart Simpson) say in a media broadcast how Scientology helps people to become gods. This is a common belief among Scientologists. I never believed that I could become a god, but I was interested in learning about our divine nature. In conversations, friends would talk about wins they had on course or in session, and say things like "I know I created the universe, so I better learn to live within it," or, "I created time, it's just a consideration, time is not real," and "Why do I worry about MEST? It's just an illusion that I created." (MEST is matter, energy, space, time). My friends and I respected each other's awareness level, which measured and reflected our beliefs and indoctrination level depending on where we were at on the bridge.

I disliked Scientology's use of words and concepts from major world religions to create the impression that similar ideas could be found in Scientology, while knowing they are not. For example, salvation and faith, two words that represent significant beliefs of Christianity, Judaism, and Islam are not found in Hubbard's materials. Yet *Scientology - Theology & Practice of a Contemporary Religion*, explains that "salvation" is attained through increasing one's spiritual awareness (p. 21). The use of a recognizable word from a religion's context is misleading, since a Scientologist seeks spiritual freedom and immortality, not salvation. This text says that faith is not part of Scientology: "In Scientology, no one is asked to accept anything on faith." I can attest to the fact that knowledge in Scientology is true for Scientologists if they actually test it and observe it to be true. Observing and testing is the opposite of faith, or belief and hope in the unseen. This book also says that Scientology "makes no effort to describe the exact nature or character of God…each person is expected to reach his own conclusions about all eight dynamics including the Supreme Being" (p. 26). A Scientologist is expected to expand his awareness across all eight dynamics of his/her life, and will ultimately arrive at the eighth dynamic, the Supreme Being (p. 25).

Dedicated Scientologists lock into the belief that Scientology holds the keys to their immortality. This conviction is a top reason why people stay in Scientology for so long, even when they have doubts about it. Members don't want to risk losing a chance for their keys to eternity. This is evidence of complete dependency on the Scientology organization, the opposite of the total spiritual freedom that they seek through Scientology.

Scientology deifies the self as an object of worship, compared to major world religions that deify their God. A Christian believes that Jesus Christ is the one and only way to everlasting life. A Jew believe in God revealed through the Torah. A Muslim beliefs in Allah revealed through the Koran, and an extremist Muslim would become a Jihadist to please Allah. A Scientologist works to understand the Supreme Being in one's Eighth dynamic. Scientologists typically spend two or more hours per day taking a Scientology course or receiving auditing, controlling one's focus on self-enhancement to develop self-knowledge, self-power, self-control. In practice, Scientologists worship and even deify themselves. (And for this, the organization gets to claim tax-exempt status as a religion?)

I mentioned Hubbard naming himself as the reincarnated Buddha in his *Hymn of Asia*, but I also saw various other mentions of God throughout Hubbard's writings. The meanings vary depending upon which text you read. Starting with *Dianetics,* Hubbard describes the importance of believing in a supreme being, but he doesn't define that being. Also, Dianetics is not a religious book, as stated in its title, *The Modern Science of Mental Health*. Again, it's self-help, mental health, not religious. And in various Scientology books, Hubbard deconstructs or does away with God and faith, or gods as being anyone other than oneself. His theme throughout all writings address self-development of godlike abilities by becoming an Operating Thetan (OT) and reaching the highest spiritual levels of Scientology, where a thetan can demonstrate control over all of life, thought, matter, energy, space and time—a role held by God in all major world religions.

## Apocalyptic thinking causes co-dependency

Getting absorbed into the Scientology world was like partici-pating in a reality show, where the participants gradually become aware of being within a labyrinth, and no one can find the way out of the "trap" of life on Earth without first learning the Scientology tech and following the closely taped path ("Safeguarding Technol-ogy," *OEC Vol. 0*, p. 186). This idea of living in a labyrinth began my sensation of feeling perpetually trapped, lost or confused. I never felt that way about my life before I got into Scientology. That's how Scientology uses coercion to create this co-dependent mindset: Before Scientology, I was enjoying life and wanted to do better, but I never considered myself trapped in a labyrinth; but now that I felt trapped in one, Scientology could help me get out of it but I had to struggle to survive.

Had I understood anything about being "co-dependent" in the beginning, I could have prevented myself a lot of wasted years, es-pecially if I had read Robert J. Lifton's 1987, "Eight Criteria of Mind Control" or Steven Hassan's book *Combating Cult Mind Con-trol* about how dependency develops within a cultic group that uses undue influence (p. 107-136). It's a type of addiction to a dysfunc-tional relationship that is emotionally destructive, abusive or one-sided.

Scientology's ongoing coercion to make rapid progress up the bridge increased this co-dependency between us and the organiza-tion. We repeatedly heard Hubbard's apocalyptic party line from the registrars who'd hard-sell us auditing, training and books: It is vital to move up the bridge NOW and go free while there is still a chance—this chance is the slim thread, this brief moment in time since Scientology arrived on earth, offering the only hope for hu-mankind before nuclear bombs destroy the planet.

When I learned about artists being prone to attacks from SPs, I thought, okay, here is a solution to fortify myself while I work in creative fields. Scientology offered solutions for artists to deal with negative influences I hadn't found anywhere else. But we were surrounded with these "dangerous world" concepts. War becomes everything, and everything becomes war. Without the impending attacks and eventual destruction of all life on Earth through nuclear war, there would be no sense of urgency to buy Scientology services and move quickly up the bridge to be safe as a spiritual being. As if the newcomers didn't know that there were lots of bad guys out there, this information seems to be revelatory, until I later realized the strategy.

The controlling actions of Scientology leaders affectively got me to relinquish control of my life to Scientology's control. This went so far as being in denial about problems between Scientology and me when I let Scientology's priorities—especially the third (group) and fourth (humankind) dynamics—dominate my feelings and personal priorities. I only felt worthwhile or valuable when helping others, while taking personal responsibility for anything that went wrong when I could have "done something about it."

Their scare tactics, as if the world was going to end tomorrow or next week, have been used in Dianetics and Scientology since the 1950s and will never change; they cannot change, because L. Ron Hubbard policy is written in stone and tells people to think, do and say this.

Peter and I relied so heavily on Scientology meeting our needs that we started becoming dysfunctional in other aspects of our life, such as family relationships fading away, not having friends outside of Scientologists, neglect of career responsibilities in place of dedicating ourselves to the "higher purpose" of saving the planet, and later, abandoning our entire career. I observed this in the lives of many of my friends, who simply could not function without being at the org in good standing so they would be allowed to practice Scientology, even if it meant doing it at great expense versus disconnecting from friends or relatives who disagreed with Scientology.

A Scientologist constantly seeks approval and acceptance from the Scientology system by trying so hard to be an on-source Scientologist who doesn't get into ethics trouble. I joined Scientology around the birth of the International Association of Scientologists

(IAS) when everyone was made to buy a one-year ($250) or lifetime membership ($2000). As a Sea Org member, I was given a "free" lifetime membership. IAS membership fulfills a Scientologist's self worth of being on-Source, and confirms their status of being in "good standing." The IAS grew into a monster within which David Miscavige set up a variety of donation levels that designated one's "status." This crush-regging practice has driven many people out of Scientology, but has also resulted in others donating millions and billions of dollars to fill the church coffers.

If my critical thinking had been in gear, I would have used logical reasoning of factual evidence to form an objective judgment about Scientology, my role in it, and how it affected my life. Instead, I moved forward on emotional impulses and short-term desires, allowing myself a vulnerability to Scientology's coercion and subversive tactics. Scientologists are taught the opposite of critical thinking skills within Scientology materials; to a Scientologist, "critical" only means faultfinding or negative thoughts and comments, especially toward Scientology. Ironically, we were lured by Hubbard's statement, "What is true for you is what you have observed, and if you have lost that you have lost everything;" when what really took place was Scientology telling us what we observed and how we should think about it—and if we didn't accept this, we were either made to feel stupid from "misunderstood words" or we were booted out of Scientology for questioning or criticizing Hubbard's works.

## The celebrity implant

Around 1990 at the International management base, Miscavige's assistant Greg Wilhere showed me a confidential LRH Advice that flabbergasted me. The advice, which is a statement from Hubbard that has not yet been converted into official church policy, was classified as for Int base staff only. The advice explains an underlying strategy for management to implement: People in the arts who are already celebrities or who are aspiring to become celebrities possess an "implant" of self-importance, of the need for fame. This implant drives their need to become well-known.

Why is this significant? Celebrity Centres are set up to exploit this to the fullest extent in recruitment efforts, knowing that artists come into Scientology to fulfill deep personal needs, to become famous. I found it fascinating to realize that the auditors at Celebrity Centres are not told this.

Yet the job of the auditor is to help their pre-clears locate and eliminate any and all implants. So if auditors aren't told these implants exist, then the don't know they are supposed to get rid of them.

The point being, if you leave the implant there, then the individual will keep trying to become famous, thus keeping them tethered to the Celebrity Centre. Of course, this means the individual will continue spending money at the CC for more and more auditing and training to help them become successful.

## Death struggle over money

Following the carefully taped path to immortality takes hundreds of thousands of dollars, and for many, goes into the millions. Every class, every hour of auditing, every book or tape is paid for at a fixed price. There are no voluntary optional donation amounts accepted for services; you pay the fixed price or you do not receive the service or product. Attaining "spiritual freedom" comes at a high price in Scientology.

Scientology's god is the almighty buck, measured by their most revered statistics: Gross Income, and the overall net worth or value of investments. The pulse of its top leadership to its street-level organizations such as the Celebrity Centre is money in. All roads point to GI, whether it's the sale of courses and auditing, books and e-meters sold, donations for buildings and IAS programs, celebrities recruited, and on. And that's the small stuff compared to their investments of real estate, oil, gold and the like.

GI is the reason the front lines organizations live and breathe and what people slave over and even die for. Remember L. Ron Hubbard's "Reason for Orgs" policy letter that I quoted: "The only reason orgs exist is to *sell* and deliver materials and service to the public, and to get in public to *sell* and deliver to. The object is totally freed customers beings."

Discovery of this almighty-buck god is ultimately a crude revelation in Scientology. I know ex-Scientologists who reached Scientology's ultimate level of OT VIII and said, *This is it? This is the ultimate mindset for which I paid how many hundreds of thousands of dollars? And gave so much more to the IAS to prove my dedication to Scientology's goal to secure this priceless technology to secure the future of humankind? For this?*

After OT VIII, and even earlier, many of these people promptly left Scientology, and some even had to escape just to get off the Freewinds.

Peter and I didn't see the big picture in the beginning. We felt the pressure of being asked for money to pay for Scientology but we chalked it up to Scientology's adage: "Able beings such as you can make it go right to pay for Scientology. The more you do it, the more able you become, and the more able you are, the more income you will earn." And our FSM who selected us into Scientology told us the same thing, while he was making 10% to 15% on everything we paid for.

In my view, L. Ron Hubbard was locked in a death struggle over money, and died before the IRS held him fully accountable for his avoidance of paying multi-millions in taxes owed by his Scientology endeavors before obtaining tax-exempt status, that he sheltered or moved around using various ploys into investments from gold to oil to real estate. His minions have followed suit, and his policies teach Scientologists how to live this way.

All that being said, it would feel incomplete to avoid a discussion of Scientology ethics tech: the molten lava of the Scientology world that heatedly shapes the ideas and behavior of every Scientologist—ethics, suppression, potential trouble sources, justice, disconnection, and fair game.

# 12

## SCIENTOLOGY'S ETHICS & JUSTICE TECHNOLOGY

"If you read that book...ultimately if it's good for Scientology and L. Ron Hubbard it's good. If it's bad for Scientology, it's evil. Period."

- Mark "Marty" Rathbun,
Dec. 22, 2014, San Antonio, TX
Deposition with Scientology attorney
Bert Deixler, accessed on tonyortega.org

THE ABOVE QUOTE FROM MARK Rathbun, former Scientology critic after leaving his role of Inspector General RTC, captures the bias of Scientology ethics. Rathbun is not an opinion leader for me; on the contrary, he lost credibility once he became the apotheosis of a turncoat for arcane reasons. But his statement made during that legal deposition captures Hubbard's mindset about ethics and justice, in the *Scientology Ethics* book.

A person like me who had been raised on the golden rule, trying to navigate life with a moral compass at least somewhat wisely to keep out of trouble, had to turn my thinking inside out when it came to making decisions based on "the greatest good." In Scientology, the greatest good only takes into consideration Scientology's greatest good. I learned the hard way that what I thought was right or wrong, good or evil, was going to be re-interpreted by Scientology policies—and that's where the danger lies. Until you know *all* the tech and policies, you really don't know when you are doing something right or wrong in the eyes of Scientology, because the ways of Scientology don't often coincide with the ways of the outside world that you came from. I believe that a religion (which in the U.S. currently includes the Scientology organization) should not be given license to practice moral exclusion, or to conduct themselves outside of or above the law under the banner of religious freedom. Yet this is modus operandi in Scientology.

Scientology also latches on to "technicism"—the belief that Scientologists will be able to control the entirety of their existence, master all problems, using his and only his technology. His auditing and training "technology" makes these promises, as does his "ethics technology." This is the notion that a scientific approach to personal ethical behavior can solve any and all human problems. Hubbard reframes questions of truth, power and control and redefines authority. He appears to offer Scientology as a path for people to take control of their present life and all future lifetimes, while actually tricking Scientologists to not see that Scientology takes control over one's life. Then he craftily plays on science to give Scientology credibility by having these "technologies," adding up to the prison of belief that ethics and Scientology technologies can solve everything.

The *Introduction to Scientology Ethics* book describes 270 pages of the philosophy of ethics and behavioral actions considered to be small transgressions, high crimes, and everything in between. The ethics conditions assess what state you are in, based on your adherence to Scientology policy or your production of statistics, with formulas for how to improve each condition. You also get a glimpse into what should be done to bring an "ethics particle" or offender to justice within Scientology's system. Although the *Ethics* book purports to help Scientologists restore and increase personal survival and freedom, the book is packed with irony. If you want to capture a profile of the organization, read this book. Scientology reveals itself as an extremist organization that grants no freedom of thought or behavior to Scientologists in its legalistic system, and grants even worse to critics or its perceived enemies. So I constantly grappled with many of Hubbard's ethics policies within it. Although the purpose of Ethics is "to get tech in," sometimes it's used more like a battering ram against individuals who deviate from leadership's dictates, or as a tool of control over a Scientologist's life.

While "ethics technology" is a control tool for Scientology, it has also become a scapegoat for why Scientologists do not experience "wins" during Scientology auditing and training. For example, Dianetics promises to solve physical problems of the human condition such as preventing accidents, getting colds or needing glasses. But Hubbard must have learned that people would start complaining about not maintaining perfect health after going "Clear," so he had to find a reason for why Dianetics didn't work. He targeted the matter of ethics. If a Scientologist's ethics are "out"—meaning, the person is involved in any kind of transgression—that Scientology tech won't "go in", meaning, Dianetics and Scientology won't work in the presence.

For more information about disconnection, suppressive persons, potential trouble sources, Scientology's version of ethics and justice, and an explanation of how ethics technology is used as a control tool, and is as much a part of Scientologists' life as the air they breathe, please visit the book website.

# 13

## RITES OF PASSAGE

"If you have built a prison for yourself little by little, brick by brick, and you are living in it, you don't know that you're in prison."

- Ron Miscavige,
*Ruthless: Scientology, My Son David Miscavige, and Me* (2016)

IN THE OUTSIDE WORLD, people celebrate marriage, births, graduations and anniversaries; Christians observe baptism; Catholics observe confirmations; Judaism observes Bar and Bat Mitzvah's. In Scientology, there are pivotal training steps, job postings, and defining moments that mark one's passage from one place in the Scientology world to another. I moved from being a general public customer to joining the Celebrity Centre, then joined Scientology's eternal Sea Organization, then completed advanced executive training, took various jobs within Celebrity Centre and moved into positions of higher responsibility. Each transition added another brick to the foundation I was building for myself as a Scientologist. I've included a few significant ones here, and have posted much more on the book website.

### Joining the Sea Org/Pacific Area Command, 1986-87

"Many are called, and few are chosen." At first glance, this phrase on a Sea Org recruitment poster struck me as a slogan for the U.S. Navy, since the man and woman in the picture wore Naval-type uniforms. Their white military caps with black visors hold a gold laurel wreath and star against the peak, instead of military insignia. With a look of fierce dedication in their eyes, their white-gloved hands gripped glistening silver swords against a galaxy of stars. Rather sci-fi, maybe, but it exudes an alluring message that reached me as a Scientologist who wanted to help change the world.

If I joined the Sea Org I only wanted to work at Celebrity Centre. And understanding CC requires understanding the Sea Org, since they are inseparable. The Sea Org is a fraternal, eternal organization of the most fanatically dedicated of all Scientologists, and lifetime members of the International Association of Scientologists (IAS). As an entity, the Sea Org (SO) is sovereign to all Scientologists through an authoritarian system that shapes, controls or influences the lives of Scientologists, including its top celebrities.

Since Scientology is in a co-dependent relationship with its celebrities, I wondered who held more influence, celebrities or the Sea Org? Scientology couldn't thrive without its celebrity members, who could more easily afford the high-dollar price tag for spiritual enlightenment than garden-variety followers; the celebrities relied on Sea Org leaders to keep the doors of Scientology open so celebs could earn the keys to their immortality.

## Sea Org Executive Training

The rite of passage to becoming an executive was through the Organization Executive Course ( OEC), and the Flag Executive Briefing Course (FEBC). An OEC executive was equivalent to a highly trained, Class VIII auditor.

Shortly after arriving at ITO, the Scientology world received news about its new leadership. An expensive looking, white glossy broadsheet boasting the RTC logo, introduced the most senior executives of Scientology command: David Miscavige as the Chairman of the Board Religious Technology Center; Captain Greg Wilhere, Inspector General RTC (IG) and his team of three deputies (D/IG): Captain Marty Rathbun, D/IG for Ethics; Captain Ray Mithoff, D/IG for Technology, and Captain Marc Yager, D/IG for Administration. With facial expressions that conveyed the meaning of the RTC logo—hard as cold chrome steel—this was the power team that would expand the Scientology world following the passing of Commodore L. Ron Hubbard.

Not long after that news, Yager and an entourage of mission-aires came storming into the ITO on a special project. Students were told to step aside as D/IG for Admin marched through the hallways with his team dressed in Class A uniform, caps and all. Their mission: to round up every copy of Hubbard's policy, "The Reason for Orgs." All copies were to be destroyed, whether printed in the church's green administrative policy volumes, or existing in individual copies in folders. These were also being rounded up eve-rywhere on the planet to obliterate the "wrong word" in them.

Hubbard's original policy sums up Scientology's goal for or-ganizations. In "The Reason for Orgs" he wrote, "The only rea-sons orgs exist is to sell and deliver materials and services to the public, and to get in public to sell and deliver to. The object is to-tally freed **customers**." I knew that policy by heart, as did most SO members and ITO students, because we had to Chinese School it over and over again at musters and meetings.

Now we were being told that "customers" was the wrong word and had to be changed to "beings." I questioned how this wrong word could have landed in Hubbard's volumes, when everything was 100% LRH Source, carefully proofread and approved by the Authority & Verification Unit in the Religious Technology Center, responsible for the copyrights and trademarks of Scientology. Surely they would have caught such a grievous error before print-ing the policies in the OEC Volumes.

The shore story for this "error" was that there were suppres-sive staff that had been handling the publication of Hubbard's sa-cred texts. They had made various alterations to Hubbard's poli-cies, so a project was being done to weed out these deviations from Hubbard's original intentions. That explanation sounded plausible since humans do make mistakes, but it didn't say much for RTC AVC's credibility.

The "customer-being" switcharoo had far-reaching public rela-tions effects for the church. By changing "customers" to "beings," Scientology's "Reason for Orgs" shifts from its true business orien-tation to a focus on the spiritual, a subliminal connection with "church" and "religion." If the IRS knew that Scientology partici-pants were called customers, that evidence would reveal the organi-zation as a business, complete with set prices paid for services and materials that are not donations. Scientology organizations determine the fixed, non-negotiable mandatory prices paid for services and materials. No pay, no product.

ITO specialized in administrative indoctrination. The course rooms were run with no teachers, only supervisors. Each student used a check sheet and moved at his/her own pace reading the policies and listening to the taped lectures. To add variety, ITO regularly used inculcation, called "Chinese school." This is the act of impressing something upon the mind by repetition. A leader stands at the front of the class with a pointer, shouts out words from the text, and then loudly asks, What is it? We'd repeat back what she said in loud and lively voices in unison. Then we'd shout out the whole policy in one round from beginning to end. In the case of Chinese schooling the revised "The Reason for Orgs," I would stumble over that word "being" because "customer" had already been instilled in my head. It took many weeks of Chinese schooling that policy for me to dis-embed its original meaning.

While reading every policy in all seven volumes of Hubbard's OEC volumes and Management Series I, II and III, I soaked up the intended mindset for Scientology executives. I would be held responsible for applying these materials exactly. There is no other way to do anything within a Scientology organization than to know what Hubbard said to do, and do it that way without questioning it. Any other way is suppressive, "off source" or "squirrel."

The Captain of CC surprised me with his order to return to CC for an executive posting. My training plan was cut short by a few months, so I didn't finish the FEBC. I returned to Celebrity Centre to become the Celebrity Public Executive Secretary (PES).

Radicalization of Sea Org members and other Scientologists is so significant in Scientology operations that it deserves a full book. Jon Atack's book, Opening Minds (2016) touches on radicalization, and describes it as the "systematic use of thought reform to divide people from other people who they come to believe should be destroyed or hated." Radicalized people come to believe they are superior to anyone outside their group, and believe they are justified to commit atrocities against their enemies. My original twenty pages on radicalization is on the book website, if you'd like to know more about it.

# 14

## COMMANDING THE CELEBRITY CENTRE NETWORK

### Hollywood Celebrity Centre, circa 1987

WHILE I WAS SO HAPPY TO BE BACK on the front lines at Celebrity Centre, being an executive was new territory for me. Now I was required to apply LRH policy, instead of working voluntarily at my own pace. This post (job) put me in charge of four public divisions that recruited new people into Celebrity Centre, got them trained in the basics, kept them in Scientology, and turned them into recruiters/FSMs.

Several seasoned Sea Org members who had worked at CC for years under Yvonne worked in my divisions: Sarah Gualtieri headed up Public Servicing, in charge of selling and delivering intro services, while Sally Esterman scheduled students for basic training and Book One Dianetics auditing. Pamela Lancaster Johnson, former CC President, was now the Div 6 Celebrity Sec, and Pat Gualtieri headed up Axiom Productions to produce CC events. Greg Labaqui and our team also sold books and supervised CC's recruitment machine of Field Staff Members (FSMs).

### On the hunt for raw meat

Our recruiters/Field Staff Members were always on the hunt for "raw meat." Hubbard coined this jocular term in one of his Saint Hill Special Briefing Course lectures (43-6410C20) to describe the general consumer who has never had Scientology auditing yet (HCOB 16 Jan 68) and who doesn't know s/he's a spiritual being and is just a body, hence the raw meat body idea.

Raw meat bodies were the greatest source for potential recruitment commissions, because a recruiter earns a percentage of everything their selectee buys while they are in Scientology, and they actively keep their selectee moving up the bridge. Recruiters are trained on the dissemination drill to "contact, handle, salvage, and bring to understanding" these raw meat people. We used a variety of tactics to hunt for raw meat celebrities and general public, and also to recover people who had fallen off the lines.

Greg Labaqui worked with the recruiters/FSMs to bring in new people and to sell them books that pumped up his key statistic, "new names to Central Files) (NNCF). This statistic measured the number of new people who have ever bought a book or first service from Scientology—hence, the number often quoted, how many people are in Scientology? This number has measured into the ten millions globally, because of the NNCF number accumulated by all orgs around the world. That doesn't mean those people became or remained Scientologists.

Recruiters/FSMs were our lifeblood that flowed new people into CC. The recruiters earned commissions of 10 or 15 percent of the courses, auditing, and materials their selectees bought. My team ensured that any new people who started an intro course or intro auditing were very well taken care of. The goal was to keep them in Scientology by bridging them over from the appetizing intro services to Scientology's full buffet, the steps to "go Clear" and then the advanced levels.

### Artists for a New Civilization

As a celebrity recruiter/FSM smitten with the CC purpose since 1983, I had envisioned a renaissance at Celebrity Centre before I ever joined the Sea Org. I spearheaded the formation of fifteen different artist associations for the revitalization of the arts

114

among our members, representing visual arts, musicians and composers, actors, cinematographers, writers, dancers, vocalists, film and theatre arts, as well as sports professionals and politics. Now we would develop these as a program within our Division 6 to boom our CC.

In 1987, we held the first annual "Artists for a New Civilization" party at Celebrity Centre, produced by Pat's Axiom Productions. The event exalted Hubbard for his philosophy that elevated the importance of the arts. Over 300 attendees enjoyed performances by CC artists and musicians including Amanda Ambrose, Peter Schless, John Novello and more. Each guest affirmed his or her commitment to abide by the Code of a Scientologist by signing their name on a scroll bearing that code. I still have the copy of the *Celebrity* magazine that covered these Artist Associations and this gala event, which began the tradition of the annual CC Gala.

That event night, we received some unexpected guests. Senior executives from the Int base streamed in, including Chairman of the Board David Miscavige, Commanding Officer of the Commodore's Messenger Org International, Captain Marc Yager, Senior Case Supervisor International Ray Mithoff, and the Executive Director International, Guillaume Lesevre. I recall several $90 bottles of wine coming into our Renaissance dining room, not items on my budget. They settled into niche of the dining room with their wine amidst the celebrity guests, seemingly enjoying the company.

Evidently, senior execs were not used to staff at my level showing initiative to create a large event such as this without first requiring orders to do so. Mithoff and Lesevre complemented my efforts for such a successful and inspiring event. Yager and Miscavige observed me but said nothing. The latter struck me as arrogant, out of place for the celebratory spirit of the night. The event revitalized the guests in their purpose as artist Scientologists, and increased some of our key statistics, such as: CBIS, "celebrities bodies in the shop." CBIS led to an increase in our pivotal statistic, Gross Income (GI). The higher our CBIS, the more money we made. The higher our CNNCF, "celebrity new names to central files," the higher our potential for expansion and more sales. Sea Org members were all about numbers. We were only as good as our last week's statistics.

I was always looking for another Sea Org recruit, so I visited other Celebrity Centres to see what prospects I could find. Executive Directors of several outer CCs joined the Sea Org through my efforts, including Lorie Segal from CC New York, and Julia Ellis from CC Las Vegas. In the San Francisco area, I recruited Karen Hollander for the Sea Org. She arrived many months later to be President of CC Int. I also went to CC Paris, where I recruited several people and got them arrived to Los Angeles within a few weeks.

I had proven that I could help expand Celebrity Centre, and received a promotion.

## Commanding Officer, Celebrity Centre Network

As the Commanding Officer of the Celebrity Centre International Network (CO CCNW), I was now responsible for overseeing the recruitment and progress of Scientology's celebrities in Hollywood, New York, Nashville, Las Vegas, Dallas, Chicago, Paris, London, Vienna—about 13 major cities total.

Celebrities are unaware of being targeted, much less viewed as the commodities we deemed them, for their value to the Scientology cause, depending on their social capital. The public were told that if Celebrity Centre could turn enough opinion leaders into dedicated Scientologists, the battles of bringing down Enemy #1, psychiatry, and making this a Scientology world could be won. The underlying strategy was to recruit Earth's wealthiest people who could keep the church's coffers filled.

The hottest seats in the Sea Org were handling celebrities, working directly for David Miscavige, being in OSA handling SPs and legal battles, and making money for Scientology. Execs across Scientology had their hands in celebrity handlings, from RTC to OSA, ASI, and ABLE. I lived within constant reminders about the value of celebrities, thus I lived and breathed Celebrity Centre's goals under threat of assignment to its prison camp, if I failed. I knew that many CC executives had failed before me. Except for Yvonne Gillham Jentzsch, the original leader of Celebrity Centre who died young, my predecessors had been removed from post, were sent to Scientology's Rehabilitation Project Force, blew, or routed out of the Sea Org.

I had no intentions of failing. My idealistic approach at the Celebrity Centre was one of vision and optimism, believing that the best was yet to come. With less than two years of experience in the Sea Org to see how Scientology really operated, my creative spirit

116

led me to the front lines where the bullets would fly. Compared to the seasoned Sea Org execs that had either worked with Hubbard on the ship or at confidential locations, or headed up other Sea Org operations, I was green.

Behind the perceived glamor of Scientology's Celebrity Centre Network is the down-and-dirty machine responsible for the Scientology celebrity scene. As an executive of a pivotal Scientology organization, I morphed into a more deeply regimented officer of the elite management corps that didn't question the group think of Keeping Scientology Working: "The whole agonized future of this planet, every man, woman and child on it, and your own destiny for the next endless trillions of years depends on what you do here and now with and in Scientology. We'd rather have you dead than incapable." "Incapable" was not in my thinking or behavior, nor could I allow any of my crew to think or feel incapable. I lived and breathed the goal of building a new civilization by expanding Scientology through opinion leaders. Now my daily beat was to oversee Celebrity Centre's internal systems and external global network to ensure that our Celebrity Scientologists became highly capable individuals who would ultimately promote Scientology and serve as mouthpieces to media.

The Los Angeles headquarters of the international CC Network designated our org's name as "CC INT", also the only Sea Org Celebrity Centre. My leadership team consisted of Franz Albisser, an enthusiastic Swiss Scientology executive who served as the internal Executive Director/Captain; Celebrity Public Secretary (and former CC President) Pamela Lancaster Johnson who now handled up-and-coming artist types, and President Sue Young McClay, who oversaw the care and recruitment of the A-list celebrities.

No one had to remind me that celebrities were the lifeblood for Scientology's expansion so I had better produce more this week than last week, or I would be "downstat" impeding the expansion of Scientology. The statistics of my post were now the combined work of all the CCs that reflected either an increase or a decrease of celebrity progress in Scientology. Every morning, I could only hope that everyone had shown up for their posts throughout the CC Network, and made all the right moves like pieces on an automated chess board, and that there would be no serious flaps on celebrity lines. I received orders from management making it perfectly clear that they expected me to do the hammer-and-pound beat, demanding products from my juniors, and handling their ethics so as to drive up the statistics. Immovable routines dictated daily and weekly strategic actions to make a significant dent in our star-high goals. I lived and died over the stats of my orgs. I was only as good as my last week's statistics.

Our outer Celebrity Centres, such as CC Paris, CC New York, CC Las Vegas and the rest had their own non-Sea Org executives. An Executive Director (ED) ran the internal workings of the organization so it makes money, while its President takes care of celebrity matters. Celebrity handlers spent time talking with celebs about how to apply Scientology to become more successful in their careers. The President would monitor each celebrity's progress up the bridge, and when she was sure that the celeb was a stable Scientologist, she'd start asking them who they knew that they could bring into CC for an orientation. This is how celebrity recruitment is nurtured.

Turning celebrity Scientologists into walking mouthpieces for Scientology was no walk in the park. The apparent glamour of my own post, as well as the purpose of Celebrity Centre, belies the working conditions of the staff behind the scenes. My daily to-do list or battle plan for my seven-day work week held names of celebrities that had to be recruited, or counseled and trained, *or else.* As I began a new week every Thursday after 2:00 p.m., I took a deep breath as I confronted the "or else" that could happen if I didn't do better in the new week. Operating under threats of punishment, such as prison camp assignment, in no way fired up my motivation; it had the opposite effect of stealing the wind from my sails and reducing my personal initiative that I otherwise would have taken on this position.

The "or else" came from the place that mattered most in the Scientology hierarchy: The Int Management base, or Gold, the senior control center from which Miscavige, Yager, Mithoff, Lesevre, and other exec including the Watchdog Committee member for the Celebrity Centre network reigned. They expected our team of about fifty Sea Org members to work like a well-oiled machine to contact and recruit opinion leaders and transform them into walking mouthpieces for Scientology's glory.

A Sea Org executive like me is expected to be a ruthless, pitiless product officer who lived and breathed statistics, particularly

Gross Income (GI) and key celebrity stats such as CDIV6MAJ, which measured the number of new celebrities who complete Division 6 introductory services and move into the big-time major services, such as training and auditing. This reflects the number of celebrities who actually become serious Scientologists and are willing to pay the price to do it.

Every hammer-and-pound day, the GI product conference convened with key staff bringing a prepared list of celebrities named to take their next course or auditing service. The emphasis of the conference was "GI cycles" that would be closed by the registrars, the staff that sold auditing, training, and materials. Each customer (a celebrity, a general paying public) was referred to as a "cycle." We'd strategize the cycles down to minutiae detail how we were going to get specific celebrities into the org and onto services. Staff worked out plans to "tag-team."

For example, after the Director of Training oversaw a celebrity completing a course, someone else would be lined up in the hallway to route that person to the registrar. The Reg hard sells them into buying an auditing package. Auditing packages started at $2,000 for a 12 1/2 hour intensive block of auditing, but specific steps on the bridge might require several intensives. They'd go for bigger chunks like $20,000 to $50,000 or more. Regges would first drill and practice their plan to ensure they brought in the GI, as these were staff who had been trained in Big League Sales—sales training written by Les Dane, a car salesman, that Hubbard used as a model to train our sales people. Electronic listening devices were also installed in sales rooms so an executive could listen to the registrar during the sales cycle, and coach them. They'd practice with another person how to handle the celebrity's objections, how to solve specific problems to ensure there would be no flaws and they would "get the cycle." They would pull out all stops when it came to resources for credit cards, loans, and notes.

**Personal life**

Peter and I had already been living in our seventh-floor suite in the Manor that we paid for, before I joined the Sea Org and got promoted. We stayed there, a highly unusual arrangement, since SO members were required to live in communal berthing. CC crew lived in the Wilcox, an old, dilapidated building in a seedy area of Hollywood, in desperate need of upgrades, repairs, and extermination of mice, rats and roaches. Senior executives were usually given a better room than general crew, more familiar with squalor. Communal living was meant to build cohesiveness among Sea Org members, but I managed to escape that since I was married to a non-Sea Org, high-profile Scientologist. I danced through my Celebrity Centre years with one foot in and one foot out of Sea Org traditions, but that didn't lessen other rigors of Sea Org life for me.

Usually on short sleep every day, there was no time for glamour in the mornings. I'd clip my long dark brown hair behind my neck, add minimal makeup, and put on my Sea Org Officer appearance that never changed: navy blue skirt with white pseudo-military style shirt, black cross tie, and black pumps. Then I would hit the stairs. I had already learned all the less-traveled passageways throughout the castle, taking the back stairs when I'd make my daily trek from the residential seventh floor to the offices on the second. I avoided the elevator so I could steal another few minutes of time descending the stairwells alone.

On the second floor across from the Captain's office, I'd slip into the office suite marked Commanding Officer. My new post came with a brevet rank of Lieutenant, giving me the symbolic authority I needed to get my job done. I wore two gold officer stripes on black shoulder boards attached to the epaulettes of my white Sea Org uniform shirt. I both loved and resented that insignia. It spoke instant authority among my Sea Org staff, but when I'd run into artist friends of mine who hadn't joined the Sea Org, I was reminded of the extreme step I took relinquishing my freedom as an independent artist.

## The bloody hatchet, Thursday at 2, and other gems

Scientology work weeks don't end on Fridays at 5:00 p.m. like most businesses, but instead end on Thursdays at 2:00 p.m. This "Thursday at 2" is a weekly event across the Scientology world. Every Registrar was on the phones or in the halls contacting public to pull in more Gross Income to drive the stats up before 2pm. Thursday at 2 also triggers a routine of statistical counts and reports, and new weekly battle plans for every staff member and every Scientology organization globally.

Every Thursday night, I carried out a bureaucratic nightmare that ended around 5:00am. From 2pm on, I would receive telexes coming in from the external CC Executive Directors around the globe who proposed their battle plans (strategic weekly to-do lists) for the upcoming weeks. I would do a statistical analysis of each CC's weekly and longer-term production, and then would respond to them by telex with their marching orders that should drive up their statistics.

I always acknowledged the accomplishments and the bright spots of their production before I told them what to do to revert key statistics that management wanted to focus on—but most of what I wrote was deleted by others. I was never allowed to email my Executive Directors directly. Herein lies the bureaucratic nightmare of the weekly stat evolution. I first had to send my proposed telex responses "uplines" to the Watchdog Committee person for the CCNW who, at that time, was Nancy Julienne, whom I had to call Mr. Julienne. I wasn't supposed to know she was a Watchdog Committee head, since that title was supposed to be unknown.

Mr. Nancy Julienne couldn't just reply to my telex directly, either. First, she had to send her response to me to AVC, the Authority and Verification International person in RTC, who had to approve it before it could go out to me. More often than not, WDC CC would entirely rewrite my response to the Executive Directors of the Celebrity Centres, or AVC would even rewrite that.

This practice was groupthink: seniors knew more than the people on the ground or had some other strategy to implement that I wasn't even briefed on, so would routinely override my actions. Feeling more like a pawn on a chessboard than a highly trained executive, this system kept me in a constant state of bypass, and short-circuited my effectiveness. I often wondered why I was even there or why I had bothered to do my executive training at ITO.

I would stay up all night, waiting for approvals from WDC CC and AVC. My feelings about the process took a turn for the worse when I got my first "bloody hatchet" telex on my computer screen. An typed linear image of a bloody hatchet, with blood dripping down the screen, appeared at the top of the telex. Underneath the hatchet were threatening words from some old poem that said something like the hatchet would fall and heads would roll if things didn't change. I wish I had written down the exact words of the threat so I could repeat them here. The closest Hubbard had come to saying anything like that was an ethics tactic of "putting a head on a pike", meaning doing the worst to someone to make an example of them for others. But I was an OEC trained executive, and never in Hubbard's training had I seen such a tactic included in his thousands of pages of policies. How would such a telex be approved through AVC RTC? Maybe it was created there?

Evidently, Int Management had its own rules and tactics. The use of threats and fear was a major one. I wondered what brand of management policy they were employing. My experiences with Nancy Julienne as WDC CC, aside from the bloody hatchet telexes, introduced me to Int Management's own way of doing things. Ironically, they'd always quote LRH policies to me about how to do my job.

That Christmas Eve, when most of our CC customers were at home for the holiday with their families, I decided to award the CC crew with a few hours off, to go pick up their children from the Cadet Org and go home around 6:30p.m. except for a skeleton crew to run essential operations. No Scientologists had come into the course room that evening. The course rooms typically closed at 9p.m. That evening around 7pm, WDC CC descended upon Celebrity Centre with a surprise visit, only to find it nearly empty of both public and staff. Mr. Nancy Julienne sent a messenger up to my office to bring me to the lobby of the CC, and then proceeded to scream at me for being reasonable with my crew and purposely crashing the stats.

Mr. Nancy Julienne ordered all the crew back into the org to call our public to come in and get into the course rooms. Many staff came back to post with children in tow. Only a few of our public responded to the phone calls to break away from their families and dribbled in. Despite the fact that our key stats were uptrending, she decided it was right to pop in, inspect my organization on a bypass, and find fault with my decision to award my crew with a few hours off for Christmas.

A few days later, Mr. Nancy Julienne and her husband, Pascal Julienne from INCOMM (who had no management authority over me or CC INT) came into my org again. They pulled me into a 3rd floor room at CC, locked the door, turned off the lights, and proceeded to scream at me in the dark. I'm talking SCREAM at full volume. In the dark! They fired questions at me like, What were your intentions? What are you hiding? What are you really doing on your post? Are you really a suppressive person? Why are you in Scientology? And more. I did everything I could to restrain from screaming back at them. I tried to "keep my TRs in," meaning, restrain my emotions and answer in an even-keeled tone that showed I was in control of myself. I was outraged that they freely subjected me to verbal abuse and intimidation, while keeping me in a locked room in the dark, to accomplish what? Intimidate me? Scare the hell out of me? Instill fear of them, of their authority? Fear of management? I knew that there was no right answer to any of these questions, so I answered each one in a calm tone of voice, trying to sound more bored than defensive.

Suddenly, Nancy stopped screaming. She stood up, smoothed her Sea Org skirt, and said, "We just wanted to see if you could take HEAT."

They got up and left the room. Dumbfounded and seriously rattled, I stayed inside and closed the door. I heard them laughing, heard her snorting out in the hall. What kind of sick people were they? This humiliating, traumatic incident did nothing to whip me into shape by instilling fear that would prevent me from noncomplying to WDC CC or management. Instead, it triggered my doubt about being a Sea Org member at all, and gave me another glimpse that senior management was off-source. My earlier intentions had been to succeed, and I didn't require orders or bypass to do my job. But this was a different game, and I didn't sign up for this. My disaffection began to grow.

I tried to separate the miserable elements of my job from the aspects of it that I loved, which were making direct contact with artists and celebrities and helping them in any way I could. Our events and activities began to fill the halls and classrooms with artists again. Some of the staff told me that CC was beginning to feel like it did in Yvonne's day.

## Celebrity Centre's Early Days

I arrived at Celebrity Centre Los Angeles about six years after its beloved founder, Yvonne Gillham Jentzsch, died in 1978. "Yvonne's day" was the term CC staff used when referring to the era after Yvonne established the first booking office and then the first Celebrity Centre on West Eighth Street in Los Angeles in 1969. Staff and Scientologists who knew Yvonne referred to her as the best of what Scientology had to offer. She exuded joy and sincere care about people, with the ability to see the best in others. The atmosphere she created at the CC was known as a safe haven for creativity, where she exemplified competency and inclusiveness. Although I had never met her, the legacy she left behind became a role model for me. I also believed that many people expected Scientology to be as wonderful as she was.

People who had worked with Yvonne seemed to love reminiscing about how she actually got started while she had worked at the Advanced Org, Los Angeles, and met many artists and celebrities in Hollywood who she felt would benefit from personal assistance through Scientology services. She got permission from Hubbard to start a booking office in Hollywood, and received specific instructions from Diana Hubbard, who then worked as the Aide over Scientology's international Public Divisions under her father, with specific things to do to get started. Yvonne's goal for the booking office was to provide special reservations for each artist and celebrity's Scientology services. Her special attention to personal care was the foundation of Yvonne's reputation for making people feel important.

Many of the CC Sea Org staff in my day, including Sally Esterman, Cathy Garcia, Pat Gualtieri, Pamela Lancaster Johnson, and Greg Labaqui, would often reminisce to me about Yvonne and her "non-Sea Org" style of management. Yvonne ran the CC as a safe, friendly place for celebs to meet and learn Scientology without being gawked at by fans, and was beloved by her staff. They said she used Hubbard's tech of ARC (affinity, reality, communication), and "admiration bombing," as the universal solvent for Celebrity Centre visitors. These and many of the other front lines CC staff continued to treat people with Yvonne's methods of personal care after she was gone. I heard all about how her staff loved the hippie-like atmosphere of the day, as did the celebrities who came in. She made no attempts to regiment the staff, who had long hair and wore regular clothing, not pseudo-military uniforms as the staff wore in my day. Artist-types flocked to the more bohemian CCLA for open mike nights, poetry readings, arts & crafts seminars, and dinner parties.

Yvonne's passion to help celebrities with their careers through Scientology had been preceded by L. Ron Hubbard's dream of doing the same. I had read a copy of Hubbard's earliest instructions in "Project Celebrity" (Scientology's *Ability Magazine,* 1955) in which he announced his original celebrity wish list, naming approximately 65 iconic people "to whom America and the world listens" in the arts and sports, such as Pablo Picasso, Liberace, Walt Disney, Ed Sullivan, Orson Welles, Ernest Hemingway, Danny Kaye.

Hubbard wrote, "It is obvious what would happen to Scientology if prime communicators benefitting from it would mention it now and then." He encouraged current Scientologists to claim a celebrity as "quarry," but to first learn what they could about their quarry, and then do everything possible to intersect with them and make contact. He advised recruiters to "put yourself at every hand across his or her path, and not permitting discouragements or "no's" or clerks or secretaries to intervene, in days or weeks or months, to bring your celebrity into a session..." The goal was that the celebrity would receive enough auditing necessary to realize what a benefit Scientology could become to them. To anyone who was successful in converting a celebrity to Scientology, he would award a small plaque as a token of Hubbard's appreciation. Hubbard also offered two weeks of special coaching, tuition-free, at the Hubbard College in Phoenix, AZ. The "Project Celebrity" bulletin is still accessible through xenu.net.

Yvonne developed a strategy of going after up-and-coming celebrities as well as celebs whose careers had faded. Their plans were written in a series of policy letters that describe the purposes of Celebrity Centres and the perspectives and tactics to use when handling celebs. "Objective Three: Celebrities" was issued in January 1963 as a policy letter emphasizing the importance of contacting celebrities who "are just beyond or just approaching their prime" and rehabilitating them with Scientology auditing and training. This reference was later used for reaching out to Isaac Hayes (RIP) who had experienced a slump in his career, but who achieved a big career bump, which Scientology attributes to its efforts. The importance of handling celebrities was so emphasized that a special Flag Order 3323 was issued, "Celebrities and the Sea Organization" on May 9, 1973, stating how important celebrities are to the expansion of Scientology. If a celebrity wanted to join the Sea Org, they were able to do so as an "honorary Sea Org member" if they had passed a test on Scientology basics and had successfully recruited other celebrities into Scientology. I knew two people who became "honorary Sea Org members" through this system—Jeff Pomerantz and Andrik Schapers. I recall this status not being warmly received by other Sea Org members who had to endure tough working conditions and low pay while the "honorary" members were not subject to Sea Org berthing, discipline, or restrictions. I don't think this honorary system lasted long.

During Yvonne's era, recognizable names came through Scientology's revolving door including John Travolta, Paul Haggis, Candace Bergen, Nicky Hopkins (pianist who had played with the Beatles and Rolling Stones), Van Morrison, Bobby Lyons, Rock Hudson, Peggy Lipton, Elvis Presley, Karen Black, Isaac Hayes, Chick Corea, William S. Burroughs, Amanda Ambrose, Mario Feninger, Dick Glass, and Milton Katsales. Some of them stayed for years. One name that usually gets erased from this display of luminary members is Charles Manson, whose infamous name was in our Central Files for years before he murdered Sharon Tate and friends in her Laurel Canyon home near Hollywood.

Since Yvonne's day, Celebrity Centre has always drawn up lists of targeted, high profile opinion leaders across the arts, sports, management, and government. To attract the targets on the list, CC staff used to put ads in the *Hollywood Reporter, Variety* and *Backstage,* hoping to lure people for career development. Maria Ferrara, the *Celebrity* Magazine editor, showed me some of the old ads that had been saved in the archives. The ads promoted services that would appeal to up-and-coming artists, such as developing greater communication skills through Hubbard's communication course, and career-building events to help artists succeed in the entertainment industry. For example, both Peter and I, as artists, started out with one of these basic communications courses.

Although years had passed since Yvonne's death, many of the CC staff still grieved over their loss of Yvonne, because they believed her death had been avoidable, and they had no closure. I was told that although she had long been complaining of dizziness and headaches, she was denied medical care with the excuse of no organizational funds to cover it. Hubbard finally gave her permission to go to Flag where she hoped to get auditing to handle her psychosomatic pain. There, she addressed her impending death and how she would "end cycle" on her role as leader of the Celebrity Centre. She suffered a stroke caused by a brain tumor that would have been operable, had doctors seen it sooner.

Since Yvonne had achieved the highly elevated status of Clear #43 under the supervision of L. Ron Hubbard himself, her early death should have never happened. According to Hubbard's claims about the miraculous role of Dianetics to heal the human condition, Clear's would never even suffer accidents or colds.

Less known about Yvonne is her background prior to her arrival in Los Angeles. I learned this through her daughter, Janis Gillham Grady, and her stories in her new book: *Commodore's Messenger: A Child Adrift in Scientology's Sea Organization - Book One* (Outback Publishing, 2017). Yvonne's upbringing in a wealthy family line of British legal authorities who moved to Australia, taught her social graces to host the local high society. She and her husband, Peter Gillham, were two of the most well-known Scientologists in the world who had expanded Scientology in Australia and trained under LRH at St. Hill. Yvonne had been one of the first Sea Org members under Hubbard, leaving her son, Peter Jr., and daughters Terri and Janis behind while she went off on the first ship with Hubbard for the original Sea Project. Later, Yvonne and Peter came to the U.S. where they were foundational building blocks for Scientology and the Sea Org in Los Angeles. Yvonne's love for Scientology and unwavering commitment to helping Ron clear the planet through the Sea Org caused her to again leave her children on the Sea Org ship *Apollo* with Ron and Mary Sue Hubbard while she went to start the Celebrity Centre in LA. Equally tragic is how Yvonne's unnecessary death was kept at first from Terri and then completely from her daughter Janis. Hearing about the lack of proper medical care for Yvonne that led to her unnecessary and untimely death serves as early evidence of how the Sea Org has long neglected proper medical care of its staff.

Pamela Lancaster Johnson, who succeeded Yvonne in caring for celebrities at the CC, often swooned over her memory of how, after Yvonne died in 1978, Hubbard awarded Yvonne the status of Kha-Khan. This was the ultimate recognition for a stellar, productive staff member who has such ethics protection that she could get away with murder "without a blink from Ethics." And if a Kha-Khan ever did anything wrong in a future lifetime, she would escape the death penalty ten times over. It made no sense why a Kha-Khan like Yvonne would have been denied medical care that led to her early death.

After Yvonne passed, the tone of the Celebrity Centre changed dramatically and never recovered until recently, per the staff's comments. I could understand why. The rigors of the Sea Org and forceful product demand over personnel dictated the militant rou-

tines of the staff. In came the regiments of Sea Org militaristic uniforms and control that strips staff of creative initiative, and out
went the casual clothes and long hair. Anyone who works at a Celebrity Centre is rigorously trained on the special policies for handling celebrities and is expected to apply them 100% perfectly in
their job, at the risk of severe punishment if a staff member makes
a mistake while caring for a celebrity. Countless staff had been removed from their posts and sent to the decks to do physical labor,
or sent to the Rehabilitation Project Force (prison camp) for making a mistake when handling a celebrity.

The elephant in the room was that L. Ron Hubbard had always
been the center of the Scientology universe as its first and biggest
celebrity, but when Yvonne Gillham Jentzsch came along and created the happy place for Scientology artists and celebrities, attention shifted to Yvonne as the brightest Scientology star. Celebrities
believed that Scientology was good because Yvonne was an outstanding leader and example of all that is good in Scientology.
Yvonne and Celebrity Centre fell under suppression by low-toned
Scientology officials, especially in the Guardian's Office, whose
vitriolic temperaments and desire to dominate by nullifying others
made Yvonne and CC a prime target for destruction.

In my day, we never called celebs "quarry," and I don't believe
Yvonne and her team referred to celebs as quarry either, but we
surely constructed weekly lists of our "celebrity cycles." Those targets drove our daily hammer-and-pound preparation steps that
would result in a new celeb in, or getting existing celebs to pay for
their next service.

**Dwindling Star Power**

One of Scientology management's worst nightmares is a decline in the number of celebrities "on lines." When the number of
celebrities that support Scientology dwindles, the church has to
spend more time and money creating interest in Scientology as a
whole, so it can depend less on the social capital of their celebrity
members. It even has to make its tax-exempt status more appealing
to those who want to get rid of some excess money for tax-
deductions so they can collect more cash donations as general contributions instead of as payments for auditing, training and books.
Or the church persuades wealthy members to invest in real estate,
open missions, or develop Ideal Orgs. Consequently, management

was never satisfied with the number of or kinds of celebs who attended CC. But the truth about insufficient or declining celebrity numbers set off a myriad of nightmarish experiences for the front line workers at Celebrity Centres.

Following Yvonne's death, her successors included Nancy Many, Pamela Lancaster-Johnson, and Sue Young, and Captains Chris Many, Val Garcia, and Franz Albisser, who ran the operations of the CC. When I stepped into leadership, and with no Internet access or informers bold enough to brief me on the dark side of Scientology's history, I hadn't yet learned about the circumstances that had challenged these former leaders who had to recruit and care for celebs during Scientology's dark era that was still having a ripple effect in my era. Ignorance was not bliss for me. It's not like I took the role in blind faith; I was only driven by personal purpose. As a green but enthusiastic Sea Org member, I embraced the responsibility with a high level of trust in Hubbard's tech, and didn't care to focus on being sideswiped by events that blackened Scientology's reputation, that hindered celebrity recruitment, or that created obstacles that kept new people from joining in greater numbers.

For a description of events that detrimentally affected recruitment of celebrities and general public into Scientology prior to the mid 1980's, too long to include here, visit the book website. As a Sea Org member supporting command intention, no excuses or challenges like any of these events were valid for not achieving the purpose of my post, and with high statistics. But I hadn't adequately prepared myself for recruiting celebrities who were savvy enough to access information that I didn't learn about in my insular world.

After Hubbard died in 1986, and just before I was transitioning from being a recruiter to joining the Sea Org, Scientology leadership accelerated efforts to recover celebs while putting pressure on FSMs and our other feeder lines to recruit new ones. Vicki Aznaran and Jesse Prince, RTC leaders before David Miscavige took over, commandeered our president Sue Young to set up a project to recover Scientology's biggest name celebrities. The project was part of a strategy to rehabilitate the celebs, get them winning in Scientology again, and shape them into becoming walking mouthpieces for Scientology, a tool that the church was lacking. Clearly, not enough of our present celebs were bringing in new people. The question became, are our celebs really winning in life with Scientology? Maybe not! Or, were our celebs "PTS" and under suppression by critics of Scientology?

One of the solutions was to get the celebs through the PTS/SP course, if we could get them into the course rooms, and also give them an auditing process called the False Purpose Rundown. This was a special form of Scientology auditing with the e-meter that addressed a person's "evil purposes," or their destructive urges that were driven by a hidden, harmful motive. If celebrities could get rid of their evil purposes, then they would be less likely to mess up important opportunities to tell other opinion leaders about Scientology. They would also be less likely to make mistakes in their careers that could lose them—and Scientology—credibility.

A small hand-picked group of auditors worked to reel back or to invigorate Stanley Clarke, John Travolta, Al Jarreau, Edgar and Monique Winter, Isaac Hayes, Karen Black, Jeff Pomerantz, and David Pomeranz, to name a few. Sue Young had invited Peter and I to receive these free auditing services to invigorate our own careers, which is how I became so familiar with it.

The project operated from a private office within CC with hand-picked, highly skilled Class VIII auditors, including Chris and Stephanie Silcock. These celebs came into the CC through a private entrance that was off-limits to non-celebrity public and staff. The president's office was remodeled so that celebs could wait in a VIP lounge and be taken care of by the president's staff. Private auditing and training rooms were set up to deliver silver-platter treatment. In the privacy of this hushed project, celebs could come and go without being seen much by other CC customers who might question them about their status in Scientology.

During this project, I met Travolta, one of the only people on the project with whom I wasn't already friends. I didn't get to know him beyond saying hello when I saw him waiting for a session. He was quite guarded while at the CC, as if uncomfortable speaking with people other than his auditors, Chris and Stephanie.

No excuses were acceptable for not getting John Travolta into session. Often Chris, and sometimes Stephanie, was flown to wherever Travolta was filming, to take him into session. Some of the other celebs didn't want auditing, or didn't want to be seen in a Scientology building. The pressure on Sue, Chris, and Stephanie to succeed sometimes seemed too much to bear against the threat of

RPF assignment for failure. The Celebrity Recovery Project was later disbanded because of the policy, "free service, free fall." Hubbard ordered to never give Scientology auditing or training for free, because it would reduce the perceived value of it in the eyes of Scientologists. It wasn't showing a high return on investment, as proven by the lack of bringing friends into Scientology and lack of praising Scientology to media, except for John Travolta. During the Larry Wollersheim trial in Los Angeles, JT told some press that Scientology was working for him.

## Recruiting celebrities

Years into my involvement at CC, I realized the underlying strategy of luring successful people into Scientology since they're the cash cows who can pay their way up the bridge and support Scientology causes through generous donations. After all, there are few legitimate professions that pay more than movie star, superstar recording artist, or professional athlete. Equally important is their ultimate value to Scientology, their social capital. Endorsing Scientology, saying it works, and talking it up to other opinion leaders is the obsession of Celebrity Centres, because only then will the celebrity membership expand, helping to guarantee Scientology's success and financial stability.

I've described some of my personal activities as a voluntary recruiter/FSM before I joined the Sea Org. I enjoyed bringing people into Scientology, motivated by the purpose of expanding Scientology through the arts. It seemed easy to Peter and me. And it didn't hurt to receive a commission as added incentive. But once I joined the Sea Org, the joy of naturally recruiting on my own was replaced by being ordered to do it, with quotas for numbers and within certain deadlines—or else.

The President CC Int was directly responsible for the care and recruitment of celebrities in Los Angeles, while I was responsible for the management of the overall CC Network. I was often ordered to intervene in celebrity recruitment and internal celebrity handlings with Sue at CC Int. Sue and I received various threats from our seniors if we didn't comply with their orders and didn't meet the quotas they gave us. We were threatened to be sent to the prison camp (RPF) unless certain named celebrities were brought in, and a specific quota of celebrities had to be brought in by a certain deadline. Imagine what it was like to be ordered to bring in a new celebrity while being threatened with a prison camp assignment if I failed. Can you imagine an artist being told told to get on the set and deliver all her lines perfectly first time through, with the threat of being jailed if she didn't?

My job existed within this very threatening environment. Between the threats of RPF assignment, the bloody hatchet telexes that would be sent to me, and the screaming phone calls I'd get with orders to contact certain celebrities, my world became a threatening place to live within. I don't recall ever being offered any rewards when we did get a new celebrity in—that was just our job.

Our office phones became hotlines for calls coming in from a Commodore's Messenger in PAC, then a 16-year-old girl who would scream at us over the phone to go and contact specific celebs that were in town on a movie set. WDC CC had ordered her to do this, which 100% violated policy about management calling into orgs, and managing by phone instead of in writing. Evidently, Int Management staff were tracking certain celebs such as Demi Moore, Brad Pitt, and Sean Penn, where they were filming. Sue developed a system for finding out which actors were filming in the Los Angeles area, what locations, and which celebrity FSM could be dispatched to different movie studio sets to make contact. Our marching orders were always to introduce them to *Dianetics*, get them into a *Dianetics* session, put an LRH book into their hands, get them to attend an event, do something with them—or be assigned to the prison camp. The crazy thing about that was not just anyone could get onto a film set to reach celebrities. It had to be someone who had been invited or who had the credentials to be allowed in. So that task was extremely daunting to achieve.

We lived along a double-edged sword: the lifeblood of Celebrity Centre was based on recruiting celebrities that our Sea Org regimentation did not always handle smoothly. The high-pressure tactics of "get it done today" were unsuitable methods for contacting and recruiting the "raw meat" we sought—celebrities—who Sue and I felt were better dealt with through softer touch arts of communication, networking, finesse and diplomacy, as Yvonne Gillham Jentzsch had done successfully. But the whip was cracked over driving up two of our lifeblood statistics: Celebrity Bodies in the Shop (CBIS) and Gross Income (GI).In the absence of big names walking in our front doors to buy Scientology services, our staff would drive up the "celebrity bodies in the shop" (CBIS) by counting celebs that came into the org for a paid acting seminar or paid dance workshop. People such as Leah Remini, Giovanni Ribisi, Elizabeth Moss and Juliette Lewis were, at that time, young in both age and career, and several were children of other celebs, but had also begun to achieve some career success. LRH policy said the entourage of celebrities and the lesser known artists who were not yet household names were equally important, because they were building careers and would achieve great success someday; also, up-and-comings networked with the A-listers, making anyone with connections important to Scientology's growth.

**Recruitment tactics**

We had many effective means to get new celebrities through our front doors. These were our friends in the field, particularly Hollywood acting coach Milton Katsales, and other celebrity recruiters/field staff members (FSMs), who developed "feeder lines," a system that would send people to Celebrity Centre. These recruiters/FSMs would earn a commission by telling others about Scientology and then bringing their "selectees" into the CC. FSMs earned a lifetime commission of 10% or 15% as long as the selectee was buying Scientology books, training, or auditing.

Milton Katsales, who had been on the ship with Hubbard, was the successful acting coach of the Beverly Hills Playhouse, whose non-Scientology student alumni include George Clooney and Michelle Pfeiffer. Milton was one of our most important and successful FSMs. By the late 1980s, we estimated that approximately 100 of his 500 students had become Scientologists. To name a few, this included Jenna Elfman, Priscilla Presley who brought in her daughter Lisa Marie, Nancy Cartwright (the voice of Bart Simpson), Giovanni Ribisi, Anne Archer and her husband Terry Jastrow, Jason Beghe, and Kelly Preston. In later years, Milton's Scientology membership at the Beverly Hills Playhouse dissipated drastically after two Scientology celebs influenced the rest of the Scientology actors to disconnect from Milton for some alleged ethics issues. They literally campaigned to get Scientologists to disconnect from him. Milton passed away in 2008, succeeded by Allen Barton, who had been mentoring under Milton for years prior.

The Enhancement Center in Sherman Oaks, masterminded by well-connected powerhouses Mimi and Jim Rogers and Francis

Godwin, was another key feeder line for us. Mimi and Francis' center actually functioned like a mini-Celebrity Centre, but was more upscale in appearance than the age-worn CC in Hollywood. Mimi eventually worked her way into her goal of acting. She landed roles in *Hill Street Blues* and some soap operas. Mimi had received auditor training thanks to her father, Phil Spickler, and capitalized on her auditing and acting abilities to contact and recruit celebrities into her Scientology field practice. They drew Sonny Bono, Kirstie Alley, and eventually Scientology's biggest catch, Tom Mapother Cruise. Their center served as a pipeline of selectees to our CC, but not without conflict. A string of Mimi-related problems threatened Scientology's goals starting with her father, a former Scientology mission holder in Palo Alto, California. He landed on Miscavige's black list of suppressive persons leaving the missions network after Scientology's finance police broke it up. Mimi and Jim Rogers got divorced, and she married Tom Cruise. But their marriage was broken up to ensure Spickler would not taint Tom Cruise.

The Enhancement Center and Celebrity Centre International played a territorial tug-of-war game over celebrities, with CC attempting to strong arm this small field practice by exerting its Sea Org power. The issues at hand were, of course, money being made and controlling the flow of celebs. Without the regimentation of CC's Sea Org rules and military uniforms, the Enhancement Center functioned quite successfully outside the control of the Sea Org. While it was an important feeder line to CC, and a more discreet place for a celebrity to find out about Scientology, our front-lines operation used high-pressure sales and control tactics moved people along at the rate we wanted them to move. We viewed Francis and Mimi's practice as a help to get recruits but more as a source of competition. The field practice was keeping the celebs too long for our liking before they finally selected them to CC.

Despite pressure from Int Management to control the Enhancement Center, both Sue and I knew that, according to Hubbard, a field auditor could deliver the lower end of the grade chart levels up to the state of Clear. They had acquired a license through I-HELP, the official network for field auditors, and paid a mandatory percentage of earnings to the Church of Scientology. Becoming a field auditor was a goal for many Scientologists who could see the incredible income they could earn outside of Scientology organizations, by charging somewhat lower rates for auditing than a customer would have to pay inside a Scientology organization. In those days, auditing cost about $2,000 for an "intensive of auditing" or 12 1/2 hours. The goal was always to sell blocks of intensives, so the sky was the limit for field auditors once they got a celebrity started on the bridge to total freedom. For example, a new Scientologist who wanted to do the steps to achieve the state of Clear might spend about $50,000 on auditing to get there. A nice chunk of change for a field auditor. The Enhancement Center was an independent field auditing practice, rightfully able to pocket the earnings of their work not controlled directly by Sea Org management. But president Sue Young was strapped with the task of enforcing the rule that they could only audit their celebrities on lower level services and were required to then "select them" to our Celebrity Centre for advanced auditing.

Since Cruise had come into the Enhancement Center under his name, Tom Mapother, his A-list celebrity status was at first undetected by Celebrity Centre and the Int Management powers. It may have been about a year until he actually got scooped up by David Miscavige and his RTC team that personally took control to ensure Scientology wouldn't lose its biggest trophy ever. Mimi Rogers and Tom Cruise married, but didn't last long. Clearly, Miscavige didn't want the church's biggest catch to waver from Scientology as some of our other biggest names, including John Travolta, had.

Some of our other recruitment tactics included strategized planning to send celebrity recruiters to certain Hollywood parties or events, so we could plant them as a guest. Their purpose would be to make contact with certain targeted individuals, and establish a good rapport so they could follow up with a "dissemination" conversation about Scientology over a drink or dinner at a later time.

Body routing was another tactic we used to bring in new people. We'd train our body routers how to go out on the streets around Celebrity Centre, start a conversation with someone, and convince them to come inside to find out more. We never knew when a director, a budding actor or a successful writer would be sitting at La Poubelle across the street enjoying a glass of wine or cup of cappuccino. This could lead that person to come in a take a personality test, watch an introductory film, get a pinch test to find out how the e-meter works, get an introductory Dianetics session, or just have a conversation with the President and a tour of the building.

The President of CC used various tactics for celebrity recruitment. Her role was to be a career nurturer, a hand-holder, and an advisor who helped guide celebs to use Scientology in their careers. She would schedule meetings for conversations with celebs to catch up on their career progress as well as progress moving up the bridge, keeping a finger on the pulse of each celebrity's progress. When she saw signs that the celebrity was becoming more and more confident as a Scientologist, she would start asking them who they knew that they wanted to tell about Scientology. She would create a strategy with each celeb by getting them to name who they were going to bring in, how they were going to go about it, and would set a goal for when they would bring in that new person. By doing this with dozens of celebrities in the Celebrity Centre, the President was to ensure that she kept a new flow of raw meat coming in regularly, by turning the celebrities into recruiters/FSMs.

## David Miscavige and personal staff recruiters

After Tom Cruise had become a Scientologist, the leader of Scientology began utilizing his personal staff to come to Celebrity Centre and talk with new recruits like Katie Holmes and others.

In what I came to know as typical Miscavige style, he considered himself to be the only one who could get anything done successfully. There was some truth to that, mainly because he wasn't being made to follow LRH policy to the letter like other Sea Org members who had to get permission to do things every step of the way, which clearly kept people gummed up and moving slowly, more robotically, than a person who could act on his own intellect, personal drive, and unlimited budget. He implemented his own strategy with a personal team that bypassed everyone whose job it was to meet his goals. Compare Int Management ninjas, like Miscavige's assistant, Mark Rathbun, to Sea Org members at CC Int. Rathbun was empowered with money for a wardrobe suitable for making celebrity contacts, funds for travel and taking celebs to dinner or other entertainment, and generally functioning closer to celebrity lifestyles while directed under the church's senior-most power. The CC Int staff in pseudo-military uniforms (before they got their new outfits) earned less than $50 week, lived in impoverished berthing, had little sense of personal pride in appearance or lifestyle. It's not hard to understand why CC crew made less impact than people who were empowered to do so.

Karen joined the Sea Org at Celebrity Centre and became the Commanding Officer of the Celebrity Centre Network in 1988.

CC leader Pat Gualtieri and Peter Schless went to Beijing for the Dianetics groups China tour circa 1986. The IAS awareded Peter the Religious Freedom Medal in 1987.

Karen Schless speaks to 300 artists and celebrities at the recent "Artists of a New Civilization" event that she put on.

Karen's passion for the Celebrity Centre purpose of expanding Scientology through the arts led to her "Artists of a New Civilization" event at Celebrity Centre, circa 1987.

Artists affirm their commitment to abide by the Code of a Scientologist at the "Artists of a New Civilization" party in the CC Int Rose Garden Theatre.

# 15

## RELIGIOUS FREEDOM MEDAL

**Paris, 1987**

PETER OFTEN WENT GLOBETROTTING as a Scientology evangelist supporting the church's expansion efforts, while I held down the fort at Celebrity Centre. We used to love traveling together in the music business or on jaunts around the U.S. on vacations, so his solo trips rubbed it in that I was anchored to my Sea Org post, not free to follow our dreams together.

He and Pat Gualtieri went to Beijing and other urban areas in China on a Friendship Tour to promote the formation of Dianetics groups. In 1987, Peter spent at least six weeks in Italy supporting Scientology's religious freedom defense efforts when the church had been under attack there and elsewhere in Europe.

Peter called me from Italy, excited about some surprising news: he had been selected by church leadership to receive the Religious Freedom Medal of the International Association of Scientologists. In those days, no higher honor had been achieved by a public Scientologist than this. This was only the second year of the award, established after the Portland religious freedom crusade. The

Chairman of the Board of RTC would bestow this award at the next IAS event to acknowledge special accomplishments in defending or dissemination Scientology.

The 1987 International Association of Scientologists' second annual event would be held in Paris, where Peter and two other Scientologists, Dennis Clark and Andrik Schapers, would also receive Freedom Medals. Without question, I decided to go to Paris to meet Peter for this event. I would be able to convince my seniors that this trip was worthwhile, not only to honor Peter as an on-purpose Scientologist, but I would also go to Celebrity Centre Paris for an inspection.

I flew to Paris, while the church flew Peter from Italy to the IAS Awards event. We checked into the Intercontinental Hotel in Paris with a view of the Champs Elysée, complements of the IAS. With a little more than a day to see Paris before the event, we explored some back streets across from the hotel where we discovered incredible French food and wines, and tables selling knock-offs of Parisienne haute couture. After exploring the Champs Elysée and the Arc de Triomphe, we indulged in some French styling in the hotel's hair salon.

The City of Lights was a brilliant location for this IAS event, a black-tie affair that drew hundreds of European Scientologists. With more than enough pomp and circumstance typical of International Management events, the Religious Freedom Medals were draped around the necks of these three Scientologists with fanfare comparable to Olympians who win a Gold Medal. As much as the awards acknowledged the three individuals, the awards also pumped up the importance of the IAS, as if creating the impression that the IAS was creating world change through their actions. I was very aware of Peter's activities, but I knew of no connection whatsoever between the actions he took and any IAS support or strategies.

The evening culminated at the Eiffel Tower, with a trip in a private elevator heading skywards to an awards dinner in a posh restaurant. How impressive to glorify these celebrity awardees at the most famous monument in Paris with the church's most senior executives.

The furnishings of the restaurant were dramatically minimalist, with the real show being the breathtaking view of Paris at night through the expansive windows. Amidst the twinkling lights of the

Parisienne spectacle that evening, I gained a close-up look at Scientology's power elite. Tuxedo'd church leaders David Miscavige, Marc Yeager, Guillaume Lesevre, and an IAS exec appeared to spare no expense entertaining their personal entourage and the IAS awardees at this lavish black-tie dinner party. While I was thrilled to be a guest and enjoyed the fine food and drink and the luxurious atmosphere, I felt strangely uncomfortable knowing that no heed was paid to the limited budget and benefits that Sea Org members back home were subject to. The evening seemed to be encased in a bubble of unreality.

This was also the second time that I came into close contact with David Miscavige and Marc Yager when both of them observed me but neither of them spoke to me; in contrast, Guillaume Lesevre, the Executive Director International, was warm and friendly to both Peter and me. I remember thinking how disingenuous Miscavige and Yager seemed, but had to keep my thoughts to myself so as to not appear disaffected towards Management in Peter's eyes.

Afterward, Peter flew back to Italy to rejoin his crusade team there, while I stayed in Paris two more days to work. I toured Celebrity Centre Paris, one of the 13 organizations CC managed from the Hollywood headquarters. I found CC Paris to be the most upscale of any Scientology organization I had been in. It was not staffed by Sea Org members, but by contracted staff whose pay depended on their productivity and sales. The Executive Director, Alain Frank Rosenberg, and the President, Sarit Rosenberg, struck me as savvy people who knew how to successfully run a business.

Alain and Sarit invited me to spend my last two nights in Paris at their home, an invitation that they told me they did not extend to other Sea Org members who come to CC Paris.

"Why is that?" I asked them.

"Because the Sea Org members who come over here from Los Angeles or Flag lack social graces, have no manners, and think they can just order everyone around." We talked the first night into the late hours, exchanging thoughts about Scientology and Sea Org life. The Rosenberg's had evidently received heavy pressure to join the Sea Org, but felt they could be more effective on the outside. What they really meant was the same as I thought: they didn't want to give up their freedom and be controlled by the Sea Org, as I had done.

I completed my inspections of CC Paris and recruited a twenty-one year old budding actor along the way. He was more than eager to go to America, especially to Hollywood. I felt reticent about describing what was in store for him in Sea Org life, and all that he would have to give up. I was, after all, looking out for the greatest good.

# 16

## SURPRISING TIMES

### Los Angeles, circa 1988

OUR WORLD SHIFTED AFTER Peter said yes to David Miscavige's invitation to join the Sea Org and become a Golden Era Musician. Hubbard's rule against people joining who have an LSD history was waived by Miscavige, who considered that Peter's stellar production record as a composer as well as his experience working with the Gold musicians, outweighed his disqualification.

This monumental change in Peter's life, walking out of his successful music career, also rocked my world. David Miscavige's father, Ron Miscavige Sr, had played a key part in Peter's decision to join. Peter and Ron had gotten to know each other during Peter's trips to the Gold music studio over the past year, during the recording and production of the *Road to Freedom* Album. When Ron came down to CC from time to time and visited with Peter in his studio, he also came to our apartment in the Manor to visit with both of us. He'd tell us about Golden Era Productions, and about his personal transition from being a professional musician and joining the Sea Org just a few years prior. Ron talked about living in Philly and taking his family to St. Hill where everyone got trained in Scientology. He had been offered a record deal years prior, which didn't come to fruition, but he really wanted to play with a band of great musicians in Gold. Ron clearly held a personal vested interest

interest in Peter's arrival. Ron showed interest in my music business experience, and started talking to me about leaving CC and moving to Gold with Peter to become the Music Manager.

Once Peter decided to join the Sea Org, this created a domino effect for the zillions of things anyone goes through to leave their private life, pay off all bills, complete many personal tasks, eliminate furniture, clothing, etc. to make the transition into a very downsized life.

## Motown Records Offer

We brainstormed about generating money to pay off all debts and put money in the bank to fall back on while we were in the Sea Org. Peter followed up on a call he had gotten from someone at Motown Records, who wanted to talk about buying the rights to "On the Wings of Love" and possibly other songs in our publishing catalog. That's the kind of call that any songwriter hopes and prays for, because selling one's songwriting catalog can generate a lot of money.

About a week later, Peter and I sat in a Motown Records conference room with Mr. Joe Jackson. Even though I had been around plenty of stars, I had never met anyone who seemed to exude as much power as did Michael Jackson's father. He lavished a good bit of praise on Peter for "Wings" being such a great song that he wanted to own it for the Motown catalog.

Joe Jackson said he wanted to buy Wings for $50,000 with other songs thrown in from Peter's catalog that they could listen to and possibly find other hits. I won't say that this wasn't tempting for both of us. But Mr. Jackson must have been counting on us to be relatively uninformed about songwriting rights, publishing rights, and copyrights. The Motown king spoke to us as if leverage was something he controlled across the entirety of the music industry, as if we had none. Fortunately, Peter and I weren't in the position of many new songwriters or publishers who would have jumped at this chance to sell a song to Motown. After setting up our music publishing company and ensuring that we copyrighted all our songs, plus maintained the publishing rights as well as songwriter's rights to Peter's music, we had set ourselves up to make almost twice the amount of money that most songwriters make who only own their songwriting rights. We felt that $50,000 was low for that song compared to what we had already earned from it, and to what we knew we would earn from future royalties.

When we thanked Mr. Jackson and let him know we would consider his offer, he was clearly shocked that we hadn't jumped at this opportunity. We later decided to pass on that offer. Peter ended up getting a better offer through Time-Warner for about that same amount, and he didn't even sell any rights to "Wings"— he just sold the rest of his catalog. Those funds paid off our bills and put money in the bank.

Ron stayed in close contact with Peter over several months to help him "get arrived." He would always make it a point to pay attention to my thoughts and concerns about the entire process, and became a friend in the process. Leaving my Celebrity Centre world and going onto the clearance lines was a radical shift for me. In the process, I lost touch within the CC world while managing the changes happening in our lives.

## A new era for Celebrity Centre

As if Scientology had spun a roulette wheel and landed on the jackpot, Tom Cruise's involvement in Scientology shifted the Scientology universe. The presence of Cruise also marked Int Management's investment of beaucoup funds into a total renovation of the Celebrity Centre and Manor Hotel in the early 1990s. The condition of the Celebrity Centre had never been updated since they moved in. Anyone who took an honest look at our worn rugs, militaristic uniforms, and less than luxury furnishings knew we needed to improve our image befitting the people we really wanted to attract.

The new WDC CC, Amy (Mortland) Scobee, ran the mission that oversaw the complete transformation of the building, a pivotal moment for not only Celebrity Centre but International Management and David Miscavige, setting off a flurry of events that hoped to transform the face of Scientology. International Management poured millions of dollars into the renovations to create the best facility possible for the best people whom they hoped to attract, now that Tom Cruise was sinking his teeth into Scientology and Scientology was sinking its teeth into him.

David Miscavige gave me the special project of designing a new image for the CC staff. My goal was to elevate their image by designing custom suits that would match the new, elegant interiors.

These new threads would help to increase the staff's confidence when servicing celebrities. Needless to say, I was thrilled to have a hand in Celebrity Centre again. I proposed the original design plan that included Italian fashion designer Claudio Lugli to work on this project with me. COB approved this plan. Claudio Lugli and I arranged for our chic new suits to be made in England.

Meanwhile, another special project worked on the appearance of the individual Celebrity Centre staff. Names of less attractive staff (too thin, too heavy, not good looking enough) and people with less developed skill sets were put on a list, and were called "coins" that were traded with better-looking staff with higher skills from other orgs. Only beautiful people could be seen in beautiful clothes for the gods of the Scientology world.

With new facilities fit for Hollywood A-listers, newly posted and uniformed good-looking staff, and Tom Cruise on board, Celebrity Centre's future—and thus Scientology's—looked bright.Management could gauge CC's overall success through its CBIS, Celebrity Bodies in the Shop statistic that started growing. While it brought hope for a new era of A-list celebrity recruitment, the inflow and retention of A-listers ebbed and flowed.

In one of my Sea Org recruitment projects, I had recruited Karen Hollander for the Sea Org, but she had not routed into the Sea Org until now. President Karen Hollander was given the newly renovated, posh offices with celebrity lounges and private entrances fit for the gods that would fill the place. Her command team also brought on Dave Pettit as the Executive Director, with Tommy Davis and Susan Watson as assistants.

I remained interested in CC's progress, and how the Scientology influence began to spread, although it hurt to feel that I had made a mistake stepping out of the CC world that I loved, to go to Gold with Peter. Being honest with myself, my enthusiasm for my "CC purpose" had drastically dwindled after I had started feeling disaffected by Int Management's vitriolic behavior. Had I stayed at CC, I would have preferred to return to my front lines action roles of personal recruitment and celebrity event planning versus holding an executive position.

My inside friends kept me somewhat informed about CC events to the extent of our limited communications. The transition to Gold was more like leaving planet Earth to go to Mars, where there was no means of communication between the Int base and the outside world—no television, no phone access, no computers, and all our mail was read by security. I was able to keep minimal tabs on CC's revolving door that was still moving, just by people at the Int base talking about CC operations. Lisa Marie Presley, whose marriage to Michael Jackson did not last long, did not recruit him into Scientology. A few celebs, such as Brad Pitt, did only one or two courses and didn't stay with it. Before I left, Sue Young had been electrified when John Travolta introduced Russian dancer Mikhail Baryshnikov to Scientology, because of the potential repercussions if he didn't like it; and indeed, he didn't stick with it. But the biggest news of all was Tom Cruise.

While I knew that Int Management staff were intervening in Tom Cruise's progress, the details were handled totally outside of my orbit. Only a few newly appointed President's Office staff knew about the transition going on within her office space that was being used by Tom Cruise to host people like Penelope Cruz. I learned of Cruise's divorce from Mimi Rogers, or marriage to Nicole Kidman, after 1990 when I began working at Int Management. I later learned that while all this new investment in Celebrity Centre was going on, Miscavige's team—which then included Tom Cruise—targeted specific millionaires and billionaires to recruit into Scientology, including James Packer, the son of Australia's richest billionaire; and Rupert Murdoch's son, Lachlan Murdoch. Packer did get involved for a few years but left by 2006, and Murdoch never arrived. Celebrities would come and go, while the world would keep turning.

# PART II

## OVER THE RAINBOW

# 17

# DOWN ANOTHER RABBIT HOLE

**Los Angeles - 1989**

THE CC PRESIDENT'S VISITS "over the rainbow" had piqued my
curiosity about visiting Scientology's control center, then the confidential Int base, Golden Era Productions, where she'd go to discuss celebrity cases with the most senior technical executives in
Scientology. In 1989, very little information about it was public
knowledge. Gold served as the dissemination arm for the church's
retail products—tapes, CDs, DVDs, e-meters, films, translated materials, but it was also the front name for Scientology's International Management headquarters, the "or else" place that I referred
to earlier.

The mystery of getting to the other side of that rainbow with
Peter, and becoming part of Scientology's elite senior-level staff
motivated me to take the journey. I think of it like jumping out of
an airplane the first time—it's crazy to take such a risk but the
once-in-a-lifetime reckless abandon-excitement is a strong motiva-
tor. I wanted us to be on the same page in our commitment to Scientology, but felt it was a grim mistake for Peter to remove himself
from the public music industry to become a Gold musician in the
Sea Org. Peter had earlier described the Gold musicians as reclu-
sive musicians who became outdated and faded into obscurity.
Why join them? Maybe he'd like being a big fish in a small pond

for a while. I harbored the idea that if we didn't like Gold, we would leave.

Peter did his Sea Org boot camp at Big Blue on Hollywood Boulevard, and seemed to love it. He and I went on "clearance lines" together, but he got pushed through faster and arrived at Gold a few months before I did. Through nearly two months of sec-checking interrogations, they looked into every detail of my personal connections, every past sex partner, connections to people with government security connections, and through all questions in the life history that I had filled out. Many of the questions them-selves intimidating; some were absurd. Some of the questions came come from a level of paranoia I had never imagined: Was I a plant for some undercover group? An operative or any kind of spy for a governmental agency or pharmaceutical company? Had I ever sub-jected myself to mental treatment such as hypnotism or electro-shock therapy? Was I wanted by the police? Had I been in jail and escaped? Did any of my family members or friends work for the government or have high security clearances? I mean, this far ex-ceeded a routine background check.

That last question caused me to think about one of my dear friends, Joe Clark, from northern Michigan. I was told that I would have to disconnect from him because of his security clearances in the Air Force! Joe, a threat to Scientology? As a former Lieutenant Colonel in the U.S. Air Force during Viet Nam and the Korean War, and part of Air Force Intelligence, this suddenly put him off limits as a friend for me. Joe had never revealed any secrets from his military days to me; he had only shared some of his back-ground. I remember sitting in the interrogation session over my life history, being asked about Joe. The security checker kept altering the question to pose it other ways to me, because the needle must have been giving a reaction that implied something was going on. Indeed, there was! I disagreed with the church trying to control who I could be friends with. I literally thought of something else to deter the needle reaction because I would never get over that dis-agreement. It was as if the church was afraid that I would tell Joe something confidential about church operations, and he'd tell someone in the government.

Sea Org members at the Int base cannot be connected to any-one who had high security clearances regardless of the circum-stances or the relationship—friend or relative. This is one of many reasons that bring about disconnection. That I balked at disconnecting from Joe just added to my interrogation time. I was made to study Hubbard's writings about suppressive persons such as the military, and specifically intelligence people who could have an influence in my life as a Sea Org member, since government officials were considered enemies of the church.

It would be years before I would learn that Scientology's interrogation process and enforced disconnection from friends is not dissimilar to accounts of the Chinese communist process as described in Dr. Robert Lifton's book, *Thought Reform and the Psychology of Totalism: A Study of 'Brainwashing' in 'China*. Lifton studied how people were detained and interrogated during Mao's regime, resulting in a nightmarish process of re-education to get people to think that what they had done in their past was bad and not the ways of Mao or of the people, thereby making them re-orient their thoughts towards "the way of the people." It was easy to compare the Maoist ways of the people with the ways of the Sea Org. My re-education into the ways of the Sea Org required ongoing compromises and changes on my part: Agreeing to give up my friendship with Joe Clark. Revealing everyone that I had ever had sex with, and what I did with them. Acknowledging that children were no longer welcome at the Int Base. I was given a document written by Executive Director International Guillaume Lesevre, that dictated how staff at the Int base could no longer get pregnant and work there. Anyone who was hoping to work there and who had children under age seven would have to leave their children in Los Angeles, and later apply for them to come up to the childcare facilities outside of the Int base. Children were considered a distraction to production for Sea Org members. I thought it was atrocious that some countries like China controlled how many children, and even what sex of children, people should have. But in America, we have Scientology regulating pregnancies within families, under the cloak of "religion"?

Nevertheless, the way of the leaders in Int Management laid down the law against kids and the value of family. Though this is just a small example of the rethinking I had to do in the Sea Org, I had to say *yes, I understand and accept this.* Saying no, I don't honestly approve of this policy as I think it's not only in violation of my human rights but I think it's cultish, would have just begun consequences of not moving up there to be with my husband, who had already been absorbed into the fold.

It was common for Sea Org couples to be split up, with one spouse at the Int base and one working in the Sea Org in Los Angeles. They might see each other on Saturday night between 1:00 a.m. and Sunday at noon, that's it. I didn't want that kind of Sea Org life. I felt that my only choice was to say *yes*. Was this a sign of my not exercising critical thinking skills when making this choice? Or, is this an example of undue influence? Or what it is like when people are radicalized into doing extremist acts? Does a person leap from normal behavior to extremist behavior in a single bound? Or are there baby steps in the process of eventually committing extremist acts?

After two months, I was approved to go to Gold. The day of the magic journey from Los Angeles over the rainbow, I received written directions to follow the back route on the Pomona Highway, which passed through industrial areas and the desert. This was also the slippery chute down the rabbit hole that dumped into Golden Era Productions.

## Gilman Hot Springs - 1989

I pulled my car up to the garage area where Claudia Olander had told me someone would be waiting for me. The old white frame garage looked like an out-building left over from the 1940s. A single spotlight glared down from the peak of the roof, highlighting a thirties-something man in navy pants, long-sleeved blue shirt with military-style epaulets, black tie, shiny black shoes, and slicked-back hair. The man waited to receive me, holding a two-way radio.

I looked beyond him at the sight before my eyes—high chain link fences along the property borders at Highway 79, topped by a foot-high twisting band of Constantine wire, barbs glistening under the street lights glaring overhead. The property struck me more like a movie set for a concentration camp than a religious organization. At first I wondered if I was in the wrong place, as this looked like pictures I had seen of Guantanamo. I didn't remember noticing that on my first visit.

The man approached my car and greeted me. "I'm Kevin O'Hare. You must be Karen Schless."

"Great to meet you." He was friendly enough, but with minimal chatting, Kevin directed me where to move my car. I wouldn't move, though, without first asking the obvious question. "What's with the barbed wire on the fences? It's kind of shocking…"

Kevin immediately responded with a smile and a calm, confident answer that sounded well rehearsed. "Oh, that's to keep out intruders."

"Who would want to intrude here? I mean, this is a church property."

"You'd be surprised. There are people who drive out here just to cause trouble." I had been briefed on this confidential location that Scientologists were not allowed to know about, with the exception of certain celebrities.

In that one-minute conversation with Kevin, I compromised my first instinct. *The fences and barbed wire are there to keep in the staff.* Little did I know that by passing through the security gates of this cultic milieu, I was relinquishing my independence. I would soon discover that adjusting to the controls of staff life in Gold at the Int base would be the single most difficult aspect of being there.

## Married couple living arrangements

That first night, I settled into our apartment that Peter had already been sharing with Russ and Linda Grielich at the Devonshire in Hemet. Russ was a sax player with the Gold musicians, and Linda worked in the Audio division. Married couples always shared an apartment, to ensure we maintained a sense of communal Sea Org living. Before I actually felt my loss of independence, I felt the loss of privacy. I liked Linda and Russ, who had already become friends with Peter. But I didn't like that our privacy was limited to a 10' x 10' room behind a closed door. I groped for positive thoughts. At least we had a bathroom off our bedroom and didn't have to traipse across a hall in bathrobes. Our bedroom was separated from the Grielich's by a tiny common room and galley kitchen. But the place was filled with Gold staff hanging out when I got there. The other option was to live at Kirby Gardens, a worn-out complex that served as communal housing where hundreds of Sea Org staff were packed into rooms like migrant workers, stuffed into rough-sawn bunk beds piled three high. The presence of Sea Org security guards belied these as public apartment complexes, since guards kept a watchful eye on us 24/7.

From day one, I feared for our marriage. Marriages at the base seemed to be under attack and divorces were used as leverage to prove loyalty to David Miscavige. Peter and I came to the Int base with a meaningful history, unlike the norm where people who barely knew each other got married and had short-lived relationships.

## Orientation to the Int Base

My first morning started with a routing form that would cover every step for my orientation—where to eat, to get uniforms and supplies, take classes, see the ethics officer or the medical officer, and find all the different organizations across the 500-acre property. The Int base is as significant to the Church of Scientology as the Vatican is to the Catholic Church. I noticed that our pope figurehead—the Chairman of the Board of the Religious Technology Center, David Miscavige—was usually out and about, along with his entourage of communicators and four-striped senior executives, roaring around the otherwise relatively peaceful property in a gang of motorcycles. Their motorcycles seemed like overkill. I wondered why they didn't use golf carts or just walk. But I was to learn that speed of particle flow determined power, and the execs were very macho.

At the top of the church's hierarchical pyramid of control stands the Religious Technology Center headquarters. The lower and upper Villas held RTC's hub of control on the north side of the property, next to the Star of California ship. The ship looked like a movie set that I had seen at Burbank Studios. Looking like the lush green Shire of Middle-earth, the Villas exuded the illusion of a luxurious resort, cloaking its existence as control-central for the church. I was told that the Int base had a Scottish motif; instead, the white stucco buildings and blue-tiled roofs looked Mediterranean.

Golden Era Productions was the lowest organization in the Int base hierarchy of power, but the largest population of Int base staff. The largest divisions of Gold included Manufacturing and HEM that produced all e-meters, tapes, CDs and films; Audio, that included the Gold Musicians who scored music for films, event videos, and commercials, and the unit that primarily remixed tapes for reproduction; Cine, that shot films and videos for Scientology dissemination and training purposes; Qual, that trained and audited the Int base crew; Estates, that maintained the entire base; and administrative divisions that serviced the base orgs with treasury, communications, personnel and security functions.

Except for a few offices on the north side, Gold was located on the south side of the property below Highway 79, which sliced through the middle of the base. In between were, from the top under RTC, Commodore's Messenger Organization International (CMOI), housed in Del Sol, an old white stucco two-story building with threadbare red carpet. This is the organization working directly for L. Ron Hubbard, comprised of Hubbard's messengers, and its Watchdog Committee (WDC) of Scientology sector supervisors. Units within CMOI were set up in satellite offices in little buildings around the property that contained the International Landlord Office, International Finance Office, Senior Case Supervisor International, L. Ron Hubbard Personal Public Relations Office, and more.

INCOMM, the highly sensitive computer operations, was tucked up at the Villas near the RTC offices. INCOMM was responsible for various computer management functions such as providing an intranet for the staff, retaining statistics, and and managing electronic libraries of LRH documents, among other things. CMO Gold operated from a little north side house, and ran the Film & Equipment unit on the south side that maintained Hubbard's archival photographs and camera equipment.

The Senior Executive Strata International, ESI, was stuffed into Del Sol on the ground floor under CMOI. ESI was headed by the Executive Director International, Guillaume Lesevre, the figurehead who took over from LRH running the Scientology organizations worldwide, who treated me kindly at CC and in Paris at the IAS event. ESI included the International Executives over their specializations of books, FSMs, new public, gross income, marketing, and more, who were supposed to expand Scientology organizations to the size of LRH's organization, Old Saint Hill, in England. ESI also included the Int Management Public Relations Office, and small but important units such as LRH Book Compilations and the Translations Unit that were located in the Ranchos, just north of Del Sol.

Added to all this was the original Bonnie View, an odd little stucco house reserved for L. Ron Hubbard's return. The messenger who toured me through it kept saying, "Isn't this great? Isn't this awesome?" I nodded as if to agree. I actually thought it was bizarre, and didn't match up to what I envisioned for Ron's home. Some of the furniture had been constructed in oversized boxy shapes, laminated with different colors of material that one might find on a cheap countertop. Some of the chairs looked like they might have been used on some odd movie set, in a style that seemed Roman but contemporary as if used by a king from another time. I couldn't wait to get out of there.

The Messenger told me that we were supposed to build a new Bonnie View, Hubbard's mansion, for LRH's reincarnated return to the base. The fact that it wasn't built yet was a flap, because Ron's new home was way overdue and this was probably holding up his return. Near the odd little BV house was parked Hubbard's Blue Bird RV, and a laundry room with washers only for Ron's clothes. She pointed out that everything we did at the Int base was to be fragrance-free for Ron (even though he had died in 1986) because he didn't allow rose water or any fragranced products to be used that could cover up dangerous odors such as chemicals used by FBI agents coming after him, that could be harmful to him. Between her orientation, and my Base Orientation course, I learned that I was never again to use any scented laundry detergent, shampoo, soap, hair spray, or anything else with a fragrance. All fragranced products were prohibited, even though Hubbard was dead, because Int base staff carried forward his paranoia of being surrounded by enemies, secret agents or infiltrators that would use fragranced products to cover up poison for weapons.

**Pseudo-military operations**

The Sea Org's entire operation at the Int base (and in certain other Sea Org bases) was organized after a U.S. naval base, complete with military ranks and lingo, musters, Masters at Arms (MAAs), a mess hall, a PX (our canteen), addressing both male and female seniors or officers as "sir," and certain military protocols, including military-style marching drills and other types of drills to instill the Sea Org attitude. This military operations mode is characteristic of the Sea Org overall, but goes to an extreme at the Int base.

All staff dressed alike in pseudo-military style uniforms. In the summer we wore our "whites:" white naval short-sleeved shirts, pants or shorts, white shoes and socks, and white webbed belts with Sea Org buckles. In the winter we wore our "blues:" navy blue pants, navy pullover sweaters with shoulder epaulettes, light blue military shirts, black ties, shoes and socks, and black webbed belts with Sea Org buckles. Our dress uniforms included insignia for ranks and ratings (gold braids for the top brass, gold stripes and black shoulder boards, campaign ribbons, the whole nine yards.

The only exceptions to this sameness of appearance were the Cine staff, the film crew who wore colored shirts and black pants; the galley crew, and estates staff. On Saturday renovations days, everyone wore their own jeans and t-shirts. Otherwise, the sameness of our appearance held together the unity of our collective identity: one Sea Org. We even had our own power generators and water reservoir, to ensure we would not be dependent on the resources around us in the case of power outages or water shortages.

On the south side of the property, a dilapidated mess hall, Massacre Canyon Inn (MCI), served military-style breakfast starting at 7:30am. For the first few years at the Int base, my rank of petty officer relegated me to sit in the north wing of MCI with other non-officers. We set our own tables, got our own food trays, and bused the tables clean. In my later years as a Midshipman officer, I was privy to sit with the other officers—including Miscavige and his entourage—in the south dining room where stewards brought platters of food to the table and cleaned up the tables.

## Unpredicted restrictions

Several simple life activities that most people take for granted were reshaped by restrictions imposed through Int base regulations. Gone were the days of picking up the phone and calling my mother or a friend, or sending a letter by dropping it in the mailbox. Or going to the store to buy someone a birthday present. Or going out to eat with Peter when we felt like it. Or driving to the doctor's office when I needed to. Little pleasures and simple freedoms people enjoy in a democratic society vanished.

We set up our TV in our bedroom, only to discover when we got back to our room that night that it had been confiscated by security guards. Why? Staff are staying up too late watching movies. The truth? Scientology officials didn't want us to hear what the world was saying about Scientology that could have influenced us to leave.

I'm an avid animal lover and have never been without a dog as part of my family. Toby was like my child, so to relegate him into what I considered to be heartless conditions is something I have never forgiven myself for. He had previously lived a life of luxury and claimed the foot of my bed as his own day and night. In our car, he had his own spot in the back seat and wore out the upholstery over the years. At the Int base, Toby found himself in a fenced area with a dog house off the Estates garage that we had built for him, but subject to daytime extreme desert heat until we picked him up late every night and dropped him off again in the morning. In contrast, the leader of the Scientology world had Dalmatians and Beagles that roamed the property, free to disrupt and in some cases terrorize other people's pets when they were let out, such as Marc and Michelle Yager's Schnauzers.

I was unable to drive my own car before I earned my place on the "OK to drive list." I first had to do Car School, which takes at least a month, before driving any of the base cars or my personal car. This training should make a Sea Org member fully capable of handling any situation if one's car breaks down or has trouble on the road. Car School included how to wash a car Sea Org style, without leaving streaks. My car wash, of course, had to be inspected and passed by someone else before I was approved. I also had to be checked out as having no PTS situations, had to be tested on the manual for the car I would drive, have no outstanding tickets, and had to be insured at my own expense. These requirements caused many Sea Org members to forgo car ownership.

When I was finally able to slip my key into my car's ignition and drive to the base, I felt that I had attained my real keys to freedom. I hadn't realized how much I counted on freedom of mobility, and what it felt like when that was regulated by an authority. Being one of the few staff members with a car gave me a small if illusory sense of personal freedom and independence.

**Those Int base buses**

Mornings dictated a routine of rise and shine at the crack of dawn before crew piled into the buses that traveled from the Hemet apartments to the base. Peter and I continued to receive outside income from songwriting royalties that enabled us to keep our car, so I escaped those bus rides.

The morning loading of staff onto the gray buses was a sight I could barely confront. It was like watching a flock of lambs stepping trustingly, blindly into the busses that would transport them to their fate. I believed that many staff convinced themselves daily that they were acting on their own free will, in control of their life, making causative choices to excel within the rigors of the Sea Org. That's what I did whenever I was forced to ride the bus. Some of us would have days as good as sheep grazing on fresh grass in a meadow; others would face circumstances that would make going to the stockyards for slaughter seem like a retreat.

The predecessors to the big grays were old school buses painted white instead of yellow, their vinyl-covered rattletrap seats split deeper from the load of two or more bodies thrust against them, and little fans that blew air from the front instead of air conditioning. I thought of them as coffins on wheels. We only switched from the white rattletraps to Greyhounds because someone discovered that the local county prisons transported their inmates in old white school busses, just like ours. There wasn't much difference in the purpose of those buses—Int base Sea Org members were another brand of prisoner—but it didn't suit our leadership to have the Sea Org compared with a prison—it wasn't good for the church's image. So he enforced the bus purchases.

While working in the Art Department, I had helped design the multicolor swooshes that a company painted on the outside of the buses for us, as well as the new interior fabric seat coverings. Our bus design submissions had to go to COB RTC, via Marc Yager, Captain of CMO Int, and went back and forth about 20 times until the swooshes finally got approved. Add up the hours spent by the head of Scientology, head of CMO Int, and two artists designing swooshes for the sides of busses.

## Acceptable truths, cover-ups and coping

Before I could have a post (job), I had to complete the Base Orientation course. The Int base had its own language, with acronyms for every building on the 500-acre property. Each building was a hub for specialized worlds, with a unique internal power structure and group dynamic, such as RTC, INCOMM, CMO Int, ESI, CMO Gold, and Gold. Each had its own culture and attitudes. I learned that RTC considered itself of a different ilk, the most pure of any staff at the Int base, who had separate berthing, separate transportation, and many RTC staff would divorce their spouse if the spouse left RTC.

The Base Security course and Public Relations course held the most indoctrination of any of the training, because I learned what a clandestine operation the Church of Scientology International actually was. Cover-ups, or "shore stories," were a way of life at the Int base, acceptable truths that were never thought of as lies.We couldn't be honest about who we were or what we were doing. From day one, we were taught how to lie, but we were always given a good reason for telling an "acceptable truth" that justified the lie. To say the base was all Golden Era Productions would protect the senior execs from being distracted by unwanted visitors and media. I later learned that this practice of shore stories started in the late '60s when Hubbard formed the Sea Organization. He trained his ship crew to lie to port officials to protect him from being arrested by the FBI or IRS, and to prevent the ship from being identified as a Scientology ship.

We were forbidden to divulge the presence of RTC, IN-COMM, Senior Executive Strata, or any Scientology management unit to a local visitor; this was all to be described only as Golden Era Productions, the film and music arm of Scientology. If we were going into Hemet or any surrounding town, we had to remove our name tags (that identified our post and organization), and instead had to identify ourselves as working at the Golden Era Productions Audio/Visual production facility for Scientology.

## Security Breach

No family visits were allowed. If we received a phone call from an outside family member or friend, that call would never be patched to us directly. Instead, a security guard or a senior would listen in on a phone extension. Sometimes we would be interrogated about details in the conversation, or the purpose for the call. Same for mail; our letters were opened and read by security before they were passed on to us, if they were passed on. If we wrote letters, we had to put them in the mail drop in open envelopes; security would read them before they were mailed, if they were mailed.

One day, Uncle George Egglefield called. Reception put his call through to Peter, because Uncle George said he wanted to see us that afternoon, since he was right down the road playing golf at the Golden Era Golf Course! Uncle George had no idea of the totalitarian controls exercised over us. He thought it was just wonderful to be able to drive up to a golf course in the desert and drop in to see his nephew by surprise. Our leadership felt that family visits were unacceptable because they disrupted our work and caused a distraction to others around us. I never did get to see Uncle George, but Peter was allowed to see him for a short time. Uncle George's visit triggered interrogations by an ethics officer and then a security check for Peter and I: "Why did your Uncle come and see you? Why did he call here? What was the motive of exposing our location to him? What secrets have you divulged to your Uncle George? What else does he know about us?" The whole incident instilled a fear between me and family, thinking *I hope family members don't call me, it just causes trouble.*

## Uber control

Our mobility was controlled and highly restricted. If we had to go into town for any reason, we could not use busses, taxis, trains, etc. We either had to have a car and be on the OK to drive list, or arrange for someone on the base to drive us. Leaving the Int base (or our living quarters) without getting approval first was considered a treasonous offense that could result in a prison camp assignment. The Int base had a special "LRH advice" about this matter: anyone who "blew" from the base was to receive an automatic SP declare. This threat created enough of a deterrent that put fear into my bones. Security policies treated this issue like the U.S. military, where a staff member would be considered AWOL if missing without an approved departure.

Int base security and the Base Perimeter Council had to constantly be on their toes to ward off threats externally and to detect them internally. To help with this overwhelming task, they maintained an auxiliary arm of well-drilled staff members like Peter who worked under the security guards as needed for temporary emergency security. Teams would fall into position for such emergencies as someone blowing (escaping from the base). Peter had pursued several staff running down Highway 79 who had managed to jump over or get through the fences, such as Captain Marc Yager, whom he had chased on his motorcycle. Other escapees like Marcus Swanson had jumped the fences on the south side of the property and ran the miles across fields toward Hemet, to catch a bus or a taxi. And others had hidden in trunks of cars just to get off the base.

We couldn't have a phone in our room nor could we own a cell phone. We couldn't receive phone calls from family or friends on an office phone during work hours without a security guard or senior listening in and then interrogating us about the content of the call. One of my later apartment-mates, Sarah Gualtieri, once hid a cell phone in her dresser drawer because her father had a medical condition and she wanted her mother to be able to reach her in case of an emergency. Security guards discovered her phone, removed it, and disciplined Sarah for defying the rule.

Our mail went to 6331 Hollywood Boulevard in Los Angeles, where none of us lived, but was the address we were told to give to friends and family. That addressed housed the Flag Bureau, the mid-level management offices, OSA and some other specialized offices, including a posh, private office for David Miscavige. A driver made several van runs daily between that building and our desert base at 19625 Highway 79 in Gilman Hot Springs. Int base security guards read the mail before it ever made it into our hands (if the mail did get delivered to us).

I once accidentally noticed a letter from my mother lying on a desk in the communication office, postmarked about fourteen days earlier. I had gone into that office to see a staff member, when I noticed that envelope lying there. Angered by the delay in the letter getting to me, I questioned why anyone had held the letter without contacting me. An ethics officer then interrogated me about my anger and asked what my mother would be writing about that would cause me such concern.

Security policies prevented us from accessing the Internet through our work computers, nor could we own a personal computer in our room, or log on to anyone else's computer in the rare instances that we went off the base, at the threat of prison camp assignment. We could never leave the base without permission, and lived under 24/7 security watch. There was no such thing as going out to eat when we wanted to, or going shopping when we felt like it. In the rare cases when we received "liberty" days off, seniors in our chain of command first had to approve requests for "libs." At the threat of being assigned an enemy condition, we couldn't wear our name tags into town, or take any Int base policies or correspondence off the property, not even to our berthing (living quarters), nor could we talk about anything related to the Int base, in the rare cases when we were off base.

Gold's "team share card system" was a debasing tool of control that yanked privileges and offered few rewards. But efforts to train and audit the Int base staff were important enough that we constructed a "Qualifications" building with course rooms and auditing rooms, where staff would also go to receive corrections called "cramming." For a short story about Gold's team share system and staff enhancement, visit the book website.

## So Many Revolts

Around 1990, Miscavige found himself in the middle of multiple mine fields. Not long after he had taken the reigns of the organization, key staff in senior positions were bailing from the Sea Org, concurrent with Internet wars starting up with people who wanted to make the Internet the first place where Scientology could be freely discussed, while the "Free Zone" emerged with independent Scientologists wanting to practice Scientology separate from the organized Church of Scientology corporate structure.

The escapes were the most troublesome. The fact that execs were walking out of Scientology management pointed to the larger problem of Miscavige's leadership, versus there being a problem with Scientology itself. Peter and I had not been involved with the uprisings or takedowns of execs in power positions from the early to late 1980s while Miscavige was on the rise to power. Consequently, we lacked full disclosure at the time about why these people left; instead, we were given blanket statements, that they were all SPs who had committed crimes against Scientology. I didn't believe that the problem was the people who were blowing, as COB and other execs would have us believe. What seemed more real was how the tyrannical actions that were becoming commonplace under the Miscavige regime had affected these long-term staff members and their unwillingness to tolerate it. I doubted that COB anticipated this kind of revolt. I imagined that dealing with staff he couldn't control badly affected his already volatile temperament. Miscavige had to cope with the out-security issues created by each of these people who blew, since anyone who left the Int base would be holding confidential knowledge about LRH and Int base operations.

While these escapes raised red flags for me that we should find out more about what was really going on, Peter expressed the opposite. I started talking to Peter about leaving Gold and getting back into our careers again. He would say, "We are trusted loyal Sea Org officers, Karen. We're not going to be like Fernando and Terri." He'd use the Gamboa's as an example for staff who blew whom he didn't want to be like. On my book website, there's a short story about several people who blew, and how it affected Peter and me.

The front name for the Int base was Golden Era Productions to obscure the presence of the headquarters of the International Management of Scientology.

When Karen arrived in 1990, barbed wire sat atop chain link fences, since replaced by speared wrought iron. Notice the razor-barrier pointing inward to keep staff in, outward to keep out intruders.

Left: The "Qual" building above was built by slave labor of the RPF. Karen worked on the roof tiles and interiors. The Scientology "cross" was placed on the steeple to give a religious appearance to the locals, as if this is a church chapel for worship.

Left: Peter's upscale work space belies the dystopian working conditions at the Int base.

Left: The Int base. HWY 79 separates the north & south sides, and was the escape route for most blowing staff when they could get out the security gates. Lakes were used for overboarding. Staff berthing is behind locked fences, preventing staff from leaving the Int base world. BV and most base buildings were built by Sea Org slave labor.

# 18

# RADICALIZATION

*"No good worker owes his work. That's slavery."*

                          - L. Ron Hubbard, *Scientology Ethics*, p. 171

UP UNTIL 1986, I HAD ALIGNED with the Scientology party line about the Sea Org, the lofty purpose of putting ethics in on the planet so the tech of Scientology could go in, and we could achieve the aims of Scientology—a world without war, criminality, and insanity. My initial reality adjustment had come after my first post assignment at Celebrity Centre, when the reality of Sea Org life changed my views. I started seeing that Sea Org members are the foot soldiers for a utopian cause, a slave labor work force that increases the Church of Scientology International's wealth while living in impoverished conditions, complying to unthinkable demands usually without question, and oftentimes within inhumane conditions.

So members forsake personal life in fanatical dedication to Keep Scientology Working. Its members live—and some even die—to ensure that Scientology flourishes and prospers. Nothing is to stop Scientology or a Sea Org member from achieving goals. This system demands secrecy, requires unquestioning obedience to a messianic leader, loyalty to the group above all else, a devout belief in the special power of its technology, and ritualistic rites of passage. After I transferred to the Int base in 1989, I discovered more troubling facts about Sea Org operations and intentions. I found an extremist culture with its own systems of communal work, lifestyle, discipline and punishment that you will soon read.

The Int base houses Scientology's highest level extremist group, where Sea Org members become radicalized for achieving Hubbard's purposes above all else. Radicalized Sea Org members here are utilized to accomplish extremist goals—such as terrorizing IRS officials to attain tax-exempt status in the US, using vigilante tactics to ruin critics' lives such as Paulette Cooper's, keeping people in "the hole" like animals, and on.

Jon Atack's book, *Opening Minds (2016)* describes radicalization as the systematic use of thought reform to divide people from other people who they come to believe should be destroyed or hated. Radicalized people come to believe they are superior to anyone outside their group, and believe they are fully justified to commit atrocities against their perceived enemies. I compare the Sea Org to the likes of German Storm Troupers or the SS in the WW II era that I've read about or seen in movies. I again redefined Sea Org members: deadly serious Scientologists who have lost personal autonomy and critical thinking skills, and will refrain from almost nothing to Keep Scientology Working. It's Scientology's parallel to a Jihadist state of mind.

Becoming radicalized starts with the rite of passage into the Sea Org as a new recruit, where undue influence is gradually used to separate Sea Org members from their families; where a "them" and "us" culture is created by Sea Org members being isolated from general society; and where Sea Org members learn from their leaders to hate a long list of enemies that can include family members who criticize Scientology. A step in this radicalization is making the Sea Org member "agree" to some radical living conditions before they even arrive at the Int base, such as not being allowed to get pregnant, not having your children live with you at the Int base, or not getting married at all, since these functions were viewed as distractions to production.

There are about twenty more pages in this chapter that go into great detail about how Sea Org members become radicalized. For the unabridged chapter, please visit this chapter in my book website.

Since the late 1960s and '70s, Sea Org overseers have headed up Scientology's command centers around the globe in continental offices called Sea Org bases, in a hierarchical bureaucracy of powers: East U.S., West U.S., Canada, Latam (Latin America), ANZO (Australia, New Zealand, Oceania), EU (Europe), AF (Africa).

The Scientology world was organized into sectors of specialization, each commanded by a senior Sea Org Watchdog Committee member, headquartered at the International Management base, where the buck stops for each sector: WDC CC for the Celebrity Centre International sector; WDC Scientology for the public Scientology organizations; WDC SO for the Advanced Sea Org orgs; WDC Flag for the Flag Land base in Clearwater; WDC WISE for the business sector of World Institute of Scientology Enterprises; WDC ABLE (Association for Better Living and Education) for the social reform programs of Narconon, Applied Scholastics, Criminon, and Way to Happiness; WDC Pubs for LRH's self-publishing machines of Bridge and New Era Publications; WDC OSA for the Office of Special Affairs International sector. Some of these sectors have since been changed, to now include a WDC for Ideal Orgs, and others.

Sea Org members are there to ensure that Scientology training and auditing is available to the area's general population. They must also defend Scientology's presence in their sector against critics and outsiders. Being "under attack" continues to fortify the group's belief that SPs are trying to tear Scientology down. War is everything and everything is war. Having a battle to fight strengthens the group's will to preserve itself, and fuels the practice that it will stop at next to nothing to defend the organization. This is the mindset behind the mantra, "Keeping Scientology Working" (KSW), and keeps Scientology involved in an ongoing war. If there was no friction, there would be no battle games or anything to fight for. If there were no enemies, there would be no game, no one to call an SP or be victimized by. "No game" would make Scientologists rebels without a cause.

I believe that people, including Peter and me, who join the Sea Org initially do so because we want to help other people and we want to support a challenging task. We believed we could help change the world through the Aims of Scientology, to make this a world without war, criminality and insanity. The Sea Org offers a game bigger than our selves, a cause to stand for. But the lifestyle of the Sea Org radically transforms those lofty goals through radicalization. You really do have to pump people up pretty hard to get them to do what Sea Org members are expected to do, within the conditions we had to do it. With Hubbard's lofty tributes paid (in words, not dollars) to Sea Org members who relinquish their personal lives to dedicate themselves 24/7 to Scientology, you have the makings of a group of individuals who draw strength from delusions of honor and sometimes grandeur instilled in them as the aristocrats, the elite of Scientology.

Sea Org members are not garden-variety Scientologists like the celebrities and other paying customers who live in private homes, have outside jobs and come and go as they please. We often criticized public Scientologists who wouldn't join the Sea Org, calling them "middle class PTS." This derogatory label demeans others for placing a higher value on income, wealth, and owning material things like classy cars and fancy homes, than on helping to clear the planet. Ironically, it's the middle-class PTS's who make the money in the wog world to pay for Scientology services and fill the church coffers with wealth.

Sea Org members forsake privacy and live in communal quarters. In Los Angeles, these quarters have been old hotel buildings like the Wilcox, in squalor conditions, in desperate need of repairs and modernization. Reportedly, some of the Sea Org housing has been upgraded in recent years, because the squalor conditions were causing public relations issues. At the International Management base headquarters, Sea Org couples lived with another couple rather than having an apartment to themselves, in an off-base apartment complex. This was prior to the "berthing buildings" constructed to keep all staff living behind fences and security guards. At lower levels of the church hierarchy, such as at the Celebrity Centre International or the Flag Land Base, Sea Org couples have their own tiny room with a bed and a bathroom, while unmarried SO members are typically packed like sardines into rooms with bunk beds.

We were reminded daily that we operated at a higher level of purpose and discipline than non-Sea Org Scientology staff who manned the lower level organizations internationally, and certainly at a higher level than the public Scientologist. We were an elite corps who could accomplish anything. Our business? Missions. Our prize? A sane planet. Thus, after signing a billion-year contract, I (and later, Peter) felt like we *owed* our work to Hubbard and to the Sea Org. By that point, we had taken on the Scientology slave mindset, as described in Hubbard's *Scientology Ethics* book: "No good worker owes his work. That's slavery.

Sea Org members pride themselves on their Sea Org attitude—make it go right, do it right the first time, be total cause over any situation (which meant being OT), quickly do whatever it takes to accomplish an assignment, getting ethics in on the planet so the planet could be cleared. All this was done with nearly no pay but a meager allowance, a bed in a room, three meals a day, and some basic uniforms. And, access to the bridge to total freedom.

Members get tougher from the internal change that occurs in the process of Sea Org life. It's not for the faint-hearted. As if a necessity to achieve Scientology's goals at any cost, Sea Org life also includes the pain and humiliation of discipline, often unjustly assigned to hard labor, sleep deprivation, or like I had seen happen to friends, being sent to the bilges of the ship for days, being thrown overboard because of a transgression, subject to public humiliation, or assignment to next to impossible tasks with inadequate time, supplies or terms in which the task had to be completed, or else.

Sea Org life had many faces, from apparent good will actions (that always had the motive to recruit people into Scientology or forward one of its causes), to dark connections and escapades. Sea Org members are expected to do any task assigned, and do it right the first time, or get sent to the Rehabilitation Project Force (RPF), aka prison camp.

How much I liked being in the Sea Org on any given day depended on how I looked at it. I sometimes felt satisfaction when working well in a team, or doing a task right the first time. Sometimes I felt pride after preventing a flap or overcoming insurmountable obstacles and Hill 10s to accomplish a goal. Sometimes after hours of focused training for a specialist assignment, or rigorous missions, and long hours, I felt I could accomplish anything, which made me feel OT. Other times, I felt that I was being used to accomplish ridiculous or useless projects while being told to "make it go right" because a senior ordered it to be done without first making provisions for the tools or money needed.

## Sea Org Indoctrination

The collective reality of being OT immortal spirits sets Sea Org members apart from Scientologists, and sets Scientologists apart from outsiders. We worked as a disciplined body of people who would undergo constant training and indoctrination in order to cooperate with one another and achieve the impossible. I liked setting high goals and striving to achieve the most insurmountable tasks, until I had to do so while often times putting my personal safety or health at risk, that the Sea Org did not try to protect for me.

I had been naive or gullible enough to not even consider that Sea Org training materials on the EPF had been purposely drafted with a hegemonic message to deceive Sea Org recruits. In my basic Sea Org training, of course no one disclosed Hubbard's alleged crimes for which the FBI, IRS or other agencies sought to bring him to justice. I wouldn't learn any of that until after 1998 when I was finally able to access the Internet and collect research unavailable in my early days. The best source of information on the outside was Jon Atack's book, *A Piece of Blue Sky* (Lyle Stuart, 1990). Atack offers the best history of the Sea Org that I have read to date, even better than more recent journalistic accounts that they draw from Atack's work.

A Sea Org recruit like me, who hadn't accessed facts through relevant background information or books like Atack's, had no chance of learning about Hubbard's motives or reasoning for his sea-bound operations, alleged crimes, unwanted governmental attention, or why he fled to international waters outside the reach of legal authorities.

In the early days, becoming indoctrinated as a Sea Org member led me to embrace the writings of L. Ron Hubbard, Commodore, without question. To depart from LRH's thinking and intention is to be treasonous to him and to the Sea Org. This is similar to any military operation where leaders issue orders and troops are expected to follow them explicitly. But an order should be questioned if it's destructive. There is one provision in the Sea Org called "Orders, Query of," but I have exercised that policy only to get in trouble for questioning a senior executive.

Every Sea Org member and Scientologist reads "Keeping Scientology Working" at the beginning of every course. The ideas within KSW are the pillars that shape Scientology's groupthink. These ideas break down old beliefs and encourage a systematic indoctrination to Hubbard's beliefs. Scientologists unassumedly learn how to live and function under totalitarianism, and succumb to top-down orders and dictates, all necessary routines to make the system work and get the job done without deviance from command intention. Individual conscience is replaced with obedience to a leader.

Maintaining a tough, Sea Org persona includes no time for niceties like conciliation or forgiveness when someone makes a mistake. Patience, kindness, and compassion don't fit well within the deadly serious job of getting ethics in on the planet, which requires a ruthless, pitiless approach by anyone who holds a Sea Org post. Legalism, judgmentalism and condemnation more commonly grease the wheels throughout Scientology's hierarchies than kindness, patience, diplomacy, or love (none of which are in Scientology's nomenclature). The words "fuck" as an exclamation and "fucking" as an adjective were two of the more common words in my and most Sea Org members' vocabulary.

Before and during my early Scientology days, I wasn't aware of cults and didn't believe that thought control existed within this organization, much less in America. Hubbard talks about it throughout his books, policy letters, and taped lectures, how thought control has been used by psychiatry and communism, and how it exists in North Korea, China and Russia. By pointing to its existence elsewhere, he deflected the fact that it existed right under my nose. Again the question, *isn't that brainwashing?* Again the answer, *Well, that's Scientology.*

Some cults like Scientology are tolerated in society simply because of prominent members, like Scientology's celebrities, while the group's harmful acts are ignored. Other cults demonstrate a variety of extremist acts. For example, after Scientology I learned that 909 followers of Jim Jones' Peoples Temple group willingly ingested cyanide in a mass suicide in Guyana. I hadn't known that Jones and Hubbard had each instilled fear in their followers through a theme of imminent nuclear devastation of Earth. They incited members to turn to People's Temple or Scientology (respectively) as the only means of survival. Similarly, Heaven's Gate leader Marshall Applewhite convinced 38 followers to drink the poison Kool-Aid in a mass suicide so their souls could board a UFO craft to reach a level of existence above human; planet Earth was about to be recycled and the only chance to survive was to leave it immediately. I finally made the connection between Applewhite's sci-fi beliefs and Scientology's apocalyptic approach to life much less its belief in Xenu, the galactic ruler. Xenu exiled millions of souls off his planet, body thetans that attached themselves to all of us on Earth. Thus, if we want to live freely again, Hubbard says we all need Scientology to purge those body thetans from ourselves. Otherwise, these "BT's" are trapped in us, driving us to destroy humankind. Scientology presents itself as the planet's only solution to gain spiritual freedom and salvage humankind, and the Sea Org's job is to make sure that happens.

Sea Org members are sometimes compared to religious orders such as Buddhist monks, or Catholic nuns and priests. There is little honest comparison. Monks, nuns and priests forsake the material world, take vows of holiness, and dedicate their lives to serve God or the ways of their beliefs for non-material satisfaction. In contrast, Sea Org members are part of a well-organized international machine, many who work for individual Church of Scientology corporations whose sole purpose is to "sell and deliver materials and service to the public, and to get in public to sell and deliver to" (Hubbard, "Reason for Orgs"). They sell courses, auditing services, books, tapes, CDs, DVDs, e-meters and other items sold at fixed retail prices through Scientology outlets around the globe. When I left Scientology in 1998, the church was making about $7 million per week internationally. This came mainly from the sale of Scientology courses, auditing, and materials, thanks to the efforts of Sea Org members, especially the registrars trained in "hard sell," and to the Flag Banking Officers (FBOs) at every Scientology organization. It's the FBO's job to get the orgs to make money, and make more money. Gross income was a key statistic, along with dollar amounts sent to International Finance Reserves.

Although Sea Org members are involved in corporately owned, well-crafted retail organizations, we defiantly called it our religion and did anything to protect that label. The church's weekly income was separate from money collected by the IAS for donations to its war chest. Monies flowed into the coffers of the Sea Org at the International Finance Office, used to buy or develop real estate to expand Scientology, or to invest in other commodities like gold to multiply church fortunes. Some of it was spent to defend legal battles and to market Scientology across the planet.

We were posted to defend every element of the Scientology empire, while receiving no pay but an allowance of about $45 per week. In my day, they even took out taxes out of my weekly allowance. After I got out of the Sea Org, I received statements from the Social Security Office that provided me an accounting of how much I would receive from Social Security when I retired. For the twelve years of my adult life that I was in the Sea Org, zero showed up as my contributions, so while I worked 16 hours per day 6 1/2 days per week, nothing was contributed for my retirement.

In the real world, Scientology celebrities are treated as the elite of Scientology, not Sea Org members, with the exception of its highest leader, David Miscavige, and his personal inner circle. In 2004, Miscavige named Tom Cruise "the most dedicated Scientologist I know," at the infamous IAS event where Cruise salutes Miscavige after receiving the Freedom Medal of Valour. Miscavige couldn't have delivered a bigger slap in the face to thousands of Sea Org members who lived and died over the statistics of their post, who knew no other pleasures in life, austere as Sea Org life was. A public Scientologist, Cruise is lavished with favors delivered on the backs of Sea Org members, and gifted with freebies paid for by church funds. Miscavige's faux pas—or was it intentional?—would surely cause irreversible damage to the hearts and egos of his dedicated ranks of Sea Org crew. That story played out over the next few years when the church saw its largest ever exodus of Sea Org members from the International headquarters.

All that being said, working at the International Management base of the Church of Scientology International with the most seasoned Sea Org members in the Scientology world, showed me a different brand of Scientology and the Sea Org.

# 19

## HUBBARD'S MOVIE COMPANY

### Golden Era Productions, 1989

"LIGHTS, CAMERA, ACTION!" can be a fun and exciting experience on the set of a well-run Hollywood studio, but Hubbard's film crew, known as the Cine Division, did things Hubbard's way. Cine (pronounced sin-ee) was L. Ron Hubbard's version of a movie company, complete with a research department and location scout, art department for sets, props and costume designs, cinematographers, talent scout, lighting gaffers, sound technicians, cameramen, sets, props, costume shop, special effects, and editing. Not that many of the staff had professional skills in any of these fields. The Sea Org mindset was to study your "hat," then "read it, drill it, do it." Presto-chango, here we have a set designer, a cameraman, props specialists, gaffers, film editors and on.

Mark Fisher, Corporate Liaison In-Charge RTC, who had assisted David Miscavige for years, seemed to be master-minding the placement of new recruits that arrived at Gold during this huge man-up campaign to build Golden Era Productions into a massive dissemination organization that would pump out training films, tapes and CDs of LRH lectures, E-meters, and other products to sell at retail prices to Scientology customers. Mark told me he planned to post me in the Cine Division.

Ironically, Peter and I had landed in the two divisions of Gold that had produced the very films and film scores that we had critiqued at Valley Org and CC for being as sophisticated as a middle-school play, and had been embarrassed to watch them with seriousness. The costumes, sets and props were amateurish, at best, and the crew acted in the films. Yet Scientology management had been sending these films out to orgs to use during Scientology training courses, and made the orgs pay about $3,000 for prints to show in their course rooms. This new Cine Division was being set up to re-shoot all the films that had been shot in the early days, plus shoot all the rest of the LRH scripts that had not yet been produced. Now Peter would be responsible for creating a beautiful music score for each film, and I would contribute a creative hand in what these films would look like.

Instead of using my professional art skills, I was posted as the Research & Assembly In-Charge, to create a replacement for Olga Ferris. Olga was a veteran Sea Org member who had worked with LRH at LaQuinta, with tons of stories in her pockets about the boss. She was also an aspiring writer, and with me to replace her, she would finally move onto her dream post of Scriptwriter to finish the rest of the LRH film scripts he had outlined. See the book website for an interesting short story of the history of LRH's film crew from the 1970s at LaQuinta.

**Fast Forward**

After W facilities moved to the newer Golden Era Productions location at Gilman Hot Springs, at first called the Summer Headquarters or "S," they moved into buildings on the new property that had earlier been a spa resort. The Lower and Upper Lodges were newly renovated to hold the Cine offices near the "Gym," that housed the studio with specially designed sets, the costume shop, make-up rooms, and props loft. This new Cine division, which was now receiving newly recruited personnel, had earlier been filled with some of LRH's original shoot crew, but otherwise manned up by Int base staff who had been removed from higher level posts to do various jobs in the film crew. The downward movement in the hierarchy of power at the Int base was a bust in ego and social status. One day, someone was a WDC commander in CMO INT; next day she was a make-up artist, or a seamstress in the costume shop.

Marcus Swanson, an LRH look-alike, headed up the Cine Division until he was demoted to cameraman. Marcus had Hubbard's red hair, large body type, same hands, and even duplicated Hubbard's handwriting. He used to pose as LRH in many of the films. One night, Marcus climbed the barbed wire fence at the south edge of the property, which must have ripped up his clothes and legs. Climbing over that fence set off a fence shaker, triggering an alarm in the main Security booth. This triggered Security's "blow drill." Marcus ran from the south fence across miles of field into the nearest town of Hemet. I don't know that he was ever apprehended. He left behind his wife, Janadair Swanson, a long-term Commodore's Messenger.

I learned that Cine held some of David Miscavige's biggest adversaries on the base, particularly our film editor, Gary Weise. Gary was a 30+ year Sea Org vet. Daily life in the Cine Division seemed to highlight some screw-up of Gary's that was loudly broadcast by DM. Miscavige would rant and rage at Saturday night base briefings about Gary Weise being an SP, always screwing up the video edits or the film edits, but I never saw DM remove him from post. I realized that public criticism of Gary Weise had become part of DM's personal vendetta for Gary, whom he called "Voldemort" and even wrote an issue called "Definition of Incorrigible--Gary Weise." I had seen Gary bully other Cine staff, but stopped thinking much of it because that seemed to be normalized as part of the Cine culture, and the Int base culture as a whole.

A basic problem with Cine was that management treated it like a band of communists. Everyone in Cine was responsible for the overall production of the Cine Division. This was management's bright idea for how to make Cine crew work as a team instead of as disjointed individuals. If the Shoot Crew screwed up on their shots, or if the Editor, Gary Weise, messed up the edits of the film, the whole division was often held culpable. If the guys in the Props loft flunked their white-glove cleaning inspection, all of Cine crew would be made to stay after post (after 11pm) to white-glove the Props loft.

Not surprisingly, the Cine division had a tarnished reputation as being unable to produce quality films. With the majority of crew being inexperienced with busted egos, expected to do highly technical or specialized work, I wonder why? The general tone in Cine was, at best, resentment, and usually some form of hostility wheth-

whether overt or covert. Crew members were often disgusted, or at best disgruntled, when fellow crew members did not function well on their jobs. Yet Cine crew were mostly people with no prior experience in film production, and expectations were unreasonably high. The individual crew were supposed to get past all that, just learn their jobs, work as a team, and do it with no counter-intention or case on post.

My first role within the Cine research department lacked excitement, but there were plenty of sparks and drama from run-ins with some of my adversaries such as Jason Bennick and Karsten Matheis, who both behaved as if they had been trained by Gestapo during WW II. This short story is on the book website if you'd like to know more.

## "We Stand Tall"

The Gold musicians had been working on a new song and music for a promotional video, "We Stand Tall" in 1990, to be used at one of the big, upcoming management events. Many people at the Int base had a hand in the video, starting with Rick Cruzen and Peter on the music and arrangement, while Scientologist David Pomeranz worked on the lyrics and recorded vocals at Gold.

COB told me to come to the music studio when the Int base execs practiced singing the song, to tell everyone what to wear for the video shoot. All of RTC, CMO Int and ESI execs filled the studio, lined in rows starting with the top execs in the front, and descending in hierarchy in rows behind them. I will never forget COB telling someone in Cine to go get an apple box that he could stand on, as he added, "Because I'm kind of short."

I advised everyone to wear business casual clothes, such as a nice blouse or shirt but no tie, maybe sweaters, preferably solids or subtle prints or stripes, nothing bold, so their clothing would not distract from the expressions on their faces and the lyrics of the song. On the day of the photo shoot, the execs lined up in their rows. David Miscavige walked in wearing a Hermes shirt with a large gold metallic circle on the front, like a big bull's eye. He stepped up on his apple box as a purposeful target for everyone's attention, while everyone surrounding and behind him wore solid color clothing. The execs watched Peter at the front of the room directing their singing. Cine crew shot the video, the Audio Division mixed it, and the Manufacturing Division produced video and CD copies.

The video was a big success at the event. The lyrics to the song seemed like a rallying cry, a collective voice proclaiming a purpose that was to lie at the heart of every Scientologist. David Pomerantz sang out: "Joining together we held our ground, and lifted our voices one mighty sound, and struck down the walls of darkness, we stood tall. We decided to take a stand, and defend the rights of man…" Gold sold thousands of copies.

## Secretive LRH Photos, Annie Tidman Broeker, and more

For a short story about the confidential photo processing performed by Hubbard's Film & Equipment Unit and Annie Broeker's role in photoshopping LRH photos, visit the book website.

## DM's Sexual Harassment of Geray Jory

David Miscavige managed to get away with sexual harassment under the guise of "putting in ethics." Geray Jory, a lifetime Scientologist from South Africa, became the object of an attack. Miscavige once ordered all the Cine crew (about 50 people) into the conference room. He ordered Geray to climb up on the conference room table where everyone was to look at her. Geray had beautiful, long red hair, hazel eyes, a creamy complexion and an hour-glass figure, and was the former wife of RTC executive Marty Rathbun. DM proceeded to tell the Cine crew how he had seen her walking around the base "protruding her boobs out" and trying to entice men. He dwelled on Geray having evil motives by sticking out her breasts to purposely distract men from what they were doing. After he had enough of humiliating Geray, he said somebody had better "put Geray's ethics in" instead of letting her dramatize her evil purposes.

I watched Geray's face turn beet red while she stood there and absorbed the criticism, with all eyes upon her. I wanted to grab her hand to help her get down from the table. Had I done that, I would have crossed COB and Cine crew who followed him unquestioningly. Instead, I along with the rest of the Cine crew, just listened to him shame and belittle her. I felt humiliated about being part of a group who would treat another human being like this. A particularly disturbing aspect of this sexual harassment session was that everyone probably assumed that what was being said about Geray was "true" because it was coming from the mouth of COB.

In the outside world, where a victim of sexual harassment could have sought legal advice, this would have become a lawsuit. Under the guise of "religious discipline" Miscavige got away with this. Geray was sent to the RPF shortly after this incident.

Geray's story underscores the way of life in Cine and across many areas of the Int base. COB's tactics seemed to successfully convince the crew that their only hope for staying in his favor is submission to his ways. This way of life groomed us as Sea Org members to carry shame about screwing up and over-working COB. In my eyes, he was stealing my and others' pride, confidence, and sense of self-worth. In this environment, I was beginning to heavily criticize myself for making even the smallest errors, and then when one of my team members would write a KR on me or confront me about an error I had made, a contempt for my own flaws began to grow.

Contrary to what I had studied in LRH policies, I had never seen written evidence of Hubbard dealing in the currency of shame, belittling, intimidation and humiliation, yet these seemed to be routine practices here. Nowhere in Scientology policies are execs told to exploit staff to make them feel unworthy, bad, and just not good enough. I would come to learn that the real world of these seasoned Sea Org members who had worked directly with LRH was a parallel universe to what was written in Hubbard's green-on-white policies and red-on-white technical bulletins.

## Way of Life in Cine

Sleeping in one's bed every night had never been seen as a basic necessity, or a right, but as a luxury. Sleep deprivation had become been a way of life, and made me and the rest of Cine crew crazy. We'd be kept up for several days to complete projects that COB demanded to be done. Or, we'd do amends to make up for being utterly dysfunctional people. During our sleep time throughout the night, we would clean and "white glove" offices and film studios; we'd lay sod to improve the grounds; we'd renovate some room or some building to improve the facilities; we'd reorganize or clean the film sets and props lofts. Whenever I was allowed to get regular sleep, I felt so thankful toward the leadership for affording basic pleasures.

Memories about the Sea Org's fanatical cleaning techniques like "white gloving" stir up another firestorm, only because this activity was the cause of so many nights of sleep deprivation. A jovial Sea Org vet named Paco Suarez was the specialist on the base for "cleaning technology." We had to forget about cleaning the way we had always cleaned our homes, if it was not the identical technique used there. One must vacuum first with a water-based vacuum cleaner, then dust. To dust, one must take a clean rag and swipe a surface or two, then walk out the door and shake out all the dust. Then come back in and swipe some more, go out and shake the rag out; come back and continue. Depending on the size of your room, this may take 50 trips out the door to shake the rag.

Paco had worked with LRH, and was presently holding a full-time post as the "LRH Cleaner" for all LRH spaces. Every day he would go in and white-glove each LRH office (that was never used) to ensure that not one speck of dust or dirt could be found anywhere on anything. In this Int base culture, the presence of dust or dirt immediately indicated "out-ethics" of the person who was responsible for that space. Senior execs would often send Paco down to check individual Cine offices for dirt. On Saturday nights, after cleaning our spaces and before we could go home, Paco had to come through Cine with his white glove to check for dust. Anytime one of us flunked, this would hold up the entirety of Cine crew from going home to sleep. Many times, dozens of people would pile into an office to clean and white-glove it until Paco passed it, just so we could go home.

## Costume Design for Films

Someone eventually realized that in my pre-Sea Org career I had been a clothing designer, and reassigned me to be the Costume Designer and Storyboard Artist in the Art Department. I assisted Mitch Brisker, a CC celebrity who directed our films, and Jennifer de Mers Cook, the Art Director, and Tim Larsen, the Set Designer, with storyboards to work out shots, and help with renderings of set designs. Other opportunities opened up to use my artistic abilities. I worked for the Int Landlord Office design team on Saturdays, drawing and rendering interior designs for Scientology properties, and for the Central Marketing Unit, helping with all-hands design layouts for promotional materials.

Working as the Cine Costume Designer put me back in my area of passion. I was also able to reconnect with many of the actors who were enlisted from Celebrity Centre to play a role in one of the Scientology films we were shooting, such as Jason Beghe and Larry Anderson. Since many of Hubbard's film scripts centered on the early development of Dianetics and Scientology in the 1950s, I researched period costume suppliers and even thrift shops that specialized in 1950s attire in the LA area. This gave me occasional chances to get off the base or design outfits for our costume shop to produce—at least a little bit of fun.

Since Cine worked nearly found the clock to produce films, it was next to impossible to get a libs day, much less a leave of absence to see family. For a short story about an unforgettable leave of absence, read it on the book website.

## Cine Crew Becomes Slave Labor Force

DM micromanaged the work of Gold crew, down to watching the daily rushes of Cine's film shoots, and even sat in the editing bay to tell Gary Weise how to edit the shots. In his early Sea Org days as a teen, David Miscavige had worked in Hubbard's film crew, so Miscavige considered himself the *expert* on filmmaking. I noted that the Cine crew were re-making all earlier films produced by Hubbard's team because they were unprofessional quality, an embarrassment to watch. Nevertheless, Cine crew were subject to Miscavige's criticisms about how bad we were at our jobs, subject to his verbal abuses and harsh discipline through deprivation of sleep.

One day, Miscavige abruptly took all Cine crew off posts. He levied this punishment because he was tired of Cine not shooting good films, and not earning our keep. Berated in front of the entire Int base staff for not being able to ever do anything right, our Cine crew of fifty was assigned to full-time physical labor to rebuild the entire mess hall. This would not be the first time that Miscavige hijacked groups of staff to use as a resource pool to complete some of his pet or urgent projects. This particular nightmare included night after night of no sleep after physical labor all day, while we were treated like scum by the rest of the Int base staff. Miscavige craftily diminished our reputation to justify his use of Cine crew as slave labor.

One night, I came down with flu symptoms including fever, chills, body ache, not to mention exhaustion. Being weak with fever made it nearly impossible to do physical labor. That night about 9:00 p.m., I walked myself to the isolation room on the north side of the property at the Old Gilman House. OGH held a few bedrooms on the ground floor where staff were required to go when sick. Laying in one of the rickety wooden bunk beds in the women's dorm felt like a place of refuge and luxury at that moment. I had fever chills and terrible body ache, and could barely turn my body over, but at least fell asleep. No Medical Officer was around to help.

Around 11:00pm, a security guard came into ISO and ordered me to get back to work. I told him I had a fever and could barely stand up. He couldn't care less. CO CMO INT, then Bitty Miscavige, had been told that I abandoned my task in the mess hall, and that I better knock off my counter-intention to COB. She was pissed that I had "abandoned my team." The guard stood outside my room until I got up and moved.

On the way from OGH down to the south side toward MCI, I took the back road behind one of the audio buildings where I knew Peter usually parked our car. I headed there to find our car as a place of refuge, in hopes of stealing a few moments of privacy to rest inside. I wanted to feel like I belonged to the real world by connecting with something I owned, versus only being part of the Int base madness. I found our car, slipped into the passenger's seat, and closed my eyes.

Within moments, another security guard patrolling the grounds blazed a flashlight beam into my car, blinding my eyes, and asked me what I was doing. I lied and told him I was looking for a flashlight so I could walk back to MCI. He told me to find it quickly and get back to work. I dutifully said "Yes, sir," so he would walk away and go find someone else to harass. My vision started to crackle, and spots swirled before my eyes like shooting stars in the blackness of the night. Either I was starting to crack up, or my fever had escalated. I felt my consciousness slipping. I blacked out. I came to with my head leaning on the dashboard. It took a few seconds to orient myself. Where in hell was I? Okay, on the north side of the property. This is my car. I had no choice but to carry on and act like everything was fine. I found a flashlight in my glove box and rejoined the workers. I shouldn't have expected or even hoped that anyone would ask me if I was feeling any better. Instead, I was berated for abandoning my group.

After two months or so, we completed most of the renovations of MCI. The Int base staff were able to move out of the temporary dining hall tents, and into a beautiful new mess hall. Cine crew returned to our posts.

The Cine division was put on a revised schedule and not allowed to have any study time until we finished a film. Ted Horner, a Cine supervisor, issued this order from CMO Gold. His order violated LRH policy, scripture in my Sea Org member eyes, that guaranteed all staff daily study time. This privilege was sacred to me and a significant reason why I joined the Sea Org. With that basic right granted by Hubbard but taken away by leadership, I disagreed. I had been told that there was an LRH Advice for the Int base that said Cine crew might benefit from going to study in between films. Int base execs used LRH Advices as if they were senior to published LRH policy. I refused to ignore the injustice. I exercised what I felt was my right, and wrote a knowledge report about Horner's off-policy order. I sent the report by Merc (Mercury, our intranet) to the ethics division.

The consequence of that report unfolds a new chapter in my Sea Org career.

# 20

## ON THE EDGE

**Int base, 1990**

MY SELF-DEFENSE USING LRH policy to report an off-policy action backfired. I thought Ted Horner had arbitrarily decided that we would only study after we finished a film. I later learned this was Miscavige's ruling that came out in Ted Horner's name, and even later learned that Tom Cruise gave Miscavige this idea.

My report went viral. The anger of the gods descended on Cine and me when at least four four-striped captains raged on motorcycles down to my office. A swarm of RTC investigators filled the rooms, slamming clipboards on desks, questioning staff about why the Cine Division fostered unethical and unproductive behavior in general. My senior, Jennifer the Art Director, was questioned for being blind to my criminal acts and not "putting in my ethics" that would have prevented me from writing this KR. Jennifer didn't tell anyone that just an hour before that, she had proofread the report I wrote on our office computer and encouraged me to send it. She felt I was applying KSW. I was so terrified by the amount of force applied by execs that I flipped into this theetie-weetie "I'm innocent" mode, hoping I would not be drawn and quartered.

A few hours later, they summoned an emergency muster of all Gold crew, about 400 staff. We fell into formation of at least 20 rows of 20 staff, dutifully standing at military attention, feet to-gether, arms hanging rigid down our sides, heads facing forward. Flanked by Miscavige's army of RTC supporters, COB wielded his verbal sledgehammer that had the power to electrify us as his audience. Profanities spewed from his mouth like I had never before heard, even from my Dad who had talked soldier trash after the war. DM's chest swelled while his reddened face quivered with rage, as though he was facing an assault of counter-intention from the 400 of us. Meanwhile, we stood motionless, like rows of chess pieces, waiting to be knocked over.

Miscavige seemed to be blowing off years of pent-up rage and frustration that felt more like contempt. *You NEVER do anything right the first time! You can't shoot films! Your hats are all over my plate! You DON'T support command intention and you cause nothing but PROBLEMS on my lines! Worthless idiots*, in other words. I wondered how other Cine or Gold staff felt about dedicating their lives to the Sea Org where nothing was ever done well enough for COB. That we cut ourselves off from the outside world, and stayed up without sleep for nights on end to try to make Miscavige happy, just wasn't enough to compensate for our flawed nature and general failure. I wondered how long many of us would stand there and absorb the verbal abuse and generalities, as if we truly deserved them. I wondered why I had the nerve to take up oxygen that could have been better used by David Miscavige.

COB ranted his nullifications until he seemed to reach a moment of gratification, when so many of us must have appeared to be transforming into objects of his desire: some of us stood stiff as stone; some looked numb and vacant; others looked crumpled in spirit, heads hung in shame. Some of us looked wide-eyed electrified. I was one of those. What would happen next? A hush fell over the group as Miscavige's rant stopped, and he stormed away, shadowed by half his entourage.

Indignant do-gooders from other divisions who were not being singled out used the moment to tongue-lash those of us who had been named, as if hoping to gain favor in the eyes of the RTC army for supporting command intention. I wondered if they felt obliged to act the part of brown nosing, sucking up generally, or was it just impossible for them to avoid joining in on the vindictive frenzy of the moment, propelled by the power of COB's voice that seemed capable of pulverizing our very essence of being.

I thought, *Wow, Miscavige dramatizes a lot of case on post. This man can't seem to control his emotions. Does he get away with this kind of dramatization a lot?* ("Case on post" is a bad thing—it's letting your mental mis-emotion spill out on other people while you're working.) I would later learn that whenever Miscavige got angry, everybody jumped, went into a frenzy, or ran around like chickens without heads to try to resolve the problem so David Miscavige wasn't affected by other people's screw-ups. I would also learn that DM's entourage of communicators and guards would tolerate any emotion he dramatized. Most staff treated him like the sole guardian of righteousness; it was everyone else who had not yet achieved his godlike perfection.

## Domination by nullification

To the truly low-toned person, emergencies are more important that constructive planning. We were constantly faced with "drop what you are doing" on our post to go and handle some situation that Miscavige said was more important. For the nullifier, compliance is commanded and lack of compliance draws punishment or destruction. In a culture ruled by this type of leader, we see indigence in the population to make it easier to control, with most of the constructive people removed. Hmmm. That probably explains why so many great people had been busted off higher posts and thrown into the dredges. Domination by nullification fit David Miscavige like the right size glove. For more information about "domination by nullification", what it looks like and how it gets used to control people, read the short story on the book website.

* * *

Security guards dutifully moved to their targets for handlings. I was led to the nearby Building 36 for interrogation in the Master at Arms' office. How could I engage in such counter-thoughts to command intention by writing that knowledge report? I groveled for an hour before Kevin Caetano, the Security Chief, and proclaimed that I had seen the light to my out-ethics. I accepted the treason assignment, and agreed to work my way back up into good standing with the crew. Surprisingly, he allowed me to go home that night instead of keeping me behind the locked fences for the night, as I had often seen happen to other staff.

The experience pushed me to the edge. While Peter drove us home that night in heavy rain, I was outraged at the injustice that had played out. I began crying hysterically about the impossible circumstances we lived within. I persuaded Peter to go for a short drive so we could talk. Had we gone to our room first and then tried to leave the premises, we wouldn't have gotten back out of the gates without questioning. We drove out to the Hemet airport, where we could watch the runway lights. We gazed blankly at flashing signals while I poured out my heart through a torrent of tears. Desperate to recover our lives and sanity, I pleaded with Peter to leave the Int base with me, and to leave the Sea Org. He disagreed that we should try to recapture our pre-Sea Org lives or start all over. He pulled that same line on me as he had before—"We are trusted officers of the Sea Org." We argued, and without resolving the festering trauma, drove home.

I laid awake for hours, wishing I had never left my private life, feeling I no longer belonged to my dreams. I always believed that when you lose hope in life, you lose your future. Coming to the Int base had been a crazy, irreversible mistake. I had only transitioned from freedom to psychological slavery and spiritual abuse and our marriage seemed to be slipping through our fingers. I was driving myself crazy, vacillating between hyperventilating and feeling suffocated. I couldn't keep living like this; this wasn't living. This was madness. My heart pounded through the night, syncopating with imagined scenes of escaping. Escaping would become a matter of courage and survival, not cowardice.

# 21

## BETRAYAL

### First escape, 1990

BEFORE DAWN, WITHOUT WAKING PETER, I tossed a few clothes
and toiletries into some white plastic garbage bags with yellow
drawstrings and crept quietly out the front door with my dog,
Toby, under my arm. Escaping in the middle of the night had less
of a chance that anyone would see me. I took a deep breath, as I
drove through the parking lot toward the gate. Since Peter had
been on the "OK to drive list," we had a remote control for the
gate in the car. Guards were on watch 24/7 at our apartment complex, but they must have fallen asleep or stopped paying attention
while changing shifts. No one stopped me!

The ease of driving through those gates belied the entrapment
that had been my state of mind. With no escape plan, I drove into
Hemet and then took back roads toward one of my favorite places,
San Diego. I called Mom and told her that I had just left Gold,
without Peter. She immediately offered to fly from Atlanta to help
me. The next day, we got through our tears of seeing each other,
and rehashed how Peter and I did not agree on the insane conditions of the base, or why I wanted to recover our life outside the
Sea Org.

We set out on our drive to Atlanta together. Outside of Gallup,
New Mexico, I broke down and called Peter, because being apart

was like separating two layers of skin. The next morning, Peter arrived with two khaki uniformed security guards and Ken Hoden, the Gold public relations port captain.Instead of feeling happy to see him, I felt betrayed. There would be no private time with Peter to talk, because Hoden wouldn't leave us alone. Scientology's extremist demands and intervention into our life just didn't quit, even while I was outside of the base trying to reclaim my life. While sitting in a booth in the hotel coffee shop, Hoden sat in a nearby booth, watching us.

As I watched Peter's facial expressions and listened to his tone of voice, I saw a man sold out to the Sea Org. For him, leaving was not an option. We argued over our commitments to our marriage versus our commitments to the Sea Org. He won with, "So are you going to throw this away and leave? I love you, KK."

He had me at KK. I didn't want to leave my husband; I only wanted to leave the Sea Org. I felt emotionally toxic, mentally broken. He persuaded me to return to the Int base and get myself sorted out.

Who had betrayed whom? Rage surged inside me, but I stifled it. Any efforts at personal autonomy seemed futile, and I felt like I was being twisted like a pretzel to conform to what he and the Sea Org wanted. I informed Mom of my decision to go back to the base, and the look in her eyes showed me how conflicted she was, knowing that I loved my husband and wanted our marriage to work.

One of the security guards drove her to the nearest airport to fly her back to Atlanta. My hopes for spending time talking with Peter while driving back to the base together was stolen by Hoden, who sent Peter back to the base with a security guard, and Hoden jumped into my front seat. When we arrived at the base, Hoden said I'd be sleeping in OGH tonight and to park my car near the Audio building for Peter's convenience.

There seemed no way out. Hoden had lied about how Peter and I would have the chance to talk things out at home. The base was surrounded by chain link fences with barbed wire, and without wire cutters, I couldn't get through the fences. Trying to hurdle the barbed wire would have torn up my body. I didn't have access to our car anymore after I gave up my keys. Even if I tried to get out of the gate and run behind some cars as they left that night, I would have walked down Highway 79 just long enough for a security team to come after me and bring me back.

I was furious for letting myself get trapped. Demanding my rights to mobility and freedom of speech would have been better than slipping into a deeper state of collapse, as I did. In Scientology terms, I "caved in." Imagine what it's like being at the bottom of a mine shaft when the supports collapse and you are covered by tons of debris. That was me, mentally.

For nearly a month, I did physical labor in the greenhouse near the Old Greenskeeper's House, received my meals from security guards who brought them to me on motorcycles, and lived in an 8 x 8 room with a bed and a table. Surprisingly, they allowed me to keep my dog Toby with me. I saw and spoke with no one, except for the greenhouse keeper, Carol Spurlock, and the guards who picked me up on motorcycles and took me to my security checking interrogations.

For a short story about an unlikely run-in with Christopher Silcock, a former celebrity auditor, visit the book website.

## The storm of August 1990

One night, while in my tiny room at OGH with the lights off and looking out the windows toward the south side of the base, a torrential rainstorm burst over the property. This storm moved in with such heavy rains that, from my vantage point, the base looked like it was flooding. Rivers of water rushed down the San Jacinto Mountains, turning into rivers of moving mud. I watched the Int base crew running in all directions laying sand bags to block the gushing waters from entering the buildings on the south side. Few staff owned rain gear, so most of them wore black plastic garbage bags over their clothes to stay somewhat dry. Compassion for the staff swept over me. I wondered where Peter was.

The base had to be in a state of emergency. I informed a security guard that I wanted to help. This was not a time when anyone cared about watching me as a security risk. I wanted to put a black plastic garbage over my clothes with the rest of them and do whatever was needed. I ran down to the south side and joined the teams hoisting sandbags to divert the flooding, and then helped a team that was digging up mud that had washed down from the mountainside. The mud had covered the freshly laid sod around the villas that we had built for Tom Cruise. Even in the middle of this crisis situation while I was helping alongside everyone else, some staff didn't want me to come near them, as I was a social pariah. Every shovel of mud that I dug, every sand bag I filled, and every piece of fresh sod I laid was another stroke of fighting for Peter and our marriage. Once the south side was gotten under control, everyone went back to their rooms to shower. I went back to OGH.

After the mud debacle, COB ordered the entire base into MCI, with Gold crew nearest the front podium. Miscavige rolled out one of his best performances reading the riot act to the Gold crew. He highlighted their gross negligence for having no emergency plan for flooding, and how this had sabotaged the security of the base and everything that LRH was working toward. Trees had fallen on cars, the villas we built for celebs had flooded and mud filled the crawl spaces. Hundreds of acres of sod were covered with mud, along with most of the roads on the south side of the property. He neglected to tell everyone about the staff member who had proposed him both a 10-year and a 100-flood plan. The plan COB chose that the Estates crew had implemented was the one that was in place when this disaster happened.

Gold was assigned a condition of confusion and would be put through other disciplinary actions. Nullification, on and on. Day after day, night after night, Gold crew labored to dig the mud out, and to repair the devastated base. Days bled into weeks and months.

# 22

# HAPPY VALLEY PRISON CAMP

## Int Base, 1990

I HAD REFUSED TO SUCCUMB to an RPF assignment, in a stalemate position for nearly three months in limbo at OGH. A security guard paid me a sudden visit one day with a special message: If I didn't willingly agree to do the RPF, I would be declared a suppressive person, and would never be able to see my husband again, or be a Scientologist.

Those words fell on my nearly deaf ears. This statement whittled away at the last vestiges of my desire to survive in the Sea Org. The guard ordered me to get on the back of his motorcycle, and drove me to Qual to see Senior C/S International, Jeff Walker. He told me to get off the fence and decide to do the RPF program, or he would issue me an SP declare.

I wanted to leave the Sea Org, but wanted Peter's and my marriage to remain intact. Now being reduced to a pawn on a chessboard dwindled my power. I had no choice but to comply to his demands if I wanted our marriage to survive. I was in denial that Peter had transformed into a fanatical Scientologist with loyalty to the Sea Org first, and a husband second. I should have questioned, what kind of marriage was I clinging to? What kind of "freedom" was I fighting for? All I could think about were some of Peter's last words to me in Gallup, "I love you, KK."

Talk about signing a document under duress. I had no legal representation when signing the paper that "voluntarily" enrolled me in the RPF, but if I had, I'm sure any attorney would have found the RPF consent form to have no legal validity. The conditions of coercion would have invalidated the whole thing, and I probably wouldn't have been found in right mind to sign it anyway.

That evening, a security guard drove me out to Happy Valley, the Int base's gulag, officially known as the Rehabilitation Project Force. Happy Valley was a suitable label for the criminal and crazy people sent out there who wanted to leave Scientology or the Int base.

I stayed in a solitary room in the Great House upstairs, away from the rest of the people on the RPF. I saw next to no one for weeks, and recall often gazing at myself in a mirror, as if to check that I was alive. I must have become only a shadow of myself; I have little recollection of functioning consciously. I slept long hours, probably making up for several years of physical and mental exhaustion. But while at Happy Valley, to receive interrogative security checking, I had to be sessionable, meaning well rested and well fed so I could be alert and bright-minded enough to engage in the interrogations. My metabolism would have to register properly on the e-meter through a breath test before I could go in session. So, I got to sleep every night at Happy Valley and eat three good meals daily.

A French RTC auditor named Frances came to HV to take me into sessions. One sweltering night during the session, when it felt like 100 degrees outside, he suggested that I take off my shirt since the building lacked air conditioning. The door to the auditing room was closed; the windows were open but there was no breeze. I thanked him for his concern about my comfort, but declined. He encouraged me again to take off my shirt, but again I declined. I guess my mind wasn't so far gone; I had heard about some Scientology auditors using the privacy of an auditing session to take advantage of their clients and have sex with them. I knew that in my diminished position, no one would have believed me if I had reported him, so I never said anything. But I didn't take off my shirt, and luckily, he didn't enforce any physical assault that I would have had to fight off.

It took me several weeks to come out of my emotionally comatose state before I became clear-minded enough to meld into the ranks of the RPF. Once a person decides to do the RPF, it's a "causative" decision and you decide, "the RPF is what you make it, the RPF is where you make it." So there's an RPF attitude of overcoming bullshit emotional barriers and just getting with the program. Now I'm in this hellhole. I'm really not thinking, *poor me*. But I do feel a bit crazy and scared with no idea what will happen from one moment to the next. Besides feeling trapped and being told that I'm here voluntarily, which I'm not, the worst thing is, my RPF status whittles down the little self-esteem I have left. And that makes me the fool for ever signing the form to do this when I was forced to "agree." It was a kind of extortion. I wish I had legal representation.

Like anyone who landed in the RPF, I didn't plan for a black wardrobe to support my sentence to hard labor. I dug through a trash barrel filled with used black clothes to find something useful to wear. These threads had been discarded by Int base staff that graduated the RPF. Without the ability to get what I needed from my room or even a store, I wrote Peter asking him to get me black clothing and send it to me in the Int base mail.

Living in a desert valley required a careful watch for rattlesnakes, scorpions and tarantulas, each of which I saw more than once. We were offered an award of $25 if we killed a rattlesnake and dragged it in. That was more than the weekly allowance of $15 we received on the RPF. I wondered how the children of the Int base staff members who were housed on the other side of the property, dealt with these poisonous creatures.

RPFers slept in rustic bunk beds with three to six people per room. We often ate rice and beans; otherwise we ate the same food as the rest of the Int base crew, brought to HV in aluminum trays covered with foil. We made coffee camping style, putting coffee grounds in the bottom of a soup pot and filling it with boiling water. RPFers were prohibited from walking anywhere. The only acceptable movement is RUN—run once you get out of bed, run to the sink, run down the path, run to your task, run back. I ran from point A to point B in the 100+ degree desert heat, every moment of every day. If I encountered staff members in good standing, I was not allowed to look them in the eyes or speak to them. RPFers were treated like dirt. No dignity, no rights.

I could barely hide my shock the moment I saw celebrity auditor, Stephanie Silcock. Stephanie had audited celebrities including

John Travolta and Priscilla Presley on RTC's special Celebrity Recovery project, with her husband Chris, while I was the CO CCNW. Stephanie and Chris Silcock were at least Class VIIIs. Stephanie had also been my auditor and Peter's before I joined the Sea Org. Now dressed in dirty black clothing, this formerly elegant South African woman stood before a pile of rocks, watering them with a hose. Grime dripped down her arms and legs as the water sprayed her body. As if I was at a zoo gawking at a creature I had never seen before, I found myself speechless. We looked each other in the eye as she placed her free hand over her mouth, and shook her head. I realized that she was telling me she wasn't allowed to speak to me. She was on the RPF's RPF, a demotion to a sub-level of the lowest caste, not allowed to speak to anyone, even other RPFers. Evidently, Stephanie had chosen to remain in the Sea Org and do the RPF while her husband Chris, whom I had talked to in the OGH kitchen a few weeks prior, was forced to divorce her, and returned to South Africa.

I learned stories of how some of the other Int base staff landed on the RPF. One guy had been accused of holding hostage a busload of RTC staff by driving them to their berthing when he knew the bus would run out of gas. He claimed that during his job in Motorpool, funds for gassing up the buses would frequently get cut due to low budgets, and he was just supposed to make it go right, so he wanted to prove a point. Social life within the RPF reminded me of movies I had seen about prison inmates, where everybody had a story.

I did physical labor for about eight hours daily, after which I would study ethics or other Scientology tech for my "rehabilitation" program another six hours. Our slave labor consisted of jobs assigned to us by the Estates Manager of the Int base. We constructed new buildings, repaired and maintained old ones, and did major landscaping projects.

Bosun Geray Jory added me to her special landscaping team to care for the grounds around the RTC villas and buildings near north side senior execs. Geray, who had been humiliated by Miscavige in Cine, had been on the RPF for months. Before I knew her, she had been one of David Miscavige's stewards in RTC, but was busted from her post, and Marty Rathbun divorced her. Geray and our special RPF team of six women were bused to the Int base at 6:30 a.m. for this privileged task, since few RPFers were allowed to come anywhere near the north side of the property where senior execs worked. Our team was praised for consistently good quality work, and we received commendations for completing special projects. This won us a little ethics presence at the base, and a menial but noteworthy elevation of status within the RPF. After the day's work, Gold Motorpool would bus us back to HV to shower, eat, and report to our evening's "rehabilitation."

RPFers can only complete the program by twinning with another RPFer and getting them through their program. My twin, Eric, had been a computer technician in Author Services Inc. before he was sent to the RPF. Eric had been accused of computer-related wrongdoings, including reading some of David Miscavige's emails. ASI was a front group on Hollywood Boulevard representing L. Ron Hubbard's writings, but primarily serving as a secret liaison between LRH in his various hiding places and the Scientology management. ASI handled the project of inscribing all of Hubbard's writings onto titanium plates and burying them in underground vaults in secret desert locations, with the Church of Religious Trust. Norman Starkey, trustee of Hubbard's estate, told us that this project was part of safeguarding the technology before the planet was blown up. The indestructible plates would survive even a nuclear explosion, thus preserving Hubbard's technology for future generations in the galaxy. So any emails going around ASI that Eric had read could have been a serious violation of internal security and confidentiality. But I wasn't sure that Eric had done what they accused him of.

Eric's presence in the RPF program seemed out-tech. Eric had a known history of epileptic seizures, a significant medical issue that should have disqualified him for auditing and for working in rough RPF conditions. But he wasn't allowed off the RPF despite his needing medical care. Neither one of us were trained auditors, so we audited each other through our correction programs, RPF style: "Read it, drill it, do it." In the Scientology world, great care was typically taken to train Scientologists how to audit: how to operate an e-meter, how to conduct a session, how to audit different auditing processes. But on the RPF, it was presto-chango, now I'm an auditor responsible for getting someone else through this program. I also wrote reports that Eric, who had a chronic medical issue, should not be receiving auditing because he continued to have seizures throughout his program. One day when the RPF crew was being transported by bus to do a project at the Int base, Eric fell to the floor and had a grand mal seizure in the aisle. I wasn't sitting near him, but staff next to him tried to keep him from swallowing his tongue. The bus arrived at the base, and several male staff carried Eric to the medical officer. I was later told that his wife demanded that he be taken to a hospital or she was going to sue Scientology. I never saw Eric again.

For me, having study time on the RPF and learning to audit was a real perk, since Miscavige had robbed Cine crew of our study time. As I progressed through my RPF program, I did well learning how to audit. The Case Supervisors at the base, who checked all RPF auditing files, said that I was doing a great job technically with my metering and session worksheets. For this, I was assigned the post of "examiner" in the RPF, so I gave meter checks after people got out of their auditing sessions. Surprisingly, some people got upset when I would give an exam and just say, "Thank you." The hope—and expectation—was that after a session, the pc would come to get their exam and I would see a floating needle, and say, "Thank you, your needle is floating."For the sake of the PC, I would not call an F/N unless it really was one. This sometimes became an upset between the auditor and me when they questioned my exam statement, and this sometimes made me question my ability to read a floating needle. That was a risk we all took with the "read it, drill it, do it" system. I knew that there was a margin of error that existed with any of us using the e-meter, but I had to call it as I saw it.

Though the RPF program is done in the setting of a concentration camp where the "voluntary" detainees have no authority over their mobility or communication with the outside world, there were several hidden benefits. We had to get enough sleep, eat enough food, and take vitamins to be sessionable for our ethics and technical rehabilitation program. And since I ran so much everyday, I lost nearly thirty pounds.

I saw Peter maybe twice during my RPF stint. Ironically, we had permission to leave the RPF on Friday nights if we wanted to go sleep together in a motel. Peter drove us to a motel in Hemet twice, but it felt so contrived and awkward that we didn't bother to request it again.

I'll never forget the moment when an exec came to my RPF unit at a landscaping project to hide me from the view of a group of celebrity visitors. A group of artists from CC, some of whom were my recording artist friends like Harriet Schock, David Pomeranz, Raven Kane Campbell, and Maxine Nightengale, were being toured through the base and then shown the Golden Era music studio. Officials wanted to ensure that those people didn't see me, the former Commanding Officer of the Celebrity Centre Network, and wife of Peter Schless, dressed in black clothes on the RPF. I was sent back to HV early to keep me out of sight. Image was everything.

Despite the stigma attached to being on the RPF, I found the physical work to be more constructive and even pleasurable than working on a post in the Orwellian environment of the Int base. The Estates Manager, Steve Willett, commented more than once that I didn't belong on the RPF because I produced good quality work and had a great attitude, atypical for us degenerate RPFers. Overall, I acquired construction-worker and landscaper skills through the RPF's physical labor. One project landed me on the roof of the new Qualifications Building under construction, where I learned to expertly install clay roofing tiles. I also worked in teams constructing the interior walls, installed foam core insulation and sheet rock, and then learned to mud and sand the walls. I was great with a paint brush, so I was trusted to paint the trim of our various projects. Around the base, I laid cabling with teams burying power lines and removing telephone poles from the property. I planted trees and shrubs, and laid sod. I even learned to operate a fire hose to wash down roads, and a gas-powered blower to clear out the roads around the base.

I had ben on the RPF for about seven months when we received news that RPF was being disbanded, and that RPFers were going to man up the Estates division to finish the base building plan and renovations. This occurred not long after my twin, Eric, had his seizure and his wife threatened to sue the church if Eric didn't receive proper medical care. I was one of a handful of people returned to a regular post and landed back in the Art Department. I had a lot of catching up to do, finding out who had blown and what were the biggest flaps. Jeff Walker, Senior C/S Int, who had enforced my RPF assignment, had since left the Sea Org by calling the Riverside County Sheriff's Office to ask for help. A sheriff served as his personal escort to get him safely off the Int base.

Most of the RPFers were posted in Estates to work as an indentured labor force to construct properties on the Int base, thus increasing its real estate value. The fruits of our labor came at no cost to Scientology, other than the food we consumed, the gas that powered the buses, and meager living quarters. In a modified version of a communistic mentality or totalitarian group think, this was "my" Scientology and the base belonged to me, so I was responsible for everything about it, despite knowing that we were not members of any Scientology church, or public stockholders, since each church is a corporation on paper. We were only members of the IAS, the International Association of Scientologists, with no shares of Scientology wealth for our membership.

Security had moved Peter into a men's dorm with a bunk and a few square feet for his personal things. My clothing and any personal things I owned and valued had been boxed up by security and stashed into the bowels of one of the Int base Greyhound buses, carried around like that for seven months. Before I could retrieve my personal belongings from the bus, I had to arrange for us to move into a couple's room. As luck had it, Ron Miscavige, Sr. and his new wife Becky had moved into a couple's room in the Devonshire Apartments. Ron and Peter were still working together in the Music Department, and I considered Ron my friend as well. But I had to get past the humiliation of convincing Ron and Becky to allow us to acquire this room and set up our new "home."

Where was my home, really? I couldn't turn back the clock or recover the years I had lost thus far. But I had found a way to survive at the Int base—I had my "secret self," my authentic self that I hid under my Sea Org personality. By recalling and reliving true memories of my life, I could retain my connection to life as I had known it. Maintaining that connection enabled me to get through my present. My past was all I had to prove that I really did have connections to a wondrous childhood and pleasurable life, to loved ones, to beautiful places and wonderful people in the world. No one could touch my true identity, not even Peter.

# 23

## CRUISE CONTROL

**Int Base, early 1990s**

I MET TOM CRUISE ACCIDENTALLY one afternoon when it was either him or me who was not supposed to be in that particular place at that moment. I was coming out of the ladies room in MCI, our mess hall, about to exit through the side door, when Cruise came bounding into the corridor like a flying bullet. We collided in the hallway outside the restrooms. In that momentary crash, I noticed that he was a little bit shorter than my 5'6." His body was a wall of moving muscle. We said our hello's and excuse me's, he apologized with an "I'm so sorry!" when we kind of laughed while adjusting our caps that had jostled off our heads, and continued on our ways. I noticed Cruise's motorcycle parked off to the side of MCI, probably making an emergency stop because he was not accompanied by a guard and usually kept out of sight of crew. It was funny to run into Cruise at this isolated location, when I had never seen him at the Celebrity Centre. This close encounter was like being on the Aaron Spelling Productions lot where stars and staff were just regular people doing their jobs. But here, Cruise didn't come to be a star; he came to become a Scientologist.

In my last days at Celebrity Centre, I had already begun to observe the impact that Thomas Mapother Cruise had on the Scientology world. His involvement showed that Miscavige and his team were effectively shaping this relationship into all that he wanted it to become.

While still married to Mimi Rogers, Cruise had been mesmerized by Nicole Kidman on screen in *Dead Calm,* leading him to get Kidman cast in his film, *Days of Thunder,* in a role where she falls in love with his stock-car-driver character, Cole Trickle. Cruise and Kidman also fell in love for real, and started coming up to the Gold base around the time the film was released. Scientology execs helped orchestrate the divorce of Tom and Mimi, solving the earlier problem of Miscavige not wanting Cruise to be tainted by Mimi's father, Phil Spickler. But there was a new problem to deal with: Nicole Kidman's father was a prominent Australian psychiatrist. Mental health professionals were at the top of the list of suppressive persons in Hubbard's views, so this automatically made Kidman and even Cruise a Potential Trouble Source. The leader of Scientology was walking on thin ice with this new Scientologist who clearly was not mindful about the psychiatrist issue as a conflict with Scientology or within this new relationship. Tom and Nicole married in late 1990. Just think, Tom Cruise would have a suppressive person as his father-in-law.

Above all else, make Tom Cruise happy. Build him a place to stay and a meadow to romp in. Flow him power because he was on the power lines of the world and could recruit the biggest opinion leaders on the planet. On Miscavige's orders, Gold Estates staff created a meadow for Cruise's delight to romp in with Nicole Kidman. This meadow was in the far back of the property where few staff ever visited unless they drove to the back of the base on motorcycles, as I sometimes did on my scooter, so many crew wouldn't have known it was going on unless somebody leaked the information in conversation. Several friends in Estates stayed up days on end tearing up sod, spreading seed and planting up a field of flowers and tall grasses, and spending countless sleepless nights redoing it until the leader of Scientology was happy with it, knowing the couple could romp in perfection.

I don't know why the church denied the existence of this meadow when asked about it in media interviews. Church spokesman Mike Rinder told the *Times* that the story was fabricated by the apostates who talked about it, not credible sources. Gold crew member, Andre Tabayoyan, who not long afterward left the Sea

Org, confirmed it in his legal affidavit, and former Cine staff Maureen Bolstad confirmed it to the *Los Angeles Times*.

Sea Org crew invested thousands of hours to build the celebrity villas, the "G's" on the outskirts of the Int base, that housed Cruise and Kidman during their stays, and helped Ron Miscavige build and outfit the exclusive gym. The villas were designed in an elegant rustic, upscale country style, supposedly in keeping with the base Scottish theme, which I could only see in some plaid fabrics, dark-stained wood trim, and some Gaelic leather decor. Teams worked like slave labor through the construction, and then finished the interiors to ensure the perfection of everything from the cabinetry to the trim work, the tile and grout, the lighting and hardware throughout, and lush landscaping. I worked on Lindy Johanssen's team trusted to do good finishing work. We made window dressings, custom bed coverings and accent pillows, created floral arrangements, and finished countless interior decor projects to make sure the place was fit for celebrity guests. Lindy often went for days without sleep to complete projects under Miscavige's dictates. In the end, the G's stood in stark luxurious contrast to the embarrassing low-end apartments in Hemet where the elite Sea Org members lived.

COB took great measures to keep the presence of Tom Cruise and Nicole Kidman secret on the base, but many staff knew about the special guests. Although Miscavige attempted to separate TC from Int base crew, it wasn't hard to learn what was going on, since many staff serviced Cruise in some capacity. In most cases, these tasks had nothing to do with regular Sea Org operations or the statistics of our posts. To that extent, Cruise's presence interrupted Int base functions and thus Scientology internationally. Not only had we become an extension unit of Celebrity Centre and David Miscavige's personal staff, but we were under Cruise control.

I caught occasional sightings of Miscavige and Cruise buzzing around the base on motorcycles. They worked out at the expensive gym financed by parishioner's funds, built by Sea Org labor, outfitted by Ron Miscavige. Cruise and Kidman had been carefully kept off the beaten paths of staff to ensure total privacy with no unplanned meetings. Miscavige's strategy to sequester the celebrity couple offended me. Why not have Cruise intermingle with Sea Org members, the elite corps? Weren't Int base staff the best of the best in the Sea Org? One reason for the separation was to prevent the guests from seeing many of the staff that, in Miscavige's eyes, had a poor image and could not communicate well. Gold crew had been ordered to avoid making eye contact with him (like an RPFer is ordered to always look down and not make eye contact) and to address him as Mr. Cruise if a meeting did occur. That order removed any options for word choices or conversations that could go wrong. In defense of the quality of Gold crew's communication, their frequent sleep deprivation would cause anyone to stumble or not speak coherently or intelligently. Gold crew frequently looked pale and sometimes slovenly because of lack of sleep and time to shower and groom; many wore worn-out uniforms that needed replacement. But Miscavige had to invalidate everyone's self-image to ensure they stayed out of the way and kept their mouths shut so as to not sabotage his strategy.

Either Shelley or David Miscavige handpicked specific staff to service Cruise and his wife. When Cruise started his basic Scientology auditor training, Pat Gualtieri was selected to be Tom Cruise's personal course supervisor. Peter and I had been friends with Pat since our earliest CC days, and ended up becoming apartment mates at the Int base. I knew Pat to be very sensitive and intuitive, highly empathetic to artists, and a great communicator with opinion leaders. His Brooklyn accent and jovial sense of humor added to his overall likability. Miscavige had chosen Pat not only because he was trained as a Scientology auditor and course supervisor, but because he was a Viet Nam vet. This made him a compatible match for Tom Cruise, who had played the role of a wounded Viet Nam vet in *Born on the Fourth of July*. Pat had survived the Tet Offensive; each of them had experienced hell in Viet Nam from different perspectives, so the two would have plenty to talk about in between TC's training breaks.

Cruise received one-on-one, silver-platter service during the rest of his Scientology journey at the Int base, under 24/7 security watch, from Int base crew who went off their own posts to service him. Instead of contributing to the dissemination and expansion of Scientology through our actual jobs, dozens of Int base crew were now focusing on one individual's personal enhancement. The big picture, of course, was to make Tom Cruise a stable Scientologist who would not falter in his commitment or teeter in his beliefs that Scientology worked, so that he would, in turn, become Scientology's greatest member, supporter, and spokesperson. There was no question that he was Scientology's biggest trophy who would expand Scientology in a way that no one else ever had, or probably ever would.

To accommodate our top celebrity, one of our teams converted part of LRH's music studio (designated for LRH's use only, off limits to everyone else) into Cruise's personal course room, where Tom Cruise would train to become an auditor as well as receive auditing, overseen by Bruce Hines from our Senior C/S International office, accompanied by Pat Gualtieri. This area connected to the hallway to Peter's music studio, so Peter would see TC from time to time, but he wasn't supposed to talk about it.

A Gold staff member, Marc Headley, was chosen to receive auditing from Cruise throughout his training. Before that, Marc had been working in Gold's manufacturing division producing LRH lecture tapes and products sold to outer Scientology organizations. Years later, Marc wrote a great story, *Blown for Good*, that gives detailed experiences with Tom Cruise and his experiences at the Int base before Marc left the Sea Org.

Cruise had been generous to Int base staff in certain ways over the years. When *Days of Thunder*, he gifted leather *Days of Thunder* jackets to Miscavige and other execs, who would wear them like hotshots around the base. I remember laughing about that because they reminded me of roadies and groupies I had seen when Peter and I were on the road in the music business. On one occasion, the whole base was treated to a night at the movies in a Moreno Valley theatre. Cruise had bought out the whole theatre that night so that we could watch his film. Most of the staff were so poor that they couldn't buy popcorn.

Tom Cruise would have to be deaf, dumb, and blind to not know of Sea Org slave-labor conditions, and the expense the church invested to please him, waiting on the couple hand and foot. I didn't begrudge Cruise and Kidman receiving special treatment; if I were in business and they were my clients or personal friends, I would do the same thing. I just didn't agree that these gifts and luxuries should be provided on the backs of sleep-deprived Sea Org crew who Miscavige often addressed as degraded beings and used us as slaves.

Years later, numerous Int base staff left the Sea Org and disclosed detailed accounts of the kinds of projects they did creating specialized gifts for Cruise. John Brousseau, who had worked for

LRH and whom I knew when he worked in Motorpool at Gold, has disclosed incredible stories about making or buying special motorcycles, cars and various personalized decorative items such as for Cruise's hangar in Burbank, and on. There is much to tell of JB's incredible story, with little room here. Google John Brousseau and you'll find stories worth reading, including about his personal escape.

The Cruise control factor that now dominated Scientology didn't offend every Sea Org member. In that bubble, Cruise was important to the expansion of Scientology. For example, Peter didn't agree that anything was wrong with what we all did for Tom Cruise; he just believed in flowing him power. But the Cruise control factor diminished my commitment to the Sea Org. My disaffection was deepened by seeing how TC received preferential treatment at the expense of Gold crew who took drastic measures to please Sea Org leaders such as having abortions just to stay there, or disconnecting from a loved one just to gain favor of the church leader who, in turn, would besmirch Gold crew. I hadn't given up my personal life and contact with my family to join the extremist organization, the Sea Org, to serve a leader under the influence of a movie star.

# 24

# RON MISCAVIGE, SR.

## Hemet, CA

DURING LATE NIGHT TALKS with our apartment mate, Ron Miscavige Sr., I began to get otherwise impossible glimpses into David Miscavige and his new best friend, Tom Cruise.

Ron and his newly wed wife, Becky, and Peter and I would come home to our off-base apartment at the Devonshire, physically exhausted after our sixteen-plus-hours workdays. Even so, it was sometimes hard to just go to bed and fall asleep while being so stressed by troubles on post and enturbulated about Int base conditions. We each worked in different areas that held their unique sets of problems, particularly as related to COB orders. I'm assuming that Ron and Becky confided in each other about every detail like Peter and I did—despite the rules about writing knowledge reports on anything that could come across as "natter."

Becky worked in the Marketing Unit—a hot seat that drew regular visits from David Miscavige who micromanaged the promotion and advertising of all Scientology projects—from strategies to designs and production of artwork for things like covers of new products and advertising campaigns.

Ron had been off and on as Music Director, another Int base hot seat. Peter and Ron's music submissions for a film or video music score would go back and forth to David Miscavige, some-

sometimes endlessly, but usually accompanied by scathing commentary criticizing their works. Here is Ron, a professional musician, and Peter, an award-winning composer, struggling to get their music approved by a man who had no experience as a musician, composer, or producer.

My post in Cine was a non-stop series of creative attempts to do well with a team that seemed to receive more criticism and discipline than any other area of the base. DM, who had worked as LRH's camera man during many of LRH's early tech films that the Cine division was now re-shooting, considered himself enough of an expert to appoint himself as the one to view all our rushes, and order re-shoots continuously.

Some nights, I'd get home and find Ron standing in our little kitchen, waiting for Becky to get home, while he seemed wound up tight like a rubber band. I'd sometimes sense that Ron wanted to talk. His personal circle of his musician friends might have been prone to report him for talking about people in casual conversation, such as his son, and the biggest celebrity in Scientology. To that extent, our occasional late night kitchen gabs were conversations over taboo topics, but between trusted friends.

I'd say, "Hey, how ya doing?" Ron would pause, rub his hand on his face, probably deliberating over what or what not to say. His intense blue eyes seemed riveted on specific troubles that added extra tension in his face. It was clear to me that as Dave's dad, Ron Miscavige Sr. carried a lot of emotional conflict in his heart about his son that no one else in the world could understand but him. I doubted that Ron could discuss his feelings about Dave in an auditing session, because an Int base auditor would be hearing things about the leader of Scientology that would put them in a position of writing a knowledge report. Being David Miscavige's father was not an easy position for Ron to be in, no matter how you look at it.

I'm sure Ron didn't talk about even half of what was ever on his mind. He once told me, "I'm so concerned about Dave, I don't even know what to do about it...I don't know what to make of it anymore. I mean, Dave is doing all kinds of things that, as his father, I think he shouldn't be doing. He puts himself at risk all the time. Like he and TC, they go out racing motorcycles recklessly and skydiving together. I mean, many people sky dive, but Dave is the leader of the Scientology world. LRH is gone. Dave shouldn't be putting himself at risk like that."

"Skydiving? Wow. That takes balls. That sounds like something either one of them would really get off on. It's one thing for anyone to jump out of a plane and have fun, but your son, you're thinking of the responsibilities he has. I can understand your concern." I knew that David had broken his ankle or leg at some point because I saw him in a cast. Some people said he had broken it while playing basketball with Tom Cruise, but the shore story was that he had broken it while skiing. Maybe he broke it while skydiving. I didn't ask Ron which story was true.

"He has no right to take those kinds of risks—he's the head of Scientology. What if something happened to him?"

"Well, have you ever talked to him about that? About not putting himself at risk?"

"Are you kidding me, KK? Dave doesn't want to hear about what he should or shouldn't or can and cannot do. I can't talk to him about anything like that. He's an adult who can make up his own mind. Problem is, no one keeps him in check. At all, about anything."

"He's an adult, but you are still his father. I think you can find a way to talk to him as your son out of concern for his well being. Out of love." I felt stupid after saying that. At the Int base, familial connections were not acknowledged, because spiritual beings do not have relatives.

Ron would look at me blankly. "You have no idea how long it's been since I have felt close to Dave." Ron wiped his face with his hand. "I am *afraid* of him, Karen. *I am afraid of my own son.*" Ron looked down for a second. "Yeah, I mean, I don't even know who he is anymore...he's getting out of control...he doesn't want me to act as his father. The other day, I called out to him near the music studio and said, 'Hey Dave!' He turned and looked at me like who the hell was I to address him that way? And I heard about it later. I've created a monster."

I wasn't sure how to respond to my friend. Ron seemed to be utterly exasperated about how to be a father to a son who, at that time, Ron could only think of as "COB." "Tell me what you mean, Ron." I had my own ideas about David Miscavige, but even in this conversation, I kept them to myself.

"You must know what I mean. Peter must tell you what happens when Dave comes into the music studio. He screams at people...I'm afraid he's going to put his fist through a wall. When I'm

211

standing there and he shouts at me in front of the musicians—I'm the Music Director—I feel like a real loser, while my own son is berating me in front of other musicians that I'm failing. I've seen him go after Steve Marlowe, punching him. Marlowe fucked up so much and Dave takes it out on him."

Peter had told me plenty of accounts of yelling and invalidation emanated by COB in the music area, most of it directed at Ron or at Peter, so I knew what Ron was talking about. I also knew there were plenty of limitations about what he and I could say, and I couldn't even imagine what it was like to be in Ron's shoes. I replied with compassionate questions because my friend clearly grappled over his role as father to his son whose power outranked their father-son relationship. In the Sea Org, particularly at the Int base, "family" played little to no role in work affairs. Yet here Ron was, brought to the base by his son, with Ron's other son, Ronnie Miscavige Jr., a senior marketing exec in the Exec Strata. As the father of two sons with power roles, and one of them being the Chairman of the Board of the Religious Technology Center, how was their father supposed to be addressed or treated? How did the role of a father fit in here at all?

The Sea Org at the Int base was an authoritarian system where power was held at the top and the orders simply spread downward. Your position in the base hierarchy of organizations and how many stripes you wore on your shoulders is what made the difference about how you spoke to others and how others would address you. "Father" had no significant place in this system. This wouldn't be a question in any other environment where the father is the head of the family and is treated with respect. But in the Sea Org at the Int base, his father role was diminished to the point of irrelevancy in Scientology operations. I realized Ron couldn't let on to his feelings about the father-son conundrum because he was never one to see himself as a victim. I didn't seem him as a victim, either; I saw this loss of his father identity as collateral damage from being at the Int base under an authoritarian ruler, son or not.

"What was Dave like when he was a kid? I mean, did he get angry easily? Was he a bully?"

Ron told me about raising the kids in Philadelphia until he found out about Scientology. He said Dave had asthma as a kid, but didn't tell me much about behavioral issues. Ron had discovered Scientology through a Dianetics center, where he took Dave for auditing, in hopes that it would help his son's asthma. He said the auditing caused a miraculous improvement for Dave, so much so that Ron wanted to know everything about Scientology. He eventually packed up his family and moved them to England when Dave was around 12, so they could immerse themselves in Scientology at Saint Hill. He said that Dave didn't even finish high school because he loved Scientology so much that he wanted to work for Hubbard, so Ron let him join the Sea Org when he was about 16. He told me enough for me to learn that Dave went to Clearwater to join the Sea Organization, and by age 17, Dave went into the Commodore's Messenger Org, and ultimately landed a cameraman position under Hubbard shooting films at the confidential Winter Headquarters near the Int base.

Dave had also tried to get both of his parents to join the Sea Org. Ron joined later, along with Dave's older brother, Ronnie, but Dave's mother, Loretta, didn't want to do it. Dave also pushed for Ron and Loretta to get divorced. When I realized that David Miscavige had been able to bully or control his parents to affect their divorce, a piece of the puzzle fell into place about why divorce seemed to be so prevalent at the Int base. Divorce was a solution for problems in Dave's early years, and he would continue to enforce it whenever he pleased. Family? Just break it up! Get rid of it. An easy solution to a problem.

When I had first met Ron circa 1988 at Celebrity Centre, I immediately liked his high energy level and his Philly accent, which wasn't too far removed from my Chicago accent. I had gotten to know him during his visits when he came to see Peter and me about coming to Gold, but knew little of his family background at that time. Now I was gaining some insight into David's humanity, apart from his role as Scientology's leader. This lessened my fear of DM because I saw that he, too, would bleed when he fell down, contrary to the hard-as-steel personality he typically exuded. Ron helped me cope with David Miscavige as an enigma.

Ron had also been given the special project of building the personal gym at the Int base for Dave to use with Tom Cruise or anyone he wanted to share it with. Ron was to select all the workout equipment, and have it shipped to the base and installed. Ron told me how nuts this project had gotten, because Dave repeatedly changed the specs for the equipment. He'd say a piece of equipment didn't do what he wanted it to do well enough, so Ron would send it back and replace it with something else. This went on an on. Dave blew the original budget out of the water, and Ron said costs had gone way out of control.

"I mean, these are church funds we're using. This is crazy, tens of thousands of dollars for gym equipment. Equipment for one person to use in a gym with TC or a few senior execs."

None of Ron's questions or concerns had immediate solutions. Dave was on his own, subject to no one's advice or control. I started to see the base as David Miscavige's personal playground with his new celebrity friend, for which Scientology's global parishioners and organizations funded the bill, and for which Int base staff labored. Of course, all this was being done under the guise of conducting the deadly serious business of Keeping Scientology Working. Scientology at its highest level belied the idealism that originally attracted me as an artist who could help change the world.

It also looked to me like Ron's son was living vicariously through Tom Cruise. Dave had joined the Sea Org at 16, and prior to that had spent extensive time at Saint Hill to become auditor trained. While Ron had provided well for his children as he and Loretta raised them, Dave's choice to enter the Sea Org so young cut out a lot of living that kids in high school otherwise experience. Had Dave latched onto Tom Cruise so solidly for more personal benefits than just helping to advance Scientology? To draw a parallel, based on how I saw Dave micromanaging people around the Int base, any staff member's product became COB's product because he was always scrutinizing other people's work and saying how he could do it better, or he made everything happen, as if he was an expert on every job in the Sea Org; likewise, any product of Tom Cruise's would become David Miscavige's. It was easy to make the projection that TC's successes would become Dave's successes, because Dave would have a hand in everything Cruise would do. I had no way of knowing just how true that would become.

# 25

# UNDER SIEGE

**Int Base, 1990-1991**

EXCEPT FOR DRIVING HOME AT NIGHT, the morning drive to the base was the most pleasurable time of my day. I'd follow the route between the base and the Hemet apartments along Sanderson Avenue and Highway 79. As I drew nearer to the Int base, the backdrop of gentle slopes and smooth curves of the San Jacinto Mountains revealed the smattering of white stucco buildings nestled within the folds of the foothills. The mountains cast morning shadows on the blue tiled roofs of each building, cooling the terrain before the sun's blazes beat down unmercilessly on us.

Large birds—hawks?—sometimes circled playfully overhead, wings outstretched to catch wind currents that lifted them higher. Mornings had been the only time of day when I could enjoy the serenity of that place—when it was just me and the landscape and no words had been exchanged by people who destroyed the peace. When I'd approach the closed security gates, I'd be greeted by a security guard through a speaker box. I'd tell him my name and the gates would roll open. Once those gates closed, I was locked in until we were allowed to leave sometime in the late hours around midnight.

Any illusion of peace created by the early morning quiet belied the turmoil of those toiling inside the buildings. Each of the buildings landscaped into the rolling terrain represented different colonies of Sea Org staff that slaved there.

While I had seen myself as practicing peaceful revolution at Celebrity Centre, I had instead become subsumed by a different bloodsport—Hubbard's war of the worlds.

## Under siege by Byrnes and Wilhere

Two tough-guy looking Sea Org officers with black-rimmed caps made a dramatic entrance at a Gold muster one day that captivated the attention of 400 crew. With blue missionaire lanyards draped across their Class A uniforms, Greg Wilhere from RTC and James Byrne from PAC announced that they were here to whip the Gold crew into shape and gain compliance to COB's orders. They spit out threats and penalties that were meant to separate the weak from the strong. We were threatened with overboarding if we were even ten seconds late to muster, and with an automatic RPF assignment in the Los Angeles prison camp if late a second time.

Wilhere and Byrnes enforced team drills and marching drills like one would see in a boot camp or a fascist military organization. These militant marching drills sounded like the marching jackboots of Mussolini's Italy that I had seen in movies. Sea Org leadership used these drills as another control tool, to eliminate free will and enforce groupthink. This went so far as marching for hours in rows, then standing still and practicing Ten Hut! At Ease! Right Face! Left Face!

## Overboarding

Byrnes and Wilhere announced that Hubbard's old sea practice of throwing people overboard was going to be implemented as a routine until it was no longer needed. We were a landlocked base, but a lake had been created on the south side of the property with a quaint stone bridge crossing over to a little island, a charming place you might use for an outdoor wedding ceremony. Now this lovely lake was going to be used for punishment.

I had read a Sea Org policy about overboarding that had been used at Hubbard's Flagship Apollo. A Sea Org member who had committed some kind of transgression, made bad mistakes on post, or did some disservice to Hubbard or the Sea Org, was blindfolded and then thrown overboard, like in pirate's days, while someone read the archaic prose, "We commit your sins to the deep..." The punished crew member would climb out of the lake, their uniforms a sopping wet mess. Most staff members only owned one or two pairs of uniform pants, and one or two uniform shirts. They were allowed to remove their shoes. Working sixteen+ hour days, when could one wash their uniform? Yet every staff member was expected to report to muster with a clean, pressed uniform every morning.

Any overboarded crew endured multiple injuries such as public and personal humiliation. The expressions on most people's faces coming out of the lake were stony, suppressed anger, humiliation, indignance, and are you fucking kidding me. I was never overboarded. I did, however, overboard a few crew after I became unwilling to tolerate other people's behavior that was putting my own survival in jeopardy. That mindset of the Int base culture crept in.

## Drills, Drills and More Drills

After plenty of verbal lacerations for how terrible we were at marching and for being such ineffective Sea Org members, we became perfectly punctual for musters, able to stand in perfect military formation. We could be further molded into good soldiers to Keep Scientology Working at any cost. Marching drills were just one of many things that eliminated individual thinking, and tightened our ability to function as a collective group.

Drilling how to handle a variety of attacks engaged us in an intense amount of practice preparing for enemy infiltrations as well as natural disasters like the flood. We drilled how to handle a fire hose, as if we were firemen. These were timed drills to attach the hose to the hydrant, to hold the hose and spray it, and to roll it up after it had been used.On Saturdays, the entire base would drill how to avoid being handed papers by anyone who came out to the base to serve us.

Our Port Captain, Ken Hoden, told us that legal officials or process servers could be hired by outsiders to serve us with legal documents, which we were forbidden to accept. We practiced how to avoid "being deceived" by a process server who would thrust papers into our hands, and how to reject anything that someone pushed toward us. We drilled how to handle "black propaganda," a Scientology term for bad or critical information spread to others about Scientology. We were told that Scientology was being "black

PR'd" by suppressive people through different media. Consequently, we refused to believe that any negative information about Scientology came from a reliable, reputable source. Anyone who spoke negatively about Scientology was not only evil-intentioned, but a suppressive person out to destroy our organization as the only hope for humankind.

## Duck, Cover and Hold

Our "duck, cover and hold" drills could have been prime fodder for a comedy script had anyone watched hundreds of crew diving under desks and covering their heads. We were trained to "protect ourselves" under the guise of intruders coming to the base to cause trouble. Security had established a base-wide alerting system—a guard would call designated "point persons" around the base who would alert everyone in their area to duck, cover, and hold within seconds. We ducked and covered by ducking under a desk or the nearest table and covered our heads with arms, books, whatever. We held that cramped position under the furniture until the drill was called off by security. Sometimes this lasted five to fifteen minutes, sometimes more than an hour.

These duck, cover and hold exercises drilled in a sense of paranoia about "enemies" coming to the base to harm us. This caused further isolation and deepened the division between "us" at the base and "them" in the outside world. I can only imagine the actual events that might have been taking place at the base while staff dove under furniture. What an effective way for executives to bring celebrities like Ron Howard or attorneys and the like onto the base that no one would ever see. I wondered how many times we had been duped to believe that a drill was just a ruse for being manipulated so we couldn't see outside what was really going on.

## War Time: Rick Behar & Time vs. Scientology

On Monday, May 6, 1991, *Time* magazine's article, "The Thriving Cult of Greed and Power," rocked the Scientology world, particularly at Int Management level. Not only had journalist Rick Behar written a story about Noah Lottick, a New York Scientologist who had plunged to his death from a New York hotel window, clutching his last $171 that his parents said he hadn't yet turned over to the Church of Scientology. Behar's story revealed the church's conflicts with the IRS, the American Psychiatric Association, and other problematic business dealings, including a quote from a judge who had deemed Hubbard a pathological liar and exposed Scientology's litigious history, contrary to the image of a church. Behar included a quote from Cynthia Kisser, director of one of the church's enemies, the Cult Awareness Network, that Scientology "was a global racket that intimidated individuals in a Mafia-like manner."*Time* also published stories about Scientology being on trial in France, and about Germany's battle against the church.

Behar's article was published by *Reader's Digest* that October and distributed in at least five European countries. Behar also described that, after publishing a prior critical article about Scientology in *Forbes,* he had been followed by private investigators and plagued by church attorneys and others who sought to defame him professionally.

Miscavige's game to expand Scientology internationally was threatened by *Time*'s article, thus it also crippled the lives of the Int base staff. Instead of working on my post and ensuring that my production statistics were up (and we lived and died over our statistics), many Int base staff including me became part of teams with our marketing and public relations units that planned an unprecedented $3 million advertising campaign to counter everything about the *Time* story. COB told us that Behar's article had been driven by the influence of Eli Lilly and Company because of the church's efforts against their killer drug, Prozac. The church had been at war over Lilly's production and use of the drug in schools. The church stayed entangled in this court case for about five years; meanwhile, the legal expenses demanded that the church coffers be filled, and had a domino effect within the Scientology world.

We designed full-age ads placed in *USA Today* every weekday that May and June for twelve weeks. Other teams, especially the Office of Special Affairs, worked on booklets to "dead agent" the author, the publication, and many of the claims. They produced a "Fact vs. Fiction" piece that attempted to correct the "falsehoods" *Time* had claimed about Scientology. One of our research team members looked for incriminating information about *Time,* and found a 1936 issue with a cover story of Adolph Hitler, thus accusing *Time* of promoting Nazi Germany and supporting fascism, and made ties between Prozac and Hitler. Ironically, the Scientology organization had already been displaying characteristics of fascism, so this was also about deflection.

Miscavige briefed the Int base on Saturday nights about the progress of the campaign, particularly his interview on *ABC Nightline* with Ted Koppel. I noted the absence of remorse about the suicide of Scientologist Noah Lottick; instead, I heard criticism of Noah's father Edward who was thought to have made his son's life intolerable. I tuned out a lot of Miscavige's rant, because by that time, it was clear to me that the frenzy of the Int base was based on Scientology's war of the worlds that sprang up through distorted notions. We never got to read any outside information about the *Time* article, the reviews of Miscavige's talk on *Nightline*, or the war against Lilly. Whatever we learned was Miscavige's version of what happened.

The court ruling on Scientology's suit against the authors eventually found that neither *Time*, nor Rick Behar, was guilty of an actual intent of malice, but was doing investigative journalism. Behar went on to receive journalism awards, as did another SP on Scientology's enemy list, Paulette Cooper, author of *The Scandal of Scientology*. In 1993, Church of Scientology International sued the CEO of Eli Lilly, Mitchell Daniels, for defamation with malice by stating that Scientology was "no church." Actual malice is knowledge of falsity or reckless disregard for the truth or falsity of the statement. The U.S. court of Appeals 4th Circuit found that Daniels was not guilty.

### Merchants of Chaos

The Int base had turned into an active war zone. I found myself sinking deeper into a collective idea about fighting a war using methods that I didn't align with. This group think focused on the enemies of Scientology who allegedly were out to destroy us. I, like other Int base staff, hadn't been allowed to read the suppressive article in *Time*, so we couldn't see all of its claims. Nor had I read Paulette Cooper's book to see what she had to say; we weren't able to get a copy of it. But this *Time* article was one of the reasons why we weren't allowed to have Internet access or a personal computer, or watch television. We might have discovered the world's view about Scientology. Instead, we were told that we didn't read outside media because we were being protected from the lies told by our enemies.

Hubbard's materials contain various mentions about "merchants of chaos," the suppressive individuals such as media, psychiatrists, police, government, and Scientology critics who paint a picture of a crazy and dangerous environment. He poses the Scientology churches as the ones providing protection from these merchants of chaos. During that time I was still detached enough from this war zone mindset to pose myself the possibility that Hubbard, Miscavige, or Scientology overall were the merchants of chaos, pumping fear into its members and offering itself as the only solution (protection). How different was that from a don in a Mafia movie whose organization provides "protection" from thugs in neighborhoods?

The war with *Time* seemed to stir Miscavige into a worsened frenzy as if Scientology was going to be imminently consumed if we didn't combat our enemies continually. The Int base built an arsenal of weapons including assault rifles, pistols, and bombs, trained attack dogs, electric fences, and a rifle range for practice. Though my post never connected with any of those war tools, this was the world of our Gold security guard friends such as Jackson Moorehead, Danny Dunnegin, Gary Connelly, Uwe Stuckenbrock and a few others who were always on watch. After 1998, I read legal affidavits that confirmed these weapons on our base, including from former Security Chief Andre Tabayoyon's and former RTC leader Jesse Prince's.

## Miscavige micromanages dirt

Although Miscavige was fighting a global battle as the leader of the Scientology world under attack, he nevertheless found time to walk through Golden Era Productions to inspect our offices on a micro level, looking for "outpoints" that could reveal any enemies within our own ranks. I learned this from other Gold crew who had been disciplined because Miscavige had personally found dust on their shelves, or clutter in their drawers, but worse, despatches or written orders that were old and non-complied to. Dirt and outdated communications were a red flag waving, a sign of out-ethics for that guilty staff member.

Now our dust and in-baskets were being monitored and controlled by COB. Out of defense, I eliminated any such signs at my own desk area. One day, protecting myself against a potentially incriminating inspection, I rearranged all the books on the shelf above my desk and put them in order of height, perfectly aligned. I cleaned out every drawer in my desk, and aligned all my art supplies in perfect parallel order. I cleared out my three-basket system that held my in, pending, and outgoing communications. This didn't say anything about how clean and orderly I really was on a daily basis; it only showed that I was alert enough to prevent a problem caused by an inspection.

Sure enough, some RTC staff came through the Art Department one day to do communication inspections. They were looking for outpoints that were sure signs to crimes having been committed. One of the officers in front of my desk said aloud, "Look, her books look so aesthetic, they are in perfect order. She is 'upstat'."

## Epidemic of abortions & attacks on families

COB assigned the Int base orgs a condition of treason because we "weren't wearing our hats" doing everything in our power to ensure that Scientology was expanding. He often spoke in sweeping generalities like this, instead of addressing one specific person. Our condition was downgraded to a condition of confusion, the lowest condition, because he said we didn't even know where we were in the world of Scientology or we would be creating better solutions for Scientology's problems.

While the base caved in from wrong condition assignments, general duress and verbal abuse, several women tried to get off the base through other means. Married couples knew it violated policy to get pregnant because children were no longer allowed there. There were two options if a couple did get pregnant: Get an abortion and stay at the Int base to prove your loyalty to the Sea Org; Stay pregnant, but leave the Int base to have the baby. Since most staff lived below poverty on $45 per week, and many staff had disconnected from their families, the second option was not workable. Who could afford to leave, get a place to live, and pay for medical expenses of having a baby? When that reality finally hit, women chose option one.

Several Cine staff, and several other women on the base, asked me if they could borrow money to pay for their abortion. I guess they asked me because it seemed to be common knowledge that Peter and I received music royalties from our pre-Sea Org music career. With desperate looks on their faces, it was extremely difficult for me to say no. But I didn't believe in helping women to get abortions to appease the Sea Org. I hadn't been able to have children, and would have considered it a blessing to get pregnant. Most of the women found someone else to borrow from.

I remember the regret and sorrow on some of the women's faces after their abortions. The ones who didn't display their emotions wrote letters to the Int base staff, describing how they had chosen a higher purpose and terminated their pregnancy so that they could continue to serve the Sea Org as the most ethical group on the planet. They passed these letters around requesting signatures of approval so that they would no longer be considered a liability to the Sea Org, and could rejoin the group again in good standing. Some eventually left the Sea Org.

• Only one couple I knew, Rick Kamen and his wife, carried out a full pregnancy and then left the base to start their family. Meanwhile, she received no special treatment or allowances for her physical condition and worked our brutal sixteen to eighteen hour work days. She and Rick were harassed a lot about choosing to leave the base to have their baby, and she received plenty of pressure to abort. I admired her grit and refusal to be deterred by peer pressure to divert from their plan. She said her family would help, but they planned to go to a Scientology organization where they could get jobs and share a place to live with other Scientologists.

I watched a gradual deterioration of family life. Divorces increased, particularly within RTC where couples were made to divorce if one spouse was booted out and the other wanted to prove loyalty by divorcing the exiled spouse. My Cine department head, Stefan Lewis, was constantly berated by Miscavige, who often called Stefan an SP in front of Cine crew. Stefan, not coincidentally, was married to Miscavige's secretary, Tanya, whom Miscavige had been trying to coerce into divorcing Stefan for months because he no longer worked in RTC. Stefan got assigned to the RPF, but eventually blew to recover his life. (In 2012, I learned the amazing story that his wife, Tanya Castle, managed to escape with Stefan's help and finally rejoined her husband.)

My section head, KK, was crazy in love with her newlywed husband, Ivano Priori. Miscavige selected Ivano for a command team sent to an organization in Canada. COB thought nothing of separating married couples. Ivano's move lasted years, which led to KK's broken heart and, of course, deterioration of their marriage leading to divorce. Former WDC CC and Cine make-up artist,

Nancy, had been married to Pascal Julienne, an INCOMM staff member. Miscavige sent Pascal on a command team to another country, which broke up their marriage. Greg and Sandy Wilhere had been married for years and their son, Darius, worked in Qual. Sandy lost her post in RTC and Greg then divorced her. My friend Geray lost her post in Miscavige's office and her husband, Marty Rathbun, an RTC exec, divorced her. The lengthy list goes on, but these are just a few examples of the collective groupthink where the group is all and the individuals nothing, leading to obliteration of families.

Neither the Int base, nor the Sea Org overall, was suitable for family life. With no time off and eighteen-hour workdays, when did we ever have time to nurture our relationship? Since we first arrived at Gold, married couples seemed to attract attacks—including Peter and me. Our relationship had changed dramatically. We would go for weeks to months without having sex; sleep deprivation made it difficult to function physically and certainly sabotaged romance. Peter's schedule was constantly torpedo'd by COB, causing him to stay up for nights on end and sleep in the studio for weeks while working on emergency videos. DM wasn't the only attacker. I once heard someone in my own division say that they were going after Peter Schless and would get him to divorce his wife—while I was in hearing range. Other women asked him to spend Sunday morning libs time with them (there was a phase in the early 90s when we actually had occasional liberty time).

Peter and I went to see the Chaplain, Ken Hoden, about this. It was a stupid mistake to think that the same man who commandeered my return to the Int base from Gallup, New Mexico, would be able to provide an unbiased ear to listen to our marriage woes. His wife, Andy Hoden, lived in Los Angeles so they only saw each other occasionally. Ken Hoden once told us, "Well, sex after so many years with the same person does get boring." That was the help we got. I once sat down with a friend of mine from RTC and confided in her about my concerns. She ended up writing a report on me that I was nattering about Peter's work schedule, which, since it was commandeered by Miscavige, was interpreted to mean that I was nattering about Miscavige. I, of course, was sent to ethics and made to write up my overts and withholds.

## Yearning for freedom

My own good sense continued to clash with the teachings of L. Ron Hubbard and the onerous leadership tactics of DM's Sea Organization. The totalitarian control stirred up such intense yearning for my pre-Sea Org life that I found the conditions increasingly unbearable. Management's crackdown on control of staff rang a loud warning bell. I think it was impossible for staff to consider themselves unfree while they dedicated their lives to fighting for total spiritual freedom through Scientology; they couldn't see the dichotomy, or this unique brand of fascism creeping into Sea Org life. Never had I imagined myself in servitude within a religious military unit with mental and physical restraints.

One day, Byrnes and Wilhere made a surprising announcement: If anyone didn't want to be here, just let them know. We could leave with no further questions asked. The strategy was to get rid of the dead wood, the SPs who were blocking command intention and keeping Scientology from expanding. Gold crew were standing in military muster formation in rows of nearly four hundred staff, and I was about four rows away from Peter, dying to make eye contact with him. I wanted to leave, but didn't have the guts to raise my hand without first talking with him. This was the first chance we'd had to actually openly discuss our discontent. Later that night on the way home I asked him, "What do you think about that open door Byrnes and Wilhere gave us?"

Peter looked at me blankly. "Yeah, that's good. We'll get rid of lots of SPs."

My heart sank, but I made a stab at it anyway. "What do you think about us? I mean, we could start all over! You know you could easily get back into the music business in LA. I know I could get design clients again. We could do it!"

"Are you kidding me, KK? There's no way we're leaving!" Peter's view hadn't changed since the last time we had talked about this. "We are trusted Sea Org officers. No way."

One day, through the windows of the MCI north dining room, I saw about a dozen crew walking in a row together. I heard someone else say, "There go the SPs. Good riddance." I entertained the thought of walking over to the Ethics office in Building 36 and joining the exodus from the Int base.

Three years after my first escape, I was nearing the edge of another cliff. If I had to make another clandestine escape again like a prisoner breaking out, I would, with or without Peter.

# 26

## DESPERATE MEASURES

**1993**

WHEN I FOUND MYSELF ON THE EDGE one night, after missing the opportunity from Byrnes and Wilhere to leave, I knew I had to survive independent of Peter. Ron and Becky Miscavige were asleep in their room, while Peter lay asleep in our room. I hated having to sneak instead of functioning like a decent human being and just honestly saying goodbye to the Sea Org, with the dignity of driving away with my husband. This time, I was angry, not fearful, lost, or confused like I was in 1990. I didn't care if there were security guards around, watching or not watching at the gate, trying to stop me. I must have been moving between molecules because no one approached my car.

This time, I had a destination. I headed toward Los Angeles, with my first stop in Glendale to withdraw some money from our bank account. I knew I could make it on my own for a little while. But to do that, I had to go to the offices of Wiseman & Burke, our Scientology accountants/financial managers. They banked our music royalties and paid our bills for us before we joined the Sea Org. We had retained them since to manage our finances after we moved up to Gold.

Bruce Wiseman and Kevin Burke were prominent Scientologists; Kevin played the role of advising us on financial investments.

I still hadn't recovered from the fact that Kevin had steered us to a bad investment that lost us a good bit of money through a bad investment with Scientologist, Reed Slatkin, who co-founded Earthlink with Sky Dayton. Kevin suggested that we invest in some great opportunities with Slatkin's enterprises that promised a high return, specifically his prison pay-phones project. Unfortunately, we were two of the many poor suckers who unwittingly fell prey to Slatkin's ponzi scheme. Neither Peter nor I knew that Slatkin's investment club was unregistered; we got involved because we trusted Kevin Burke and his recommendations. Not until 1998 did I discover that the Securities & Exchange Commission discovered Slatkin's unregistered business in Santa Barbara after he had scammed about $593 million from Scientologists and other investors. I don't know whether our money landed in his Zurich account at NAA Financial or not. Investigators found that he owned a fleet of cars, about 35 real estate properties, a significant art collection, and a private jet. Slatkin pleaded guilty to 15 counts of fraud, conspiracy, and money laundering. He was sentenced to 14 years in prison, and was ordered to pay $240 million in restitution. To my knowledge, we never recovered a cent after investing thousands of dollars. And I could only imagine how much money Slatkin channeled into his Scientology accounts, or into Wiseman & Burke who, I imagine, received commissions on these investments.

Showing up at a Scientology-run business during day hours revealed the fact that I, as a known Sea Org member, was not where I was supposed to be at that time of day. The Wiseman & Burke staff were all dedicated Scientologists who knew that Peter and I worked at Gold. But I walked into the offices, and asked the assistant to write me a check out of our Schlessmusik account. He put me off for a while, telling me he had to balance our account before they could withdraw funds. I wouldn't be surprised if they called Peter or Gold security to alert them of my sudden presence. Knowing that I had the right to withdraw money from my own account, I refused to be delayed or intimidated and held my ground. I was outraged that two of the staff asked me questions about my withdrawal, as if I owed them any answers. This was my money, not theirs, but there seemed to be an air of authority over me.

I don't know whether they contacted Peter, but since they delayed so long, I imagine they tried. I felt victorious about exercising my right to access my funds, despite their questioning. A little paranoia began to move in as I walked down Glendale Boulevard, now that an alert might have gone to the Int base about my whereabouts. I wanted to get off the streets to reduce the chance of being seen by anyone who knew me, who would notice that I was not where I was supposed to be at that hour of the day. I checked into a small Holiday Inn in Glendale and paid cash. I didn't want to use a credit card because Gold Security would be tracking my expenses through their computer system to see where I was and what I was doing.

Safe in my Holiday Inn refuge, I drew the blinds, took a shower, and crawled under the covers. My dog Toby cuddled next to me and, other than taking him out and feeding him, I slept for two days straight. I don't remember eating.

My next priority was to see Peter's brother Ely and his wife Krista, both very dear to me. I called Krista to tell her I had left Scientology, and that Peter was not with me. She welcomed me to come to their home in Burbank and stay as long as I wanted. After Krista got over her shock that I had left Scientology without Peter, she and later Ely talked with me about how our fanatical commitment to Scientology had affected them as our family. Ely and Krista had been upset with Peter and me for never getting in touch, even though they lived in the Los Angeles area. They had just had their first child, Kyle. Ely was deeply disappointed that we had made no efforts to be an aunt and uncle to their first child, much less to have a relationship with him and Krista. I saw just how much we had hurt them, made them feel excluded because of Scientology policies, particularly the Int base rules about no time off, no opportunities to see family, no family visits at the base, and no phone calls unless they were monitored by security.

I stayed with my in-laws for several days, and can barely describe how wonderful it felt to wake up under their roof and feel loved. The issue of love really broke me. I wanted to share this family relationship as the four of us, with Peter. I eventually broke down and called Peter, I just couldn't take the separation. Peter, of course, passed the information on to security, who began calling me at Ely and Krista's house. I finally accepted a phone call from an Int base security guard, Paul Kellerhaus, and agreed to meet with PK to discuss my situation.

PK's messages to me about Peter were persuasive enough to make me think that I was unable to leave the Sea Org if it meant that Peter and I would have to split up. PK's coercion was effective, holding my commitment to the Sea Org over my head, reminding me of Hubbard's words that people who leave the Sea Org are degraded beings who cannot make it on the outside. In other words, Sea Org members are so institutionalized that we can't function on our own, like ex-cons who just can't stay out of prison and have to get back in.

After all that I had told them about my life, I felt so conflicted about telling them I was going back to Peter. They questioned our lifestyle and our commitment to Scientology as being extremist. We said our goodbyes, with me knowing that it might be a very long time before we would ever talk or see each other again.

PK followed me in his car back to the Int base. When I returned to the property, I of course was not allowed to see my husband. I was made to stay at the Old Gilman House again under security watch. The base was still surrounded by chain link fences with barbed wire, so trying to get out would have been a formidable task. I didn't bother to try, and didn't even think about trying.

I remained isolated for at least three months at the Old Gilman House while getting security check interrogations. This time, I was not threatened with an RPF assignment. I worked around the OGH premises, cleaning rooms and working on the grounds. I learned that I wasn't totally alone in the OGH area, after catching a glimpse of Marc Yager, the former Commanding Officer of the Commodore's Messenger Organization International, flanked by several security guards, working in the high weeds behind OGH.

Marc Yager had been a close compadre to David Miscavige for years. I remembered an emergency briefing that Miscavige had called one day a few months prior. He said that Yager had committed seriously suppressive acts against him personally and against the church. I noted that Miscavige was effectively "black PRing" Marc Yager here, because everyone would swallow Miscavige's opinions and turn against Yager. I had never observed Marc Yager doing anything abusive or destructive to another Sea Org member. Yager had blown the Int base, but was recovered by an emergency security team sent after him on motorcycles. Since then, he had been held captive at OGH, but I hadn't known that before I had left. I also didn't find out until later that Peter had served on the emergency security team who chased Yager down Highway 79 on motorcycles, and brought him back. Yager had been sequestered near OGH for at least five months that I could estimate. A nasty swamp of thick green water filled with bullrushes, weeds, snakes, algae and other undesirable things had edged the back side of OGH in its pre-Scientology days in the 1930s, when the property had been a warm mineral springs resort. Dead, tangled brush lay at the base of OGH where no one ever walked because of mucky ground and impassable thicket. For months, Yager worked at that swamp carving through the thicket with a machete, cutting down stalks of bamboo, clearing out brush and doing I don't know what else, while under 24/7 security watch. His full-time punishment stretched on for months. No one was supposed to see him and certainly not talk to him if they did. I later heard that he was made to build a cage for himself made out of bamboo shafts, and live in it there. Meanwhile, Marc's wife Michelle was told to divorce him. Michelle wanted to leave the Sea Org at one point after Marc was taken captive, and was also sequestered out at OGH for months until she changed her mind to stay in the Sea Org. She did eventually divorce him.

Like Marc Yager, I had been left to decay at OGH with plenty of time to think. I knew that I reacted differently than Peter to Miscavige's abuses. Peter lived within the four walls of his music studio. I saw Miscavige in many different settings with different people than Peter did. Maybe I just had a little more objectivity, because I saw Miscavige's power games of abuse and control, which Peter said didn't exist. I came to believe that there was no way to win in Miscavige's Sea Org. Whenever Miscavige accused us of committing overts and crimes, he labeled us with an ethics condition (confusion, treason, enemy, doubt, liability, non-existence, never the higher conditions of normal, affluence or power). However, his labels were always wrong, because he used ethics to manipulate and disempower us, instead of helping us to improve. For example, the formula for no longer being perceived as an enemy of the group was "find out who you really are." The only "right" answer to that question in the Sea Org was to find out that one is really a Sea Org member, dedicated to the only technology that exists to save mankind. Outside of that answer, there was no way to find out who you *really* are. One could never discover or expose their true self if that self differed with the one that fit the "right" answer.

The way people thought of me was never my *true* self, but the identity I had to maintain to function in the group. To be who I *really* am, I had to be out of the Sea Org. I knew I was *not* the pseudo-military officer depicted by my uniform; I was not a Sea Org member who would sacrifice this and all my future lifetimes to the cause of this fanatical group. There were no handcuffs on me, no bars around me, but I couldn't get out. The mental gyrations at play became confusing and erratic, like tangled strands in a web of dissonant thought:

*Yes, I am miserable, but it is so hard to leave.*

*Yes, I want to recapture my chance at living with my family in society again, but what about the people I am leaving behind?*

*Yes, I believe I could recover my career and create a fresh new start, but Sea Org members who left Scientology are degraded and would never make it. That includes me.*

*No, I no longer want to give my life to the aims of Scientology that had deceived me. But what if it was all true and it was me who was all wrong?*

*No, I no longer believed that L. Ron Hubbard or his writings were Source because I knew other people wrote Hubbard's materials under his name. But wasn't RTC trustworthy enough to preserve the sanctity of Source materials? They wouldn't purposely deceive us, would they?*

...and on.

After being in confinement for three months, I broke. I knew I didn't want to leave Peter and I didn't want Miscavige to win by splitting us up. My desire for keeping our marriage intact won me over. I told one of the security guards that I decided to stay in the Sea Org. That set off a chain of events, starting with a motorcycle ride to Building 36 to meet with the Chief Master at Arms. He had to upgrade me from each ethics condition before I could move forward. Then it was time to write my Liability formula, to show that I had made amends, and was no longer a liability to the group. I gained nearly 400 signatures from Gold crew, but some hard-nose crew who believed that no one should ever try to leave the Sea Org, refused to sign it. I only needed a little more than 50 per cent. In two days, I earned the majority and was accepted back into the group.

Next, I was allowed to see my husband. I have an indelible memory of Peter telling me that I had to decide to be a Sea Org member first before we could talk about restoring our marriage. The very thing I had been in denial over was the very thing I was now being faced with: Peter's total indoctrination to the Sea Org. In his mind, it was okay to enforce these criteria for us to stay married, criteria that had never been a part of our marriage vows. I had convinced myself that I was a Sea Org member first, which is how I ended my doubt condition.

Peter had been moved out of our apartment with Ron and Becky Miscavige to a room for single men while I was sequestered. Now, for the second time, I made arrangements for us to move into a couple's apartment. This time, it was with Pat and Sarah Gualtieri at Kirby Gardens. We moved into a 12' x 12' bedroom with a small bathroom attached, a sink in the bedroom, and a closet with heavy sliding doors. I hung some artwork and photographs and dressed the room to look like us again.

I recommitted myself to become a stellar Sea Org member, and privately vowed that I would move up in the ranks to gain more responsibility and power where fewer seniors had authority over me. I had no other choice but to succeed Sea Org style, because I had convinced myself that it was impossible to get out and stay out.

# 27

# REPRIEVE

## North side of the Int base - 1993

MIRACULOUSLY, I WAS POSTED in the Senior Executive Strata in the LRH Book Compilations Unit, instead of going back to the Gold Art Department. Being treated like a respectable human being again was a highlight while working as a proofreader of LRH originals. A story about working in RComps is on the book website, if you'd like to know more. But my role in RComps was short lived. One surprising day, COB Assistant informed me that my design skills were needed for a special project at Saint Hill in England right away.

Against objections from Cheryl Sutter and my RComps proofreading partner, Rachel, who didn't want me to leave without a trained replacement, I went on the uniform design project. I felt torn, because I respected my senior and partner, and didn't want to leave them in the lurch. But COB's assistants told them to support command intention.

This project was run as a mission from the Action Bureau in CMO Int. I was sent to the UK on mission orders (that I cowrote). CMO UK would give me an office and assign me an assistant to help me get the project done. To make it official so that I could be in charge of a Sea Org mission, I went on full-time study to complete First Class Missionaire training and PRO TRs. The one drawback was that I would be in England for at least three months and Peter didn't want me to go. Although Peter and I had been living together, we hardly saw each other. We worked sixteen-plus hours per day, had no time off, and Peter often worked all-nighters producing music for the next event videos, with no time for relationship building, romance, or any sort of enjoyable lifestyle.

## East Grinstead, Sussex, England - 1993

Why rush to Saint Hill? Scientology's Advanced Organization at Saint Hill (AOSH) near East Grinstead would host the IAS annual conference in October. Miscavige wanted all the AOSH staff to be transformed from their present slovenly state to sparkling examples of what Scientology technology could do for them and the world. Hubbard's 17th century Manor in the UK that he had purchased from a Maharajah was the heart of Saint Hill and the symbol for Scientology since the 1960s. Saint Hill still held the magic of the 1960s era when Hubbard wrote hundreds of policy letters and technical bulletins there, that comprise the tech of Scientology, while building what became the ideal org, or a Saint Hill size organization.

My days at Saint Hill kept me busy doing work I loved. A woman named Lyndell was selected by CMO UK to be my assistant. The day I met her, my heart broke for her. She was dangerously thin, with pasty skin and straggly hair. Her teeth needed cleaning and repair, and her Sea Org uniform looked like she had worn it daily for years. Lyndell had been on the waiting lines to get out of the Sea Org, unhappy about the horrific conditions in which her children were being raised and "educated" while she and her husband dedicated their lives to working at Saint Hill 15 hours per day. Bullard's provided insufficient heat to the already drafty stone building where the crew lived. The children's "day care" facilities were below substandard in cleanliness, looking impoverished rather than a facility that should be taking care of the organization's elite corps Sea Org members' children. Hot running water was a scarcity rather than a normal provision, so cleanliness for herself and her children was not something she could count on.

Lyndell and her family opened my eyes to the fact that Sea Org members outside of the U.S. lived in far worse conditions than what I had observed in LA, which were pathetic and embarrassing.

My first order of business was to somehow help change Lyndell's mind about leaving the Sea Org, which I almost felt guilty about doing. Simultaneously, I wanted to help improve her personal wellness.

Lyndell didn't want to do anything to help management that had led to the decline of her family; she only wanted out. My good sense as well as my conscience told me to understand Lyndell's grievances and to not judge her for her desire to leave. Even though I was a Sea Org member from the most senior org in the Scientology world, I didn't blame Lyndell for feeling the way she did, since I had been in her spot more than once. I addressed her as a woman buried under a mass of conflicts and circumstances that she felt unable to control. I pushed through some expense money to buy her some new clothing (Uniform K, plain clothes) to wear when we traveled to London to do some of the project tasks. I required AOSH to purchase her some new uniform parts, starting with some new shoes and a Class A uniform that she could wear with pride. I also cut and styled her hair, and encouraged her to wear makeup again. Most importantly, I made sure she left on time at the end of the day, so that she could pick up her children on time, and get a decent night's sleep. That's something I also afforded myself while I was on this project. There was no need to work 16 - 18 hours daily and sabotage my personal wellness, as was the trend at the Int base.

Lyndell's quality of life became a personal project for me, as important as the uniform project. I'm certain that my empathy toward her and my lack of judging her for her doubt in the Sea Org helped her to open up to me. I never once told her that I had tried to get out of the Sea Org twice myself. Lyndell and her husband were able to move to better, more respectable living quarters. However, nothing changed with the childcare situation. Pulling her out of her decline from doing grunt work around Saint Hill in dirty clothes while on the "routing out lines" waiting to go into sec checking sessions, helped to clear her mind. Working on a project to improve staff conditions, and working in a clean office also helped to diffuse her disgust about Sea Org conditions.

I had been warned by the senior execs at the Int base that the Saint Hill staff smelled of body odor. One of the problems had been their lack of hot water; thus, staff didn't bathe often enough. So, I ordered that the plumbing problems be financed and fixed, and had all the staff restudy the Sea Org issues about grooming and cleanliness. Lack of cleanliness was rampant at AOSH. I had been given a bunk in a dorm room of CMO girls who lived at the Stables. I'll never forget discovering that two of the girls in my room had head lice. I've never had this and it gave me the creeps knowing that the people sleeping above me and next to me had lice. I could understand why this might have happened to them: it was so difficult and inconvenient for them to bathe frequently. When you have to walk down the hall and wait in line after working 16 hours, and the water is not hot, sometimes it's easier to skip the shower. Plus, impoverished Sea Org members probably couldn't afford shampoo and soap. I also took it upon myself to do a personal makeover on nearly all the men and women at Saint Hill. This included hairstyling and cuts, and makeup and grooming instructions on more than one hundred staff.

Since my project required so much research of sources to buy other uniform accessories, we traveled all over London and parts of England. We'd take the train from East Grinstead to Victoria Station, and get on the Tube or jump on the red double-decker buses. I learned my way around London and justified ways to combine sightseeing with my research. I toured Greenwich and saw the lines of demarcation that have marked international time zones since the 1500s. Sights of Roman walls, the Tower of London, Westminster Abbey, Oxford University, all became part of my research trips. I studied coats of arms that I saw throughout England, which influenced my design for Saint Hill's uniform emblem and the overall sense of style for this project.

I researched clothing manufacturers in London, Ireland and Scotland, before I selected Adrian Hewitt at Burlington Uniforms in London to be our primary supplier. Burlington utilized manufacturing facilities in northern England where fine wool suits had traditionally been made. We selected a shirt manufacturing company in Northern Ireland, and a sweater manufacturer in Glasgow, Scotland. Burlington Uniforms was just a few streets away from Savile Row, the historic center of hand-tailored suits made at the pleasure of His Majesty. I'd frequent the tailor shops on Savile Row, studying the tailoring details of fine clothiers, acquiring a set of standards that I applied to my own design projects. My travels also included visits to local places in East Grinstead where I met some of the shopkeepers in town, and specifically to the living quarters for Sea Org crew at Bullard's and Stonelands.

Adrian Hewitt, the director of Burlington's, manufactured many of my uniform accessories. I designed a new Sea Org button that Hewitt produced for me in Italy. I designed an embroidered jacket emblem for AOSH, and got the original prototype made by a team of artists who stitched accessories for the Queen of England. Hewitt and his staff took this prototype to Pakistan to oversee quality control, since these patches (hundreds) were individually hand-stitched.

We went to Edinburgh, Scotland to do a little sightseeing around the Edinburgh Castle before we picked up the train to Glasgow, where we inspected the production of our uniform sweaters. There, I caught my Sea Org buttons being sewn onto the cardigan sweaters upside down. Doing quality control of my products proved to be the best investment of my time that guaranteed excellent results in the end. On another excursion, we went to the northern tip of Ireland, overlooking the North Sea, where my uniform shirts were being made. I had never seen shirts mass produced in individual pieces before. I watched one woman doing the same thing all day—machine stitching buttons into place. I would have gone crazy doing a repetitive job like that, but I was told that these jobs were valuable to the residents of this northern Island area.

The journey to Ireland had been a great adventure. We took the speed train to Manchester and then flew to Belfast. There we got picked up by an Irish cabbie who drove us to the coast between Coleraine and Bushmills. I ate homemade shortbread hot out of the ovens of a tiny village bakery in Ayr. We had lunch in an inn overlooking the North Sea, where I devoured fresh caught whitefish and chips served with malt vinegar. Hewitt took me out to Giant's Causeway for a walk along Ireland's legendary coast, which I believed should be added as an eighth wonder of the world.

Lyndell and I accomplished the incredible feat of getting everything manufactured and delivered as planned and on time. She did an excellent job setting up the Saint Hill Chapel as the showroom and distribution center for the initial uniform release. Rows of tables held a variety of shoes and boots, socks and stockings, ties for men and women, sweaters, Sea Org insignia, and racks of suit jackets, skirts, pants and shirts, coats, gloves, scarves—everything a Sea Org member needed for the harsh English weather.

Faces of staff eager to get in the Chapel beamed through the door windows for an hour before the release. When we opened the Chapel doors, staff rushed in to get their allocation list that showed the parts they were entitled to receive. Staff went through the aisles filling their arms as if on a magical but frenetic shopping spree. I recall the joy of helping to transform at least their outer image from slovenly to dignified. For these Sea Org members who, before this, only had one pair of pants and one shirt that they washed every few nights, this was beyond anything like the best Christmas they could imagine.

The Saint Hill staff transformation was ultimately gratifying. From the auditors and supervisors in the technical division, to the servers in the mess hall, the executive staff, and the estates crew, their faces glowed with appreciation. I couldn't help but notice that some staff even carried themselves differently, as if walking with a little more pride.

Lyndell decided to remain in the Sea Org, to work as the Uniform In-Charge for the Saint Hill base. My work would be finished when I had documented the lines for taking care of the uniform parts, and knew that Lyndell was fully set-up to successfully maintain the uniform system.

While at Saint Hill, I never received one phone call or letter from my husband. I called Peter from time to time, defying policy: Phone calls from lower organizations (AOSH) were not allowed to be made to higher organizations (Int base). Policy also said that higher organizations could not call into lower organizations.

I finished my project well before the IAS event that October. Int base advance crew who came to Saint Hill to produce the event raved about how great the staff looked. David Miscavige and Marc Yager arrived to preview the setups for the upcoming event. One day in LRH's Manor, Miscavige and Yager told me that I was doing an incredible job with transforming the staff image. This put another notch in my belt for a job well done, inspected personally and approved by COB.

"I have plans for a new post for you when you get back, Karen," COB told me. My imagination ran wild, hoping that a permanent post would be created for me to take care of staff image. "You'll work in the events unit in the Int Management PR office in Exec Strata, as Cindy Rainer's design assistant. And you'll get to see Peter for Christmas."

Seeing Peter would be great, but regarding the post news, I had to feign appreciation. Working in the IMPR event unit would be as chaotic as working in Cine, even though the job was in a senior org. Being back at the Int base for Christmas would be nice, but in reality, this just meant working over that holiday and, at best, having maybe one-half day off with Peter on Christmas day. Had I stayed at Saint Hill, I wouldn't like being alone without Peter on my favorite holiday, but having a white Christmas and going into London to enjoy a few hours of holiday celebration would partially make up for that.

I responded before I thought about my words. "Oh, but Sir, I can't go home yet because I'm not done with this project." Miscavige's fading smile and furrowed eyebrows showed me that was the wrong thing to say. Yager raised his eyebrows with a crooked smile. But I think COB took my comment as coming from a person very dedicated to my work. That was, in fact, true but certainly not the total truth.

"Sir, what I mean is, I want to make sure that my assistant who is taking over the uniform project here is set up to be successful. I have to document everything and make sure she can run the program without me. But otherwise, I can't wait to get back. Thank you so much."

"Well done, Karen."

# INT FINANCE OFFICE UNIFORM PROJECT I/C

Above: Karen used her clothing design skills to improve the image of Scientology and Sea Org staff internationally. The name badges showed one's job title, never a person's name.

The black Uniform Project In-Charge shows the last post she held in the Sea Org.

Right: Karen designed and produced this Sea Org button in England, used on Sea Org uniforms since 1993.

Above: Lyndell Warren, Sea Org member at AOSH UK, assists Karen on the Saint Hill uniform project, setting up the Chapel for the uniform distribution to the Saint Hill staff, 1993.

Right: Karen changed the image at the Flag Land Base in the mid-1990s, replacing the pseudo-military Sea Org uniforms with business dress more suitable for the Clearwater tropical climate.

Debbie Cook, Captain FSO, left the Sea Org in 2007 and alerted the Scientology world to the dangers of Miscavige's Scientology.

# 28

## MAKING SCIENTOLOGY LOOK GOOD

### The War Is Over, 1993

AS IF FATE WAS ON MY SIDE, I did not return to the Int base before the infamous event at the Los Angeles Sports Arena. David Miscavige announced that the WAR IS OVER with the IRS, and that he was the victor in the years-long battle to gain tax-exemption for the Church of Scientology. The International Management Public Relations (IMPR) office and its Events Unit, working closely with the Gold crew, was responsible for planning and producing this pivotal event.

Although this monumental event released monumental news in the church's monumental history, it also marks one of the most monumental "flaps" ever at the Int base. This level of flap was just one reason why I didn't want to work in the hot-seat office of the IMPR Events Unit. NOTHING was more important to David Miscavige than his announcement at this event. In 1967, Scientology entities had lost tax-exempt status in the U.S. because the IRS had declared Scientology a commercial enterprise. Scientology leaders had been suing and losing almost annually over this issue since then. Once David Miscavige, Marty Rathbun, and some OSA folks performed their black magic over the IRS Commissioner and team, the "war" to gain tax-exemption was over. They were able to dig up enough dirt on key people and threaten enough lawsuits that threaten enough lawsuits that it behooved the IRS to issue the tax-exempt status. Scientology got off easy by paying only $12.5 million of the nearly billion it owed and received the coveted exemption.

This victory held huge ramifications for Scientology organizations and its followers. Being tax-exempt meant Scientology was no longer to be subject to many business regulations and, instead, would be treated like other nonprofit "churches." Followers could claim their "donations" to Scientology as tax deductions. Even though Scientology was set up as a network of corporations that sold self-help services and retail material products to its customers (whom they would later call parishioners), they were to be treated as a "religion" instead of the business that they actually are, with tax-exempt status. Quite an incredible feat.

By the time I got back from the UK, fires were still smoldering around the base following the debacle of that event production. Many staff recounted the gory details to me. I had thought that the flood of 1990 had been and would ever be the worse situation we lived through, but this sounded like a worse blood bath. Was it any wonder that so many crew would screw up their work at the event, after going so many days without sleep? Teleprompter operators messed up, so Miscavige could barely read his speech. Camera, lighting and sound crew were nearly defunct and messed up on key parts of Miscavige's speech, particularly his big announcement. An overhead light had nearly caught fire that almost fell on COB. Nearly a dozen Gold production crew received a justice action, and at least two people were sent to the prison camp for their mistakes. Many other Sea Org members on the base were stripped of their officer rank, even though many of these people had worked dedicatedly for years to earn it.

## Designing Int Management Events

COB placed me in the Int Management Public Relations Office as an artist to assist the Events Art Director, Cindy Rainer, with making Scientology management look good. As the Assistant Art Director, I also maintained my unofficial double-hat of being the International Staff Image Officer and Uniform Project In-Charge. Because of the ongoing need for improvements to Scientology's staff image worldwide, I was continuously used as a resource to help staff to look good at Sea Org bases around the globe.

Gone were the days of holding an event with a simple podium and an LRH photo hanging in the background. I could write a hundred pages on the ridiculous events that happened from day to day in the events unit, like designing awards, handling flaps, and beautifying the Int execs. I put a short story on the book website that describes some interesting details if you'd like to know more.

## Another Promotion: Deputy to Diana Hubbard

One surprising day, COB and COB Assistant briefed me on a new post they had created for me. I would work in the Senior Executive Strata as Commander Diana Hubbard's deputy. Diana Hubbard Ryan Horwich was the Division Six Internal Executive International (DSIEI), responsible for the recruitment and basic training of new people coming into Scientology around the globe. As her deputy, I would continue doing my staff image projects that implemented Hubbard's policy about the cleanliness of quarters and the image of staff as being the single-most important factor that would raise the income of Scientology organizations. Diana Hubbard was exceedingly creative and talented, and loved to write. If you'd like to know some of the details about how working under Diana Hubbard had it's advantages and disadvantages, please visit the book website.

## Int Landlord's Office: International Properties & Staff Image

Since I had worked with the Int Landlord staff on many design projects for Scientology buildings, they welcomed me into their office as a squatter who needed a place to work. The Int Landlord's office was in CMO Int in the International Finance Bureau, and the Int Finance Director and the Int Landlord were constantly on COB's radar. The Int Landlord post was a such a hot seat; Bill Brugger and Sarah Cunningham were just two who headed that office in my time there.

Working in this office was a perfect fit, although I was technically still posted in Exec Strata. Once I had a larger more functional workspace, I began to feel like a professional designer again. I enjoyed working with Geray Jory, Anna Caneen, Barry and Carol Stein, Marco, Laurence Barram, Jeff the landscape architect, and more. Anna, Barry, Carol and Jeff had been professionals in their field prior to the Sea Org, as I had been a professional designer. I also assisted the designers on their drawings and color renderings of Scientology buildings, including Bonnie View (Hubbard's mansion on the Int base), Building 50 (the new RTC building at Int), and the Super Power Building at the Flag Land Base. Consequently, I saw the extent to which the designers and COB changed plans again and again, sometimes monumentally, to create the showplace that Miscavige desired.

On the book website, there's a story about the SuperPower debacle, and how COB used to walk through the Int Landlord's office bragging about winning the IRS tax exemption. I also jumped another hurdle by taking the initiative to solve a problem about flaws in Gold's film production that had been on COB's plate, which led to another promotion. I had forged my way deeper into the group, according to my 1993 plan to be the best version of myself I could be within the Sea Org. I thought that dragging my feet before taking the IMPR post made it clear that I didn't want to do it.

# 29

## INTERNATIONAL MANAGEMENT
## PUBLIC RELATIONS

### IMPR Office, 1995

MY BIGGEST DILEMMA HAD TO BE kept secret: How would I do public relations for the International Management of Scientology, when COB said over and over that no one in International Management knew what they were doing? I had no confidence in International Management. To accomplish this feat, I would have to understand public relations, Scientology style, along with the many programs developed by the Int base execs, present them to the Scientology world, and then persuade the people down the echelons of organizations to embrace them. I had done public relations for our company, Schlessmusik, but had no training in Scientology PR.

David Miscavige reached out to me several times, probably sensing that I was floundering in how to approach this challenge. One day, he sent me a despatch telling me to watch the 1995 movie, "The American President," where Michael J. Fox plays the president's PR man. One of COB's staff brought me a CD of the movie so I could watch it for training purposes. COB liked the way the PR man advises the president about what the people are thinking, what the polls say, and how the president should respond according to what the public wanted to hear. This idealized persona for a PR, however, did not align with our authoritarian manage-ment structure built on ego, know-best, and rigid adherence to LRH management policies. Michael J. Fox's stylized role was in no way conducive for someone like IMPR who is lower on the org board and only a junior officer to advise senior execs that wore three or four stripes on their shoulder boards.

Hubbard required PRs to study the 1952 book, *Effective Public Relations* by Scott Cutlip and Allen Center. My first stumbling block came on page one, where its definition of public relations clashed with Hubbard's definition. Hubbard's writings were always senior to other sources and I never resolved that quandary.

I had known previous IMPR's such as Jean-Michel Wargniez who held the post for years, who fried in the hot seat of that job. Katie Paquette didn't make it. Cindy Rainer didn't want it. The IMPR worked closely with COB and most of the senior execs, along with OSA (Office of Special Affairs) execs. This IMPR posi-tion was subject to a degree of heat, pressure and demand from COB that I wasn't sure I could bear. I had to stay true to my prom-ise to myself that I would be the best I could be.

Thanks to the talks with Ron Miscavige about David, and my experiences with COB directly, I had lost my fear of DM and de-veloped a thicker skin. I had already left twice, so what more did I have to lose? I wasn't afraid of being booted out. Minimally, they could send me to the prison camp if I failed. But so far, I hadn't yet been shot with physical bullets, so how bad could it really get?

Since 1993, I had gotten along well with COB and won his fa-vor by doing a good job on my projects. As a designer, I was on my game. He showed favor to highly-productive staff displaying personal creativity. But that became part of my playbook. Being in his presence was walking in the company of power. Being on his bad side made the pits of hell appear to be a more habitable place. The gravest mistake anyone could make was thinking that we had any power just because we were close to power. I also believed that he drew pleasure from watching people experience pain that he caused directly or indirectly. Ever since I had done the RPF, I learned to avoid pain by doing nothing but my job, and doing it extremely well. I did not believe that pain is good and extreme pain is extremely good, which seemed to be an unstated mantra of oth-ers who lived in a pain zone I didn't want to enter. I had written my own playbook on my designer post that I would use as a model for my IMPR job:

- Know my area of expertise and excel within that sphere.
- Don't leave any holes in my work where COB can find fault.
- Take initiative; don't require orders to do my job.
- Work way ahead of my present project by lining up other projects that were waiting in the wings for me to get to.
- Impress COB with personal initiative.
- Cherish and protect my ethics protection on the Int base.

The most challenging job for the IMPR was to produce International events that featured COB and the senior executive entourage. COB expected masses of Scientologists at every event. That meant thousands of seats had to be filled at each major location, and that was the IMPR office's job. We ran the international call-in units, headed up by Monica Grannis, implemented at the regional and local levels. Hundreds of Scientologist staff and volunteers manned the phones every day for weeks before events, calling every Scientologist in central files at least three times to confirm attendance.

Event call-in was rough, but speechwriting was a nightmare that really didn't need to be that way. COB had posted Jane Janney, a new OT VII recruited from Flag, in the IMPR office as a speechwriter. Jane was quite flippant about her OT abilities when she first arrived in the office, which only drew attacks. She walked in confident that she could write fabulous speeches, but COB shredded them and nearly shredded her and everyone else in my office for not jumping in and writing excellent speeches. Bill Dendiu, long-term Sea Org member known for creative marketing genius, and former head of our Central Marketing Unit prior to Jeff Hawkins, was posted in our IMPR office and put on speechwriting. In fact, everybody in our office was put onto speech writing.

We were trying to create great stories out of skimpy statistics to squeeze blood out of rocks. That was the problem; we were lousy at cover-ups. ESI execs including Ronnie Miscavige (Marketing Exec Int), Greg Hughes (World Institute of Scientology Enterprises Exec Int), Diana Hubbard (Div 6 Internal Exec Int), Fran Harris (Books Exec Int), Sherry Murphy (Fields Exec Int) and others would jump in and try to write the speeches. Ray Mithoff (then Senior Case Supervisor International) and Guillaume Lesevre (then

Executive Director International) would work on writing their own speeches.. We'd all be up for nights on end writing speeches, screaming about speeches, crying over speeches. Time after time, COB shredded all speeches. My conclusion? The only words David Miscavige wanted to hear were his own. He finally put Danny Sherman, the LRH Biographer, onto speechwriting, and David Miscavige also edited those speeches.

Danny shared a little office with Andy Lenarcic, the LRH Biographer. I'd visit Danny to see what I could do to share the burden by at least providing research, or to just talk so I could learn from him. Danny finally warmed up to me after lambasting me for not getting speeches written by my office, causing him not do his primary job writing the LRH Biography.

COB made Exec Strata and CMO Int pay dearly for Dan writing speeches. Shelly Miscavige ordered me to put together a wardrobe of new clothes for Dan Sherman to wear at the Maiden Voyage event, when he would give talks as the LRH Biographer to the Freewinds guests. I was given a budget of $5,000 by COB orders, but the funds were to come out of CMO Int's and ESI's budgets, since he was doing our job. Danny and I went through catalogs and magazines to discover his tastes before I developed his look. He loved finely tailored classic clothing in natural fabrics like linen and wool with a 1940s influence. I showed COB Assistant my design plan; she loved it and gave me the green light.

I leveraged all my resources for the Dan Sherman event wardrobe project. This led to several shopping sprees in Beverly Hills boutiques such as Ralph Lauren, Hermes, Cole Haan and others. I'd bring back shopping bags full of things Danny loved. He let COB and COB Assistant know that he was as happy as he could be with these new threads when he went off for the Maiden Voyage event, looking like a million bucks. CMO Int and ESI funded the bill. This was on top of buying him a convertible sports car. Pleasing Dan Sherman was pleasing COB and COB Assistant, overshadowing my office's failure at speechwriting.

Being part of numerous senior executive planning meetings gave me insight into the workings of Scientology in a deeper way than I could have imagined. I learned how we routinely covered up problems with public relations solutions, despite Hubbard's policy to not lie in PR. For example, ED INT Guillaume Lesevre revealed that he had falsified the reports of several organizations achieving the coveted Saint Hill Size Award, including Los Angeles Day organization. In Guillaume's world, the work that goes into making a Saint Hill Size organization beats the work of an entire country's Olympics athletes to win a gold medal. In the Scientology world, the magnitude of falsifying these expansion awards could be compared to the U.S. President saying that the U.S. had paid off its national debt when it hadn't.

Using PR cover-ups to blanket Scientology technology flaps were the worst. Scientologists held one thing to be totally sacred: LRH's materials were 100% pure LRH. As just one example, I learned that a particular Exec Strata executive, who had also worked with the LRH Book Compilations project, had revised one of LRH's policies, the Danger Formula Expanded. Meanwhile, Scientologists around the world were applying this formula thinking it was pure LRH tech. I later learned that he wasn't the only one who had revised LRH's policies, which got approved by the Issue Authority RTC, and then issued in the OEC and HCOB volumes as being pure LRH tech. Plenty of other Scientology materials had been written by Sea Org staff and issued in LRH's name, and approved through AVC and RTC. Greg Wilhere wrote the Key to Life book that drew from LRH materials. Ray Mithoff and a team of the highest trained technical staff were writing the NOTS Rundowns. Mithoff was constantly in trouble for the ongoing flap of the NOTS Rundowns and Super Power Rundowns not being done, that drew Miscavige's wrath due to their lack of completion. This was all shattered glass for me. I had unquestioningly believed that anything that came out in LRH's name was 100% LRH. The fact that other people wrote or edited LRH materials is covered up at the most senior level to prevent public Scientologists from knowing this. If Scientologists knew the truth, the empire could crumble.

It was all about cover-ups—that's what I was learning about public relations, Scientology style. I began connecting the dots that church operations and missions were, in great part, set up to do cover-ups. Since the 1970s, Hubbard and the early Sea Org crew moved into Clearwater, Florida under a false name (United Churches of Florida) to cover up that they were the Church of Scientology. Sea Org ships were banned from many ports around Europe, the Mediterranean and Africa, so they have covered up their true identity by painting the ship a different color, or going through

through a name change while changing countries to sail under a different flag. Early Sea Org members continuously covered up their identity as Church of Scientology members, calling themselves everything from archaeologists to engineering projects. LRH's true location and identity has been covered up for years, in defense against the IRS and FBI. When I arrived at the base, the Port Captain normalized the action of having different shore stories ready to tell locals about what we were doing here. We covered up the truth about this being the Int base for the leaders of Scientology and instead called it Golden Era Productions. When going into town, we couldn't wear our name tags identifying our job titles. The LRH Biography project...the death of LRH...the death of Lisa McPherson...cover-ups.

My IMPR office on the first floor of Del Sol was a few doors down from ED Int, Guillaume Lesevre's office, and directly across the hall from Captain Ray Mithoff, then the Senior C/S International. Mithoff used to be Miscavige's Inspector General for Technology RTC, the person responsible for the tech, the most sacred element of Scientology. It is still hard for me, as I write this a decade later, to turn off the sounds attached to memories from that time. The sounds of heavy footsteps stomping down the hallway of Del Sol from the front door, the shouting, the cussing, knowing it was COB followed by at least five staff, going to rip the faces of either Ray Mithoff or Guillaume Lesevre.

COB would stop at Mithoff's office when the shouting would start. "WHY ARENT' THOSE RUNDOWNS DONE YET? Ray didn't have an answer. "YOU'RE A F'KING SP, THAT'S WHY! YOU'RE STOPPING THE PROGRESS OF SCIENTOLOGY! YOU ARE SABOTAGING LRH'S INTENTIONS FOR THE BRIDGE!" Ray Mithoff was supposed to be writing the OT V NOTS rundowns, and they weren't done. Anyway, the accusations would fly out of Miscavige's mouth, regardless of Ray's reasoning. In between the shouting, I could hear physical jostling in the hallway because my desk was just a few feet from the door to the hall. I knew what was happening, again and again, because I had seen it enough.

One time, I couldn't just sit there and not do anything, so I stepped into the hallway. Miscavige had pushed Ray up against the wall, and held Ray's black uniform tie in his grip, pushing it up into his chin, smashing his neck. Considering that Ray was at least 6' tall and Miscavige was around 5'2", it seemed like a ludicrous effort to try to overpower him. I was on the outside of the circle of people watching, but I instinctively wanted to jump in and help Ray, whose face was turning purplish red. I looked around at the the inner circle--Shelley Miscavige, Laurisse Stuckenbrock, several communicators, and the IG MAA Chris Guider—and wondered why the hell aren't they restraining Dave from hurting Ray? How was this physical abuse justified? I could answer my own question—it was justified because David Miscavige says Ray Mithoff is an SP, and he is bloodthirsty for SPs. Human rights are no factor in this equation.

In another similar incident, Miscavige was on a rant in Mithoff's office. I saw him order Mithoff to get down on his hands and knees like a dog, and move on all fours from his office vestibule to the bathroom in his office. COB made Mithoff start scrubbing the toilet and the tile floor with a toothbrush. Later, Miscavige relegated Ray Mithoff to sleep outside on the hillside above the RTC building. He was given a pup tent and told that when he had to pee, to just do it in the grass.

Not long after that, Ray Mithoff was dressed up in a tuxedo like a prop and spoke on stage at the next International Management event, as if it was situation normal. Ray played the role as if he was in good standing. COB held true to his values, that image was everything. Public perception was more important than the people involved. Scientologists should feel secure and confident knowing that Ray Mithoff was consistently overseeing the priceless LRH tech that everyone in the Scientology world believed in. After that event, Ray Mithoff was back to being treated as a dog in a tent.

While IMPR, I observed a deeper level of David Miscavige's humiliation and nullification game than what I had seen in Cine. One afternoon I was called to the Upper Villas to meet with COB. In the driveway in front of the villas, I saw Norman Starkey and Warren McShane walking toward COB. Starkey had been a senior executive at ASI and LRH's Trustee of his estate. McShane had been entrusted to deal with RTC copyrights and other similar legalities. Both had been stripped of their three gold-striped shoulder bars. Now, a cardboard sign hung from a string around Starkey's neck that said something like, "I don't know what my hat is." His laminated name badge, which said "LRH Estate Trustee" that had Velcro on the back, was stuck on his shirt upside down. COB laughed at Starkey's upside down name tag, evidently enjoying this spectacle of humiliation.

Meetings in COB's War Room in the RTC Upper Villas were the most abrasive encounters with the power elite. The War Room held a graphic colored map of the world in a light box on the wall, overlooking a contemporary conference table, with a high-tech telephone in the middle for speakerphone conversations.

One day, ED Int Guillaume Lesevre came storming into my IMPR office and said that COB wanted to see us right away in the War Room. SNR C/S INT Ray Mithoff was with us. We each jumped on our motorcycles and roared up to the Upper Villas. CO CMO Int Marc Yager was already there, along with CO Gold, Wendell Reynolds. Three four-striped captains and one three-striped commander, and me, a single-stripe Midshipman, stood there, not knowing exactly why we were in the War Room. I noticed a box of photographs or slides on the War Room table. *What flap is it this time?* was all I could think.

The five of us were lined up in a row, when COB came in and began his verbal thrashing. "YOUR F'KING POSTS ARE ALL OVER MY PLATE! WHY ISN'T THIS SLIDE SHOW DONE WITH THE SPEECH THAT GOES ALONG WITH IT?!" Guillaume Lesevre put his head down and shook it, and then looked at Wendell. I didn't know what slide show or speech COB was even talking about. None of the senior execs tried to answer COB's question.

"Karen, do YOU know why this isn't done?" COB asked me.

"No Sir, I do not. I am sorry, Sir, and I apologize for not being aware that I was supposed to be doing a slide show right now. I need to grab my hat and find out what is needed and wanted on this."

COB spit out, "You didn't get the order from your senior?" COB looked at Guillaume Lesevre, my senior. "DON'T YOU F'KING TALK TO YOUR JUNIORS OR TELL THEM WHAT THEY ARE SUPPOSED TO DO?" Miscavige pushed Guillaume in the chest which knocked him backwards a few steps, although he didn't fall on the floor.

"WENDELL, WHY ISN'T THE CINE EDITOR WORKING ON THIS SLIDE SHOW FOR THE EVENT?" COB paused. "LET ME GUESS! BECAUSE YOU DIDN'T F'KING KNOW ABOUT IT?" He pushed Wendell in the chest, but

Wendell was over six feet tall and, like a punching bag, just absorbed the brunt of the blow. Beads of sweat burst on his forehead.

To Marc Yager he said "YOU'RE EVEN WORSE. YOU'RE HOPELESS. YOU'RE STOPPING SCIENTOLOGY!" He punched Marc Yager in the upper arm and then pushed him. "YOU'RE A F'KING SP, YOU COCK SUCKER!"

"GET THE F___ OUT OF MY OFFICE. YOU ARE USELESS! "He said to everyone. COB walked over to the War Room table and picked up some papers from the table.

The senior execs stood there, frozen. I broke the line, walked over to the table, and stood next to COB as he was looking through some of the slides. I picked up the box of slides and pictures and started looking through them. "Sir, let me sort through these. I will do this, I'm sorry, I didn't know this was needed right now. I will also find out about the script." What I didn't tell him was that I had no idea what he was talking about, no idea of this project, my senior had never forwarded me any order or despatch about this mystery slide show, or that COB had set a deadline. COB looked sideways at me, clearly surprised that I would have the courage or the gall to stand next to him or to speak after that thrashing. I looked him in the eyes, not fearing that he would push or hit me. He didn't.

While looking at me, he called out, "Shelley, get me a copy of the despatch to Guillaume and Wendell where I said this slide show had to get done. Give it to Karen. She's the only one who will bother to even try to do it." COB and I started looking at the slide pictures through a loupe and started stacking them by topic. I had no idea what I was doing, but made the effort to at least physically contribute to the act. I sensed that COB's emotional thermometer, which had reached a boiling point, was coming down. Shelley brought me the despatch, and COB told me to just go back to my office. I don't know what happened to the rest of the execs.

Far greater battles were being fought by Miscavige, RTC and OSA staff than the smaller problems most of us dealt with. Circa 1995, there were many raids and court cases that kept Miscavige embroiled dealing with huge legal and financial risks. Without a doubt, these issues affected his temperament and treatment of staff. Much of this related to Scientology's Internet battles and ongoing conflicts related to freedom of speech and information. Scott

Goehring had created alt.religion.Scientology a few years prior, which posted anti-Scientology information that became a place where confidential Scientology information was posted. Dennis Erlich was raided at his place in Glendale, CA; Arnie Lerma, a Usenet poster, was raided at his home in Arlington, VA when Scientology attorneys brought in US Marshalls to take Arnie's computers and disks; Larry Wollersheim and Fact Net Director Bob Penny were also raided. Lawsuits were tied to each of these individuals that demanded ongoing strategies, legal counsel, and financial investment.

Clearly, David Miscavige had his own ways of addressing problems and conflicts. And his state of mind seemed to be outside of our experiences; we were always expecting to refer to a policy or some Scientology tech that would help to handle a problem. Miscavige didn't lead with Scientology like that. He always talked and even screamed about Scientology and getting ethics and tech in. He talked the talk that he didn't walk. DM lived in a different world than the rest of us as Scientologists. He became an enigma to me; it was hard to comprehend who he really was. One thing I knew for sure: David held a strange advantage over the rest of us who had consciences that kept us in line. He seemed to behave with unhampered liberty to do just as he pleased. He made himself out to be flawless, and overworked because of us. I wondered if he ever had a pang of conscience after he verbally or physically abused one of his staff. I began to question whether he had a conscience at all. He seemed to have ice water in his veins. He didn't seem to exercise any restraints on himself when it came to expressing frustration or anger. He would scream in someone's face, push or hit them, and then walk away and start a new conversation as if nothing had just happened. I never once saw anyone confront him about his abusive behavior and case dramatizations.

Perhaps the real problem at the Int base was not that everyone who worked here was so incompetent or suppressive, as Miscavige said. Perhaps the problem was that David Miscavige possessed the ability to conceal his true psychological make-up that we couldn't understand. Did he even believe in Scientology or L. Ron Hubbard any more? I often wondered. David Miscavige was far from my role model for an on-source Scientologist. But it would work to his benefit that who he *really* was would remain invisible to the rest of us. This would enable him to continue exercising a strange advantage over our handicapped minds.

During the nine months of serving in the IMPR position, I realized what we were doing in around the world in a scope that I had not been able to see before: We were all about fake news and cover-ups on a global scale. I had traveled to the Scientology bases on every continent except Africa and Latin America, and had became aware of staff poverty conditions and the slovenly quarters of most organizations. I also saw the pressure on the FSO to increase their $7 million weekly income, along with the international moneymaking actions of the Flag Banking Officers in each org sucking as much money as possible from their local orgs and sending it up to the Int Finance Office where the IFD, Int Finance Director, managed our burgeoning Sea Org Reserves and holdings in real estate, stocks, gold bullion, and the like. I tried to explain my views to Peter, but he immediately rejected anything I described.

I broke one Thursday afternoon after two o'clock when I calculated that my weekly statistics were down. I got my weekly meter check along with everyone else. Evidently, the e-meter picked up that I was troubled. "Has a withhold been missed?" he asked.

I answered immediately, "Yes. I do not want my post."

"You do not want your post?"

"Correct. I do not want my post."

The meter checker wrote down what I said and ended it immediately. I was told to wait. Two RTC MAA's (Master at Arms) came down to interrogate me. I was now considered an "ethics particle" for doing the ungodly—the treasonous act of refusing to serve on a post, especially one that had been designated for me by COB RTC.

A security guard escorted me to the drainage canal area on the north side of the property, where Estates crew were building a retaining wall made of rocks. I was told to fill wire baskets with rocks and haul the baskets to line this steep-walled river bed. It was about 100 degrees outside in the sun. I was wearing a long-sleeved blue uniform shirt and navy blue wool pants and black leather shoes.

Other people who had gotten into trouble were made to labor there, with RPFers. This was how work got done around the Int base—slave labor performed on the backs of ethics particles. Two other Senior Executive Strata staff joined forces with me in the drainage canal—Fred Schwartz had just been removed from the post of GIEI, Gross Income Executive International, and Fran Harris, who had been removed from her post as BEI, Books Executive International. As our trio hauled rocks, I cared less about the weight of the rocks, and more about the brutal heat along with the rattlesnakes and scorpions that I expected to see. Hauling rocks was a great way to vent my anger and frustration. I was happier slaving in the desert heat than coping with the insanity in Del Sol and the IMPR post. With every rock I picked up and shoved into the wire baskets, and then with every basket I lodged into the retaining wall, I felt freer. I would no longer have to take part in the charade called public relations for international management. I was done.

After weeks in the drainage canal, they found other things for me to do. But first, I was brought before a "justice" action, a Committee of Evidence, which felt more like a witch hunt into my background for every mistake I had ever made, including back to when I worked in Cine. I'll never forget the goldenrod-color issue that summarized my committee's findings. Among other things, they accused me of treason, not wanting to do my post (true) and being "worker oriented" wanting to work on uniform projects for the staff, caring more about helping Sea Org crew than supporting command intention—true. While being "worker oriented" was considered a derogatory charge, I smiled. At least someone had noticed that I cared about the Sea Org staff. They cancelled my training certificates as a graduate of the Organization Executive Course. They also assigned me lower conditions with I don't remember how many hundreds more hours of amends that I was to do to make up the damage of leaving my IMPR post.

Working at this level of Scientology and seeing what I had seen, built a web of cognitive dissonance so dense that I could have lost further touch with reality. I believe the senior execs who stood there and took Miscavige's abuse were losing touch with reality and believed the lies he said about them. I knew Guillaume Lesevre lived with his own cognitive dissonance; he had made it clear to me that he was conflicted about his role and his work. But like the other execs, I saw ED INT handle his own dissonance by continually convincing himself to bring the conflicts into balance. Guillaume Lesevre and Ray Mithoff would get up at Int Management events in front of the Scientology world and proclaim the greatness of Scientology. Then they would go back to the Int base and live their miserable existence.

This was also very telling of the condition of Scientology and David Miscavige's leadership. If people like Ray and Guillaume made statements contrary to their own feelings or beliefs, this implied that there was a reward for them doing it, or more likely, the absence of a threatened discipline. I had been convincing myself every day that staying in the Sea Org was the right thing to do, even though I felt deep down that the Sea Org operation was suppressive of Sea Org members.

I never once saw anyone confront Miscavige about his abusive behavior and case dramatizations. No one ever stopped him from punching, pushing, twisting, slapping, hitting a staff member. I had seen enough human rights violations that could have gotten Miscavige or his assistants arrested, or would have won a court case if I had decided to call the police or to sue Miscavige or the Church of Scientology. Why didn't I call the police? Our groupthink was so regimented, so separate from the outside world, the police weren't an option; they didn't even exist as a resource in my mind. But my reaction to this IMPR mess did not include a thought or plan to escape again. I had ruled out that option in 1993 after escape #2. I believed I couldn't get out, so why try and fail again?

# 30

## COVER-UP EXPERTS

**December 1995**

MY EXPERIENCES WITH DAVID MISCAVIGE confirmed that what mattered most to him was the public perception of Scientology versus the people involved. Beautiful buildings, beautiful celebrities in the seats, beautiful staff, beautiful book covers, publications and promotional pieces, mattered. If something or someone was beautiful, then it had more credibility. Creating beautiful images was in my area of expertise. Since I didn't have a post, I found things to do that helped the IMPR office with some of my former responsibilities. I went to the Central Marketing Unit (CMU) headed by Jeff Hawkins, where the IMPR office and Gold's Marketing staff were planning the next issue of the *International Scientology News*. While helping with research for one of the upcoming *ISN* articles, I sent a Merc message to Shelley Miscavige. COB Assistant had always been kind to me, and I was hoping to find a way to help with Scientology image somewhere. She responded to my message almost immediately.

Shelley told me that they were heading to Clearwater for a massive undertaking, without saying what they were doing or why. She said they would like me to completely refurbish the image of the 1,000 Flag Land Base staff. I could help with removing the social barrier between Scientology and the local Clearwater public, by by transforming the appearance of staff and thus the church's image to make it more acceptable to Clearwater locals. I wondered why all of a sudden this was the biggest priority, but didn't ask.

There were many reasons why the Church of Scientology in Clearwater had not been at peace with the local government, businesses or residents, starting with the lies and cover-ups when they moved into town in the 1970s. Hubbard's front group, Southern Land Sales and Development Corporation, bought the Fort Harrison Hotel in downtown Clearwater and leased it to his other front group, United Churches of Florida, instead of forthrightly buying it as the Scientology organization. Clearwater Mayor Gabe Cezares and the Scientology organization clashed over community battles on a plethora of issues.

One of the more basic problems was that Sea Org staff looked like militaristic cult members that didn't match anyone's idea of what "church" staff should look like—which caused fear and alienation. Clearwater residents dressed in tropical clothes fitting for a coastal town surrounded by white sand and crystal blue Gulf waters.

COB Assistant said there was no time to do a full design submission. She wanted me to come to Flag, set up in an office in CMO CW, and start working. She and COB would be there to approve my design submissions on the spot. I went from being a woman with no post and a tarnished identity to being someone that COB's office needed again. After doing well on this FLB project, I could earn back COB's trust and refurbish my reputation.

## Lisa McPherson Cover-Up

My arrival at the Flag Land Base coincided with the aftermath of a tragic event that RTC staff were handling with a frenzy. Senior executives stayed tightlipped on the matter so that Int base staff wouldn't learn the details or become affected by the news: Scientologist and former Sea Org member, Lisa McPherson, had just died a horrible death in Scientology's Fort Harrison Hotel in Clearwater. Since Int base staff weren't allowed to watch television, read newspapers or access the Internet, I hadn't heard any media about this tragedy, nor had there been any base announcements.

The first details I got about Lisa McPherson came the day I arrived in CW from the LRH Personal Public Relations Officer in CMO CW. She was the first person I spoke with as I entered the second floor CMO offices to find out where my office would be. She said, "I don't have time to help you get set up here right now because FLB is in this big flap, because some chick died in the Fort Harrison. This is a big flap because her case supervisor messed up, and some heads are gonna roll."

One of Flag's public had died at our mecca of technical perfection? I asked who was responsible for her in the Hubbard Guidance Center (HGC) or in Qual, where every Scientologist had confidence that they would receive the best quality technical services. She said they were finding that out now during the invest, but that "the whole tech and Qual divisions are electrified." She added, "This is just huge dev-t."

Dev-t is Scientology slang for "developed traffic," meaning unwanted, annoying interruption by someone or something. She told me that CMO had just started the investigation to gather all the details. I didn't learn a fuller story with the circumstances of Lisa's medical neglect and gross mishandling, or the lawsuit filed by her family, until after I got out of Scientology. All details were covered up internally, with information known by only the few RTC, CMO and FSO staff who had been directly involved or who were responsible for repairing the mess.

In brief, for readers unaware of this tragic case: Lisa had spent about $175,000 on Scientology services, including an introspection rundown due to mental instability, and then was declared "Clear" in the summer 1995. She began exhibiting emotional problems, including a breakdown after she was in a car accident. She was taken to a hospital, but Flag Sea Org members took Lisa out of that hospital and placed her in a cabana room in their Fort Harrison Hotel, under 24-hour watch. Reportedly, Scientologist and physician David Minkoff prescribed medication for Lisa without examining her. About seventeen days after she was placed in the FH, the Sea Org members watching over Lisa saw that her condition had become grave. She had severe pocks on her face and bug bites on her body, was severely dehydrated, had been refusing food, and was comatose for about 2 days. They drove her to Dr. Minkoff's office about 45 minutes away, meanwhile passing up closer hospitals. Lisa died along the way. The Florida medical examiner's report at first indicated that she died of a pulmonary embolism, and that Lisa was a victim of negligent homicide. The Church of Scientology was to be indicted on two felony charges, "abuse and/or neglect of a disabled adult" and "practicing medicine without a license," but in 2000, the state's medical examiner changed the cause of death to "accident." Full reports on the criminal and medical details of this case are available online. Later, the *St. Petersburg Times* reported that David Miscavige responded to a question about Lisa saying, "At the time I don't think it was really thought to be that significant an issue. She died. People die."

Had I known Miscavige's views about this tragedy at the time it happened, I wouldn't have carried on my end of the charade by trying to improve the public perception of Scientology. The faster we could transform staff image and remove the objections to Scientology's image in Clearwater, the less negative attention there would be on Scientology while the aftermath of Lisa McPherson's tragedy raged on.

Although I was no longer IMPR, my project was, in fact, an external public relations handling for Scientology with the people of Clearwater, called PRO Area Control. My tiny slice of the PR area control in Clearwater got completed over that year. I transformed the image of about 1,000 staff to clothing more fitting for a Florida coastal town, with more than 50 different specialist uniforms to fit the functions of the many jobs across the FLB, including specialty looks for each restaurant, from servers to cooks and cleaners, each of the five hotels, the security teams, the auditors and technical staff. The Flag Service Org received a carefully planned clothing program that distinguished executives from staff, and auditors and other technical crew from administrators.

As I worked out each of the specialist uniforms, I'd submit them to COB via COB Assistant, whose offices were down the hall from mine in the CMO CW Building. I involved Burlington Uniforms from England to manufacture the basic line of executive and administrator's suits, and outsourced countless other clothing parts from local and national suppliers. I also brought in a stylist from Los Angeles, Jill Kirsch, who did a personal makeover on nearly every staff member at the Flag Land Base. She did color consultations to determine the best makeup and clothing colors for each staff member, and outfitted each woman with a makeup kit specifically for her color tone. I personally did hundreds of haircuts and stylings, giving the FLB staff fresh, updated looks.

The good result from the overall project gave me the courage to step over Scientology's boundary lines with city officials, and I attended a City Council meeting. I informed Mayor Rita Garvey and city officials what the Church of Scientology was doing to improve their relations in Clearwater by outfitting the staff in tropical clothing. I told them that our hope was to remove the stigmatized military image by replacing it with a welcoming image more fitting for a coastal town, thus attracting rather than repelling tourists to the area. While she and the others were quite wary of my presentation and questioned the motive for doing it, they said they found the idea to be a positive effort and thanked us for it.

Thomas Tobin from the *St. Petersburg Times* wrote a story published April 19, 1997, "Scientologists get away from military look." He wrote that the Church of Scientology was "addressing a long-standing complaint," and unveiled a new look in an attempt to improve its image in downtown Clearwater and fit in with Clearwater's tropical environment. Tobin said, "merchants, city officials and residents have complained about what they said was a somewhat jarring, even intimidating, sight of hundreds of Scientology staff members massing through the streets of downtown as if there were a Naval base nearby." His story noted that locals feared the military uniforms kept people away from downtown. He added a photo featuring Carol Nyburg, Lorie Houghton and Tamar Egosi in their new hotel uniforms to provide an example. This story earned small but positive press for our public relations bureau.

Through these image projects, I felt complicit in Scientology's cover-ups. A Scientologist only thinks within the framework of "the greatest good" for Scientology; but what about Lisa McPherson, her family, the people of Clearwater, and justice? I had not done anything illegal, but I can't say that for the rest of the team working on this case. I knew that RTC was heavily involved, but didn't learn until years later how David Miscavige, Marty Rathbun, Elliot Abelson and others navigated the outcome of the legal battle that got Scientology off the hook for Lisa's death, including covering up the fact that David Miscavige had personally supervised Lisa McPherson's auditing prior to her death. For additional information about Marty Rathbun's role in this cover-up and excerpts from his legal deposition about destroying evidence of Miscavige's involvement, visit the book website.

## Another Promotion: A Sea Org Dream Job

❀ I went back to the Int base with a good production record and restored reputation. With the IMPR debacle long forgotten, I was reposted in the highest ecclesiastical organization within the church's management hierarchy, the Commodore's Messenger Organization International. I officially landed on the post of the International Uniform Officer, in the International Finance Network, situated in the Int Landlord's office.

I had worked my way into a position where I required no orders to do my job. No senior watched over my shoulder while I did my work. I received messages direct from Shelley Miscavige letting me know the priorities for which units I should focus on, and I would coordinate with the WDC member responsible for the sector I was working in, while COB would approve my planning.

The fact that I had two reasons for *why* I did this work explains my point about having two "selves": My Sea Org persona was doing it to help improve the image of the Sea Org so that Scientology would be accepted in their locale and this would help drive up gross income, per LRH policy that income comes from high image. My true self was my heart for the people who had dedicated their lives to this group, and needed to be cared for by someone who made an effort to help. That is how I separated myself from the reality of contributing to Scientology's cover-ups, and how I lived with myself while doing this work.

COB sent me to Copenhagen to handle the "smelly staff" (his words) at AOSH EU. I also re-dressed the Freewinds crew, the IAS, the Int base orgs, the PAC Orgs including AOLA, ASHO, and LA Day, also CC DC, a project in Sydney, and a project for Church of Spiritual Trust (CST). The stories are available on the book website.

Between the time of my FLB project and the summer of 1998, Miscavige twice awarded me with a certificate of "most productive staff member on the base" at Saturday night base briefings before the entire Int base crew. Nothing could boost one's ethics protection like a commendation and public acknowledgement from COB RTC.

## Scientology defrauds its customers

Although Scientology was now looking better internationally with improved staff appearances around the world, it wasn't looking so good in its most important area, the tech of Scientology. Miscavige announced at a base briefing about Jan Norton, then the Director of Processing at the Flag Land Base. He said Jan had allowed nearly 700 people to attest to Scientology's highest level at Flag, OT VII, when they hadn't really achieved it. He describe how she and her staff hadn't interpreted the e-meter correctly when the Scientologists came in to attest to completing the level. In summary, all the OT VIIs were, by Scientology's own standards, overt products—flawed, and not real completions. To add to that, he said ALL OT VII's were going to be made to redo their levels, and *really* make it.

Miscavige pulled Jan Norton from Flag along with Ron Norton, the Captain, and put her on the RPF at the Int base. He did this sanctimoniously, as if he had saved the day for the Scientology world. He also proclaimed a mind-boggling problem in our Scientology world: "NO ONE KNOWS HOW TO AUDIT." If no one knows how to audit, then what were Scientology organizations doing all day every day, and why would they be allowed to sell auditing if they didn't know what the hell they were doing? If NO ONE knew how to audit, and that was the primary service Scientology sold nearly $7 million weekly, then they should have put training on hold until it was fixed. I put my personal progress up the bridge on hold after Miscavige shook my confidence in Scientology.

Bottom line was, the Church of Scientology and the Flag Land Base were overt product makers. In one technical bulletin of 10 May 72, Hubbard says that overt products are called so "because they are not useful, something no one wants, and are overt acts, such as inedible biscuits or a 'repair' that is just further breakage." In an administrative policy HCOPL 7 Aug 76 II, Hubbard defines "overt product" as "a bad one that will not be accepted or cannot be traded or exchanged and has more waste and liability connected with it than it has value." I have never heard the organization take responsibility for one overt product, correct their mistakes at their expense, or willingly give a refund to unhappy customers.

Hubbard describes "exchange levels" in Scientology; that to be successful, you must produce a high level of exchange and give more to the customer than what they even paid for. Yet, this example proves the opposite. By Hubbard's standards, this shows a criminal exchange level: nothing from the criminal for something from the customer. Hubbard says in HCO PL 4 April 1972, "One has to produce something to exchange for money. If he gives nothing in return for what he gets, the money does not belong to him." Like a car manufacturer who knows that a car part is faulty, they do a recall, fix the parts at no charge to the customer, or give them a new car. But no, not Scientology management. The public customers would pay dearly for this.

Instead of fixing the criminal exchange level with Scientologists, and repairing the overt products at church expense, Miscavige created a PR solution to con the Scientology world: The Golden Age of Tech (GAT). GAT was launched as a mandatory requirement for all Scientologists and staff to enroll in the new GAT courses to "finally" become 100% standard auditors. The courses consisted of hundreds of drills that the student auditors would learn using their e-meter, their new drills simulator, their new drills materials, and the Scientology processes used in auditing. GAT was presented as a means of raising the bar on standards that LRH always intended but that had never been implemented. A longer description of the Golden Age of Tech and its consequences is on the book website.

# 31

# Tough Questions

**Int base, 1997**

SCIENTOLOGY IS FULL OF PARADOXES. For some people like me, who had been born on the outside and enjoyed a vibrant career and personal life, Sea Org life at the Int base was torturous. It was not in my DNA to be the kind of woman who could or would support command intention unconditionally while throwing my integrity out the window while calendar days rolled by, while my mother was aging and I couldn't be a part of my family's life. I had done that for spurts of time, but not without showing my dissidence.

Since my last escape in 1993, I had traveled the world improving staff image to increase public acceptance of Scientology internationally. The behind-the-scenes truth about Scientology's global operations brought a final reckoning. I could not turn a blind eye to intolerable staff working conditions, poverty level pay, substandard housing, and unacceptable child-care conditions, particularly while knowing the income and bonus levels of management's senior executives. Not to mention ongoing sleep deprivation, lack of insurance and sufficient medical care, and unreasonable working hours that prevented staff from being able to have a family life, a healthy schedule, and a healthy mind. Our $7 million sales per week was being earned on the backs of Sea Org members living and working in dishonorable conditions that parallel those of corpora-

parallel those of corporations who produce goods through low-wage labor overseas to ensure high profits.

Our Int base Security Chief, Gary "Jackson" Morehead and his wife Sheri left the Int base in 1997, which rocked Peter's world. Despite the negativity and challenges of his post, such as being responsible for recovering any staff who blew the base, Jackson was a super-likable guy and a friend. A guy who could survive as long as he had on that post had to stay clean. I didn't buy it when leaders tried to defame Jackson for his crimes against Scientology; to me it was more about what did he knew or saw that others didn't, that broke his willingness to tolerate base conditions any more.

COB's personal public relations machine that specialized in cover-ups clarified for me that Scientology was a global fraud, a for-profit business using a unique brand of slavery, justifying abuse under the banner of religious freedom. These realizations fast-forwarded my soul-searching about my affiliation with it, and confirmed my loss of confidence in Hubbard, in management, in Scientology technology, and in both Peter and myself for buying into it at all.

I hadn't talked with Peter about leaving the Sea Org since I recommitted myself around 1993. By 1997, I started carrying on with Peter about wanting to get our lives back together outside of the Sea Org. Weeks would go by, and I would not say a word to him about my desire to leave. Then, I would barrage him with pleas at night in our crowded little bedroom across the hall from Pat and Sarah Gualtieri. I would have to turn on the radio to talk with Peter so that Pat and Sarah could not hear us. I tried to convince Peter that he could get back into the music business. The success of "On the Wings of Love" could still be his ticket back into songwriting and help to reestablish ourselves in music centers like L.A., Nashville, or New York. As a fashion designer, I would be able to find new clients wherever I lived.

Again Peter replied, "We are trusted loyal officers, Karen. We are never going to be like Fernando and Terri." He used the Gamboa's as an example for who he didn't want to be like, and I always felt the opposite. I had been in management; he worked in Golden Era Productions' music studio, two completely different worlds within one. He did see some of the wretched conditions of Sea Org life when the Gold musicians traveled to Scientology bases in Europe and the UK, but he turned a blind eye, promising me that we would never live like that. That was enough for him—to decide that he and I personally would live better than 99% of other Sea Org members, and only because we still received songwriting royalties from our prior music business.

Human rights violations against staff didn't bother Peter enough to affect his conscience as it was doing to me. Peter was content with his array of keyboards in his luxurious composing room at Gold, and we received our personal music royalties that lined our bank account. I understood it was more pleasurable for him being a big fish in a small pond at Gold than continuing to compete in the Hollywood music business dominated by drugs and politics, neither of which we wanted any part of. Being able to practice piano all day and not worry about paying bills or maintaining a home was an idyllic arrangement for Peter. I believe he did consider leaving at times, but he lacked the gumption, courage and desire to even attempt to make a break with me, knowing we would have to start completely over with new careers, home, and people in our lives. Worse, we would have to eat crow and admit that we had made a mistake in judgment about dedicating our lives to Scientology.

In 1997, a glimmer of hope arose about us leaving. During our second leave of absence (a 3-day vacation) in nine years, we went to see my family in Atlanta for a day and then attended his family reunion in upstate New York. During that trip, we talked about leaving the Sea Org. We rented a red convertible Mustang at the Atlanta airport and drove up to the Smoky Mountains the day before we visited my family. The weather was cool, overcast, and ready to rain, a fresh relief from the southern California desert climate. The clouds burst while we were speeding up the highway with the convertible top down. We let the rain pour down on us, turned up the radio, and laughed and sang at the top of our lungs until our voices reached the sky and we got drenched. That was the last time I could remember feeling anywhere close to joyful or free during my Sea Org years. That night, we stayed in a hotel outside of Cherokee in the Smokies, and drove back the next day with the convertible top down. My hair whipped in the wind while I appealed to Peter about leaving the Sea Org. As he listened, I could tell by his pause that he was trying the idea on for size. But then his face grimaced and twisted, as if his mind was pierced by fears about the consequences of failed attempts. His body froze.

"The thought of Marty Rathbun or Greg Wilhere coming after me with an e-meter if I got caught terrifies me. No way. Couldn't do it," Peter told me. That's the way he would think about it—"if I got caught." I understood his fear of Marty Rathbun, the Inspector General, who I perceived to be an egomaniacal hothead who walked in Miscavige's footsteps. He was a bully on the base known for doing underhanded things called "the greatest good" to protect Miscavige and Scientology. I wouldn't enjoy Rathbun coming after me either, but I would care only if I wanted to remain a staff member.

As we sped through the foothills of the Smokies and headed toward Atlanta, thousands of miles away from the Int base, no chains physically binding us as slaves or prisoners would be bound, but we were both trapped in the Sea Org in our minds.

Peter suddenly spoke. "No. We have made a commitment and we are trusted officers in the Sea Org. We are not going to leave." As Peter gave me his decision while keeping his eyes fixed on the road, I realized that I had lost my husband, probably a long time prior to that. Peter was not a free man at all. He had become institutionalized—a person who didn't believe he could make it on the outside. He belonged to the Sea Org, instead of to himself. I couldn't understand what kind of freedom he thought he was dedicating his life to, when he was so trapped. It wouldn't do me any good to keep pressing this issue. I let it go. I had been naive enough or too hopeful to believe that everything I had done (leaving and coming back and re-committing myself) would ever lead to resolution with Peter. We didn't talk about leaving the Sea Org together again since that trip out of the Smoky Mountains.

# 32

# CHAIRMAN OF THE BOARD RTC

**Int base, 1997**

FOR YEARS, I HAD SECRETLY harbored thoughts about Miscavige being a suppressive person. His type of suppression was harder to detect because of his charisma and his claims of caring about Scientology's expansion and preservation. But it was really a no brainer after doing the PTS/SP Course, because *Science of Survival* provides plenty of "tech" that describes the low-toned, aberrative personality, and how domination by nullification is used to destroy higher-toned people, such as the dedicated Sea Org staff who surround him at the Int base. A suppressive person exhibits specific antisocial characteristics that squelch individuals and bring decline to organizations.

One evening, behind David Miscavige's curtain of control, in the privacy of his plush office within the hallowed upper villa of the Religious Technology Center, Shelley Miscavige called me to COB's office to review one of my design plans. I used to get nervous and flustered whenever I got called to his office because I had seen him toast other people for doing work he didn't like. By this point, my attitude was that I had nothing much left to lose, so I never worried or feared anything when I met with him. Plus, I had been in his favor since the Flag project. I leaned into that confidence.

Whenever I was in his private office, I had learned to not let my eyes rove around his room or stare at his expensive audio/visual equipment, the cupful of a dozen Mont Blanc pens on his desk, or the fine furniture built to fit the scale of his small physique. I just absorbed details through my peripheral vision while keeping my focus on Miscavige's face. If I didn't maintain comfortable eye contact with him, I'd be accused of withholding transgressions from him. I had learned to be there comfortably.

We stood just outside of his private office at the island, a cabinet with a large countertop where he would review large presentations. My design submission, a 24" x 36" spiral-bound art book, laid open on the island. COB stood over it, looking down at the first page with his hands behind his back, when Shelley took me in.

In this calm atmosphere, he examined the submission with me, commenting on a few details and asked questions here and there. In that moment, I felt a fresh sense that the image of Scientology meant more to him than the actual human beings who worked tirelessly on Scientology's front lines and behind the scenes. Anyone who allied themselves to this cause as I had, was considered a trusted member of the inner sanctum upon which the defense of him and Scientology rests. I was not part of his inner circle of people who he would sit down and have a glass of scotch with after post time, but I had moved quantum leaps from where I had been.

In the calm sanctity of his inner office, he slipped. While gazing down at my designs covered with logos and insignia that would solidify Scientology for that organization, he must have been thinking out loud, perhaps making a comment not meant for my ears. I always looked in COB's eyes while he spoke to me, and watched his facial expressions.

COB said, "We can't get people to pay for Scientology services. But we can get them to give plenty of money to the International Association of Scientologists for nothing."

*For nothing?* I was dumbstruck. I looked down, and struggled to not gasp, and kept my jaw from dropping. What a time to be without a tape recorder! This moment was a real test in TRs. I wanted to ask him what he meant by *for nothing,* but I wouldn't let myself react. His temper could turn as hot as molten lava in a split second and I wanted to avoid being turned into ash. I looked into his marbleized, ice-blue eyes, searching for a glimmer of conscience.

I successfully sat there with a blank face that showed no signs of the firestorm raging inside me. Scientologists who donate to the IAS are giving money *for nothing?* Scientologists believe that their millions of dollars paid out for services and IAS members and additional donations are used to buy legal defense against enemies of the church to protect the priceless treasure of religious freedom. People took out bank loans and drove their credit cards to the limit to donate to *nothing.* We sweated buckets over working for Scientology. We aborted our babies, worked like slaves, and disconnected from friends and families over our dedication to the cause—the cause of *nothing.*

I held David Miscavige's gaze perfunctorily. The silence was deafening. Maybe he had expected me to comment. He straightened his back and, as if startled by his own words, began to rephrase his statement, and started jabbering like a talking head. I normally hung on his every word, as if hearing a god speak—as did all sycophantic management staff—but at that moment, I didn't hear anything. My perception of David Miscavige morphed before my eyes. He generally overcame his small physical stature by wielding a larger-than-life image, intimidating staff by the numbers in his entourage of assistants and body guards who fawned over him and drove around the base on their motorcycles like a gang of hoods. But at that moment in my eyes, he had shrunk to the size of a gecko standing on hind legs, trapped within his own system, devoid of conscience.

I had worked under him for nearly nine years. He had steadily challenged me to become what he wanted me to be in the Sea Org—a dedicated ally who could carry out command intention without independent thought. I had always carried a dual opinion about him being sometimes quite charismatic and someone who I really wanted to like me; versus feeling that he was a monster disguised as a church leader. What seemed to be his hunger for power also seemed to be fed by a steadily increasing diet rich in defamation and nullification of others through verbal and physical abuse. His daily rants would involve denouncing us for our ineptitude while pontificating on his own effectiveness. In his mind, he was the only one who ever got anything done. And the sycophantic staff who agreed with him on that matter earned the privilege of being part of his inner sanctum and inner RTC circle.

Miscavige had become a source not only of fear, humiliation, and enforced dependency, but also of solace. The hope of a kind word from him, his approval of our work, or our receiving some other ordinary human comfort like being allowed to go home on time or to have study time in our schedule, had become compelling. It seemed that the more we feared him, the more we acted in adoration and humble appreciation for granting us simple basics that he bestowed as favors, instead of respecting as rights. We craved his approval and worshipped the ground he walked on. We'd stand by as if supporters of his imperiousness while watching him abuse others, when we were actually in fear of revealing our disapproval of his actions. For me, this was more than confused or sycophantic. It was a relinquishment of my integrity, inner autonomy, world view, and moral principles—loathsome consequences for repressing my inner doubts about Scientology and objections to totalitarian leadership tactics.

I doubted whether David Miscavige even believed in Scientology anymore. He was showing me that he knew Scientology and the IAS were a scam. Both Winston Churchill and Lord Acton have been quoted to say, "Power tends to corrupt and absolute power corrupts absolutely." I had witnessed enough incidents to see that this man lived for the power he held over the Scientology empire, and he was already becoming trapped within his own addiction to it. Ron Miscavige Sr. had told me about how much Dave loved Scientology auditing in the early days. But since then, David had been able to see what worked and what didn't work in Scientology. He, of anyone, would know whether Scientologists were achieving the gains promised through the upper levels. He had already told us that no one knew how to audit, and that all the OT VII and OT VIII completions were invalid. So this is a man running a multi-billion dollar corporation selling Scientology services that don't work, but he had to continue running the charade to keep the empire propped up, because he isn't going to relinquish the power that he appeared to covet. Rick Behar's *Time* magazine article, "The Thriving Cult of Greed and Power" nailed what this group is about.

While Sea Org members lived under totalitarian restrictions that he had established, Miscavige carved out his own world and way of living far above basic Sea Org conditions. He had found ways to milk the system that awarded him with homes around the

United States and overseas, numerous cars, $10,000 suits, lavish gym equipment, and a soon-to-be 70,000 square foot private office building for himself as the leader of RTC and the Scientology empire. I knew about some of these things only because I was on good terms with his public relations secretary, Marion Pouw Dendiu, and had even helped her with some ideas for renderings of apartments she wanted to acquire for him in the U.S. and abroad. I privately questioned some of his privileges, never questioning Marion about her planning. I sucked up her explanations when she volunteered her opinion that "he deserved it" because, after all, he was COB RTC. He was the only one at the Int base who ever got anything done and he did everyone else's job. *He deserved it.*

Throughout my last years at the Int base, with the desire to be allowed to survive, keep my design job, and remain in his good graces, I had tried to discover David Miscavige's humanity. From time to time, I would connect with him, enjoy moments with him, and hope he would stay kind for longer than a few moments or days. The Int base, and the Scientology empire as a whole, had become a platform for supporting the ego, lifestyle and antics of David Miscavige. Put if I pull the lens back and look at the origin of his story, I have to ask myself, had he been shaped by Scientology, and was Hubbard responsible for him as a product of its technology, beliefs and practices? Absolutely.

But behavior is nevertheless a choice. Perhaps some behavior is in our DNA. Miscavige was a man who had worked hard to maneuver himself to the top of an empire that had no checks or balances, as if he deserves to be there, where he can act as if he is above the law. Miscavige's dangerous over-confidence and inflated self-perception defied my understanding, and I believe, defied the understanding of most staff at the base. I imagined David Miscavige becoming a notable example of hubris in some encyclopedia one day, like the spiritual descent of the angel Lucifer into Satan in John Milton's *Paradise Lost*. Lucifer attempts to compel the other angels to worship him, but God and the innocent angels cast Lucifer into hell. Lucifer says, "Better to reign in hell than serve in heaven." I didn't need to hear a statement from DM like Lucifer's to know where he had already fallen.

While I saw Miscavige managing Scientology as a business, not a religion, he nevertheless seemed to live for pledges of personal loyalty in return for some kind of favor. I believed that loyalty should not have been to Miscavige, or even to Hubbard; if at all, it should have been to the code of a Scientologist. I held not one shred of loyalty to him within me. I had long ago seen through the patina of Scientology, created by David Miscavige's personal bent for making Scientology look good in the disneylandish environment he presented to Scientologists through annual events and publications loaded with fake news. But even the best marketing in the world can't work if it doesn't resonate with people as truth. By presenting Scientology to the world this way, he has created a vacuum of credibility, and steps in to fill any void as the self-appointed guardian for mankind, who cares first for himself.

While there were plenty of perks that lavished COB's cushy life as the Scientology leader that others were not privy to, I nevertheless pitied him and never envied his lifestyle. He couldn't be honest, he would always have to put on a show, and he would never be able to leave. Did his days bleed into weeks and his months bleed into years, as they did for so many of his Int base crew who slaved for him? Outside of Scientology, he would have no empire, no minions to rule, unless he held his inner circle captive and moved like a cult leader to some remote place to live. He would be as significant and vulnerable as a bug on a sidewalk, able to be squashed by any random shoe. No, he would continue to rule his empire but I saw him as a despot behind his curtain on the north side of the property, or in one of his many residences where he would live reclusively, where perhaps only Tom Cruise or a select few could visit. Where on the planet could an ex-Scientology leader hide, and still have a life?

While Sea Org members think of ourselves as OTs, we actually lived within individual bubbles within a totalitarian system of controls. We were a group of people who were living someone else's life—David Miscavige's. The staff relied on him to control the next move, too confused or in fear to take initiative because it would be invalidated as not good enough or not right in Miscavige's eyes. I had already started believing that LRH was a damaged individual who had built his insanities into Scientology, and felt that David Miscavige should be removed from his position. There was no place for a self-serving fascist leader in Scientology for it to grow and expand. It was going to fall apart unless someone like a Nelson Mandela could get above the riot at the Int base and serve as a leader who brings reasoning to the Scientology world.

Not to mention that David Miscavige controlled Peter. I nevertheless still clung to a strand of hope that somehow this would miraculously change, something would break the spell Scientology held over him, and Peter would eventually leave with me. Hope had been a powerful weapon that kept me going all these years. At times I would vacillate. Why keep alive the hope and expectation that people should be treated fairly and humanely? Religions should not set themselves apart from those expectations. Why fight against this anymore? I wasn't getting any younger and there was still plenty of life to enjoy. I had accumulated so many turning points, moments of disillusionment and anger about this Scientology game that I had parked on a shelf in my mind as indelible memories, I knew that shelf would eventually break some day.

# 33

# BREAKING POINT

"...We will never betray your faith in us so long as you are one of us."

L. Ron Hubbard, *Scientology 0-8*, p. 16

## July 31, 1998

CMO INT STAFF CRAMMED into the largest space in the double-wide trailers filled with folding chairs for our weekly Friday night staff meeting. As usual, we listened to flaps and handlings, typically filled with more flaps than good news. Flaps included announcements about staff who had messed up on their posts and required ethics and justice actions, financial flaps about international planning, slows in the development of new training drills, the usual. That particular night seemed to offer the worst I could remember.

Andy, responsible for writing the LRH biography, announced a flap. He confessed that he had falsified many of his writings in *The Ron Series*, individual biographical magazines profiling Hubbard's backgrounds in philosophy, writing, cinematography, and the like. The problem was that he and Dan Sherman were collecting information from live interviews with Hubbard's past associates and friends that conflicted with information they had already published

published in earlier *Ron Series* issues. His quandary was, how could he recall the earlier issues without incriminating the integrity of the publications? Andy said he could not continue writing the ominous, decades-old project like this. Andy had taken over after the prior debacle with Gerry Armstrong and Omar Garrison, who had attempted to write this biography and got as declared SPs after running into similar challenges.

Andy's news took me to a place where no Scientologist wants to go—the discovery of falsehoods published about LRH. How could I have been so gullible to believe that what was written about LRH had been true, based on historical facts? The natural question became, what then is really true about L. Ron Hubbard, if the *Ron Series* is fabricated full of lies? Now that I'm hearing I have been deceived about the founder's background and he's not really who I have believed him to be, I was afraid to consider other levels at which I had been duped by Scientology. How deep was this mess?

I remember looking around at the faces of other staff. I saw a sea of blank stares. What did those blank faces mean? Were they suppressing their anger, or were they just plain numb? Or did they already know that what was in the *Ron Series* was bogus? Didn't they feel they had reason to immediately question their affiliation with this group, like I did? Did they feel they were part of a sham, like I did? We weren't allowed to discuss such matters at the risk of appearing disaffected, so I kept my mouth shut and slumped in my chair. I withheld my urge to get up and walk out.

Next, one of my friends and coworkers, Laurence, announced that she had rescinded on her decision to leave the Sea Org with her husband Danny to start a family and give birth to the child she was carrying. Instead, she proclaimed that she had made a decision according to the "greatest good for the greatest number of dynamics," to stay in the Sea Org. This was another way of saying, *I decided that being a Sea Org member is superior to being a mother, and I've made amends by getting an abortion so I am no longer a liability to the group.* I considered abortion to be murder in alignment with Hubbard's reference to abortion as murder in *Dianetics: The Modern Science of Mental Health*.

The issue of abortion and children reminded me of a previous staff meeting when we were told about Jenny, the "suppressive" eight-year old daughter of Jacqueline Kavenaar, then a Watchdog Committee commander over the Office of Special Affairs. The "flap" was that Jackie had blown the Int base to spend time with her daughter Jenny in Los Angeles, under the guise of checking out a base car and just going down for Saturday night with a promise to return at Sunday lunch muster. When she failed to report back, we had sent a team to LA to find Jackie and her daughter. Jackie had been apprehended in Los Angeles by base security and brought back. We were told that eight-year old Jenny would be "handled" for her suppressive actions of distracting her mother off post. Jackie was to be assigned to the RPF (prison camp) for blowing the base. Jenny had been complaining about not seeing her mother often enough because Jackie lived at the Int base and Jenny lived at the Los Angeles childcare unit. Sea Org supervisors were raising eight-year old Jenny instead of her mother, which clearly made Jenny and Jackie unhappy. This arrangement was common with Int base staff whose children lived separately from them full-time. Jenny's unhappiness caused a great deal of stress in Jackie's life, and thus "distracted" her from working.

Jackie's RPF program might last years; what was to happen to her eight-year old daughter in Los Angles in the meantime? Jenny would be about 11 years old before she would see her mother again! My heart went out to Jenny for wanting a normal life growing up with her mother. I couldn't believe how we had sunk to these extremist measures. The last I saw Jacqueline Kavenaar, she had broken down emotionally, crying hysterically, curled up in a ball on the floor in a hallway of the WDC office. I watched as four WDC commanders carried Jackie by her hands and feet like a sack of potatoes to a room off the hall.

These announcements added to the tip of the iceberg. We had been working for nearly a year with no breaks because COB had assigned CMO INT and ESI a condition of confusion, and according to him, we were unable to improve. He said that neither ethics nor tech would "go in" on us. This problem kept persisting. According to Hubbard, the only reason a problem persists is because of a lie. So there had to be a lie underneath the problem of staff "never improving." One lie had to be that "everyone" was committing constant overts and withholds on our posts as COB said. The ultimate lie had to be that David Miscavige was the good guy, the only one Keeping Scientology Working.

I reflected on a recent conversation Shelley Miscavige and I had, sitting in one of the upper Villa offices. She had been reminiscing about being a Commodore's Messenger on the Apollo when they wore uniforms of shorts and white boots and tie-ties. We laughed about me having no idea what a tie-tie was, and that she had trouble describing a tie-tie other than calling it, you know, a tie-tie. She had also told me about a movie she had recently seen, "The English Patient," that I seen once. A French-Canadian nurse was living in a bombed-out Italian monastery after World War II, nursing a critically-burned English-speaking man who reveals his past working in the 1930s as a cartographer in the Egyptian/Libyan deserts. Shelley was smitten with the styling of this film; she loved the clothing the actors wore from that period. She told me to research that movie and propose a uniform for COB's office staff based on this. It had a Banana Republic influence, with 1930s khaki pants and white cotton shirts.

In the midst of this light-hearted conversation, COB Assistant asked me, "What tone level do you think the Int base staff are in?"

With little hesitation, I said, "I think most everyone is numb, or in fear." (That's below 1.1 covert hostility, around 1.0 on a scale of 0 to 40. Individuals ridden by fear are afraid to be or to own anything.)

COB Assistant responded, "I think they're lower, like in apathy" (that's .5 on the tone scale).

I wanted to ask her why she thought the staff had fallen into apathy, but felt a bit cautious of treading too far into what was a comfortable conversation. I did say, "I think many people don't know how to do what's wanted on their post. They are afraid of screwing up and angering COB."

She replied, "So many people have no clue how to do work without requiring orders. They wait for orders before they will do anything."

I responded, "Sir, do you think they wait for orders to do anything because they are in fear of doing something on their own that is wrong?"

"No, that's just being a robot. Not doing anything is apathy," Shelley said.

LRH tech on SPs and potential trouble sources says that a sign of an SP in the area is that people around them are not doing well, are sick and failing in life. I wanted to ask Shelley whether she had ever considered getting the Int base staff through the PTS/SP course. That was one thing that had never been tried in terms of correcting what seemed to be the impossible situation of uncorrectable Int base staff. But I didn't feel free to ask her that question, nor was Shelley free enough in her own thinking to consider that her husband might be an SP, causing many staff to stumble in their effectiveness. After reflecting on that conversation, and after the staff meeting that night, I concluded that this base was a sorry mess of PTSness that would never resolve using Scientology, because no one could see the SP who was causing the real problems.

My epiphany was that Scientology didn't work at the Int base, and I wondered if it worked at all. Miscavige didn't use it. Or maybe he WAS using it—and THAT was the problem.

I now felt personally at risk, as if my future and my sanity were threatened. I looked around the room feeling totally out of alignment with my group. Why are their eyes vacant, while I feel passionately outraged? Why am I able to hear this and sense the madness? What seemed acceptable to the others was no longer acceptable to me. Some people chatted about what they had to do on their post that night before they went home. Others moved ahead, looking apathetic, withdrawn.

One of Hubbard's statements wedged itself into my thoughts: "…We will never betray your faith in us so long as you are one of us" (*Scientology 0-8*, p. 16). What would happen if I were no longer one of "us"? I liken this to what a person should know before joining a gang or organized crime family. As long as I was on the inside, they would never betray my faith in them. Leaving the safety net of groupthink implied that I would step into the domain of the enemy, and suffer the consequences of a defector. Better to never join at all than to join and then leave.

I WAS DONE. I left the staff meeting and walked out of the CMO INT trailers, for once NOT feeling like one of the herd of sheep meandering out of the corral as I usually did when that meeting let out. I had never imagined that these CMO INT trailers would serve as the eventual prison cells for "the hole" in upcoming years where Miscavige would banish erring executives who berated each other until they would confess their suppressive acts, and where Miscavige would beat on them with others standing by watching.

DONE. I made my way down the paved path, crossing under the Highway 79 bridge over to my desk in the Int Landlord's Office. I looked around at my drafting table, my bookshelves and display walls that held years of accomplishments. Two framed awards from COB for being the most productive base staff member hung above my art supply cabinet.

I was done. But the reality of physically departing started to scare me. I had failed two escapes already, and that couldn't happen again. I would lose everything I had, menial as it was. And Peter! Right now he was preparing to play with the Gold musicians at the annual CC Gala. Hundreds of celebrities would be mingling throughout the property. Random fears became mental upheaval. Things started swimming around me, swirling on the walls. I began to feel suffocated. The ground under my feet felt like sinking sand. Things on bookshelves started swirling. I reached for the side of my drawing board to steady myself. But the conflict exploded in my head. I was slipping over the edge of a wall in my mind.

In one split second, a compelling strength suddenly arrested me. As if this strength cut through the whirling confusion, everything stopped spinning. My surroundings stood still. A strength steadied me that I didn't understand. It was as if two loving hands had reached into me to hold everything still, and reached into my heart to lift out my anxiety. A sense of peace washed over me, bringing calmness over my body. An unfamiliar feeling of comfort enveloped me in total. A deep, powerful love filled me, as if washing me.

My anxiety and confusion was replaced by what I can only describe as a transfusion of peace that brought a calming, and a sense of overwhelming love. With it came the knowledge that there would be no end to this love, that it would never leave me. A small, still voice sounded through me like a quiet roar, as if surging from an infinite well. The voice was not my voice or any recognizable voice of human quality that had ever before reached my ears. Resounding from this deep well were the words, "It's okay. You need to leave. You need to be with God in the new millennium."

For a few seconds, I felt suspended in time. God? New millennium? Voices from within? I had to be cracking up. I looked around the room to see if anyone near me had heard what I had heard; no one seemed to. I was surrounded by staff at their desks, but no one was watching me. Whatever was happening to me must not have been evident to anyone else. I was still standing at my desk. But I don't know for how long; I had no sense of time. The presence of that voice was within me only. There was no rational explanation for what had just happened. That voice had reached out to me like a lifeline across a chasm, an intangible helping hand of love connecting me to a safe point, like someone throwing me a mental life preserver.

The incident insulted my logical mind. I didn't know if I still had a logical mind, or what condition it was in. For that split second, was I anchored, or going crazy? God? I wasn't looking for God, didn't believe in God. And why did the voice refer to God in the third person? If it was God speaking, wouldn't the voice have said, "You need to be with me..."? I had long lost the belief that I would come to know God through Scientology. I suddenly saw myself as what I had become: a void, a Godless soul. So why did I need to be with God? Who or what was that? A source of power outside myself was not part of my spiritual equation.

And the new millennium? What was that? It was 1998. What I thought of as the new millennium was to start in 2000 and I didn't believe in any prophesied disasters of the upcoming Y2K. Is that what the voice meant about the new millennium? I could make no sense of what seemed to be a supernatural experience. Had I been touched by the divine? Had God revealed himself to me? Or was this a psychotic break like other Scientologists had experienced? Had I gone Type III? Was this a moment of madness, a crackup, a mental slip from reality?

As likely as any of those could possibly be, several of my actions suggested that I had not cracked up. I conducted myself in a normal manner within minutes, cleaned my office, handled some Merc messages, packed some things in a box, and drove home while planning to escape the next day. Whatever had just happened to me, I wasn't sure. But one thing I believed is that I would never be someone who said that I didn't know what it was like to have a divine revelation. No matter the explanation for what had just happened, my life had been changed. I had heard a small, still voice emanate from the silence of my soul—or void of my mind—and a filling of love, calming, comfort and peace, so compelling that I wanted to know God beyond this incident. Not God of any religion, just God through personal discovery.

Whether it was fear or blind faith that moved me along after that, it was hard to say. When I left the base that night around midnight, I felt confident that my decision to escape on Saturday would be successful.

I drove back to my room at Kirby Gardens in Hemet around 12:30 a.m. I closed my bedroom door, knowing that Pat and Sarah would be home soon, and I wanted no encounters. I didn't want to slip that I was going to leave the next day, and didn't want to reveal any fear or anxiety that would arouse suspicions. The bed was empty; Peter wouldn't be there that night. What I was about to do hit me again with the emotional force of a head-on collision. *Get through it! This will be over soon.* Did those words come to me from my conscience, or did I now have a guardian angel on my shoulder talking to me? Or was I now officially crazy?

Peter and I didn't have cell phones or computers, nor could I call him at CC to tell him what had happened to me. I looked around our room. A 12' x 12' bedroom defined the extent of our private world. We had gotten rid of everything else we owned except for the meager pieces of furniture that fit into this space, and some boxes we put in a storage closet at Kirby. Our two favorite photographs hung over our dresser and near the door. In 1983, our friend Wayne Masserelli, make-up artist for Melissa Manchester, had treated us to a photo shoot with photographer Dick Zimmerman for our third wedding anniversary gift. Zimmerman captured a passion in our eyes that exemplified his photography as a work of art. Those cherished photos were two of the most valuable things we still possessed. I wanted to take one of them, but it was too large to carry with me on my breakaway, so I left them both on the wall.

Sadly, our bedroom summarized our life—what was once great had been reduced to what Scientology controlled. But the most incomprehensible aspect of this mess was Peter's choice of his commitment to Scientology over regaining our free life together again. I knew I had lost him, but held onto a sliver of hope that he wasn't so far gone that he would come to his senses and be bold enough to make his own break after I left.

*Back to packing.* I sat cross-legged on the floor facing my opened closet of the only stuff I had left from my entire life with Peter. I forced myself to dig through boxes and files of our paperwork, looking for things that I might need out on my own. I found a box of photographs of places we had traveled and times we had shared over the past 20 years. I couldn't bear to look at them, but put one small album to the side, hoping to remember to grab it before I left. Tears came easily and I stuffed the box back into the closet.

I found copies of some tax returns and music royalty statements. I might need my account numbers for future correspondence with our accountants, Wiseman and Burke. My passport! I had stashed it in my closet after I returned from my last trip to Europe. Scientology officials <u>always</u> took away our passports when we returned from a trip, on the grounds that they didn't want us to lose it. But I had managed to circumvent a stop at our legal department after my last trip, and they or Security forgot to retrieve my passport. Holding passports was really a control measure, a ruse for preventing staff from leaving and going back home if they lived outside of the U.S.

Packing? I knew I couldn't take much with me. I couldn't chance walking out of my room with a suitcase. My fears went into full throttle again. I couldn't even pack up a box and stash it in the closet until tomorrow, because what if security came into my room to do inspections in the meantime and found that I had packed?

I couldn't leave now or in the morning because I wanted to bring some of my art supplies and books from my office, the few things that held value to me. So I would have to leave after renos, and would only be able to throw some things together Saturday at 5:00, the one window of time when we'd come home after renos to shower and change, when there was reduced security watch.

The fear of failing began to overpower me. My heart raced. I started to hyperventilate.

I couldn't break down now. I had to get out; I had to carry this through. A sense of peace moved in on me and my breathing calmed down:

*Take these papers and put them in a plastic bag on the floor of the closet,* I told myself. *It won't look suspicious. Saturday at 5:00, I'll put the bag in the laundry basket. Use the basket to carry a few clothes and put it in the car. No one will observe anything out of the ordinary.*

When I finally went to bed, I thought I'd lay awake all night, working out the details for my escape. Instead, I quickly drifted off to sleep.

# PART III

## ESCAPING SCIENTOLOGY

# 34

## THROUGH THE LABYRINTH

**Int base - August 1, 1998**

THE QUICKENING OF MY HEART was the only thing that made this day different than any day before. I had no trouble waking up at 6:30am and getting ready. I sprang out my front door at Kirby Garden Apartments, anxious to carry out my plan. Adrenaline pumped through every inch of my body. Pausing for a minute on our tiny concrete patio enclosed by a warped wooden fence, my bare feet singed from the heat already radiating from the concrete while I knew this was my last day here.

I rolled through the security-monitored gates encasing Kirby Gardens and drove 15 minutes up Sanderson Road to turn right on Highway 79; I could have done it in my sleep. But that morning I was unusually alert. The view around me seemed lovely—a word I had rarely used for the past ten years. Softly muted summer colors of purple, green and gold desert shrubs speckled the sands near the highway. I had stopped noticing that desert scene long ago.

Heading to the security gate at the west end of the property, I waited behind a few other cars as they passed through the security checkpoint. That morning, as always, the gate closed behind me and I was locked in for the day. The Saturday morning routine unfolded—inhale breakfast, fall into formation with 800 Int base staff for our paramilitary style muster. *Attention! At ease,* the Master at at Arms would bark. Instead of dreading today's labor, I basked in pleasure knowing that I would cross the 100-mile expanse between Hemet and Los Angeles that stretched before me like open arms and by 6:00pm would be outside the Int base boundaries for good.

Saturday morning's muster was held for all 800 base crew in one place with roll call at 8:00am in front of the Estates building. We showed up in ragtag clothes--holey, paint-covered shorts and t-shirts, cruddy old boots and sneakers. We repaired old and constructed new buildings, maintained the grounds and landscaping, laid electrical lines, working on plumbing and electrical projects, and did architectural planning for Scientology properties.

All weekly routines were abandoned on Saturdays, including the arrangement of security guards at various watch points. Saturday was the one day I could get off the base potentially unnoticed because of the small window of time between 5:00 and 6:00pm when all staff went back to Kirby to shower and change and then came back for dinner and worked the rest of the evening until we were allowed to go home.

That day I had been assigned to a special renos team, working on a privileged project. Bonnie View, or BV. L. Ron Hubbard's new mansion had cost us more than $8.5 million by that point to build and furnish. Miscavige had insisted that it be prepared with haste because Hubbard would live in BV upon his reincarnation back into Scientology. After muster, we reviewed our project orders, collected the tools and materials we'd need to complete our tasks, and then eight hundred people ran off in all directions. My friend Anna Caneen jumped on the back of my Zuma scooter, and we puttered under the tunnel to BV. My assignments included touching up the Jacobean stain on the trim along the hallway to Hubbard's sauna and exercise rooms. I would also smooth the grout in the tile floor of the changing area, using a toothbrush and small trowel to remove imperfections. I would spend about seven hours on my hands and knees, ensuring everything was perfect for L. Ron Hubbard and David Miscavige.

Less than about three dozen staff out of 800 at the Int base were allowed to step foot in BV, myself included. We were known to complete cycles of action to a good result and could be trusted with materials being installed in LRH's house.

Many of Hubbard's clothes, shoes, hats, ties, jewelry, and other personal effects from his St. Hill Manor estate near London had already been shipped to BV. Only specially appointed crew handled his personal items and placed them in his closets and drawers. I had been to St. Hill several times and, because I had been the staff clothing designer with a reputation for good taste, Hubbard's personal stewards took a liking to me and gave me a tour of his Manor bedroom and dressing room. We had looked through his bureau drawers filled with folded-up shirts, sweater vests, and jumpers (pullover sweaters) that had been meticulously stored. His closets held many of the wool tweed jackets, trousers, and shoes that I had seen him wear in various photographs. At BV, Hubbard's clothing, books and records, cigarette cases, photography equipment, and countless other personal effects from his estate had been placed in the house as if he already lived here.

That BV wasn't finished yet was an ongoing flap. Projects not completed perfectly this day could result in dozens to hundreds of people having to fix a mess or complete a job before they were allowed to leave. Of course one person who never caused a flap who was highly experienced in finger pointing was David Miscavige. Today it was especially important that I carried out my assignments perfectly. If my work didn't pass, I might be made to stay over dinner until it met my inspector's satisfaction. I couldn't afford to miss the one moment when the buses pulled out of the gate at 5:00 p.m. with me in my car right behind them. That was the only moment when I could get off the base and head back to Kirby Gardens when I could grab some personal items, and drive off.

During the morning, I took a few breaks to stretch my back and legs by pretending to need some supplies from the BV garage. We were never allowed to take breaks during physical labor; leadership believed we were independent of the outside world, so such things as labor laws covering work breaks were ignored. I took the long way to get the supplies, walking along BV's front terrace sidewalk toward the garage. Along the way I caught the spectacular view down into the valley, overlooking the lush green Golden Era Golf Course toward the left, and the Moreno desert valley south of Highway 79 that stretched to Hemet and Kirby Garden apartments. I couldn't stop and gaze at the view; a Master at Arms could catch me being idle and admonish me for wasting time. I would never again partake in this panoramic view of the desert valley that had been my home since 1989, and felt no traces of nostalgia.

Back on my hands and knees scraping the tile grout with my toothbrush, I got lost in my plans for my freedom. Then I saw Miscavige's 7 ½ EEE shoes approaching and another's walking toward me. I could distinguish DM's shoes from others without looking up because I had bought clothing for him and knew his sizes.

"How are you doing, Karen? The tile's looking good there." I couldn't tell him my back and knees were killing me, or that I considered myself an enslaved minion whom he would never see again after my escape later today.

"Thank you, Sir." I perched up on my knees to greet the Chairman of the Board RTC. I watched him walk around the room inspecting the stain on the trim behind the exercise equipment.

"There are some stain spots on the carpet over here." He pointed to an area of the room. "See if you can get these out."

"Yes Sir." I had learned how to acknowledge an order without "backflashing." Adding comments to my reply instead of just complying, or giving an explanation of why it couldn't be done or my opinion about it, is backflashing and that is forbidden. Perfect compliance to an order and precisely towing the line by doing my job was in my playbook, the best way to gain DM's acceptance and stay in his favor.

I watched Miscavige and Captain Mark Ingber, then Commanding Officer of CMO INT, walk out to the lap pool room about twenty-five feet away, out of my vision. I heard them ask a few questions to a male staff worker in that room, and heard a heated discussion about some flaws in the concrete along the edge of the pool. I winced as I heard the staff member backflash to COB. Hadn't he learned how to play the game yet? I heard a raucous splash in the pool and assumed the worker had been pushed, thrown, or told to jump into the water. I had to ignore what I had just overheard. We were expected to confront fellow staff when they messed up, but when it came to confronting a senior exec for inappropriate behavior, I kept my mouth shut. The worker who went into the pool was ordered to re-fill the pool with clean water after he fixed the concrete because he had dirtied the pool by going in with his shoes on.

My watch said 11:45am, time for lunch. I drove my scooter to MCI and grabbed a quick lunch before I ran over to my desk in the Int Landlord's Office to decide what I could take with me at 5:00. I rummaged through my desk drawers and set aside art supplies that I had bought with my own money. I collected my calligraphy pens, fine-tipped art markers, colored pencils, and my mechanical drawing pencils. I grabbed two empty boxes from near the trash and put them under my desk. I hoped to have time to fill the boxes with my supplier binders, design sketches, some OEC volumes, and small books and pictures.

My watch showed 12:27, so I ran over to the 12:30 muster. Fear pumped my heart, flowed through my veins, and gripped my very bones. The July midday sun beat down on 800 leaders and workers standing in formation. Beads of sweat rolled down faces in the heat radiating from the pavement. I looked around at the crew, some who joked and laughed together, some who just stood silently waiting for the next order. I was surrounded by some people I loved, some I barely knew, and some who had controlled some aspect of my life that had brought me great pain. Trying to act natural while standing in line at muster seemed farcical when, in only a few more hours, I would attempt to walk out of this life.

Between 1:00 and 4:30, my emotions thrashed between anxiety and fear, numbness, and anguish about leaving Peter. All I could do was hope that at 4:30, the usual would happen: The whole base would stop their renos projects like a well-drilled military outfit, pack up the tools, get to muster at 4:45, get on the bus at 5:00, and go to our rooms in Hemet for cleanup.

Four-thirty arrived. I putted my scooter to the south side where 800 of us would muster for the third time that day. I could barely breathe through the 15 minutes of announcements. My throat was tight with short inhales/exhales. My vision began to blur and my head felt light. Done with announcements and orders? Unbelievable! We were all allowed to leave on time.

I would drive out behind the convoy of buses. That gave me about ten minutes to pack up my things and load my car. I ran to my office. I grabbed the two boxes and casually opened the top drawer of my drafting table as if it were business as usual. I withdrew personal photos, fountain pens and art supplies and filled one box. I pulled personal books off the shelves above my computer and filled up another box.

Lurie Belotti, an RTC officer, stopped at my desk to question me about a uniform project. I matter-of-factly continued to fill the box right in front of her while we talked. Had she asked me why I was putting things in a box, I would have said I was de-cluttering my desk. After she walked away, I carried one box to my scooter, and put it on the floorboard. I drove to my car parked near the buses and put the box in my trunk. I raced back to my office to get the second box and repeated my moves. No one seemed to notice what I was doing, until two RTC officers with cars parked near mine looked over at me and waved.

I parked my scooter against the fence near the front of my car and left the key in the ignition. Sweaty staff piled into the buses, engines humming, waiting for clearance to leave and the gates to roll open. Hundreds of staff would shower, change and get back on the buses within 45 minutes to return to the base for dinner and a base briefing by COB.

At the security checkpoint at the gate, Danny Dunnegin's voice sounded through the intercom when he got a visual on me. "Hey, Karen. Going back home to change?"

"Yep, I am. See ya Danny." The cheerful tone of my voice didn't belie my fear or reveal the nausea churning in my stomach.

"See ya Karen." The gate rolled open.

The fifteen-minute drive down Sanderson should have been exhilarating, but I could have easily puked from the fear surging through my stomach and up my throat. I had less than 45 minutes to shower, change, pack, and make it out the apartment gates.

I parked in my usual place near our corner apartment. I raced inside the front door only to find our roommate, Pat Gualtieri, was on security watch! He was standing in the kitchen grabbing some dinner before he went on rounds, chewing a sandwich while holding a two-way radio. I glanced at his rotund body perched at the edge of the table. We had been friends since our Celebrity Centre days in the mid-1980s. I'd have to restrain myself from getting into any conversation with him; I had little time. "Hi Pat. You on watch today?"

"Yeah. Just grabbing dinner. When's Peter getting back from the CC gala?"

"Tomorrow afternoon. The event will be over late tonight; they're staying over at the complex. The musicians have to pack up all the equipment and drive it back—"

Pat's radio beeped to receive a call! How lucky could I get? He replied to the call and waved 'bye as he walked out the door speaking into his radio. Saved! I watched him for a few seconds to ensure he headed away from the apartment, then raced down the eight-foot hall to my bedroom. I shut the door behind me, breathless. I grabbed our white plastic laundry basket and threw in the bag of papers that I had packed last night. My short breaths and panic-blurred eyes kept me from focusing enough to pick out clothes. My heart pumped up my throat.

Single staccato thoughts ordered my steps.

*Jeans. A polo shirt, take this one. Grab those sneakers. Get some underwear. Toothbrush. Makeup. Hairbrush. That's enough.*

How could I get this collection of stuff out the door in a laundry basket? Talk about looking conspicuous!

*Towels. Cover the basket with towels. Tuck 'em down the sides so it looks like a load of laundry. Yes. Shower. Dress. Run.*

I bounded out the front door but caught myself to slow down. The busses had left. I had blown it! Now my car would look conspicuous leaving off-schedule and the guards in front of Kirby would notice. As I walked down the short sidewalk toward my parking space, Pat came around the corner! He was talking into his radio while making the rounds, and broke from the radio to look up at me.

"Hey Pat." I continued moving toward my car and opened the back seat door.

"Getting an early start on your laundry?"

"Yeah. Thought I'd throw it in now and pick it up tonight. You know how it is." I slipped the laundry basket into the back seat.

"Hey, I hear that. See ya."

Thanks to the radio conversation, Pat was not paying attention to my reasoning. The coin laundry room was less than 50 feet away from the front door of our apartment in the opposite direction from my car, so we never drove to do our laundry. "See ya, Pat."

I casually let myself into my driver's seat and locked my door. Pat had turned left around the corner, speaking into his radio. I could barely steady my hand to put the key in the ignition, hyperventilating again. I took a deep breath and held it.

*Get a grip.* I backed up slowly and then drove slowly toward the gate. I saw no other security guards on rounds. I clicked the remote gate opener.

The gate began to roll open when I noticed someone in my right peripheral vision moving toward my car. *Keep driving but go slow.* I slowed my car, turned my head toward them and saw a staff member on security watch with a radio. I waved to him and he waved back. He didn't stop me to question why I was leaving late!

I turned right as usual, and turned left at the next corner, as usual. I kept driving smoothly because I didn't want to break any patterns. I drove up the side street toward Sanderson Road and flipped on my right turn signal. I was out.

The drive north on Sanderson toward the base was glorious. I opened all four windows of the car. The fresh air swirled freely around me and whipped my hair whatever way it wanted to. Along Sanderson, a petite dust devil twisted its way through idle tumbleweeds across a patch of barren land parallel to the road. The sky resounded a brilliant cobalt blue.

I had a clear view ahead to the base nestled into the foothills of the San Jacinto Mountains, with Bonnie View elevated slightly above the other base buildings. Miscavige was most likely strolling through BV looking at all the work that had been completed that day, maybe even reveling in the fact that he had squeezed thousands of dollars of slave labor out of us that added to the real estate value of Scientology properties. Behind me, the view of Hemet receded in my rear view mirror. To the distant far right, the mountains rising above Palm Springs peaked crisply against the cobalt sky. To my left, the sunset would be kissing the horizon off the Los Angeles beaches in just a few sweet hours.

At the intersection of Highway 79, aka Gilman Hot Springs Road, where I had turned right automatically for the past nine years to the base, I looked right and left and in my rear view mirror to see if there were any familiar cars around who would see me defying my usual routine. I drove straight ahead up Lamb Canyon Highway that cut through the San Jacinto Mountains toward Beaumont and ultimately led to the I-10 San Bernardino Freeway. The temperature seemed at least fifteen degrees cooler here than the desert roads, and made me shiver. The chilliness of the mountain shade and higher oxygen level brought relief from the scorched desert air that my lungs had breathed every day for nine years.

My beeper's sudden vibration against my waist startled me. I had unthinkingly clipped the beeper to my pants when I got dressed. The screen showed CMO Int Reception's phone number. Someone reported me missing at 6:30 muster. I immediately felt guilty for not answering the call as I had done so obediently hundreds of times before.

I tossed the beeper that bounced onto the passenger's seat. The power that beeper had held over me didn't control me anymore. I would have preferred to say, Look, I'm leaving, I'm sorry. Goodbye, don't worry about me. But I would never answer to the authority behind that beeper again. Another piece of control disengaged from my life.

My car ascended the mountain highway toward the crest when the vibrating beeper bounced and squealed on the seat again. CALL RECEPTION. Normally, an order like that would cause me to comply without hesitation. Only senior executives, security, or staff who answered up directly to COB RTC or his immediate staff carried beepers. Today I defied that damned beeper.

Call in. CALL IN. Finally, base security's number showed in the text message with an order. CALL SECURITY. Did they really think that anyone not showing up to muster was going to comply and call security? I thought about throwing the beeper out the window to be free of it at last. But it wasn't mine to discard; I'd have to return it at some point.

The highway dropped in a declining elevation into Beaumont, the scrubby little town on the other side whose saving grace was its 24-hour Denny's Restaurant. Detour signs led me roundabout the town before I finally saw the sign I was looking for—I-10, west to Los Angeles.

While waiting at the light, my left blinker clicked like a tongue tsk-ing against the roof of a mouth. *You naughty girl, what do you think you are doing?* The stark reality of having only $48 in my wallet, a half tank of gas, a gas credit card that shouldn't be used, and no destination, hit me.

I needed to find someone in LA who could help me. Chaz! He was the only one in my address book—in my world—who was not a Scientologist who would care about my circumstances and assist me. Peter and I had plenty of friends in LA but we had lost touch over the past nine years, so I couldn't suddenly call any of them. Ely and Krista had moved out of state, so we no longer had any family in the area.

Chaz owned a shop in L.A.'s garment district. I had gotten to know him quite well as one of my vendors who manufactured different clothing parts for my uniform projects, and we had become friends over the past year. I often stopped at his shop to pick up samples for my projects, or check on his progress with other parts. We would chat about work, about life, about his religion, and about stuff unrelated to Scientology. He was a member of the Ba'hai faith and believed in God, but we had not gone so far as to try to convert each other. I wasn't interested so much in what Bahai's believed, as I was interested in how kind, understanding, and caring Chaz was as an individual who seemed to draw a lot of peace from his religion. He had shared his story with me of how his family had to escape his country when the Shah of Iran took over. His family had fled the country and came to the US where they built a new life. I had gone to Italy the year before with Chaz and another Sea Org member to establish sources for manufacturing fabrics for several Scientology building's interior design projects, as well as several of my uniform projects. Chaz had met us in Milan and introduced us to a fabric manufacturer. He was also the only person in my address book who believed in God. I knew I could ask him to help me through this crisis.

It was nearly 6:45pm. I pulled over to a gas station and called Chaz from a pay phone. No answer. I left a message that I was in desperate need of help, asked if he could meet me later somewhere at his convenience, and to call my beeper. I felt guilty about using that beeper for a personal reason, but put the thought out of my mind. Finally, that beeper would serve a good purpose.

# 35

## MY ACCOMPLICE

**Los Angeles – August 1, 1998**

I KEPT LOOKING IN MY REAR VIEW MIRRORS, not wanting to see Int base security guards on motorcycles trying to flag me off to the side of the highway or edge me off the road. Peter wouldn't find out what happened until Sunday afternoon when he got back to the base. He would be made to participate in the emergency recovery drill. Security guards would make him list every place I could have possibly gone—what places did I like to visit, where might my destination be—and whom would I call. He'd check my use of our credit cards. I knew they would check Yosemite National Park, my favorite place in California, so I decided not to go there. I wanted to move back with my family that was now in Atlanta, but also thought I would benefit from being alone for a while. I always wanted to go to Seattle, one of the few places that offered the best environment for me of urban mixed with mountains and ocean. I had no money to travel or sustain myself, so those options were out.

Driving through the San Bernardino National Forest area was my favorite stretch of the freeway. The air was cool and fresh, and felt especially welcoming now. Late afternoons in July typically exuded the thick brown L.A. smog that cloaks the city on bad days unless strong ocean winds clear the skies. The drama of the day

303

paled against the painted sky that hung like a giant backdrop over Los Angeles. The sunset seemed more like a private showing of an original painting with vivid brush strokes of orange, pink, and purple across a cobalt blue backdrop. This unexpected surprise showed me that a very real and magnificent world awaited me.

I veered west on I-10; its name changing to the Santa Monica Freeway showed me that I was about twenty-five minutes from the Pacific Ocean. If I couldn't meet Chaz and get his help, I would sleep in my car somewhere at the beach. Now a refugee, I had no place else to go, and no cash to pay for a room. I couldn't reveal my whereabouts by using our credit card. Int base security had a computer system to track reservations, plus Peter would even stop my ability to use the gas card as he had done before.

My beeper bounced on the seat, announcing my caller. I pulled off the highway to find a pay phone. I gasped when he answered. "Chaz, you're there? Hi Chaz, hello, this is Karen Schless. You got the message that I left you!"

"Karen, hello, calm down—yes, I did get it. I beeped you—are you okay? You sound stressed."

He had no idea. "Chaz, would you be able to meet me somewhere tonight? I need help. I didn't have anyone else to call."

"When and where? I'm at dinner with my family. But yes, I can meet you afterwards. Are you going to be okay?"

"I can't think straight, I don't know where to go. Just name a place, somewhere in Santa Monica. That's where I'm headed. A restaurant parking lot maybe?"

"I can meet you at 9:30." Chaz gave me directions that I kept repeating to myself as I couldn't trust them to memory. Just the sound of the Pacific Coast Highway in Santa Monica eased my tensions, knowing I was near the ocean, the one place that could always refresh me like no other. My thinking started to slip out of gear again. I could barely follow the street signs. This is crazy, meeting a businessman in a parking lot in Santa Monica in the dark and my husband doesn't even know I'm gone and—there's the place Chaz described.

I pulled my car into the covered parking lot next to the restaurant he selected. Couples walked holding hands and laughing, ready for a night out. Lamppost lights glowed softly around gently swaying palm trees that lined the driveway into the parking garage. The scene offered an inviting setting, but I couldn't enjoy it. Instead I pulled into the concrete garage lit only by sporadic overhead lamps that cast a harsh glaring brightness. Within minutes, Chaz's white van pulled next to me.

The unavoidable reality of events gripped me. Someone else had now witnessed the fact that I had walked out of my life. The black-and-whiteness of what I had done morphed into a suffocating fear that crackled over my face. Spots sprinkled across my vision. *Focus, come on girl, focus. You're tougher than this.* I gestured to Chaz to come into my car. I felt immobilized.

Chaz settled himself in my passenger's seat and turned toward me, lifting my hands and placed them between his. "Are you okay, Karen? I've been worried about you. What happened?" Chaz was a soft-spoken Persian man who spoke clear English with an ancient accent. His dark, kind eyes gazed at me in wonderment.

The spots dissipated; my tears broke loose. I poured out my story while he just listened and nodded his head, occasionally patting my hand. "The worst part about all this is that my husband doesn't even know yet that I have walked out of our life. He and I had talked about leaving but he kept saying no. He had no idea that I was leaving tonight, on my own."

"Can't you call Peter and tell him where you are?" Chaz asked.

"No! Our circumstances are nuts. We're not allowed to have a cell phone. I have no way of reaching Peter. This may sound even more insane, but let me tell you about the other obstacle I'm facing." I explained how Scientology's security system works. "Security uses a travel agency-type system that tracks reservations for planes, buses, trains and hotels. Security scrutinizes all reservations to find names. Had I made a reservation for a plane flight, security staff would have known when and from where I would be departing. They'd send security teams to the airport to find me with the intent to bring me back. That's why I haven't made a reservation yet—at least, that's one reason." I was about to express my financial needs to Chaz, but I went on.

"Security works like a finely tuned clock. Upon an alert, the Int Base Perimeter Council fires security teams to to track down defectors, with the intention to escort people like me back to the base—"

Chaz interrupted me. "Karen, how have you lived with this? You never told me this before. I mean, they sound like Gestapo."

"It's hard to believe, I know. I mean, that's why I tried getting out twice before—I just could never stay out. I couldn't get Peter to leave with me. He is just too far gone, too indoctrinated to be able to see the madness."

Chaz shook his head. "You're courageous to even try to make this break, Karen. I'll do anything I can to help you."

I didn't tell Chaz that I didn't want to be alone if challenged by their ability to overwhelm me at an airport because I didn't feel I could resist much coercion. Nor did I want to scare Chaz off, thinking his own safety could be in jeopardy. If any security guards did find us together, they wouldn't try to hurt Chaz; they would just intimidate him to go away and leave me alone. Afterwards, they'd collect information about him and then go after him for trying to help me. They'd try to damage his business or his reputation. I hated pulling Chaz into this, risking his being harmed in any way.

Chaz asked me gently, "How was it that you chose me to help you?"

Because Chaz had always been so kind to me despite our differences in religion, and the fact that Chaz believed in God was why I had called him. I hesitated to divulge my "God experience" to him because there was no rational sense to be made about it. I was not a believer in any religion. Telling him what happened could have made me look even more like a lunatic. Though I was unsure of most other things that night, I was sure of one thing: I believed that Chaz seemed to be placed in my path, as if my designated helper.

"I came to you for help because you were the only one I knew who believes in God. I don't think anyone in my family does, so you were the only one I could call. I don't even understand why that is important to me right now. I probably sound like a lunatic, don't I?" I buried my face in my hands, embarrassed by my mixed-up thoughts. "I just felt I could ask you for help."

"You know that I am a Ba'hai."

"Yes, but you know I don't believe in messiahs or prophets and I'm not looking for religion. I have a spiritual connection with you that I don't understand. You don't realize...I have so many needs at the moment, I'm embarrassed to tell you what I'm down to..."

"How can I help you, Karen?"

"Chaz, I need—I have $48 in my wallet. I need a place to stay tonight. I need to borrow some money. I need some cash to live on until I can get my feet on the ground and get a job. I need a suitcase. I want to go to Atlanta, my whole family is there. I need a plane ticket—I want to stay with my mother." Words barely made it through my lips, humiliated by explaining my needs to a man who had been one of my vendors and for whom I had always tried to make Scientology look good. I knew I was asking for a miracle. It would take a few thousand dollars to cover my requests.

"Let's think about the first thing. You need a place to stay tonight."

I instantly feared that my helper would misinterpret my needs, but discarded the idea that he would try to take advantage of my vulnerable circumstances.

"If you are concerned about total obscurity where no one could track you down, you can stay at my house. My parents and some cousins live with me in Encino; I own a ranch house with five bedrooms. And you will be safe there." I realized that as a family who had escaped the clutches of the 1970s Iranian revolution, they had already gone through a worse exodus but similar to mine.

"Thank you so much for opening up your home to me, Chaz, but I wouldn't feel comfortable doing that—I mean, I wouldn't want to give your parents the wrong impression—"

"I understand. Don't worry. There is a nice hotel off Ventura Boulevard, down the street from where I live. You can stay there. No one will find you."

How could he be so confident that no one would find me? Chances were slim that anyone would notice my car in the lot among so many others.

"If you think that's a safe place, I'll stay there."

"You can get a good night's sleep there. I will go home and look under my mattress to see if I have any cash to lend you," Chaz laughed. "In the morning, we'll figure out your plane ticket and I will buy you a suitcase."

Through my blurred eyes I saw the face of a dark-haired, bearded man who seemed pleased to be on a mission. It was as if he had been brought into my life for such a time as this.

"I want to repay you for all of this, Chaz. Please just give me some time to get myself established, get my feet back on the ground, get a job. If you lend me some money, how long can I have to repay you?"

Chaz raised his hands and smiled. "If God only uses me once in a lifetime to help another, then let this be the time." He rested his hands back on his lap. "You pay me back when you can. I have needed help before, and God provided for me. Now I provide for you."

I wasn't used to this kind of unconditional help and didn't know how to accept it. His peaceful presence subdued my anxiety.

I followed him on the 405 Freeway and southeast on the 101 Hollywood Freeway, which unleashed a flood of good memories. This part of the Valley had been Peter's and my stomping grounds in my happiest pre-Sea Org days. Chaz was leading me to Sherman Oaks, bordering on Studio City, on the north side of the Hollywood Hills that separated the valley from Hollywood, near where Peter and I had lived in Coldwater Canyon. What sweet irony—the thing that had stolen my life was now returning me to it.

I had seen this hotel many times before; now it would be my place of refuge for the night. We parked our cars behind the hotel. My laundry basket was perched in the back seat as if beckoning me to carry it into my room. I popped my trunk open to see if anything worthwhile in there could help me now. I noticed a clear plastic bag of old clothes and shoes stuffed into the side of my trunk. I had meant to give those things away and had forgotten about them. Things I had once tired of now seemed like recovered treasures. I dropped the bag into my basket, suddenly feeling far from destitute, ad carried it inside.

Chaz used a credit card to check me into a room under his name so Security would be unable to track me through a reservation in my name. He stepped away from the lobby desk, and handed me the room key. He tapped my hand gently, bidding me a good night's rest.

"I'll call you in the morning around 10:00, okay? Then we'll have coffee and talk."

### Sherman Oaks, CA - August 1, 1998

My home away from home that first night of freedom was just a few miles from my beloved home in Coldwater Canyon. My room was void of anything personal, but the surroundings nevertheless assuaged my anguish, like a friend providing refuge. The room's beige walls and tan Berber carpet offered a quiet backdrop that helped to neutralize the chaos of my thoughts. I savored the room's simple comforts: a dark-green patterned easy chair, a traditional walnut desk, a telephone with buttons for room service and front desk, a black television, a copy of *USA Today*, sweetly fra-granced soap in the bathroom, and privacy—all strangers to the life I had just left.

My white plastic laundry basket with teal-color handles sat atop the wooden luggage stand that would normally hold a suitcase. My appreciation for that basket had grown dramatically over the past day. I had bought it at Target last year during a rare three-hour Christmas shopping break in Hemet. Now that basket and this room were the closest things I had to a friend, next to Chaz.

A time to celebrate! But there would be no corks popping to-night. This victory was bittersweet. My husband of twenty years had no idea of my whereabouts. I had left behind everything I owned except for my old red car, the two boxes of things I had packed and stashed in my trunk, the stuff in my basket that I had grabbed randomly before I escaped, an empty wallet, and the clothes on my body.

I could no longer claim an address—even the bogus one we all used of 6331 Hollywood Boulevard, Los Angeles, California, where none of us lived—or a way for anyone to reach me, other than the beeper. I had no cell phone, computer, or Internet access. I was transient, homeless.

A room phone! I could call my mother in Atlanta without get-ting permission from anyone first. And no one would track my calls. "Oh my God, you finally left? Where *are* you?" My mother was fully aware of why I went back after my two previous attempts to leave. "And what about Peter?"

"I'm at a hotel in LA near my old house. Peter didn't know I was leaving today. I've lost him, he's too far gone, Mom." Tears started flooding all over again. "Someone is helping me get to At-lanta tomorrow. I'll call you back once I have a plan. I'm ex-hausted, and just need to sleep." I gave Mom the name and address of my hotel, in case something happened through the night and she didn't hear from me the next day.

"Love you, Karen."

"Love you too, Mom."

Scientology had tried to get me to disconnect from my mother several times over recent years. Now Mom and Chaz were my life preservers.

How surreal to move freely around the room, enjoying the idea that from that moment on, I would live unencumbered by any real or implied control over my life. I didn't care whether my reasoning made sense. All the structure that had been in place in my mind was now being dismantled.

I felt blanketed with peace and quiet. There would be no more screaming or abuse from any church leader. No more prison camp. No more sleep deprivation. No more…Was this the kind of relief a refugee might feel as they floated away in a boat, drifting in the dark, leaving it all behind?

I dipped into my laundry basket to find the few toiletries I had brought with me. I felt grateful for having a clean bed to sleep in at a safe hotel that provided things I didn't have. I buried my nose in the stack of thick white towels with a hint of scented detergent and breathed in the fragrance. I hadn't been allowed to use scented laundry detergent in nine years. I climbed into the tub to soak for a while, and then showered afterward with fragranced soap.

The amount of pleasure this brought me was more than a normal person should have felt. It brought me such pathetic delight knowing I would never again have to follow Scientology's paranoid rules about using fragranced shampoo, makeup, deodorants, air fresheners, hairsprays, and soaps. There I was, having just walked out of my life, and I was thinking about how good it was to use sweet smelling soap.

No one prevented me from watching television that night. I hadn't watched TV in our room for nine years, but that night I couldn't tolerate sound. I needed to hear myself think, to order my thoughts. I was free to watch TV, but freely chose not to. Thoughts vacillated like a pendulum swinging from one extreme to another:

I made a terrible mistake. *No, this is the right thing to do.*

I cannot bear the thought of being without Peter. *Don't think about him, it's too painful right now.*

How will I make it outside of Scientology? *Survival won't happen inside Scientology so don't even think about going back.*

If I persisted longer, I could have persuaded Peter to leave with me. *That's hopeless; he's too far gone. There's been plenty of opportunity.*

Pick up the phone and call; I want to keep our marriage together. *Call? Peter has chosen Scientology and the Sea Org over our marriage years ago. Who am I kidding?*

Have I abandoned my husband? *He abandoned me when he shifted his commitment from our marriage to the Sea Org.*

I felt guilty for being even a little bit happy about my decision, as if I had claimed a sliver of happiness that was not meant for me. I fought to stay awake; I didn't want to turn out the light and lose visual contact with this priceless moment.

### Sunday, August 2, 1998

The gentle purr of the phone ringing was just loud enough to wake me from a sound sleep. I had been unable to hear a phone ring by my bed for over nine years. When I answered, a security guard would not be listening on an extension. "Good morning, Karen. Did I wake you?"

"Chaz! Is it 10:00 already?" How odd to feel even the slightest bit lighthearted! Then I felt guilty that a man other than my husband was calling me.

"Indeed it is. Let me remind you where you are—I know you were pretty mixed up last night. I am about three miles away in Encino. There's a Starbucks next to your hotel. Why don't you meet me down there at 10:45? Does that give you enough time to get ready?"

"That sounds wonderful. See you shortly." Sunbeams glowed between the drapery panels over my window. I stretched my legs under the covers and relished the subtle fragrance and softness of the bed sheets against my skin. Anguish replaced pleasure as I felt Peter's absence. Should I go back? Tears began to sting again. NO! I could barely breathe, just thinking about him.

That first morning of my new life, I showered with richly lathered sweet-smelling soap, washed my hair with the hotel's herbal fragrance shampoo and conditioner, and dried my body with a thick, white, lavender-fragranced towel. Not bad for a homeless person. Despite my limited options, getting dressed was a pleasure. My laundry basket filled with small treasures held more value than I could describe. I put on my one clean pair of jeans and a white polo shirt, and met my friend at 10:45 at Starbucks.

"Chaz, you can't possibly know how much I appreciate…" He broke me off with a wave of his hand. He bought two coffees, and sat down in the green wrought iron chair across from me at our round table. Life on Ventura Boulevard carried on as a backdrop of laughter, brakes, motorcycles, kids squealing, music drifting.

"The good news is that I searched between my mattresses and found the money you need." Chaz handed me a thick white enve-

311

lope. Tears swelled in my eyes. He waved his hands in front of me. "No, no. It's time to start new. Come now. Let's make our plans."

I told Chaz I feared venturing into any airport terminal.

"Why don't we drive to the airport in Las Vegas? It's only about four hours from here." Chaz's willingness to solve everything amazed me.

"Las Vegas? You would drive there with me? I can't ask you to do that."

"Why not? It's Sunday, I'm not working today. We'll fill our tanks with gas, and you follow me. You'll park your car in long-term parking. Some day you can come back for it."

"We still can't make a plane reservation. They'll see it on their computer screens, and they will come after me."

"We won't make a reservation. We'll just walk up to the ticket counter, find the next flight to Atlanta out of Vegas, and I will buy your ticket with cash."

I couldn't think of any reason why his plan wouldn't work. I didn't believe in angels, but this man seemed to be the closest thing I could imagine to one. "It's a perfect plan. That you would do this for me…"

"Come. There is a luggage store down the street. You need a suitcase."

Thirty minutes later I wheeled a new forest-green Atlantic Tourister suitcase down the sidewalk of Ventura Boulevard from the luggage shop to the hotel, with my friend at my side.

"I have to work out how to repay you for all this."

"Quit worrying about it. I have a better idea. Do some designs for silk fabrics that I can manufacture in Italy. I will make men's ties and sell them in my shop. Send me a couple dozen different designs with a variety of color schemes. I will pick the ones I want and get them made."

"Will that be enough? I mean, will you make enough profit on them to cover all these expenses?"

"It could be more than enough. I'm not worried about it."

Chaz knew my passion for design while he manufactured items for several of our uniform projects. He encouraged me to keep designing as a profession, and not allow the loss of my Scientology position to be the end of my design career. I couldn't recall anyone extending such a kind or compassionate gesture to me in years.

Relaxing outside at this boulevard bistro, I delighted in the goodness of this man. I enjoyed the breeze blowing gently through the people's hair around me and at Chaz's shirt collar flitting in the light wind. We finished our coffees while I relished in the luxury of free time. A half-hour later, I packed my few belongings in my new green suitcase and wheeled it, topped by my now empty laundry basket, to the elevator. I said I felt idiotic with my laundry basket perched on top of my suitcase. Chaz said, "Don't care about what people think!"

We stopped at the hotel's rear exit, while I scanned the parking lot before I moved toward my car, concerned I was being watched. My car hadn't been stolen; my tires weren't flat; there were no hate notes attached to my windshield wiper. I breathed a sigh of relief while tucking my laundry basket into my trunk, got in my car, and locked the doors. I followed Chaz down Ventura Boulevard to the nearest gas station. He gassed up our cars and paid for both with his credit card.

We headed toward downtown LA where we picked up the I-10 freeway heading east. I dreaded heading back in the direction of the Int base. We would pick up Highway 15 just outside of Ontario, to take 15 north. Chaz said we'd take a break in Barstow. I had driven those miles through the Mojave Desert and Death Valley numerous times alone, when Peter played with Melissa Manchester at the MGM Grand. For details about our desert trip, visit the book website.

I could have become transfixed by the illusion that the desert never ends, and stretches infinitely beyond the horizon—until Chaz's red blinker flickered on, alerting me that McLaren Airport appeared in the distance, wavering in the heat like a mirage.

My friend's van led me toward the long-term parking section. I parked my car in a spot near the elevator, despairing over leaving my car behind. Chaz tucked my suitcase inside his van while I locked up my car and climbed in beside him. He parked at the short-term parking area and we walked to the Delta ticket counter. The chiming of nearby slot machines and the sounds of coins tumbling into winner's cups clanged in my ears, adding a raucous, freakish effect, clashing with my somber mood. Chaz ignored the casino attractions and found that the next flight left for Atlanta in a few hours. He bought me a one-way ticket with cash.

When Chaz handed me my ticket and boarding pass, my stomach flipped. I stumbled through my thank you's and hugs before my protector exited through the glass doors. Suddenly alone, I felt strangely frightened. I had traveled around the world by myself on numerous adventures. But I had never been in a vulnerable position like this, feeling like a frayed electrical wire. I found my gate and settled into a seat in the waiting area facing the window. The rhythm of planes taxiing down the runway for takeoff while other planes landed provided a balanced, comforting sense of a world under control.

I slipped my hand into my purse to find the envelope Chaz had given me this morning. Two thousand dollars in cash.

I was one of the first to board the plane and settle in with a blanket and pillow. I tuned out everything but inner anguish. As the wheels of the plane left the ground, my body felt even heavier with the weight of what I had done. I looked out the window into the clouds—soft, white erasers that I wished could wipe everything away.

What would happen once I hit the airport terminal in Atlanta? Would uniformed guards be waiting for me, or my husband's frowning face, judging me? My mother had given me directions on taking the train and then a taxi to her house in the suburbs. I had asked her to not tell anyone who called from Scientology that I was coming to her house. She would be the first person Security would call once they started looking for me, and I didn't want anyone harassing her.

When the captain announced our approach to Atlanta's Hartsfield Airport, he headed into a smooth landing as if to say, we're safely home. I let passengers pass me in the aisle before I stepped into the stream of people departing through the front exit. I preferred to emerge as part of a crowd rather than as a distinct individual. A sigh of relief escaped my lungs as I made my way through the crowd and headed toward the baggage terminal, just moving with the flow of people. Past the restaurants and magazine stands; *no surprises.* Down the escalators and into the baggage terminal; *okay, good.* My green suitcase circled around the baggage carousel and fell into my hands. *Uninterrupted so far.*

# 36

## BRACE FOR IMPACT

**Atlanta - August 2, 1998**

JIM AND DENISE'S PORCH LIGHT illuminated the stairway down the side of their home to Mom's deck downstairs. As I pulled my suitcase down the steps, tears spilled down my cheeks. There was no place on earth I'd rather be than right here, right now.

I rang Mom's doorbell, watching through the door window as her Sheltie, Jenny, went crazy barking and leaping at the door. Mom walked toward me, breaking into tears as she saw me. We hugged and cried, hugged and laughed. I stepped back and surveyed my mother. "You've gotten really short since the last time I saw you. Are you shrinking?"

Mom's red eyes, smeared lipstick, and happy face overwhelmed me with joy. She smudged her tears with balled up fingers and laughed. "Well, yeah, you know that happens when you get old."

Her words stabbed my heart. A song called "My Father's Eyes" expresses how he wished he would have told his father many things in his living years. The song kept the flame alive in me to rejoin my parents, thinking how I had missed so many years with my dad before he passed, and how Mom's living years were flying by.

Jim, Denise, Josh, Nicole and Lucy the Bulldog streamed into Mom's apartment. Lots of tears flowed with hugs and kisses that night. I had seen everyone a few years ago, but the kids had grown up. Nicole was tall and slender with beautiful long blonde hair and huge blue eyes like her dad's. I found out she had dreams of singing in a band. Josh was developing his pitcher's arm for a hopeful career in baseball. Jim and Denise looked happy together, and I envied the fact that they had been married since 1979 and were still going strong.

We talked for hours before I crawled into bed, but mostly cried together. My mother loved Peter dearly and was sorry to see us separated. But she was glad to see me finally make the break from Sea Org life, knowing how unhappy I had been for years.

"Karen, Peter called earlier this evening."

My stomach flip-flopped. "What did you tell him? You didn't tell him I was coming here, did you?" Memories of the nightmare in Gallup, New Mexico flooded over me.

"Of course not. I felt badly about lying to him. I told him I hadn't heard from you. You didn't want me to say anything, right?"

"I'm so sorry to put you in this position, Mom. I don't want you to lie to him. I want him to know where I am, but I'm so afraid what will happen once he finds out..."

"You think I don't remember those Gestapo-like security guards showing up at the motel in New Mexico? I don't want them here either, believe me. Isn't there a way to talk to Peter without security listening in?"

"No way, especially now that I'm gone. It will be impossible for me to get through to Peter privately."

I stayed in Mom's craft room that night on her guest bed. She had put fresh ivy-print sheets on the bed for me, and made some room in the closet for my clothes. Shelves overhead spewed with stacks of fabrics and sewing supplies. I fell asleep that night realizing that I had regained, not lost, my life.

Calls started coming in from Peter the next day and every day for the next three days. Mom always took the calls; I stayed away from the phone. I didn't trust myself, knowing I was highly vulnerable to Peter's voice. He could have easily persuaded me to jump on a plane and fly back, so I couldn't let myself take his calls. Mom and I both felt terrible when Mom told him she didn't know where I was. By the fourth day, Peter said he was going to file a missing person's report if I didn't surface. We finally decided to tell him I was there.

Mom told Peter how distraught I was, and asked him repeatedly to come to Atlanta alone so we could resolve this. I believed Peter knew I was not going to break down this time, and that I would hold my position and stay out. Mom told me that Peter seemed to be worried about consequences, why I did this and what was my plan. She said he seemed to be under pressure specifically about why I left, since my last years at the Int base had been so successful.

In one of his last calls, Peter told Mom that he wouldn't be able to talk to me, even if I did take the phone. He said he couldn't handle hearing my voice, because it would be too painful. After the fourth day, Peter stopped calling. I imagined all kinds of reasons why he stopped. If he had been off post working with security in an attempt to recover me, which was most likely the case, then he would be getting in trouble for that. Work would be falling behind; seniors would be screaming; production schedules in the studio would be falling off target, causing a domino effect in other departments.

Peter stopped calling, but the phone kept ringing. The Int Base port captain Ken Hoden was hot on the trail attempting to recover me. I refused his calls, so he spoke with my mother. Mom told me about Hoden's persuasive techniques, how he was trying to get her to become a vessel for him to get through to me.

Passing time was like a war of attrition, being without Peter, away from the routines of the Sea Org, with no Scientology people, with waking hours wracked with anxiety, fear, a crazy kind of withdrawal sensation, confusion about my decision to make this break, and doubt about whether I could persevere on my own. The biggest saving grace was that my escape from Scientology lifted the burden I carried about missing the growing up years of my nieces and nephews, my brothers and sisters-in-laws, and particularly my mother's aging.

# 37

## LAST CHANCE

### ATLANTA, LAS VEGAS, LOS ANGELES

**September, 1998**

HODEN'S PHONE CALLS FINALLY got through to me after one month, mostly because I didn't want my mother to bear the stress of his coercive tactics. He acted as if I had no right to my privacy, and that his mission was to pervade any peace or pleasure with my family I had hoped to achieve. Hoden was using many of the skills we were so well drilled on, including various Scientology communication training routines. His use of "TR 3" worked. TR 3 teaches a Scientologist to keep confronting an individual and repeating one's question until they got an answer, not just any answer, but the specific answer they wanted to get.

I got tired of repeating why I wouldn't come back to LA. The pain of losing Peter was excruciating. My fears about leaving Scientology non-standardly, and being the target of Scientology's fair game practices added complications I didn't want to deal with. His tactics focused on me reconciling with Peter, because he knew that was my biggest button; second to that was routing out on Scientology's terms—signing bonds attesting to never speak about Scien-

Scientology in a negative manner or to never reveal confidential information. Some people signed a $500,000 bond of confidentiality. I couldn't imagine how they believed their documents could ever hold up in a court case between themselves and an apostate like me, since it violates one's First Amendment rights to sign away one's freedom of speech, especially without any legal representation. I would never do that.

To be in good standing and not be declared suppressive, I would be required to complete a brutal interrogation called a security check. The worksheets of my sessions would be read by security, senior executives, and other personnel, and are not confidential. Anything I said could be held against me, but would, in their eyes, restore the balance and clean the slate because now they would have dirt on me that they could hold against me if needed.

Scientology never holds itself responsible for making any mistakes of any kind with the staff member; the individual is always to blame. Hubbard's policies say that if a person leaves Scientology, the only reason they do so is because of transgressions against Scientology organizations, against their post in the Sea org, against Scientology management, and against Hubbard.

I could care less about being labeled suppressive; it's a ludicrous label that no one cares about except other Scientologists. If my friends wanted to disconnect from me for being true to myself and departing Scientology, then so be it. I was much more concerned about what would happen after the sec check, questioning my ability to stay *out* of the Sea Org, away from Peter.

Mom and I talked it over. I decided to go back, partly because I had to get my car anyway, but mostly because he promised that Peter and I would talk things out. Hoden promised to cover a plane ticket, hotel costs, and food until I completed the procedure in three or four days. I would also retrieve my personal belongings from Peter's and my apartment.

Denise convinced Mom to go with me as a form of insurance that would guarantee my return to Atlanta. My mother was a sprightly 76 going on 56 in her physical energy level, so I knew she could tolerate the trip and endure at least a few days of the process with me.

Mom and I took the trip in September, leery of how we might be greeted at the airport. Thankfully, no navy-blue trench-coated Sea Org members or security guards awaited us at the Vegas airport. We found our way through the sprawling parking garage until we located my old red BMW covered with a layer of sand. My first attempt at starting the ignition failed. An airport attendant helped me jump the battery while we brushed off the sand, cleaned the windows, and loaded the luggage. I paid over $200.00 in parking fees covered by Chaz's cash gift.

As Mom and I headed through the desert, I felt like I was going the wrong direction and wanted to cancel my agreement with Hoden. Compromising myself had long been my nemesis, but here I was, doing it again. Four hours later, Mom and I broke through the mountain passes and saw the sprawling outskirts of Los Angeles suburbs. Signs for San Bernardino and Riverside made me feel queasy, though we headed the other direction toward Hollywood and the Big Blue. That old familiar, suffocating feeling spread over me, just from being in the church's proximity. Thoughts about Sea Org members laboring on the RPF, new Sea Org recruits doing their EPF boot camp, and me getting swallowed up in the claustrophobic bowels of the blue buildings nearly made me drive away.

We pulled into the horseshoe parking area outside the PAC Security office, where Hoden had told me to check in. I saw a few confused looks in the eyes of several PAC Security guards who knew me from the project I had recently done that upgraded their security gear with far higher quality gear than they had ever had. Mom stayed in the car while I went inside, because I thought I would just meet Hoden to let him know I was there and then check into the motel room that he was to reserve. But PAC security guards ushered me into one of the back rooms, and I waited and waited. I became increasingly concerned about my mother sitting in the hot car. While I was in that back room, Mom attempted to find me because I had been gone so long. She went to the security doors where I entered the building and banged on them. Through the tinted window, while knocking, she saw someone standing on the inside, but they wouldn't let her in. She called loudly, "I'm looking for my daughter!"

The guard shouted, "You can't come in. She'll be out when she's done." Mom turned around and went back to the car. They cared nothing about her sitting in the heat. An hour later, I ignored their efforts to restrain me when I insisted on returning to the car to care for Mom.

Security guards told me that I was going to stay in one of the PAC rooms that night. Hoden had made no motel arrangements for us, and had lied to me about covering the basic expenses. I made it clear that Hoden had promised to cover our expenses and I would in no way agree to stay in their blue building under security watch. I told the guard we were going back to Atlanta now.

At least this undid Hoden's manipulations. Mom and I checked into a motel room paid for by Hoden. I felt terrible about Mom experiencing this madness, and knew it wasn't going to get any better until we were gone in a few days. I disparaged myself for returning to their turf, and just hung my hopes on seeing Peter, retrieving my belongings, and getting the hell away from Scientology.

I planned to cooperate to get it over with in a few days. I knew that anything I disclosed could be distributed throughout the Scientology world, made broad public knowledge, and used against me, providing fuel for fair-game hate attacks. So be it. Contrary to Hoden that the sec checks might take a few days, they dragged on for weeks. My interrogator was Jane Jentzsch, wife of Heber Jentzsch, president of the Church of Scientology. Her partner was Kirsten Caetano, an OSA investigator. Kirsten's demeanor reminded me of SS troops from World War II movie scenes in which they acted as if they could do or say anything they wanted to those who were at their mercy.

Mom and I moved to three or four different motel rooms paid for by my org, CMO Int, during those weeks. I hated that I was dragging my mom and I through this, but wanted to complete the process so they couldn't say I refused to cooperate. Those weeks served as solid evidence why I needed to sever all ties with this group, as it made it even more clearly how nuts Scientology operations were—in case I had any thread of doubt.

I had never considered Peter as having a suppressive effect on me until then. Inside the group, it's very difficult to do any subjective thinking about oneself or to rationally analyze one's circumstances. While I had been addicted to Scientology's solidarity—believing that Scientology held the keys to my salvation, my immortality, so I couldn't leave—I concluded that I had been a minion in a psycho-political philosophy cleverly disguised as a church that functioned, in effect, as a retail religion. Scientology's economics grew only from work done on the backs of Sea Org slaves.

During a moment when I couldn't stop clinging to the hope that Peter would join me, I asked Jane Jentzsch and Kirsten Caetano if someone would go to Gold and talk with Peter to find out his intentions. Two days later, Kirsten told me that she had met with Peter, and that he said, "I am the happiest that I have been in years." For a moment, I thought she was telling the truth. Then I realized she was nothing but an OSA investigator trained to lie and trained to execute orders without a conscience. Kirsten's loyalty as a Sea Org member would go first to Peter as an ally who had chosen to stay in the Sea Org, not to me as an escapee.

If part of OSA's strategy was to drive me into doubt about leaving so that I would remain the Sea Org, they failed. But the pressure to comply with their process versus my desire to get on with my life sometimes felt like too much to bear. Prying myself apart from my husband of twenty years felt like separating two layers of skin. Mom and I dealt with stress by going out for drives in the mornings or evenings following my sessions. On one trip, we drove to Malibu to walk on the beach. I pulled off at a roadside access that required a short climb down a steep, sandy bank to get to the beach. Mom decided to wait in the car to let me have some private time on the sand while she would enjoy the view of the ocean from the car. As I ventured onto the sandy path jutting with seaside foliage, my foot got caught in a root protruding from the ground. I tumbled down the dune and sprained my left ankle.

Mom and I drove back to PAC and I called Jane to let her know of my accident. This caused a total upheaval in my sec-checking sessions. If a person has an accident, they are labeled PTS, potential trouble source. A PTS condition prevents auditing and case gain. They bandaged my swollen ankle and gave me crutches to walk with. I spent usual session time receiving "touch assists" to help the injuries, which slowed down the whole process. The first suspected SP in my vicinity was my mother. There was no way I would succumb to any coercion to disconnect from her, one of the steps to resolving a PTS condition. I couldn't tell them what I honestly thought—that Scientology itself, and more specifically David Miscavige, was the SP. So instead, I said that I was PTS to myself. I was the one pushing myself out of Scientology, I was the one leaving the Sea Org, I was my own suppressor. Jane said this was really the only right answer. We resumed the sec-checking again that led to a final breaking point.

In one session, I told Jane about something that transpired while David and Shelley Miscavige and I were at the Flag Land Base, when I was working on the uniform project down the hall from their office. I won't repeat the details here, but I told Jane exactly what happened. Jane put down her pen, looked up at me and said, "I'm not going to write that in these worksheets."

"Are you kidding me? That's what happened, Jane!"

She shook her head and said, "I can't believe what you are saying. Even if it was true...I can't put it in the worksheets."

I asked, "If I didn't disclose this in my session, then I would be withholding something, and we both know about withholds. So, how could you refuse to include this statement in my worksheets?" Here we were, arguing about the session content and procedure during the sec check.

"It would cause more harm than good to report that. I'm making the call—I'm not going to do it." Jane pushed her pen aside and looked visibly rattled by what I had told her.

"I've been troubled about that incident ever since it happened. You want me to tell you the things that have pushed me away from Scientology? I'm telling you this, and you don't believe me?"

"I'm not going to do anything that would hurt COB's reputation. I'm just not going to do it," Jane said.

"If you don't want to put this in the worksheets, don't. I'm not trying to hurt his reputation. I'm telling the truth. I also know that other people read session worksheets, although I don't know who reads David Miscavige's files. I just want to resolve this." This incident coalesced my negative conceptions about auditing, confidentiality or lack thereof, and that the Golden Age of Tech was the sham I thought it to be. I had enough auditor training under my belt to know that auditors are trained to never react to a pre-clear in session. This was a sec check, not an auditing session, but the same rules apply. This was the first time in my 16 Scientology years that an auditor reacted to something I said in session. And Jane was a re-trained Golden Age of Tech auditor for OSA.

Jane's reaction to me in the session is not included here for the intentional purpose of incriminating her, and I'm sorry if it does. My point is only that auditors are fallible, sessions are imperfect and this was, I'm sorry to say, an example of an imperfect session by a fallible Golden Age of Tech auditor/sec checker. This auditor was more willing to protect the reputation of a senior Scientology executive than to apply standard tech in session and report the truth.

Mom's patience was drawing to an end. She had been prepared for a few days, but not for four weeks. She was mostly concerned that I was unable to cut ties. I didn't know how to draw an end to this without having seen Peter yet. I had asked Hoden repeatedly to see Peter. He would say, "Probably this weekend" or "We'll work it out for one day next week." He'd string me on, and that did kept me hoping.

Hoden came to our motel several times to talk while I was in session, trying to convince Mom that I shouldn't leave the Sea Org. Mom told Hoden that it was my decision and that there was no way she would accept another plane ticket to be flown home as what had happened in Gallup, New Mexico.

Meanwhile, large boxes started arriving at the OSA office, addressed to me, in response to me telling Hoden that I was going to drive to the Int base to pack up my things and ship them to Atlanta. They forbid me to arrive at the gate of Kirby Gardens and go inside to pack up my personal possessions. I still had the gate opener and would have been able to get in.

Despite these loathsome circumstances, it was nevertheless so damn hard for me to break ties with the church. I liken the process of cutting ties with Scientology to that of a heroin addict using methadone to get through a withdrawal period rather than making a cold-turkey break.

Mom and I knew we had to get off of Scientology's treadmill that was wearing us down. Scientology's official routing out procedure of endless interrogations was nothing but a game of survival of the fittest.

No more games. I called the OSA office and told Jane "no more sessions, that's it." I would leave on my terms, without meeting Hoden again, without seeing Peter, without signing the bonds, covenants or any other legal papers as part of their official routing out process. Miscavige and minions would once again destroy another marriage. This was the one battle that I had fought so hard to win, and was frankly tired of battling over a husband controlled by David Miscavige. I didn't want them to win that battle, but I was determined to win the war over my own freedom.

Mom threw up her hands and said, "Let's pack right now." We started making trips to the post office to ship out the 12 boxes that

I had received. After our second trip, Mom and I pulled up to our motel room, only to find Ken Hoden, Jane Jentzsch, and Kirsten Caetano standing in front of our door.

It was a déjà vu of Gallup, New Mexico, only different faces. Kirsten and Jane were in full Sea Org pseudo-military style uniforms and there was Hoden, like in Gallup, here to coerce me again to stay in Scientology. Wearing their U.S. Naval-styled dark-blue double-breasted suits with shiny brass buttons, shoulder boards with officer stripes, white shirts, black ties, shiny black shoes, and white naval caps with black patent rims that bore the Sea Org symbol—the gold laurel wreath encasing an ascending star, they must have hoped that the Sea Org symbology would exert some degree of power over me. It had none.

They formed a physical block that prevented Mom and me from getting through the doorway.

"Get out of the doorway!" I shouted.

They wouldn't move, staying there with locked arms.

"Get out! Move!" I repeatedly yelled until they finally stepped aside. My mother and I walked in, grabbed our luggage and walked toward my car carrying the bags. Each of them used a different tactic and tone with me. Kirsten maintained her SS-Gestapo fear tactics. Hoden kept lying and said, "You and Peter still need to talk." Jane kept saying that she wanted to take me into session just one more time. I sympathized, knowing she could get into trouble for me leaving like this. I made the last compromise I would ever make in my Scientology life—I agreed to go into one last session with her in a motel room down from ours before we left.

She told me that she had left something incomplete from our last session, so she took it up with me. Within moments I was cloudily looking at something that appeared to be in Nazi Germany, straight out of a movie I had seen. For a second I gave it a try, and told her I was uncertain of some of the details and the identity of the individual with me, or who I was in that memory. Jane actually suggested names to me of who this person might be and who I might have been. I had never before ever known an auditor to make suggestions of the identities of people in past-life incidents.

Discerning what was real and what was imagined when looking into past life memories was all bullshit and we were both wasting each other's time. "That's it! No more! This is over!"

I put down the cans and walked out the door. I felt disgusted overall but actually felt bad for Jane. I cared about her as an individual, and didn't want to see harm come to her just because of my decision to leave. She called after me while scrambling to collect up her e-meter from the motel room. I walked back to my room where I found Mom with Hoden and I told him to get away from my mother, and to leave the area. Mom and I tried to finish packing the car, and tried to get into our front seats. But first, Jane flung open the passenger door on the driver's side and jumped into my back seat.

"I'm going with you. I'll take you into session when we stop at night, and we'll sort this out," Jane insisted. Seeing this OSA officer uninvited in my car, with her uniform skirt and shirt all disheveled from squashing herself against the luggage in my back seat, trying to control the situation down to the last second, was a sight that even I, as a departing Sea Org member, found humiliating.

The desperate look on Jane's face triggered my compassion for her as a woman trapped in Scientology. She thought her only option was to carry out her duties without question, even at the risk of compromising her own dignity. Her desperation, though, made me feel humiliated for having been part of a group that would stoop to this level of action. But Jane's choice was to be part of this group; my choice was to regain my independence. Jane would have to fend for herself. I was done compromising.

My mother looked at me questioningly about how to respond to Jane in my back seat. I made eye contact with Jane and mouthed the words, "Jane, preserve your own dignity here." Jane didn't move.

"Jane. Please. Get. Out. Of. My. Car."

Jane finally extricated herself, but not without making claims that she would get me back into session as soon as she could, even if it meant flying to Atlanta. She stepped away and smoothed her uniform and hair as I slipped into the driver's seat. At least Hoden and Kirsten could report that she had made every effort to salvage me.

As we backed out of the parking space, the threesome moved in front of my car. I pressed the button that locked all four doors, but lowered my window and told them to step away. As a last-ditch effort to keep me from leaving, Hoden threw up his arms and said,

"What's Peter going to say? He was expecting you to work this out and come home."

I should have gotten out of my car to slap him. Or push him into the wall and scream at the top of my lungs into his face, frothing and spitting, as I had seen Miscavige do to staff. Hoden was a liar and a manipulator. But I didn't want to stoop to mirroring Miscavige, Hoden, Kirsten, or compromise my dignity. I was free to be me now. I replied dispassionately, "Tell Peter he had four weeks to see me and never bothered to show up. Tell him time is up."

As I drove away, I felt like a different person gripping the steering wheel of my car. I pitied the three workers reflected in my rear view mirror, standing in the parking lot in front of that motel room watching us leave. The Church of Scientology wasn't used to losing battles.

My old BMW traveled well across the country as the driving machine it was built to be. Surprisingly, my often 90-miles per hour in a red car attracted no highway patrol or tickets along the way. We arrived in Atlanta two and a half days later, and all I could remember about the trip was a few thousand miles of stripes in the road.

# 38

# ON THE OUTSIDE

"It comes down to a simple choice: Get busy living, or get busy dying."

- Andy Dufresne, *Shawshank Redemption*

**Atlanta - Fall 1998**

MY FEELINGS ABOUT ARRIVING at my family's home in Atlanta could be compared to what an ex-con might feel after getting out of prison, institutionalized after years inside: Sweet freedom, finally, but many years of life lost. I felt like a stranger in a strange land finding new ways of seeing, thinking, and forming opinions not influenced by Scientology views.

This bittersweet homecoming marked my final exit from Scientology, empty handed without my husband. Mom's return was also bittersweet. Her Sheltie, Jenny, was gaunt like an abandoned child, missing clumps of fur. Jim and Denise were glad to have us safely back, with me out of Scientology for good. Denise had been right about Mom being the insurance that guaranteed my return home.

As if I had tapped my red shoes together like Dorothy in *Wizard of Oz* and landed in my bed in Mom's, I echoed Dorothy's thoughts that there is no place like home. Mom's crowded but cozy craft room became my safe haven for many months.

Scientology's aftermath played itself out. I couldn't have made it on the outside without being surrounded by people I loved and who loved me back.

Other than the joy I felt every day from reconnecting with my family, the first year was beyond painful. Assimilating back into American culture while in my forties was like making a transition through a twilight zone. Nearly everything about me had been foundational in Scientology—my thinking processes, my opinions, my worldview, my friends, and our marriage. I was exhilarated about being free when I wasn't feeling mixed up by uncertain opinions, painful memories, erratic emotions, mixed with an inability to reason clearly or to trust my own judgment, seasoned with a high dosage of trauma from losing a 20-year marriage.

I made the radical decision to purge all things Scientology from my life—language, ideas, behavior. I knew it would take a lot of time. The process was really about recovering from the uneasy balance of my Scientology life, having walked that tight rope for sixteen years. I'm a survivor who has found that writing about my experiences has helped me to heal from it—from that mindset with twisted ideas about what was true or real. The hard cold fact that I had been lied to all those years. The trauma of physical, spiritual and psychological abuse in the Sea Org at the Int Base that required PTSD counseling to diffuse its effects in me. That ongoing questioning of beliefs, what was right, wrong, wise, foolish, normal, extreme. That alluring addiction of Scientology's Celebrity Centre and its glorification of celebrities and artists. My intrigue with, and doubts about, acquiring ultimate control over life, matter, energy, space and time through the Scientology system. My dislike for much of L. Ron Hubbard's bizarre behavior and beliefs that I wasn't free to express and tried to ignore. The responsibility I felt to help make this a better world and save the planet through Scientology, while having ongoing regret about being separated from my family. The ambition I had for myself outside of Scientology as a fashion designer who wanted to leave, with dissonance in my life with a gifted husband and award-winning musician-composer who wanted to stay. That constant struggle with what was the greatest good for my life and for the planet. Constant dissonance.

This "adjustment" period was not about feeling like a victim. It was about feeling the impact of having lost sixteen years of my prime adult life, a time when many people reach their peak of professional accomplishments that build toward future retirement. So yes, I had to deal with a lot of anger—anger toward myself for my choices; anger toward Scientology and the Sea Org for lying about so many things; and anger mixed with loss and disappointment toward Peter. The loss of my husband and the world we had built together, and loss of the belief system we had dedicated ourselves to (destructive or not) had the greatest impact on me. The world Peter and I had built together provided a solidarity that I had become dependent on. Actually, this had probably become a problem of co-dependency, which is why it had been hard for me to cut ties, and to adjust on the outside.

When I was around other people, I often had to force a happy face. My mind and heartstrings remained wrapped around friends and loved ones I had left behind. Their faces stayed vivid in my recollections, even in my dreams, and even after repeating nightmares. To the degree that the past fades but never disappears, the people of my past stayed with me. Emotional trauma held me in a fragile condition, easily triggered by memories and feelings about Peter. Everywhere I went, I heard *On the Wings of Love* playing, and believed it was a sign that something positive was about to happen, or Peter would be coming back to me. Every time I spotted a yellow motorcycle on the street, I thought Peter had finally come to join me.

I had little idea what happened in popular culture between 1987 and 1998. People would say, wasn't Seinfeld funny last night? I'd laugh and think, *what's Seinfeld?* Or they'd ask, did you see *Everybody Loves Raymond* last night? When I admitted that I hadn't heard of those shows, people would look at me as if I was from another planet. They had no idea.

I sought ways to heal. I turned to new friends, groups, authors and journalists, scholars and college education, ministry and preachers, religious critics, cynics and skeptics, business blogs, movies, the media and the Internet. I questioned just about everything—who am I, really? What cultural issues did I agree with, apart from the Scientology filters in my thoughts? Was I a Republican? A Democrat? What were my political leanings? What did I think about social and political issues of the times, like Roe vs.

Wade? Same sex marriages? Prayer in schools? The war in the Middle East? Gun control? For the past sixteen years, none of those social issues impacted my life, so I had no personal convictions about any of them.

The one thing I did know about was everything to do with Scientology. The only thing that had mattered to me while a Scientologist was clearing the planet. We paid little attention to world events; we never watched television, rarely saw a newspaper, and only listened to a radio on the way home at night. I had lived in a social time warp while the world moved on and culture changed.

I reached out to only one friend in Scientology, my dear friend Valerie Schomer Page, who worked with me in the Big Blue project implementing the new uniform program there. I called Val to let her know I left, knowing that she and I would not be able to stay in touch, because she would be required to disconnect from me. I told her about my new life and asked her if she wanted to join me on the outside. I offered to send her a plane ticket, help her get a job in Atlanta, and help her finish high school. She said there was no way, because Sea Org life was all she had known since she was a child, and how would she support her daughter Alyssa. She had never been outside the Scientology structure, so had no clue how to function on the outside.

The ending of my friendship with Valerie was one of many sad stories that illustrate Scientology's cruel disconnection rule, like Val's own traumatic disconnection story. She had been born into Scientology. Her father, Homer Schomer, joined the Sea Org when Val was about 5, and went to work on Hubbard's flagship, the Apollo. Meanwhile, her dad had left Val in the care of friends until she reached age 10 when she was allowed to come to join him on the Flagship Apollo in 1972. There, she was nicknamed "Shortie," and worked for a time as a Commodore's Messenger assistant, but hit the RPF by age 11. Homer had to write a petition to see his daughter due to their conflicting work schedules, even while she was a child. She told me stories about living in roach-infested quarters there, all the while not getting an education. But it was the only life she knew.

Val's father went from the Apollo to the Flag Land Base and then to Author Services Inc. in Los Angeles to handle Hubbard's finances. After the infamous "corporate sort-out" of Scientology, when he was told to hide LRH's assets and shield Hubbard from liability for tax or fraud, Val's dad escaped the Sea Org in 1982. By 1984, attorney Michael Flynn filed a lawsuit for him, demanding a jury trial and damages exceeding mega-millions of dollars, naming ASI, Miscavige and Hubbard's right hand person, Pat Broeker in the suit that centered on Scientology's deception about Hubbard's qualifications and the true nature of the Scientology organization as a for-profit organization. His suit cited numerous charges including physical abuse, intentional infliction of emotional distress, false imprisonment, and violation of his civil rights. Homer described Scientology as an elaborate scheme to obtain money and assets from followers by creating organizations for allegedly tax exempt purposes, while the assets obtained were used for Hubbard's personal use—as he could testify after having been responsible for Hubbard's finances for years. As the person who managed Treasury, it became clear to Homer that LRH was controlling all assets for the church, even though Scientology had deliberately established the corporate sort-out to shield LRH and protect the assets and LRH from investigations by the IRS, FBI and other governmental agencies. The whole idea was to shield LRH from inurement, from liability for taxes and tax fraud. Because Valerie's dad had been working at Flag, he had also been aware of the Guardian's Office vigilante fair game attack on Clearwater Mayor Gabe Cezares, who was not a Scientology supporter. All these factors deemed Homer Schomer a major threat in the eyes of Scientology.

Valerie was made to disconnect from her father because she was told that he had been declared a suppressive person, but she knew little about what her father had discovered, that her father had been abused in the RPF, had been spit on by three different ASI executives and humiliated. In blind faith to her church, Valerie wrote her disconnection letter to him, confirming that she would never see or speak to him again. For more than two decades, she had no contact with her father. Val told me that she saw her father one day while she was at the Los Angeles airport. She never ran up to him to say, Dad it's me! She never spoke to him, just watched her father pass by as if he was just someone that she used to know. When I asked her how she felt about that, she said, "Well, it was weird. But he's an SP. So what else could I do?"

Valerie struggled to this day with literacy. This young woman had devoted her life to the Sea Org, was a hard worker and an officer, but had not moved up the bridge and couldn't get trained in

Scientology because she had trouble learning due to no education in her early years. Despite that, she felt unwilling to leave it. My dear friend and I said our goodbyes.

I had lost my husband and dear friend so far; now what about my in-laws? I contacted Peter's mother, brothers Beau and Ely, and sister Lacy, as well as Peter's daughter Heather, to let them know I left Scientology and Peter stayed in. They were each shocked, but glad to hear that I had made it out. Peter knew that I would be in touch with my in-laws, so he had already started to damage my reputation with them. My brother-in-law Beau Schless told me that Peter had already called and gave him a string of stories about me, including that I had committed crimes against Scientology, had committed financial irregularities, and had falsified my post statistics. Beau said he could care less about those claims, but said that it seemed to make Peter feel better to have reasons like that for why I left, instead of my departure being a personal thing between us that affected his ego.

My mother-in-law Shirley Egglefield Schless was so glad to hear that I was out of Scientology. Regretfully, we hadn't seen her in a while, even though we knew she had been going downhill with emphysema and had been hooked up to an oxygen tank for years. She told me that Peter had called and claimed that he was happy, which she said she didn't believe for a minute. Shirley asked me to stay in touch, and I promised I would. She said she hoped that Peter would come to his senses and get out of Scientology.

Each of my in-laws encouraged me to stay connected with the Schless and Egglefield family, even if Peter and I got divorced. We had been family for nearly twenty years, and were very close despite the miles between us. I would continue to hear from his cousins Lori and Lynn Egglefield, or his sister Lacy Schless Rezak off and on. But I couldn't handle the emotional pain without Peter involved, so I had to tuck all my in-law family relationships into my memories, and let them go.

I avoided connecting with people (friend or foe) who had come out of Scientology, because I didn't know whom I could trust. I knew about Sea Org members in OSA doing counter-intelligence and had no interest in being spied on or having anyone infiltrate my life pretending to be a friend, as what happened to Paulette Cooper.

I also didn't want to talk with people who spoke in Scientology words because I was determined to stop thinking in that language. For this reason, I missed the opportunity to build friendships with many people who had left. Jon Horwich called me after he left the Sea Org in the early to mid-2000s, a shock considering he had been a fixture in the Sea Org for decades, worked for LRH on the ship and had been Diana Hubbard's husband and father to Roanne Hubbard. He moved to Chicago to work in radio. I told Jon that I believed David Miscavige was an SP since the early 1990s, and he said that many Int base staff were just now coming to that conclusion.

I regret not staying in touch with Jon and others, but at the time I wasn't capable of having friendships with ex-Int base staff. I am truly sorry to anyone reading this if I acted rude, arrogant, or cold. I hope you understand why I didn't respond, and I apologize. I was often tempted to join other former Scientologists picketing Scientology organizations or doing other forms of protest. But for me, starting over had to be cold turkey with no Scientology influences in my life that would prolong my recovery. I also didn't want to be consumed with vengeance, or remain angry toward anyone personally who had harmed me while I was in. I tried to take the high road of holding myself accountable for the bad choices I had made of ever joining Scientology and the Sea Organization.

There were a few exceptions. Chuck Beatty, who had been in INCOMM and started an online message board for exes of the Int base, reached out to me online. He was a compassionate man who made it safe to communicate about my experiences through Operation Clambake Message Board or Ex-Scientology Message Board. He also fielded contacts from media requesting interviews, and sent some of them my way, which got me started doing interviews.

Tory Bezazian Christman also reached out to me. I knew Tory since the Portland Crusade, and knew she had been working for OSA. She went through a traumatic departure from Scientology because of her OSA connections and her husband disconnected from her. She began posting her story as Torymagoo44, which became an incredible voice on ex-member sites, with YouTube videos providing detailed descriptions of what had happened to her, to others who had been harmed by Scientology, and to other people who were being attacked as critics of Scientology. She has boldly picketed Scientology organizations for destroying families.

She was one of the people with whom I wanted to be friends, but kept my distance only because I was not yet ready to trust former OSA staff. Years later, I had the opportunity of working with her and Steve Hassan on a project to help a family learn to deal with a son who had gotten sucked into Scientology. I've always thought of Tory as an incredible force to reckon with.

I re-connected with Nancy Many, a former President of Celebrity Centre. Nancy and her husband Chris left the Sea Org a few years before me; Nancy made a miraculous recovery after having a psychotic break. She was extremely kind to me, knowing what I was going through. As much as I liked Nancy and appreciated her kindness, I had trouble trusting her only because she had been in OSA counterintelligence. I wasn't mentally sharp enough yet to discern whether she was she just doing black ops on me. She went on to help the Lisa McPherson trust. We later got back in touch while contributing to Andrew Morton's *An Unauthorized Biography of Tom Cruise,* and I read her draft of her wonderful memoir, *My Billion Year Contract.*

Nancy's story, and others like it, had a strong healing effect on me, because they corroborated so many of my own experiences at Celebrity Centre, at Flag, with the RPF, and with the abusive culture and madness within Scientology. Nancy and I followed similar paths with education; we each finished an undergraduate degree and then a Master's Degree. She went on to become a non-denominational Chaplain, and has remained an outspoken critic of Scientology's human rights violations.

On a visit to a relative's house, while answering questions about my Scientology life, she said, "You need to get a life!" Her cut and dry, blatant honesty was hard to swallow, but jarred me into realizing I had to stop wallowing in grief and move on. Each of my family members helped me in every way they could, starting with helping me get a job. When someone leaves the Sea Org and rejoins society, where's the resume? How would I truthfully explain what I had been doing for the past decade?

During that first year out, I kept in touch with Chaz. As promised, I produced a series of fabric designs for him in a variety of color combinations, in hopes that he would manufacture them for his shop. Chaz selected about ten of the designs, produced the silk fabrics in Italy, and made them into men's ties. He sold out at a clothing convention; those ties were bought by retailers in England,

Belgium, and other European areas. I asked Chaz if those designs had been remunerative for him, and had I repaid him for all the help he had given me? He said, "Yes, tenfold."

My brother Tom got me my first part-time job as a host in a subdivision showing model homes to homebuyers. I worked a few hours on weekends, which brought in more money than what I had made in the Sea Org working more than 100 hours per week. It felt great to start earning a paycheck again so I could buy groceries, put gas in my car, and got me back into contact with other people again. Tom's lifestyle centered on gastronomic rhapsodies. He included me in get-togethers at his favorite restaurants like Van Gogh's and Stony River in Roswell, where good food and drink was shared with good friends. Before the Sea Org, I had lived a good life in Los Angeles, so I was no stranger to these delights. I just had trouble hanging out with people because I could barely see past my emotionally damaged self and enjoy fun moments.

Jim and Denise gave me a full-time job at their company working in the office, and then selling home remodeling projects and materials in Atlanta. This job was a lifesaver that helped me get my feet on the ground to actually support myself. I loved being with them and helping with something they had worked so hard to develop. I was lucky that Jim and Denise tolerated my highly sensitive emotional condition over those first few years, while I was working for them and often a basket case, even at work. I had many bad habits, baggage from my Scientology indoctrination, to which I subjected them unthinkingly. I had an arrogant attitude, was bossy, impatient and demanding, all learned from the Int base culture. I'm sorry for those attitudes, and I'm just so thankful that they tolerated me while I worked through it all.

My greatest challenge was handling social relationships. I had all kinds of issues getting along with people at work, and even in forming friendships. I discovered that my ability to roll over people like a steamroller, an ex-Sea Org member, an OT Scientologist who could accomplish anything, only worked within the Scientology culture. In the outside world, that attitude comes across as arrogant, bossy, dominating and overly-confident, being a bully and know-it-all, and is downright offensive to many people, especially in the South that values social graces.

Once I realized who I was in relation to other people—as myself, not as a Scientologist—I broke through the Scientologist delusion: I was not part of any superior breed, as we believed in Scientology; on the contrary, I had been living within Scientology's groupthink, which included delusions of grandeur. I ran into one circumstance after another that made me realize that there was nothing superior about my knowledge gained in Scientology, as I had thought. I had to purge myself of this "superior" persona. This process of increased self-awareness in social settings helped to chisel away at some of the narcissistic tendencies I had developed.

### How do you think now?

A new friend invited me to a Christian Apologetics meeting, where people study how to defend their beliefs. The leader, Don, heard I had been in Scientology. He approached me and asked, "So, how do you think now?" Stunned by this question, I asked what he meant by that.

"What I mean is, how do you think, now that you're out of Scientology? Because Scientology uses brainwashing." "Oh no," I said, "Scientology doesn't use brainwashing. A Scientologist is in control of everything. We did everything through our own choices, our own will." I gazed back at him, feeling like he was talking down to me. "Haven't you read the verse in Romans that says, 'Be transformed by the renewal of your mind'? That's how I think." He stood there looking at me, searching my eyes. I walked away from that meeting, realizing that while I knew I had been very messed up emotionally, I hadn't considered that I had been brainwashed or subject to thought control.

I wondered if Christians know that many non-Christians think Christianity uses brainwashing through its preaching, and legalistic operations and regulations to control people's lives and donations. I had questioned whether Scientology used it, but had always rejected it as having been done to me. I had many new things to think about.

His question marked the beginning of my journey to understand brainwashing, mind control, undue influence, and my personal study of cultic groups and recovery methods. I share some of my discoveries in my last chapter.

My friend Tal Davis from the North American Mission Board reached out to an acquisitions editor at Broadman & Holman Publishers to tell him about my experiences in Scientology. This led to my first book contract, which I describe in, "Merchants of Fear,

Fair Gaming & Vigilante Justice." I started looking at my life like I was peeling layers of an onion; everything I did seemed to bring on new realizations about Scientology's influence in my life, about my cultic personality that was changing, about changes in attitude and awareness.

A new friend read me a modernized biblical passage that resonated with me: "…Are you tired? Worn out? Burned out on religion? Come to me. Get away with me and you'll discover a real rest…learn to live freely and lightly within unforced rhythms of grace…" Live freely and lightly, unforced? As someone who wanted to know God but had zero interest in organized religion, dogma, or religious regulations, these words offered an appealing approach that contrasted sharply with the force, control and regimentation of the Scientology world. I gradually dumped more and more baggage. I let go bit by bit of my regrets about the past, my losses, fears about spending my future alone. All of that unnecessary pain had weighed me down like a heavy yoke that was not meant for my neck. I became a seeker, free to be, unhindered by rules, codes or policies.

In late 1999, I went to the Holy Land—holy to people of three world religions. In that tiny region of the Middle East, I saw Muslims, Christians and Jews in pursuit of knowing God, carrying out ancient cultural traditions in Israel that had monumental impact on the world, while clashing culturally. Young Israeli soldiers walked around Jerusalem with machine guns slung over their shoulders. I was not permitted to tour the Muslim temple until I changed out of my dress into long pants and a head cover. I walked down the ancient cobblestone streets where Christians believed Jesus dragged a heavy cross to Calvary under whippings by Roman guards. At the Wailing Wall, male Hasidic Jews rocked back and forth praying aloud while stuffing prayer notes into cracks in the walls. So much heaviness, tradition and force attached to each of these religions.

Prior to this trip, I had paid little attention to how Muslims, Jews and Christians had simultaneously attempted to survive there through their faiths. Like Scientology, each has its unique dogma, truths, rules and regulations, and each believes in itself to be the superior religion. Although there is no God in Scientology, the similarities between these groups rocked me—each is rigidly sequestered into their own way of life, and each believe that their way is the one and only truth.

My newfound freedom to explore spirituality allowed me to explore myself outside of a belief system—who I had been before Scientology, how I had lost myself while in Scientology, and who I was now outside of Scientology's influence. There was so much to figure out about my true identity, and how Peter's and my cultish beliefs and lifestyle in Scientology had sent our marriage into oblivion.

I often recalled that event back in my office at the Int base on July 31, 1998, the night I decided to leave, when I had that incredible experience. I had long questioned whether I had cracked up or whether I had been touched by God. Who is to say? One thing I did know—I had received an immeasurable filling of love that had washed me with peace, and calmed me. The experience had nothing to do with religion, a denomination, or force—nothing to do with the religious traditions I had witnessed on my trip to Israel.

# 39

## WHAT'S LOVE GOT TO DO WITH IT?

"I want to say that I'm sorry for the way things turned out. It wasn't supposed to go like this, but it has and that's the reality of the situation."

- Peter Schless, July 7, 1999

**Atlanta - 1999**

ON DECEMBER 31, 1999, WHILE MILLIONS celebrated the turn of the millennium, I celebrated the one-year anniversary of my personal victory breaking free of Scientology. For the first time in ten years, I watched Dick Clark's New Year's Eve party broadcast from Times Square, so grateful to just be alive and free.

I wrote my first letter to Peter before I went to Los Angeles in September 1998. He didn't respond before I went to LA, and we didn't see each other during my four weeks there. On January 6, 1999, I received a letterhead envelope from Golden Era Productions with Peter Schless' name typed under the return address. Enclosed was a copy of papers dated September 4, 1998, filed in the Superior Court of Hemet, California for the dissolution of our marriage. These papers had already been filed while Ken Hoden was calling me before I flew back to Los Angeles! Peter's signature showed him as the "petitioner in propria persona." A form dated December 31, 1998 was also attached with Ken Hoden's return address typed in, and signature at the bottom, with a yellow sticky note attached that said, "sign and date and send this page to Peter." Hoden wanted me to simply sign the papers and dissolve our marriage through the mail, just like that. I wouldn't do it.

I had no contact with Scientology representatives until I received a letter from my OSA interrogator, Jane Jentzsch, of April 17, 1999. Excerpts:

*Dear Karen,*

*I have been thinking a lot about your cycle recently as it is not a complete cycle and this is something that doesn't sit well with me, as it is not Scientology...I had really thought we had an agreement to apply the tech to a complete result. We did agree on this...I am a person who likes to complete cycles of action, it is not a matter other than this is what should be done as it is not good to not complete what one sets out to do. Since I audited you, I have done some training and I know what went wrong in our sessions and I want to fix this. I have a new program and from my viewpoint this is purely a technical matter. I am not interested in anything else than pure application of tech to this situation. I have worked out how this could work and my obligation is to not leave tech uncorrected, nor cycles incomplete...I have looked at how this could be made to happen and I have worked out a plan I think that you will like and agree with, but I need to talk to you on the phone to go over this. Please call me.*

*Much love,*

*Jane*

While I appreciated Jane's admission of technical mistakes, and her desire to set things straight, I would never do more auditing. Jane called and called. She flew to Atlanta, planning to take me into session. She stayed in a nearby motel, and I invited her to Mom's home. We talked about Scientology, Peter, and my new life. I refused to go in session. We attended my mother's church the next morning; I knew it was part of Jane's mission to find out about my new life. Afterwards, Jane shared personal stories about how Christianity had not been fulfilling in her youth. We shared common experiences that we had both walked away from Christianity and held no spiritual beliefs until Scientology.

Jane said, "I can see that you have found something you believe in, although I'm sorry you are not continuing in Scientology. But I am at least glad that you have not gone to the dark side."

The dark side? To me, Scientology was the dark side. To Jane, the dark side was where people practice Scientology outside of corporate church control. The dark side includes going on the Internet to read criticisms, dig into the background of Scientology, read the confidential OT level materials, and post critical comments.

"Jane, I have no interest in any of that. I am building a new life." Jane left that afternoon saying she wanted to continue our conversation the next day, but failed to show up. I contacted OSA to ask about Jane, and received a letter dated June 8, 1999 from the Case Supervisor. He explained that Jane left because it was clear to her that my beliefs no longer align with Scientology practices.

Peter's first letter to me was dated July 7, 1999, eleven months after I left. A few excerpts:

*Dear KK,*

*Well, I felt I needed to write to you for a number of reasons. This hasn't been an easy time for me and I'm sure it's been even harder for you. I want to say that I'm sorry for the way things turned out. It wasn't supposed to go like this, but it has and that's the reality of the situation.*

*I am told you have found a new life with your family and for that I'm glad as I know they'll take care of you. I know that I could have picked up the telephone at any point over the past year and called you but you must understand that the pain in doing that was something I could not confront. I think you knew it was going to turn out this way when you decided to leave and that made it all the more hard for you.*

*I'm writing this letter to you. Not to Alice, Tom or Jim or anyone else. Please respect this. It's not that I don't have feelings for them (which I do) but now I need to communicate with you. Obviously you will do what you want, but I am talking about wrapping up our marriage and that is between you and me. We're the ones who spent 20 years of our life together, so I want to handle our own laundry.*

*In order to end cycle on this, we've got to split up our mest. It's been almost one year since I sent you 12 boxes of clothes and stuff I packed not long after you left. Do you want the boxes of pictures? I have a hard time going through them, but I will send whatever you want.*

*I think that your family probably wants you to take 50% of the income of the song from here on out. You are totally within your rights to do that. You were there when the song was written and worked to get the publishing company set up.*

*…I do wish you well and I know that you are going to be very successful in whatever you've planned out for your life. Financially, you are in a position to make whatever you need to live the lifestyle you choose since you are so competent in the job arena.*

*It is my recommendation from me to you that we put this thing to bed. It's nobody's business but yours and mine…I guess the good news is we don't have kids to handle. So, please let's end cycle on this as friends.*

*As I said before, if you see fit to go another direction with this, there's nothing I can do or say. I'm only hoping that twenty years of our life together means something to you and that you will make a good decision which both you and I can live with. I've tried to make it as simple as I could by keeping this between you and me. It's your decision and whatever you decide, I want to know that it was your decision alone.*

*Peter*

It's hard to describe my reaction, since this was his first contact with me after his last phone call to my mother August 5, 1998. I'm wondering if he even knew that I had been in LA to see him for four weeks; Security probably withheld this information from him. His words "end cycle" and "wrap up our marriage" brought such pain, I can barely express it. Our "Scientologese" in the letters reflected the cultic tone that had once defined us but now posed a stark contrast between us. I knew our letters passed through the hands of minimally one Security guard and other Scientology officials before they would get off or on the base.

The "I was there during the songwriting and publishing company" statement hurtfully minimized my contributions to our accomplishments. I was struck by the irony of him asking me to make my own decisions and not allow my family's thoughts to influence me when, at the Int base, he was totally under the influence of Scientology with leaders telling him what to think, do and say.

On July 29, I finally answered his letter. I accepted his apology and repeated mine. I addressed our religious differences, and explained how love of God and family was changing my life. I pointed out that he was under the influence of Miscavige and Sea Org leaders while addressing our message, yet he was asking me to not be influ-

enced by my family. I had to let him know that while he has the right
to his beliefs, I did not feel obligated to support them financially, and
asked him to have compassion for my new life as he was asking me
to have for his. On August 24, 1999 he replied. Excerpts:

*Dear Karen,*

*Thank you for your letter. I would have answered sooner, but to be
honest, I was a bit shocked by the contents. While I am totally OK on
working this out amicably, I want you to know that it's totally counter
productive for you to send a communication which is filled with slanted in-
nuendoes, invalidation and insulting remarks about Scientology which is
<u>my</u> religion. That's going to cease from this point on… there is a bunch of
memorabilia/artwork from our travels that I will box up and send along
with linens…The particular photo you requested (from Wayne Masserelli)
was thrown out the week after you left. I'm sending the frame.*

*…In summary, I have put together a settlement that is
even…However, I must say one more thing. We both joined the Sea Organization and agreed to abide by its principles. You broke that agreement
when you left…you are attempting to rewrite history because the fact of the
matter is that you abandoned me and took off with our car. You never
asked me to leave with you because you knew down deep what that answer
would be. I tried to contact you repeatedly after you left but you were totally
out of comm. Yet you imply that I was the one who was not communicating. I even talked with your mother on a number of occasions when I was
trying to find you and I'm certain you were right there in the room with
her. Totally suppressive.*

*So, if you want to justify your suppressive acts behind your newly found
religion, so be it. Just spare me the entheta in any future communications we
have. Realize that I know in my heart that the real reason for your blow
and antagonism is your transgressions against the only group on this planet
that holds the answers to spiritual freedom. And yes, this <u>is</u> me talking.*

*Peter*

No, this wasn't Peter talking. I knew the tones of my husband
of 20 years. This is David Miscavige's voice—cold, domineering,
nullifying and it drastically conflicts with his first letter. I understood why Peter had to lie about us talking about leaving. If he
admitted that, he would have been an accessory to my "suppressive" act. He had still not told them the truth.

Scientology leeched the lifeblood out of our marriage. Our outcome is typical for couples that break up where one wants to leave Scientology and the other one wants to remain in. Disconnection is cruel. The exile is called the SP with no rights, and the one staying in is the good guy.

Years later, I got a call from a former Gold musician whom I will call Sam, who worked with Peter directly and who was also my friend. Sam said that after I left, Peter was in rough shape for a long time, and couldn't bring himself to end cycle on our marriage. Hearing this made me feel that I had made a mistake by moving on. Sam said DM kept pushing Peter to divorce me and write the final disconnection letter. Miscavige required that Peter submit a draft of the letter to him first, like a project submission, and get his approval. Sam said the folder went back and forth for nearly two months. The letter was even brought up as a flap at Gold staff meetings in front of all the crew, because it wasn't getting done according to Miscavige's desires. Miscavige put words into Peter's mouth, just as I suspected. My husband's final words to me were not even his.

I finally stopped denying that I had lost Peter as my husband long before I finally left. Peter had lost himself, I had lost myself, and thus we had lost our marriage. We had coexisted under the guise of marriage that was under Sea Org control, not our control.

We revised and Fed-Ex'd settlement papers back and forth, until November 9, 1999. The dissolution of our 20-year marriage was finalized in the Superior Court at Riverside, California, through the mail controlled by the Church of Scientology.

Several Scientology spokespeople (Tommy Davis, Karin Pouw, Mike Rinder) have denied the disconnection procedure. My experience is just one in a string of hundreds, maybe thousands by now. Our divorce is just one of dozens of examples I could name of Scientologists divorcing each other under pressure from Scientology officials. I later learned from Peter's older brother, Beau Schless, that Peter had disconnected from him as well.

Peter Schless has never since composed a song for the outside world. I can devise no rational explanation for what void Peter filled or what need he satisfied by staying at the Int base. His glory days as a musician and composer were behind him.

Who needs a heart when a heart can be broken.

Peter and Karen took their 2nd leave of absence from the Int base in 1997. They went to see Karen's family in Atlanta, and drove up to the Smokies one day, when Karen asked Peter to leave the Sea Org with her.

Peter and Karen attended the Celebrity Centre Gala event, 1996, when Peter performed with the Golden Era Musicians. This was the last Scientology event they attended together.

Karen, circa 2015, out of Scientology since 1998.

Karen found this online photo of Peter, accessed around 2015. Peter had already been in "the hole" at the Int base before this. As of 2017, Peter is still at the Int base.

# 40

## MERCHANTS OF FEAR, FAIR GAME & VIGILANTE JUSTICE

"Vigilante justice - n. any person who takes the law into his or her own hands, as by avenging a crime…done violently and summarily, without recourse to lawful procedures"
- *Random House Webster's Unabridged Dictionary, 1997*

"Make enough threat or clamor to cause the enemy to quail … always find or manufacture enough threat against them to cause them to sue for peace. Don't ever defend. Always attack. Don't ever do nothing. Unexpected attacks in the rear of the enemy's front ranks works best."
- *L. Ron Hubbard, HCO PL 15 Aug 1960*
*"Dept. of Governmental Affairs"*

**Since 1999**

PART OF THE PRICE I HAVE HAPPILY PAID for my freedom from Scientology has been finding ways to help others to protect theirs. Like me, many people who eventually made it out of Scientology alive, with our mind and ability to think clearly at least partially intact, tell our stories in public arenas. Many of my ex-Scientology friends agree on the importance of communicating about our experiences as a way to heal, to come to terms with our past, to inform the public, and to alert authorities. Some have chosen picketing, YouTube activism, blogging, writing books, helping individuals personally, doing media interviews, demonstrating with Anonymous, and on, to express their views. I have been writing articles and book manuscripts, teaching, speaking at public events, doing media interviews, and helping families or individuals one on one.

Any word uttered by critics about Scientology is immediately rejected by Scientologists. The critic is labeled a "merchant of fear" or "merchant of chaos." Hubbard describes the "disturbing elements" or suppressive persons in our civilization as critics, journalists and other media, police, government officials who go up against Scientology, psychiatrists, and a long string of professions. He calls these "merchants of fear" who earn their daily bread by making our environment seem as threatening as possible, causing confusion and upset, and "trying people's sanity." In other words, any Scientologist who hears any critical words about Scientology is trained to automatically think that any criticism is coming from a suppressive person, so there is no validity to the criticism. References to these undesirables can be found in a variety of Hubbard's works, including *New Slant on Life*, his 1965 policy letter "Handling the Suppressive Person," the *Scientology Ethics Book*, *Science of Survival*, and *Scientology Technical Dictionary*. The fact that Hubbard writes about this so much, and Scientologists have to study and know this, points to Hubbard's fixation on enemies, war, and being prepared for defense against them in his ongoing battle.

One of the more striking characteristics of Scientology actions towards its enemies who were once active Scientologists, is that they never share in the criticism of these people. Ex-Scientologists went through the Scientology or Sea Org system, and are products of Scientology. Yet Scientology leadership refuses to acknowledge that Scientology made Scientology a bad word—not the critics.

I had no intention of speaking out about Scientology, and tried to distance myself from anything to do with it so I could heal and build a new life, but I often found myself back in the sweep of it. I'd get involved in activism exposing the cult, and would then withdraw for months or years to get on with my life. Keeping silent—which is exactly why Scientology implants you with phobias about speaking out—enhanced Scientology's ability to survive and spread, like malignant cancer. One of my favorite words of wisdom by Dr. Martin Luther King became a personal mantra: "Our lives begin to end the day we become silent about things that matter." When I didn't want to do an interview or a speaking engagement, I would think about the importance of not being silent, and instead, not allowing Scientology to bully me and others. Breaking my silence was as much of a mental challenge as a social one. Another statement from Dr. King also resonated with me: "There comes a time when silence is betrayal." I knew I had to make it public knowledge what had happened to me, because this could help to prevent Scientology from continuing to harm others as I had been harmed.

Sharing my story began by speaking in churches after I started working at the North American Mission Board in 2000. Pastors invited me to share my experiences so their congregations could compare and contrast Scientology to their own beliefs. Christian journalists started interviewing me for their papers, radio, TV shows. Speaking out mushroomed from there. round 2002, I developed Wings of Love Ministry to help people who had come out of Scientology or other cults, and affiliated with Atlanta Community Ministries. I simply offered a listening ear and a caring heart; I had no counseling experience or training. I signed on with the Robinson Agency in Atlanta that booked me for speaking engagements at churches, women's and youth groups, and special events across Georgia, Alabama, Florida, the Carolinas, Mississippi, Kansas, Missouri, and to Oregon. I also partnered with the Interfaith Evangelism team at the North American Mission Board, the Evangelical Ministries to New Religions (EMNR), and the International Cultic Studies Association.

I often wanted to avoid activism. It would have been easier to stay quiet and keep the past behind me. But it's equally troubling to know of injustices and people being bullied by Scientology, so I can't do nothing.

My activism in speaking out about Scientology from 2000 to the present originally consumed 60 pages of this book, covering speaking at events, university classes, media interviews with CNN, Dateline NBC, and CBS; and written articles and presentations.

For the sake of printed brevity, I posted the original chapter on the book website, so please visit that page to get a fuller picture.

## Calvary Baptist Church, Clearwater

Working with religious groups in the Clearwater, Florida area was an especially moving experience for me, because Scientology was known of but not understood, so I felt I could help. I had never visited Calvary Baptist Church next to the Fort Harrison while a Scientologist, but passed it frequently. To be invited to speak to Pastor Bill Anderson's congregation was a humbling experience. They consider Scientology to be deceptive and dangerous, since Hubbard's entrance into Clearwater was based on lies, and since the organization had framed Clearwater's Mayor Gabe Cezares. After speaking at a Sunday service to 800 of Pastor Anderson's parishioners around 2004, many people expressed appreciation for explaining things they had always wondered about dealing with Scientologists. I held a workshop that taught them how to reach out to Scientologists, which they practiced that day by starting up conversations with Scientologists on the sidewalks carrying e-meters.

Calvary Baptist Church built a new larger facility in north Clearwater. In 2007, I was invited to speak at the new location for an event sponsored by Watchman Fellowship. On my way to the church, I noticed someone tailing me while I passed through a shopping plaza. Not very good at being obtrusive, he was easy to see dodging behind columns and other people in my peripheral vision. I let him tail me, and hoped he would come to the event so he could hear my description of how Scientology was harming people.

Several Scientologists attended, including two female OT VIIIs who asked one of the staff to arrange a face-to-face with me afterwards. The OT VIIIs were a French and an Italian Scientologist, one who drove a fancy yellow sports car around Clearwater that I recognized. She got in my face with her super OT confront level and in an antagonistic tone, asked "Why are you using this opportunity to talk to people and tell them lies about Scientology when you could be telling them the truth?"

I held her penetrating gaze while replying calmly, "Everything I have said tonight is what I experienced in Scientology, and what I observed. ALL OF THAT is true to me. Your reality does not enable you to see any truth but what you believe to be true in Scientology."

She snapped back, "If you are out of Scientology, why are you talking like a Scientologist?"

"Because that is all you understand," I replied, "and I wanted to make sure I got through to you." Her pursed lips and tense forehead told me she didn't like my answer. She had no reply.

Her other friend reached out to shake my hand. "I would be glad to talk with you some day." I reciprocated and let her know that I would be glad to talk with her, too. I never heard from either one again.

Watchman Fellowship recorded my talk, Escaping Scientology, and sold CDs online.

## Scientology's Vigilante Justice

We don't know how much our "rights" actually protect us until we go to claim them, and then find out whether the system works, or malfunctions. In a nation that goes to war to protect our democracy and to preserve and enlarge our zones of freedoms of speech and religion, it is quite disillusioning that there would be any risks reporting on any "religious" group in America, much less Scientology that takes it upon itself to retaliate with its vigilante justice. I would expect risk from investigating a terrorist network, a drug cartel and organized crime, but a group that calls itself a religion and a church that has its own spy ring and intelligence collection branch?

At Int base briefings, we heard announcements from Miscavige or an OSA executive about fair gaming tactics used on enemies. Our crowd of 800 staff would hoot, holler and applaud wildly whenever we heard that another critic's life or reputation had been damaged or destroyed.

How was damage done to our enemies? The radicalization of Sea Org members and its guns for hire is the systematic use of Scientology as thought reform to divide people from other people (critics, SPs, psychiatrists, government, media) who they believe should be destroyed or hated. The actions in Hubbard's original Fair Game policy have continued long since the policy itself was cancelled for PR reasons. Scientology's vigilante fair game actions played out in my life and in the lives of others whom I have mentioned.

Church officials, other Sea Org members, certain public Scientologists who volunteer or are paid by OSA, and private investigators work as vigilante operatives who act above the law when it comes to defending Scientology. Scientology vigilantes use their own brand of frontier justice—terrorism in today's terms—taking the law into its own hands, seeking vengeance against people without having legal authority to do so. I explain several experiences of my own here and more on the book website.

## Andrew Morton's Unauthorized Biography of Tom Cruise & a French documentary

In 2006, British journalist Andrew Morton interviewed many exes for *An Unauthorized Biography of Tom Cruise* (St. Martin's Press, 2008), including me. His objective was to determine whether Cruise was heterosexual. His story provided the first detailed background about Cruise as a Scientology celebrity, about Scientology's leader and management headquarters.

Contributing to Morton's research brought beneficial experiences that exceeded the opportunity to provide information for the book. The weekend I was to meet Morton in Santa Monica, I had flown to Los Angeles to first meet with a French television producer of *Secrets d'Actualité* on the M6 network in Paris. He was interviewing exes at the Bonaventure Hotel for his documentary on Scientology celebrities, particularly Tom Cruise. He later asked me to contribute to a second French documentary on France 2 National Network in 2009 covering Cruise's role in spreading Scientology throughout Europe. After the documentary interview, I drove to Santa Monica to meet Andrew Morton at Shutters, a beachfront hotel with an outdoor veranda and magnificent view of the Pacific. The ocean has always been the one place where I found solace and balance—a perfect setting to talk about my dark era. We settled in some white club chairs at a small round table dressed with tropical napkins and fresh flowers. Ocean waves rhythmically lapped onto shore while the sun sparkled so brightly that I turned my chair to let the sun fall on my back.

An aspiring writer myself, I studied everything about Andrew Morton. A tanned, 6'2" man with intense eyes and light brown hair that toppled nonchalantly down his forehead, he seemed intensely focused despite his casual appearance in khaki shorts and a breezy linen shirt. I was familiar with Morton's biographies of Madonna and Princess Diana, so as a writer in training, I observed his information-gathering process, how he took notes, asked interview questions, and later how he fact-checked and compiled the biography. He was on a journey to discover every detail that would piece together an account of Cruise the individual, the Scientologist, the man of questionable sexual preference, and best friend to the leader of Scientology.

I enjoyed my salad with a glass of chilled pinot grigio while Andrew waited patiently as I deliberated with answers to each of his questions. He started with, "What do you think of David Miscavige?"

As seagulls squawked around me and I breathed the salt air, my thoughts went into lockdown when trying to dredge up memories of COB. In every other interview I had done, journalists had only asked about celebrities in Scientology. I liken my frozen frame of mind to that of an abused child who finds herself in the presence of someone who could help, but the child is unable to say, *that is the man who did those things to me.*

Talking about Miscavige had always been forbidden; my criticisms lived only in my private thoughts and I had written few words about them. The first words out of my mouth were not from my own wellspring, but from a line in one of Hubbard's policies. I answered, "Miscavige is a ruthless, pitiless, product officer."

"A what?" He was trying to be kind, despite my cryptic answer.

"A product officer is an executive who inspects areas under his control and uses various tactics to make staff produce results on their job. 'Product officer' is a Scientology term."

"Describe how a 'product officer' can be ruthless."

"Ruthlessness is the essence of being an executive in Scientology. You are merciless. You never accept excuses for why something doesn't get done. This is David Miscavige. Everyone else emulates him. But 'ruthlessness' is required by L. Ron Hubbard." I wanted to say more about ruthless, but I couldn't go there. I wanted to talk about pitiless, but the words remained trapped behind a mental firewall. I wanted to tell him how Miscavige had coerced my husband Peter into captivity, and abused and humiliated him and many others, but I couldn't go there either. Not the ocean breezes nor the lapping waves or the intoxication of salt air helped me to access the ineffable, what I wanted to say about the abusive culture at the Int base. Miscavige had used his own brand of psychological terrorism to harm me versus laying a hand on me. But while sitting before Andrew, my deepest thoughts about Miscavige remained under lockdown. I freely described the Celebrity Centre operations of recruitment, gave ample details of life and operations at the Int base, and many observations of Cruise and his friendship with Miscavige. After hours of taped interview, we watched the fiery orange sun shoot pink and orange rays across the sky as it sunk into the horizon, and called it a day.

I drove up the Pacific Coast Highway to my hotel, relishing my freedom, while realizing that some of the most deeply disturbing details of my past were still inaccessible to me. I'd like to say that violence and abuse were an anomaly at the Int base, but many exes, including some who have since left such as Mike Rinder and Marty Rathbun, had perpetrated terrorism that made them two of my most-feared people. Int base violence had not struck me as something to disclose about my Scientology experiences, partly because violence and abuse had become **normalized**.

Being interviewed by an experienced writer who knew how to deep dive for the information he needed for his story helped me to see that I had to come to terms with the perpetrators of my past within myself. I had to stop minimizing the level of evil at the Int base, stop thinking that abuse was normal, and clear up the confusions and old ideas about what happened. I had peeled away layers of trauma and emotional blindness, but evidently had more work to do.

I reorganized *Chasing After the Wind* that we had done for Broadman & Holman in 2000, with a new timeline, new chapters, and many more accurate details and vivid descriptions that my first co-writer didn't pull out of me during our interview. Through the healing process of writing, I faced details of traumatic instances, had to privately deal with consequences of my actions, and cracked apart the shell of influence that had confused my thinking. Writing helped to free me from confusions and emotional burdens of the past. Details started becoming as sharp and clear as broken glass.

In late 2005, after speaking at a national collegiate conference in Albuquerque, New Mexico, a representative from New Hope Publishers handed me his business card and said, "You need to write your story for us." Soon after, I signed a contract with New Hope to write *Escaping Scientology: An Insider's True Story*. They did the cover design and launched the marketing campaign while my manuscript was in editorial production. New Hope put the book on Amazon.com and promoted it in their catalog of upcoming releases distributed at a national book convention. My publisher told me that my title was #1 on their list for pre-orders, a 2006 release. Exposure of the book brought my title to Scientology's attention again. I'll explain the legal steps against me that started to unfold, but first, the prelude: Scientology's vigilante justice at play.

## Fair Gaming Me

Around 2006, OSA implemented their plan to hurt me in Atlanta, revealing itself as a psycho-political organization that seeks to be a law unto itself, using lawyers, threats and intimidation to impose its will on others. The onslaught began behind the scenes without my knowledge a year prior, but came to my attention when I received a letter from Elliot Abelson, legal counsel for Scientology. His letter notes my interviews with the French television shows and other media, and orders me to cease and desist from talking about Scientology.

The threatening letter intended to overwhelm me through pressure designed to put me as their enemy into a more amenable frame of mind. This is known as Black Dianetics and Black PR, as was done to Paulette Cooper and other "merchants of fear." They try to weaken the enemy psychologically, by infiltrating the enemy's personal life and mining the person's connections, thus embedding OSA in a way that the people close to the enemy serve OSA's purpose in influencing the enemy to become ineffective and silent. OSA only stops once the price to own the enemy is low enough to satisfy their sense of domination over the individual.

This is a good place to mention Marty Rathbun, Miscavige's former Inspector General and right hand man, for making public OSA's plan to harm me in 2006. (He left Scientology in 2004, became a figurehead for the Independent Scientology movement, but turned again in 2017.) Thank you, Marty, for posting this on your blog, "Moving on Up a Little Higher," Jan. 9, 2012:

He starts with the Debbie Cook story. As Captain of the Flag Land Base for 17 years, Debbie's departure from the Sea Org rocked the Scientology world after she sent an email to all Scientologists that Miscavige was destroying Scientology and engaging everyone in off-policy fund raising. Her image as a stellar leader of Flag had come to represent aspirations for what a Scientologist could become. However, she had been sent to "the hole," subject to psychological abuse in physically humiliating conditions. She was sent back to Flag, but escaped with her husband, and sent that pivotal email that led to an exodus of Scientologists.

Rathbun followed Debbie's story with a report "to give Debbie and the public at large more reality on how Black Dianetics was applied to one Karen Pressley, once wife of musician/composer 'On the Wings of Love' Peter Schless." Rathbun provides context that the actions planned against me were far below what OSA was going to do to Debbie Cook. He wrote, "Though Debbie and those similarly situated would love to believe they will be treated differently because they are not condemning Scientology as a philosophy as was Ms. Pressley, they have misread Miscavige entirely. No, **when one dissents in order to ensure the survival of the philosophy of Scientology, the programs to destroy such an individual rise to a whole new level of treachery, force and vengeance.** Debbie can take it to the bank, Miscavige is already going far beyond what is contained in the following document when it comes to Debbie. Where they have contacted the preacher that baptized Karen, you can bet they have already contacted the doctor that delivered Debbie."

"THE OFFICIAL CHURCH OF SCIENTOLOGY REPORT, OPERATIONS AGAINST KAREN PRESSLEY

February 8, 2006

Both the [Director of Special Affairs] DSA Atlanta and DSA Austin have been talking to their Christian ministry contacts about Pressley.

The DSA Atlanta contacted Stacy Robinson of the Robinson Agency who books Pressley for Christian speaking engagements. Robinson has a website which contains information about Pressley and how to book her to speak at an event.

The DSA asked Robinson to help her as she had attempted to speak to Pressley unsuccessfully and would like to somehow influence Pressley to stop bashing her Church [Scientology] and stick to ministering Christianity. Ms. Robinson asked the DSA what she wanted of Pressley and the DSA expressed her frustration with the content of Karen's "speeches" and that her fellow parishioners were deeply distressed with the falsehoods spread by Pressley and we needed Ms. Robinson's help to get these lies stopped. Ms. Robinson told the DSA that she could do nothing about the content of Pressley's lectures and that the "Biblical" thing to do is to speak directly with her. The DSA told Ms. Robinson, she was hoping she could help by promoting Pressley less or not at all so long as the subject was bashing another church and its followers. Ms. Robinson said all she could do is give her name and number to Pressley and that if Pressley wanted to talk to her she could. The DSA told Robinson if she could encourage Pressley to call her so we could end all this, she would very much appreciate it. Ms. Robinson said she will see what she could do.

The DSA also spoke to Rev. Johnny Hunt, pastor of the First Baptist Church Woodstock. He runs the church where Pressley was baptized. He told the DSA that Pressley rarely attends his Church any more as she moved out of the area but that her family still attends. He said that Pressley now attends Roswell Street Baptist Church.

Hunt told the DSA that if he saw Pressley any of her family members he would give them the DSA's name, message and number so that Pressley could contact the DSA herself. There is nothing he could do about the situation.

The DSA has a call in to Dan Hayes, Executive Director of the Atlanta Community Ministries of which Pressley's ministry is a part as well as Stacy Buchanan, Ministry Manager. (This is the woman who screens and approves all ministries that will function through ACM.) The DSA has not had a call back yet. The DSA has also e-mailed to a list of Christians terminals on Pressley's lines.

The DSA Austin [Cathy Norman] has spoken with one of the board members of the Evangelical Ministry to New Religions (EMNR) and sent emails to two other board members concerning the misrepresentations that have come up in Pressley's past speeches. The DSA will be attending their annual conference starting Thursday and will be talking directly with different members of the group. Pressley was scheduled to speak there but said that she may not attend."

It creeps me out knowing that Rathbun, Rinder, and anyone from RTC and the OSA network in three states intentionally implemented a plan to bring harm to me. This plan embedded Cathy Norman, Director of Special Affairs at the Church of Scientology in Austin, Texas, into my life. Cathy attended every conference I spoke at through EMNR and NAMB. She'd pretend to be a friend to Christian ministry leaders, and inevitably get a seat at my table where guest speakers are hosted by the leaders. Cathy chit-chatted with the table guests like a nice person who was there to objectively learn about Christianity, while her true purpose was to spy and gather information about my thoughts, statements, friends and professional connections. She even emailed me prior to some of these conferences, asking to review my speech to ensure the information about Scientology was accurate! I would always assure her that I was perfectly capable of disclosing verifiable facts. I cautioned the EMNR leaders about Cathy Norman's destructive intentions, but the conference leaders chose to turn the other cheek. They also hoped that Cathy would hear things in the conference presentations that could turn her away from Scientology.

In Atlanta, I started getting phone calls from several of my professional associates, including the Executive Director of Atlanta Community Ministries, Dan Hayes; the Ministry Manager at ACM, Stacy Buchanan; and the Director of the Robinson Agency, Stacy Robinson. They said Scientology representatives were making waves and applying pressure to keep me from public speaking and giving media interviews. The infiltrator told Stacy Robinson "it wasn't very Christian of her to book someone like Karen Schless at a Christian conference."

Robinson, Buchanan and Hayes not only informed me of these attempts, but expressed full support for whatever I chose to do. I didn't change anything, and neither did they. Dan told me that the Scientology person tried to damage my repute with the ACM Board of Directors, but considering the source of the information, they ignored the Scientology claims. Scientology just lost more credibility in the eyes of people who found out what the organization had tried to do to me.

## Legal Leverage, 2006

When Elliot J. Abelson, General Counsel for the Church of Scientology International came after me for criticizing Scientology, I had to learn about legal leverage, and who possesses it when it's me versus Scientology. I'll start with his letter of March 8, 2006. This letter "placed me on notice," demanding I "cease and desist from further public disclosure of information obtained during my tenure as a CSI employee." This threat was no surprise; I had only wondered when I would start hearing from them, since I already knew they had gone after my publishers.

After reviewing the letter, I noticed Abelson's first foot bullet: he did not refer to me as doing religious/ministerial duties as an eternal member of the fraternal Sea Organization during my tenure from 1989 and 1998, but specifically referred to me as a "CSI employee." His acknowledgement that I had actually been employed by the Church of Scientology International gave me the first edge, because employees have rights and are subject to labor laws; employers must abide by human rights and labor codes.

His letter is centered on the claim, albeit false, that I had signed a bond of confidentiality, agreeing to never disclose information that I possessed or learned about the organization. He said that in this alleged document, I "bound myself to CSI in the amount of $500,000 as liquidated damages in the event of a breach of that contract." These were stunning claims, considering that I had never signed this bond. Leaving Los Angeles without signing any such document lived bright and clear in my memory.

Abelson continued, "It is certainly no secret that you have violated this covenant on several occasions, most recently by appearing on a television program in France. Your public utterances in violation of your unequivocal contractual obligations to CSI are incontestable and documented."

By this point, I'm incredulous. So far, he has no grounds for his letter or claims. But it gets better. "Accordingly, I am placing you on notice that such actions are in breach of your obligations...(and) constitutes a formal demand that you cease and desist from any further conduct contrary to your legal obligations.... including but not limited to further public disclosure...CSI reserves the right to take any further legal action to protect its rights and obtain recourse in this matter without further notice."

I never signed this covenant, yet he's holding me responsible for violating it—and putting me on notice. In response, I would reserve the right to take legal action to protect my rights and obtain recourse in this matter as well. But how much did Abelson's threat really matter? I knew I hadn't signed any such bond, and knew that Abelson dealt in commodities of fear. Abelson was one of Scientology's legal honchos who scared many ex-Scientologists. He had been the Assistant District Attorney in Los Angeles before he defended organized crime syndicate leaders on pornography distribution charges, before he became Scientology's legal counsel. Abelson has been part of the Scientology team that brings people to their knees through lawsuits backed by a bottomless money pit financed mainly by IAS donations. Abelson has worked closely with the top guns of Scientology in RTC and OSA, who routinely use PIs to collect incriminating information for smear campaigns against enemies.

This was now the third time this bond had been used as leverage against me, when my signature on it didn't even exist. How much more time would be wasted getting embroiled in this ludicrous claim? That was the plan—wear me down. This alleged bond deserves attention. Some staff sign it under coercion when they leave the Church of Scientology International, as Hoden tried with me.. Signing it is a type of expatiation, a trade of one's freedom of speech for "protection" from CSI's attack team. The power of the Scientology community exerts a mafia-like or vigilante force against you by acting as if nothing matters other than what the Church of Scientology thinks or wants. Stock-in-trade for a criminal organization, extortion even. "Protection" entitles the Scientologist to be active in the Scientology community once their freeloader debt is paid—usually six figures, the retail value of the training and counseling received throughout their employment for which they've signed promissory notes.

After I left in '98, Scientology started paying people off with large sums of money to shut up and go away after signing a similar document. To others, they paid small sums like $500 as a leaving compensation. To not sign it and leave on one's own terms usually results in being labeled a suppressive person, expelled, becoming fair game subject to vigilante hate tactics such as personal and professional defamation, physical threats, financial or legal framing, friend and familial disconnection, anything that could lead to your demise.

Abelson's letter mattered now only because he had stopped my book publication in 2000 with Broadman & Holman. Someone had tipped off Scientology attorneys about my book when B&H sent my manuscript for a standard libel reading to a Washington, D.C. law firm. B&H was told they would be held liable for $500,000 in damages if they published my book—fraudulent leverage. The CEO of B&H decided to not engage their financial resources in a legal battle. Scientology officials attempted a similar scare tactic with St. Martin's Press when they published Andrew Morton's *Unauthorized Biography of Tom Cruise* around 2008, but St. Martin's withstood the threat, and published Morton's book anyway, without a lawsuit.

The repeat performance in 2005 between Scientology lawyers and New Hope Publishers used the same fraudulent leverage to stop *Escaping Scientology: An Insider's True Story*. Abelson called my publisher and tried to pump her for information about the publication of my book. He planted doubt in her mind about how it would help to forward the publisher's ministry objectives by putting the publishing company at a financial disadvantage, on the grounds that New Hope would be culpable for this half-million dollar breach of covenant. She asked me to speak with New Hope's attorney, who told me that until he saw copies of the alleged covenant document, he wouldn't be able to move forward with publishing my book. What? The most absurd aspect of this situation was I hadn't even signed this document but had to deal with it anyway.

Before I responded to Abelson, I consulted two California attorneys to educate myself on the legal aspects of this situation. Could a lawyer get away with threatening legal action against my publisher or me based on false pretenses? What recourse did I have against a lawyer who sabotaged my professional advancement to defend his client? Did the Church of Scientology International have the right to enforce confidentiality of a staff member who lacked access to legal counsel to protect her rights? What happens to an attorney (like Abelson) for lying about me signing a bond of confidentiality and using it as a threat a leverage for a lawsuit, when I hadn't signed it?

Both attorneys told me that the church's coercion of staff signing any documents of confidentiality was ludicrous, particularly if the church was doing so while also enforcing an employment contract, and without allowing for legal representation that protected the employee's interests. Abelson had referred to me as an employee of Scientology. We have something here.

Abelson knew that his claim of my signing the bond of confidentiality was a lie. I could have sued him. But this did not solve the problem with the New Hope publisher or its attorney, who would not move forward without this document that didn't exist. On August 9, 2006, I replied to Abelson's letter. An excerpt:

"Thank you for your letter of March 8, 2006, expressing concerns for the Church of Scientology International regarding my public utterances about experiences as a CSI employee. You stated that I signed various legal documents concerning my access to 'privileged, proprietary, confidential, and other information' that you said included a confidentiality covenant and bond. Though I never did sign a $500,000 bond, and do not recall signing any other confidentiality agreements which I would have since violated, I am, however, interested in informing myself of said contents and any responsibilities I may have."

I requested Abelson to send me copies of any documents he referred to in his letter that bear my signature, including a copy of my Sea Org contract. After receiving no response to my letter, nor did I receive the copies of these alleged documents, I called Abelson at CSI's law offices in Los Angeles in mid-August 2006. I left more messages over the next few days and weeks before Abelson finally returned my call later that month.

"I never signed any covenant bond that you referred to in your letter, and you know it—unless someone there forged my signature and gave you a phony document to look at," I told Abelson.

"You didn't sign it?" he queried in his gritty, bass voice.

I reminded him of the circumstances under which I left Los Angeles without ever signing Ken Hoden's papers, and said that if he has that document with my signature on it, it's forged.

"Well, why are you contacting me now then, when I wrote you the letter in March 2006?" Abelson asked.

"If I have signed any documents that CSI thinks legally bind me, then I need to see the originals. I need to see the terms and take responsibility for them—and settle the issues, or adjust my actions."

"That sounds like a reasonable request. I will send you some copies," Abelson said. In a covertly hostile tone, he added, "We do like to win."

Did he think I didn't know that? Having been on the dark side fighting battles with them longer than I had been on the outside. I replied, "I like to win, too."

He didn't respond. I filled the momentary silence with a question. "Do you have copies of many documents?" I asked this more out of curiosity about how he would fabricate his reply than expecting an honest answer.

Abelson responded, "I've got a few." I knew that the only documents I had signed were promises around 1986 to not disclose information from celebrity auditing files; promises around 1989 to not disclose the confidential location of the Int base, and lots of promissory notes for training and auditing services. I knew I had not violated the first issue, and that the secrecy of the Int base location had since become public knowledge through countless publications. Abelson had nothing on me.

I called Abelson's office through September 2006 because he had defaulted on his promise of sending copies—because there were no copies to send. I could have sued Abelson and the church. I was in college and had no interest in dropping out of school to pursue a legal battle. I understood why some ex-members sought legal recourse to right the injustices, and I admire their resilience, but I had been a soldier long enough. Life was too short and I had a lot of catching up to do. Connecting with such negative energy was not the path I wanted to travel at this time.

I placed Abelson's letter in my scrapbook, next to the letters from Peter/David Miscavige. We choose our battles, and I had made mistakes about which ones to engage in. There would be plenty of books to write, speeches to make, people to help. I considered myself the victor thus far, because I didn't cease and desist as Abelson demanded.

### Janet Reitman's Inside Scientology

In 2006, *Rolling Stone* published a controversial article about Scientology by contributing editor Janet Reitman. Reitman developed her Scientology research into a book, *Inside Scientology: The Story of America's Most Secretive Religion* (Houghton Mifflin, 2011). In 2008, Reitman contacted many exes, including me, to collect in-depth details, insight and context that helped her take readers deeper inside Scientology's world. I provided her with insight into and experience with celebrity recruitment and the operation of Celebrity Centres. While she also drew from Jon Atack's *A Piece of Blue Sky* (Lyle Stuart, 1990), Reitman produced an updated history of Scientology that Gary Willis' *New York Times* book review (2013) called "The most complete picture of Scientology so far."

## Lunatic fringe

❁ In response to media interviews from exes (self included), Scientology spokespeople dish out denials and cookie-cutter responses such as "...the church regrets that excommunicated self-serving apostates are sadly exploiting private family matters to further their hate-filled agendas against their former *faith*. Having left the church many years ago, these sources have no current knowledge about the church and their recollections are distorted by their animosity" (Karin Pouw to CNN, July 10, 2012). Yet the opposite is true. Hubbard's policies are written in stone and don't change. Events and personal details change from day to day, but facts are readily accessible through ex-members, legal affidavits, memoirs, credible journalist reports, and on.

Pouw had used the word "faith" to equate Scientology with "religion," a ludicrous comment by an organization whose members don't engage in faith. Its materials clearly state that "no one is asked to accept anything on faith" but is expected to "test beliefs for themselves on a purely personal level" (*Scientology*, 1998, p. 26). Evidently Pouw and Scientology officials aren't aware that faith is the <u>opposite</u> of personal testing and observation that is the basis of Scientology.

She strategically avoids Hubbard's most foundational premise, one as important to a Scientologist as the Constitution is to Americans: *Something is only true to you when you actually observe it, and determine its truth according to your own determinism.* Thus, public testimony like mine, like the authors of the self-published memoirs, like Debbie Cook's and the many individuals who filed legal affidavits or testified in lawsuits, is drawn from actual observation that stands up as truth. Cookie-cutter responses that deny any thread of truth or validity to any critic's testimonies are strong reflections on the group's inability to recognize that people outside of their organization have valid viewpoints.

I can't help but compare these Scientology denials to other similar denials reported by author Deborah Lipstadt in her impassioned work, *Denying the Holocaust: the Growing Assault on Truth and Memory*. She provides claims from people who insist that the Nazi holocaust of the Jews was nothing but a hoax perpetrated by a Zionist conspiracy. Apart from the obvious differences in magnitude and actions between Scientology and the Nazis, there are notable similarities. Lipstadt suggests that some of the Nazi concentration camp survivors and some of the Nazi sympathizers might have developed Stockholm syndrome, because they denied that the Holocaust even happened, that gas chambers ever existed, that people were ever killed at all, much less killed systematically. Lipstadt refers to some of the Holocaust deniers as a "lunatic fringe creating anti-Semitic diatribe." I can't avoid this comparison because of the Scientology mentality of blanket denials—what critics say happened "didn't actually happen" despite the proof, the circumstances or the people involved.

Using Lipstadt's statement for an analogy, I describe the Scientology spokespeople as "extremist Scientology fringe creating anti-critic diatribe."

While it's possible that Scientology's inner circle of spokespeople and even certain staff suffer from Stockholm syndrome, in which people who are held captive become sympathetic to their captors, I think it's unlikely. Sea Org members believe they are voluntarily participating by their own free will. Also, certain Sea Org members are *trained* in the skill of denial. It's a learned and even required process for OSA staff, for Scientology Public Relations. Having been there and done PR training, however, I know that such denial occurs under conditions of undue influence that could lead to a variety of syndromes. I am not a mental health professional and refer readers to credible resources such as Robert Lifton, Steve Hassan, Janja Lalich, Judith Herman, and others mentioned herein.

## "Ruthless: Scientology, My Son David Miscavige, and Me"

Well after Ron Miscavige Sr. and his wife Becky escaped the Sea Org in 2012, word traveled on private Scientology watcher Internet groups that Ron would be releasing a book. St. Martin's Press published it in 2016 and it became a New York Times best-seller.

After Ron's book release, I witnessed a sad act from Peter Schless. He recorded a video for Scientology's hate site in response to Ron's book, which Peter couldn't have read. He throws his former good friend Ron under the bus, such as: Ron "couldn't produce," was a "weak musician," "a slob," "enjoyed putting people down," "vile and disgusting," "a complete disappointment," and "Put it in neon lights on his gravestone: con man Ron Miscavige."

But Peter's statement, "the amount of talent the guy had could fit on my little finger," surprised me. What did Peter's opinion of his 20-plus-years band member's talent have to do with the book content? Of course, nothing. This personally demeaning comment is a reflection on Peter as a Scientologist who has lost his moral compass as a result of building his own mental prison with Scientology's help.

My stomach churned as I watched Peter motivated by words that would prove his loyalty to David Miscavige, while denying any friendship or camaraderie had ever been shared between Peter and Ron, after surviving so many tumultuous situations together in the Gold music studio and achieving so many products as a team; as if no bonds had ever existed between them as apartment-mates over the years; not to mention that Ron recruited Peter up to Gold.

I had come to terms with the fact that the will of the Sea Org had overcome Peter's individual will many years prior. But this video showed that he had lost his heart, his conscience, his human compassion, and had become a wind-up toy for COB, because Peter made those statements without reading Ron's book. Peter would have been told about the book, but would never be allowed to read a publication by a blown Int base Sea Org member who had been declared a suppressive person. So by only being told what was in the content, Peter felt it suitable to say Ron is "selling out his family for a fast buck." I wondered if Peter had given any thought to question why the entire Miscavige family had left the Sea Org.

Peter's fabrications about Ron are consistent with his other similar statements such as: "This place is a dream to work in," "If I wanted to leave, I'd leave," "as a musician you'd be nuts to leave," "I come and go as I need to, I go to the store, I go to the doctor, it's such a non-issue," and "we have a five-star pastry chef, we eat these pastries all the time," and "the meals are totally terrific." Peter has worked it out in his mind to spout off these fluffy claims with the mindset of "greatest good for the greatest number" to stand in defense of David Miscavige, of Gold, of the Sea Org, and against Ron as an enemy.

Peter lives and works behind locked fences censored by Security. He isn't free to just drive off the base or go anywhere without pre-arranged approval or a companion with him. He has been sleep deprived for so long, this has probably become normalized to him.

He lived on beans and rice or left overs for years while he was in the hole or long stretches of being in trouble. I doubt he is served up pastries on a daily basis as he portrays. Yes, there is a beautiful kitchen in MCI with a five-star chef, but those meals cater to COB, his staff, and other staff in good standing who are allowed to eat it—not the other staff who are served beans and rice and leftovers. Peter's statements portray a regrettable picture of his actual existence that I have always wished I could have reversed.

Tony Ortega addressed Peter's claims in his story, "ABC's '20/20' let Scientology trash Ron Miscavige—but here's what you didn't get to hear" (tonyortega.org). Tony challenged why Scientology would have put Ron in charge as a music director at its top international management compound, and trust him with the musical entertainment at a Tom Cruise birthday party, at Celebrity Centre's annual gala events, and on, if he were really such a failure, as Peter's and others' statements claimed him to be. Tony described Ron's pre-Sea Org musical life with his earlier band, performances and record deals in London. When Tony contacted me to find out more about Peter and why he would have said this about Ron, I explained Peter and Ron's friendship covering 20+ years. Peter must have made these vitriolic statements about Ron because Peter had simply sold out after nearly 25 years at Gold. Peter had been in "the hole," so he most likely made this video as some kind of amends for an ethics handling or to simply appease Miscavige to prove his loyalty to him. I also know that Peter is a man who lives within his own mental prison that Scientology helped him to build, just as I had done. I can only hope that someday he will free himself.

Karen's activism exposing Scientology earned her a legal threat from Scientology's attorney. Note that Abelson refers to Karen as a church employee—which also means the "church" should have been observing labor laws. He also includes a lie about Karen signing a "$500,000 bond of confidentiality" that she never signed.

LAW OFFICES OF ELLIOT J. ABELSON
8491 WEST SUNSET BOULEVARD • SUITE 1100 • LOS ANGELES, CALIFORNIA 90069-1911
TELEPHONE (323) 960-1935 • FAX (323) 650-0398

March 8, 2006

Karen Pressley
311 Clarinbridge Parkway NW
Kennesaw, Georgia 30144

Dear Ms. Pressley,

I am General Counsel to Church of Scientology International ("CSI") and address this letter to you in that capacity.

Between 1989 and 1998, you were a CSI employee. From time to time during that period, you signed various legal documents concerning your access to various privileged, proprietary, confidential and other information to which your position in CSI gave you access. Those documents include a confidentiality covenant and bond which you executed as obligor, in which you agreed that you would never disclose any information you "[have] or will learn about the organization of the Church ... including but not limited to their internal structures, functions or activities..." By that document, you bound yourself to CSI in the amount of $500,000 as liquidated damages in the event of a breach of that covenant.

It is certainly no secret that you have violated this covenant on several occasions, most recently by appearing on a television program in France. Your public utterances in violation of your unequivocal contractual obligations to CSI are incontestable and documented.

Accordingly, by this letter, I am placing you on notice that such actions are in breach of your obligations under various bonds and other binding agreements and covenants you executed during your employment by CSI. This letter constitutes a formal demand that you cease and desist from any further conduct contrary to your legal obligations as to CSI including, but not limited to, any further public disclosure of information obtained during your tenure as a CSI employee. CSI reserves the right to take any further legal action to protect its

rights and obtain recourse in this matter without further notice.

Very truly yours,

Elliot J. Abelson

EJA:gs

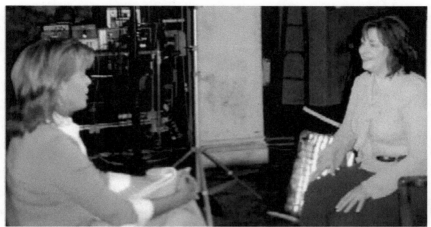

Hoda Kotb interviews Karen for NBC Dateline, circa 2005.

Calvary Baptist Church, Clearwater, FL 2007 collaborated with Watchman Fellowship and Karen Pressley to speak about Scientology to the Calvary congregation. Karen spoke about escaping Scientology and its abuses at approximately 100 events from 2000 – 2009.

Leah shot this selfie after they finished filming for *Leah Remini: Scientology and the Aftermath*, July 2017. They sat at a table in a restaurant and talked, all impromptu with no script. Karen is humbled to be a contributor to their exceptional efforts exposing the abuses of Scientology that call for justice.

# 41

## ESCAPING SCIENTOLOGY

"It's not easy to come out of a cult. Not many people understand it unless they are in…I'm a big supporter of people who
get that…. We are maneuvering our way through this life
without a cult, that's not an easy thing to do…You still have to
find who you are. We need each other. We have to support
each other…"

> \- Leah Remini,
> from an interview by Chris Crimy 6/9/17
> www.blogtalkradio.com "Come Get Sum"

### Epilogue 2017

IT SEEMS IMPOSSIBLE FOR A SEA ORG MEMBER to walk off the Int
base, or a Scientologist to leave Scientology, and just shrug off their
experiences without questioning what the hell happened, and experiencing at least some degree of difficulty re-adjusting to life on
the outside. People recover faster or differently than others, depending on what level of Scientology they had been at, or what
echelon of the Sea Org they worked in, and for how many years.

My journey has shown me that "escaping Scientology" is more
than just the physical break-out. It's a process of mental withdrawal

and psychological adjustment. Escaping starts with a change of mind, a questioning or a rebellion before the physical departure ever happens. Escaping the belief system is not cold turkey; it takes recovery time. Everyone will experience some kind of an aftermath, which is really the process of escaping Scientology.

My process of escaping was already in play before I made my first break from the Int base in 1990. Prior to that, I harbored a growing unwillingness to endure the offensive conditions that were so prominent in that culture. I did leave, but I couldn't totally withdraw from it because I hung onto the hope that Peter would leave with me. I went back, and repeated the process, when I escaped again in 1993, went back again, and stayed five more years. Clearly, I had different issues to deal with than couples that escape together.

When I wrote about life on the outside after August 1, 1998, I described the aftermath of dealing with disconnection, divorce, personal loss, reconnecting with family, re-acclimation to society, building relationships and learning to trust people again, coming to terms with who and what I had been as a Scientologist, and all the tough challenges related to rediscovering myself. I'm not sure if the aftermath ever ends completely, since life brings an ongoing stream of events, changes and realizations.

This leads me to the afterclap—the most unexpected repercussion that took place in my sequel to Scientology on the outside. I never anticipated having to deal with the kinds of corrosive, emotional and psychological side-effects that Scientology imprinted on me. This affects my sleep, my temperament and communication, my personal relationships, my ability to trust or to work under authority figures, and even my willingness to do certain kinds of work or participate in groups.

Scientology caused trauma in me for reasons described throughout my story. Hubbard's system was set up to provide thoughts, philosophy, policy, desired behaviors, and orders about everything in life, so he wanted Scientologists to think with all this instead of thinking independently. Leaders and policies demand 100% obedience and conformity through unconditional support of command intention. Hubbard wanted to mold a behavior and a mindset within each Scientologist, with him as the author and arbiter of both. This produced dependence, numbness and fear, not independent intellect, love, growth, freedom, individuality, or the ability to trust one's own feelings and judgement.

Thanks to my mother being the most tenacious woman I have ever known, I inherited her tenacity and the resilience that goes along with it, which adds up to me becoming a strong survivor. The fact that she was still going strong in her mid 70s when I got out, and she lived until age 92, had everything to do with the fact that I survived Scientology and built a new life. Before I left, she wrote me letters and never gave up on me getting out. I never gave in to the group's efforts to enforce disconnection from her; had I made that horrendous mistake, I would have lost my greatest supporter and my only source of unconditional love. Mom constantly inspired me by her defiance against the effects of aging, and believed she could overcome anything. She even tolerated getting calls from Scientology orgs who were trying to get her to come back for services—after 30 years away—and she would tell them what she thought of Scientology.

There was no way I was going to be another casualty of Scientology with a life down the tubes from inability to recover from trauma incurred during my Scientology years. Just as there had been signs leading to my unhealthy relationship with religion, there have also been signs that pointed to a road of recovery. For me, recovery has been possible—and even accelerated by— relationships with family, new friends, and empowering connections on the outside, such as getting a college education, being a lifelong learner, doing creative work, getting some therapy, loving others and being loved back, traveling, and building healthy relationships with critical thinkers.

Because of all this, I built competence, regained my autonomy and initiative, and experience trust and intimacy with friends and loved ones again. Being able to recognize various syndromes such as Post-Traumatic Stress Disorder (PTSD) and phobias in myself and seeking wellness therapy, helped me to end repeating nightmares and troubled dreams, and restore my emotional and mental well-being. PTSD counseling was a life changer for me.

On the book website, I've written about aspects of living that had everything to do with my ability to fully escape Scientology, to restore my sense of well-being, and my ability to think and reason independently. I've posted the content from the original chapter and will continue to add to these topics on the website, including:

- a detailed description of PTSD symptoms with real-life examples
- a discussion of phobias and nightmares
- disarming the power of Scientology's undue influence
- disarming the power of Scientology in one's life by disarming the power of their words
- handling insults in the aftermath of Scientology
- the importance of establishing trustworthy relationships with new friends and family
- exercising the freedom to explore spirituality
- the life-changing effects of getting an education that helps built critical thinking skills and starts a renaissance
- the synergy of creativity and wellness and their role in creating your new life

## Full Circle Anecdotes

I love it when things in life come full circle, especially when they bring catharsis or epiphanies. I include two anecdotes here. There are more on the book website: "We Stand Tall"; "Disconnection of Raven Kane & Roger Weller"; "The Specter, Marty Rathbun"; "Mike Rinder;: "Jeff Hawkins;" and "The irony of the IAS "for nothing" event; and "the Reconnect Event 2017."

## Mom and me

My most beloved supporter—my mother—has been a pillar of strength for me. We had our conflicts while I was growing up, but our relationship came full circle in the last 17 years of her life together. Defying Scientology's coercion to disconnect from her, I rejoined her and my family in 1998, in what I described as my "safe harbor." She was so proud of me as she attended my college graduation and graduation for my Master's degree. She had lived with Jim and Denise as well as Greg and me in our homes over the years, until she decided it was time to live in an independent senior facility. I was at her side during many tough age-related transitions, such as her giving up her car keys at age 87 because of her macular degeneration, several hospitalizations, having her home reconfigured by low-vision specialists, and her personal preparations of details knowing her time was running out. She had always told me that she hoped to die in her sleep, the easiest way to go, as her mother had. Mom died from a stroke in her sleep in May 2015. She had never married anyone else since Dad passed away in 1985, and she died on my father's birthday. It's cathartic to know that she and I had been a significant part of each other's lives over the last 17 years, and now she is resting in peace. Our memories together keep her very alive in my heart. Mom had saved me from drowning twice in my life. We were at a resort in Michigan when I was eight years old, swimming in the pool. She had been panning her movie camera across the pool when she saw me bobbing in the deep end, and jumped in to pull me out. After she ensured I was okay, she told me to go back in the pool in the shallow end and have fun, because she didn't want me to be afraid of the water. Mom had also tried to prevent me from drowning in Scientology, years before I finally got out, and was there for me when I did. I only regret not publishing this story before she passed, so she could have enjoyed the satisfaction of knowing that I had not remained silenced about things that mattered to me and to her. I deeply miss her.

## Janis Gillham Grady

An extra special highlight of the Reconnect 2017 event was seeing Janis Gillham Grady, the organizer of the event, whom I had been closely connected with in recent months, but who I hadn't seen since 1990. She and I mused over the fact that her mother, Yvonne Gillham, had created the Celebrity Centre in the 1960s—the project that caused Yvonne to leave Janis and her siblings on the Flagship Apollo with no parents; and I had stepped into her mother's position as the head of Celebrity Centre about eight years after her mother's death, but I had never met Janis, Terri or Peter. Janis and I met at the Int base in 1990, but Janis and her husband Paul left shortly after Peter and I arrived there. In 2017, our mutual friend, Roger Weller, told Janis that I was a writer and editor, and thought I might be able to help Janis finish her book. After reviewing her chapters, I knew I wanted to help Janis complete her story, and she asked me to edit her book. She unfolds a history of the Sea Org since its inception, but offers the unique perspective of Hubbard and Scientology through the eyes of a child, and as an original Commodore's Messenger, in Book One. She details how her mother Yvonne birthed the Celebrity Centre in Los Angeles, and how Janis and her siblings fended for themselves while her parents supported the goals of the Sea Org as their priority. To be someone who had stepped into her mother's role at CC, and then met Janis two decades later at the Int base, was ironic and karmic. At the party, when she announced the upcoming release of *Commodore's Messenger: A Child Adrift in the Scientology Sea Organization - Book One* that I had edited for her, which is coming out July 2017, it is both satisfying and cathartic to be someone who is helping Janis tell her incredible story.

\* \* \*

The full circle anecdotes, particularly "The Reconnect Event 2017," bring to mind the power of the narrative that I describe in my workbook, "Coming to Terms With Your Story" that I mentioned a few times. One author/researcher I reference in it is Maria Pia Lara, author of *Narrating Evil,* who also draws from philosophers Immanuel Kant and Hannah Arendt. Lara writes,

> "Narrative plays a key role in helping societies acknowledge their pasts. Stories haunt our consciousness and lead to a kind of examination and dialogue that shape notions of morality...debate over these narratives allow us to construct a more accurate picture of historical truth, leading to a better understanding of why it was possible."

This book, and the Reconnect event is all about sharing stories. I look at each of us in the ex-community as a historian of sorts. I believe it's important for exes to document experiences, to make connections that wouldn't otherwise be possible to know. It's like allowing puzzle-pieces to connect. As Lara wrote,

> "Life stories can help us reconcile human burdens...even in the darkest of times we have the right to expect some illumination...Human understanding depends on giving meaning to our actions...a way of demonstrating that those actions have a permanent significance that allowed a single story to enter into history" (p. 44).

Experiences such as seeing great people and making new friends at the Reconnect weekend in June 2017 have become pinnacles in my journey of escaping Scientology—connecting with people on the outside, communicating freely with others and discovering their truth, discovering their humanity, building relationships free from the cult's influence on who we really are.

The release of this book celebrates my 19th anniversary of escaping Scientology. It's never too late to reach out to someone whose life you might be able to help by simply sharing a listening ear or a caring heart.

Dr. Liza Davis oversaw Karen's undergraduate studies in the KSU Honors College from 2004-2009. Karen completed her Master of Arts in Professional Writing degree with honors in 2011.

Dr. Anne Richards, professor of English in KSU's Master of Arts in Professional Writing program, mentored Karen from 2009 - 2011. Anne, Karen and Sandy Simpson where they and other writer friends incubated each other's writing project. Photo: St. Petersburg, FL, 2016.

Karen Pressley and Mike Rinder each made a "Sophie's Choice" when escaping Scientology and leaving loved ones behind. Karen told Mike she feared him while he headed OSA, but now respects and appreciates his efforts for exposing Scientology's abuses. Photo was taken in Tampa after watching Cathy Schenkelburg's Squeeze My Cans, 2017.

# INDEX

Index

CPSIA information can be obtained
at www.ICGtesting.com
Printed in the USA
LVHW02*1559221017
553341LV00002B/5/P